JUST
SCHOOLS

JUST SCHOOLS

The Idea of Racial Equality
in American Education

DAVID L. KIRP

University of California Press
Berkeley / Los Angeles / London

LC
214.2
.K57
1982

University of California Press
Berkeley and Los Angeles, California
University of California Press, Ltd.
London, England
© 1982 by
The Regents of the University of California
First Paperback Printing 1983
ISBN 0-520-05084-3
Printed in the United States of America

1   2   3   4   5   6   7   8   9   0

Library of Congress Cataloging in Publication Data

Kirp, David L.
    Just schools. The idea of racial equality
in American education.
    Includes index.
    1. School integration—United States—Case
studies.   2. Educational equalization—United
States—Case studies.   I. Title.
LC214.2.K57   370.19′342   81-16497
                                    AACR2

To the memory of Murray Kirp

The school board must . . . fashion steps which promise realistically to convert promptly to a system without a "white" school and a "Negro" school, but just schools.

Green v. County School Board, 391 U.S. 430 (1968)

Contents

Acknowledgments

For the past five years, I have been trying to understand the evolution of American race and schooling policy, focusing on five Bay Area communities as a way of gaining perspective on that broader puzzle. My own concern with the issue considerably predates this research. As director of the Harvard Center for Law and Education from 1968 to 1971, I was involved in shaping desegregation strategies for the North and West. Several years later, as advisor to the Berkeley Unified School District, I counseled the district in its negotiations with the Office of Civil Rights over the fate of Black House, an all-black alternative school in that otherwise desegregated district; subsequently, I drafted a proposed new integration plan for the San Francisco district, as consultant to a state-appointed review commission. In short, I am not a disinterested observer; while I have sought to pay particular attention to my own biases and to stress the inconvenient truths, personal history colors this work.

This enterprise would never have gotten off the ground were it not for the encouragement of Howard Kalodner, who asked me to examine the desegregation of San Francisco's schools as part of a larger study of judicial management of school desegregation sponsored by the Institute for Judicial Administration. It was Kalodner who urged that the court case not be isolated from its political and social context, a point of view that has shaped the case studies in general.

The Spencer Foundation provided the support necessary to look at four additional communities and to reflect on what was to be learned from their experience. Spencer is a remarkable foundation, whose relationships with grantees are characterized by trust and encouragement; that institutional stance is largely attributable to its president, H. Thomas James, whose advice I have much valued. The Spencer Foundation had the good sense to urge that I involve social scientists with diverse perspectives in shaping the project: Luvern Cunningham, Martin Trow, and David Tyack have been persistent and positive critics.

I have depended greatly on the kindness of friends. Colleagues at Berkeley and elsewhere, including Eugene Bardach, Paul Berman, Robert Church, William Clune, David Cohen, Richard Elmore, Paula Fass, Hugh Hawkins, Robert Kagan, Marvin Lazerson, Martin Levin, John Meyer, Paul Peterson, Ann Swidler, Martin Trow, Stephen Weiner, and Mark Yudof, read and provided invaluable detailed criticisms of all or part of the manuscript. Discussions with fellow members of the American Academy of Arts and Sciences Study Group on Urban School Desegregation, which met during the academic year 1977–78, and with the Berkeley-Stanford Seminar on Law, Governance, and Schooling, which began meeting in 1980, have helped to focus my thinking.

My study of British race and schooling policy, *Doing Good by Doing Little: Race and Schooling in Britain* (Berkeley: University of California Press, 1979) sharpened my sense of what is distinctive about the American experience. I am especially indebted to Maurice Kogan and Stuart Maclure for their counsel in that enterprise.

The students who over the years worked with me in preparing the case studies included in Part 2 were invaluable colleagues. Steven Angelides, Kenneth Bloch, Robert Gamble, Patrick Hayashi, Kevin Koshar, Donna Leff, and Lois Meyer each contributed to one of the case studies. Joy Hansen and George Perlee tracked down stray references, checked quotations, and updated some of the data. I am especially grateful to Doris Fine, a collaborator from the beginning, who participated in the San Francisco, Berkeley, and Richmond case-study research and whose own parallel examination of San Francisco broadened my analytic framework, and to Michael Doyen, whose efforts to bring into order the vast corpus of materials concerning the evolving idea of equality with respect to race and education are reflected in Part 1, and whose research concerning the social and political character of the Bay Area informs chapter 5. Bette Francis and Marleen Fouché attended to the manuscript with scrupulous attention to detail, serving as editors and proofreaders as well as secretaries.

My debt to the University of California Press is substantial. Grant Barnes' enthusiasm for the project has eased the agonies of revision. Helen Tartar's meticulous editing has added an element of clarity and grace to the volume.

Several of the case studies have appeared in different form in various places. An early version of the San Francisco study was published in the *Harvard Educational Review*, and a more detailed account may be found in Howard Kalodner and James Fishman, editors, *Limits of Justice: The Courts' Role in School Desegregation* (Cambridge, Mass.: Ballinger, 1978). The Richmond study appeared in *School Review*, the Oakland study in the *American Journal of Education*, and the Sausalito study in *Urban Education*. Each of these has been updated and significantly refined. Trace elements of my treatment of courts as policy shapers are drawn from "School Desegregation and the Limits of Legalism," an essay published in *Public Interest*.

The title for this book was inadvertently borrowed from a report to the National Institute of Education co-authored by Doris Fine and Philippe Nonet; I am grateful to both of them for their indulgence of my misfeasance.

PART ONE

The Aspiration to Equality

Everything begins in sentiment and assumption
and finds its issue
in political action and institutions.

Lionel Trilling,
The Liberal Imagination

CHAPTER
1

Uniformity and Idiosyncrasy: A Delicate Balance

I

The quest for racial justice in education is an old and ceaselessly vital theme in American social policy. The issue has been at least nascent since the founding of the republic, for even then there was debate about how black children should be treated. The Supreme Court's 1954 declaration, in *Brown v. Board of Education*,[1] that officially maintained racial separation was unconstitutional, thrust it onto center stage. The issue is immensely complex. It links racial fairness with educational equity; both ideas are morally and constitutionally salient, technically perplexing, and politically volatile. Small wonder, then, that the effort to achieve racial justice in the schools appears a vexed, and to some a quixotic, undertaking.

The puzzles fall into two broad and interrelated categories. The first is substantive: Should race and schooling policy be defined as a single standard applied nationally, or is there room for variability? The second concerns the mode of decision: Is the issue best resolved through the constitutional apparatus of the courts, or does politics deserve pride of place?

Whatever the positions of the partisans, whether a racially balanced school system or neighborhood attendance zones are being urged, conventional policy aspires to uniformity.[2] Policy is proposed for the country as if equality had an unvarying meaning from place to place, and in terms of fixed goals, as if there existed an ideal end state. Such remedies as extensive busing, vouchers, special "magnet" schools, or metropolitan-wide districts are proffered with little attention to context; each is advanced as if it were a panacea for the ills of racism.

Similarly, the recommended process of decision, whether judicial action or (more rarely these days) legislative or administrative initiative, specifies a uniform and authoritative standard. There is little room for adaptation to circumstance, since the task of government is seen as one of ensuring compliance with the norm. The process envisioned is described in moral or constitutional, not political, terms. Those who oppose the prevailing approach as excessively interventionist would take the issue of race and schooling out of the political and judicial system. Those who would have the government do more bring to the task a belief in social engineering and a certain moral absolutism, neither of which brooks much attention to the complications posed by variability. In either event, uniformity is the hallmark of analysis.

If thinking about racial justice solely in terms of uniformity is inappropriate—and that is a central argument of this book—the reasons for this emphasis are nonetheless readily understandable. One is eminently practical. National-level issues dominate the attention of policymakers, not just in education but in all areas. It is the American experience—not that of Albany, New York, or Americus, Georgia—that commands their interest. And focusing on policy at the national level often implies specifying a single policy for the entire nation, whichever branch of government bears primary responsibility for carrying it out. The judiciary proceeds on the assumption that once a question has been resolved by the Supreme Court, the lower courts will faithfully and consistently apply that definitive standard; the history of the race cases is in some measure a history of bringing the federal judiciary to heel.[3] Legislation typically speaks to broad categories of situations, not to isolated and particular instances. Congress proscribes racial discrimination or calls for appropriate education without further specification. The executive branch departments routinely rely on rules in administering programs. The uniform application of rules has conventionally been regarded as sensible and fair administrative practice. When officials are faced with myriad claimants, differentiations are hard to make and harder to defend; the possibility of favoritism or of making arbitrary distinctions also diminishes in a regime of rules.[4] This view acquires particular force in the context of racial policy, where rule enforcement historically betokened effectiveness, whereas attention to differences was viewed as signaling administrative vacillation and weakness.[5] Attention to specificity and nuance could, of course, be incorporated into national policy, but such concern is readily confused with a mean and unprincipled parochialism.

Principle as well as practicality buttresses the emphasis on uniformity. If everyone is treated alike, questions of the "Why us and not them?" variety do not so frequently arise. Because in a uniform world distinctions are not drawn, it becomes harder to complain of arbitrariness. Requiring uniformity thus reflects a more general idea of justice. This conception sharply distinguishes justice from politics or policy: justice bespeaks clear, fixed, and universal principles, claims of right rooted in the moral traditions of the republic, not instrumental calculations or compromises.[6] The victims of injustice are said to hold "political trumps,"[7] which enable them to impose a principled and uniform resolution, whatever the outcome of the political give-and-take.

Equality is one of the central elements in this peculiarly American conception of justice. The power of the ideal of equality has been reiterated by three centuries of European observers—St. John de Crèvecoeur, Alexis de Tocqueville, James Bryce, and Denis Brogan among them—who saw the seriousness of the quest for this ideal as distinguishing America from its antecedents.[8] To another European, Gunnar Myrdal, the egalitarian tradition was so pervasive as to constitute an American Creed, so powerful that it would eventually bring down racial injustice, in the schools as elsewhere.[9] While equality need not be defined as uniformity, the two can readily be equated. In that sense, uniformity not only coincides with the conventional view of the capabilities of a national government but is also regarded as normatively right.

II

The *Brown* decision appears to embrace a uniform and egalitarian understanding of racial justice, marking the triumph of this point of view. The Supreme Court's opinion recorded a consensus—or at least a consensus among those who might be termed the enlightened—concerning racial justice with respect to schooling. Official segregation of the races constituted bad law and bad social policy, and segregation could be undone by an authoritative judicial decision.

Segregation was legally wrong because it denied blacks the respect that the constitution bestows equally on all individuals. Segregation embodied a persisting badge of slavery, a symbol of caste, and was for that reason "inherently unequal." At the level of constitutional law, the *Brown* decree seemingly resolved the American dilemma identified by Myrdal—the disparity between the nation's formal commitment to equal treatment and its palpably unequal treatment of blacks.

In terms of social policy, segregation was equally misguided, for it kept blacks from achieving equality of educational opportunity. This denial mattered in its own right. Segregation wounded the "hearts and minds" of black youngsters. It also had important long-term consequences. Because education was widely viewed as a vehicle of social and economic mobility, unequal education was held to doom blacks to life in the underclass.

Thus were education, race, and equality linked in the prevailing consensus. The remedy for the sins *Brown* identified followed directly from the recital of the wrong: abolish state-imposed racial separation. Once racial barriers were lifted, it was supposed, there would exist neither white schools nor black schools, but "just schools." [10] When the dual school system was dismantled, the constitutional rights of blacks would be secured; so too would their opportunity for social and economic equality. Blacks, like whites, would then be free to succeed or fail on the basis of merit, not caste.

The *Brown* decision changed the terms of the policy debate on race and schooling. In pronouncing segregation unconstitutional, the opinion placed supporters of the policy on the defensive, obliging them to revise what had been revealed as part of the republic's organic law. Often in its history, the Supreme Court has functioned as "teacher in a vital national seminar"; [11] it did so here.

That the decision was unanimous underscored the importance of the lesson and thus gave further impetus to the enlightened consensus: as the justices well understood, even one dissenting opinion encourages doubts about authoritativeness. There was also hope that the consensus could be swiftly and surely converted into social reality because the Court rather than one of the avowedly political branches of government had spoken. That the Supreme Court had announced the law was regarded as reason enough to secure its realization. There were, to be sure, details to be worked out, but the underlying question was settled.

When challenged, the justices themselves adhered to this view. In the 1957 Little Rock case, faced with resistance to desegregation nurtured by Arkansas' governor, the Supreme Court made plain that it would brook no defiance of its decision. [12] Each member of the Court signed the opinion, a gesture without contemporary precedent, undertaken by the justices as an affirmation of their determination. *Brown* was the unquestioned law of the land, to which government officials and ordinary citizens owed allegiance.

While squarely grounded in positive law, *Brown* also touched profound normative aspirations whose sources lay deeper than the Constitution. The case at once confirmed and gave rise to a social movement committed to the moral rectitude of civil rights. It is not by accident that the language of the movement was visionary, that Martin Luther King spoke in terms of his "dream" for the nation, that the leading chronicle of the movement is entitled *My Soul Is Rested*.[13] It is an exaggeration, but only a slight one, to equate the ideal of uniform and authoritative justice evoked by the Supreme Court with the image of the Heavenly City. To its most devoted adherents, the *Brown* decree promised a kind of secular salvation.

III

What once seemed right and inevitable—a great declaration of law, morality, and politics—has been remade and in some sense diminished by subsequent history. Details that were thought trivial now dominate discussion. What is the meaning of "intentional discrimination" in desegregation cases? Just how should the benefits of desegregation—changes in student attitude and achievement, for example—be measured?[14] What happens when the intended beneficiaries of racial equality resist the practical consequences of desegregation? In contrast with the lofty themes of *Brown*, these seem mere cavils, but they have come to occupy a central place in working out the meaning of equality.

The contemporary reality of race and schooling policy also makes a shambles of the hoped-for uniformity. What prevails is not a single national standard, authoritatively set and effectively implemented, but rather a bewildering diversity of arrangements, ad hoc in nature, varying enormously both in content and in implementation. Some communities have undertaken to balance their schools racially; others have retained neighborhood schools while improving the quality of instruction in predominantly black schools; still others have done nothing at all. The processes by which these policies come into being similarly vary from place to place. Court orders, as well as federal, state, and local initiatives, have played a part. Within communities, the structure of the school bureaucracy, the views of the professionals, and relationships between professional administrators and elected school boards have had significant influence. The outcome in a particular community has frequently been brought about by sustained bargaining among political and bureaucratic forces. Race and schooling policy is thus predominantly localist, significantly political, and widely varying.

The stories publicized by the media at the onset of the 1980s illustrate this variability. These tales are less dramatic than those of some years ago, when Berkeley's apparently effortless racial mixing seemed the very embodiment of the Heavenly City, while the bus burning in Pontiac and the riots in Boston resembled scenes from the *Inferno*. Yet they are no less distinctive. The football team at a predominantly white St. Louis high school welcomes incoming black students; in Los Angeles, whites quietly withdraw from the public schools in sizable numbers in the face of badly managed desegregation; and parents in a Louisiana community, supported by a state judge, seek to defy a federal judge's order assigning their daughters to a newly desegregated school. The ways in which policy takes shape are equally miscellaneous. Chicago negotiates an agreement with the Justice Department (subsequently jeopardized by school board changes of heart) to accomplish both some desegregation and substantial improvement in the remaining all-black schools. Seattle, which earlier had voluntarily adopted a modest busing plan, enlarges that plan on its own initiative. In contrast, the federal district court in Cleveland, pronouncing that district's efforts to comply with court-ordered desegregation a failure, in effect takes over the management of the system. At the national level, Court and Congress seem intent on undoing the work of one another, as the Supreme Court expands school district liability for segregation and Congress again limits the authority of the Executive to enforce racial remedies.[15]

Some of the variability—notably the tug and pull of legislature and judiciary—is troubling because it appears to jeopardize the national commitment to equality. Yet variability itself is not necessarily a concession to parochialism, a stubborn problem that can be overcome with will and imagination. Rather, justice with respect to race and schooling is in good measure idiosyncratic. One reason for this is the vagueness of the substantive aspiration. The greater the degree of policy consensus, the greater the basis for uniform action: in the realm of equality, though, agreement is hard to come by. Equality carries no single coherent meaning either in race or education. It is the tensions among meanings that have been historically most important. Consider the issues. With respect to race, does equal treatment refer to opportunity or to result? Is equality defined with reference to the individual or to the group? Is it equal educational opportunity or equal educational outcome that is sought? And who is to be made equal to whom? These are troubling matters when posed normatively. They become harder still when practical exigencies—the feasibility of achieving a particular outcome, for instance—are permitted to intrude.

The specifics bespeak a larger truth: equality does not assume a single, simple, unitary, and invariant form. It is at root ambiguous, and this very ambiguity gives the concept much of its power to motivate, incite, and disappoint. Equality seems at once luminous and elusive, or perhaps luminous *because* elusive, evolving as a consequence of altered social circumstance and moral perception. It is not just that as a society we attend to smaller and smaller degrees of differentness, but also that the differences we find offensive change over time. In this sense, loyalty to equality resides not in allying oneself with a firmly settled principle but rather in the very process of pursuing the elusive, for it is the pursuit itself that counts. As Tocqueville observed: "Democratic institutions awaken and flatter the passion for equality without ever being able to satisfy it entirely. Thus complete equality is always slipping through the people's fingers at the moment when they think to grasp it."[16] Progress entails capturing the meaning of equality in a specific setting and translating that meaning into official action, not securing a single coherent, timeless understanding.[17]

In an environment where the objective is uncertain and changing, the way policy gets made may be as significant as the policy itself. The lack of substantive consensus underscores the crucial importance of the process of policymaking. If the rightness of the end were unquestioned, imposing it on the recalcitrant would occasion little objection: that is how the "second Reconstruction" of the South was carried out during the 1960s.[18] But the contemporary variability of equality makes such imposition illegitimate. To the extent that we don't know what "right" means, it makes sense to let those affected settle the matter for themselves. Representativeness, not substantive rightness, becomes a measure of the legitimacy of the outcome as racial justice is thus transformed into a significantly political concern. A key promise of what Lord Bryce termed "government by discussion" is that political behavior—"mutual adjustment,"[19] incorporating the bargaining and compromise characteristic of traditional interest politics—may offer the best hedge against misguided action. Reliance on political decision making within the affected community is an essential part of determining what equality signifies, and it assures that the policy outcomes will differ.

The issue is still more complicated. Race and schooling policy, while importantly idiosyncratic, cannot be *merely* idiosyncratic, a matter of adding up the votes or market preferences. For one thing, the health of the political process has to be reckoned an open question. The classic concern with respect to race policy is that politics shuts out minority voices, systematically disadvantaging this "discrete and insular minority."[20] Blacks thus suffer from decisions that they had no hand in shaping. When that happens, the process itself needs to be recalibrated, often by the constitutionally based decision of a court, to ensure their conclusion.[21] A less frequently discussed pathology entails abandoning the field of decision making to the historical victims, with a concomitant loss of policy sensibility: acceptance of black separatism, with its anti-white overtones and emphasis on indoctrination, is the best illustration. It is easy enough to understand how sentiment can dissolve into sentimentality, to the long-range detriment of both blacks and whites. As Daniel Bell writes, "when a nation has publicly admitted moral guilt, it is difficult to say no to those it has offended."[22] In these circumstances, the cure for the political system is likely to be self-administered, a reassertion of authority by the broader community. Too little responsiveness to the schools' constituencies thus imposes majoritarian policy on blacks, while too much responsiveness to black extremism sets the schools at odds with social norms. Fixing the balance between these pathologies of process presents a continuing quandary, one that may call into question the persuasiveness of idiosyncratic decisions.[23]

This concern about the process of decision making helps to explain why idiosyncrasy is not to be honored unquestioningly. There are also substantive limits to the policies concerning race and schooling that would be thought just. Imagine a community whose citizens vote unanimously to maintain racially separate schools. We would think that decision unjust and wrong, regardless of the views of the voters. Had the voters unanimously rejected the proposed construction of a municipal subway system, for instance, we would be indifferent to the outcome. Race and schooling is somewhat different. It is not a public works project, but rather a public good; decisions affect those who are not party to them, and that licenses outsiders to have some say.

Because the policy question concerns the fair treatment of persons it has a constitutional dimension—a suprapolitical dimension, if you will—as well as a political one. The implementation process, with all its variability and ambiguity, remains essential in defining what we mean by racial equality, but that process does not operate unchecked. Individual rights recognized by the nation's compact with itself are at stake. The constitutional salience of race and schooling does not give a "political trump" to the losers, but nonetheless it bounds the process: in this respect, *Brown* still speaks powerfully. Put differently, there remain substantive standards, unaffected by how a decision gets reached, summed up in the constitutional command of fair treatment. The idea of equality as a uniform norm is indeed ambiguous, but it retains a core and controlling meaning.[24]

Process and substance, politics and principle, are not so separate as this discussion may suggest. On the one side, the health of political decision making is gauged in part by fidelity to constitutional values. Constitutionalism is relevant whether or not a community dispute over race and schooling ever winds up in court. On the other side, courts attend to political considerations, often enough seeking to rescue constitutional principle from the fact of compromise. In each instance, both nationally and locally derived norms come into play; in that respect, the value of a federal system of decision making, with its implied balance among the several levels of government, is affirmed.[25] Not that the enterprise works effortlessly or smoothly: the thrust and parry of diverse substantive aspirations and distinctive decision-making apparatuses make conflict an inevitable and persistent feature of the quest for racial justice.

The story of race and schooling policy was once told as a tale of high drama, culminating in *Brown v. Board of Education* with the triumph of a powerful and particular national vision.[26] The hope for racial equality in schools remains as luminous and as elusive as ever, but it is now less certain that official policy has frustrated achievement of that end or that any particular remedy convincingly relates to the wrong. With this altered perception, what was once taken for granted becomes suitable for debate.[27] What seems most significant today are not central tendencies but the vital dualities, the interaction of contending forces: constitutionalism and politics, uniformity and idiosyncrasy, self-interest and shared visions. The central puzzle of this book is: How does an essentially political process involving each branch and level of government shape race and schooling policy over time, in light of the larger normative concerns summoned up by the question? What substantive outcomes does that process yield? And to what extent is increased minority participation in the process of decision—increased inclusion in the forms of politics—noteworthy in itself? That descriptive inquiry leads to a prescriptive concern: What mix of politics and constitutionalism, and federal and local decision-making best serves the ends of racial justice?

Because the answers to both the descriptive and prescriptive queries depend in good measure on the particulars of local experience, Part 2 traces the way in which five communities—San Francisco, Oakland, Berkeley, Richmond, and Sausalito, Bay Area cities that are geographically contiguous but in most salient respects very different—have gone about the task of framing a race and schooling policy.

The balance of Part 1 confronts these questions from a more global perspective. It traces thematically the enduring debates about substantive equality and decisional process that have been alluded to here. Chapters 2 and 3 explore diverse understandings of equality in the respective contexts of race and education. Although the specifics are very different in each chapter, the central theme is much the same. The meaning of equality, whether it concerns race or schooling, has been the subject of contention among those holding conflicting views of this country's mission and the place of blacks in that mission. Only in its weakest form has any single vision, whether of equal educational opportunity or of racial justice, commanded national assent. Until the *Brown* decision, racial justice and equal educational opportunity were distinct spheres. Debate over schooling largely ignored the situation of blacks; the racial struggle was broadly concerned with segregation in all spheres of life, not just with education. It is the Supreme Court that brought together these two ancient quarrels and produced the apparent consensus earlier detailed. By noting the diversity of understandings of equality before and after *Brown*, these chapters underscore the tenuous quality of that consensus. They also describe the shifting climate of national opinion within which the five Bay Area communities debated race and schooling questions.

Chapter 4 stresses the relationship between constitutional and political understandings of racial justice. The thesis of the chapter is straightforward, if unconventional: the opinions of the Supreme Court from *Brown* to the present have invited an essentially political resolution of race and schooling disputes, within the capacious bounds fixed by the Fourteenth Amendment. Politics and principle shape both the development of doctrine by the courts and the course of any particular dispute, whether or not it is brought to court. Part 1 sets the contours of national policy and puts into perspective the strategies pursued by each of the five Bay Area communities.

CHAPTER
2

Race: The Persisting American Dilemma

I

The central tenet of the *Brown* decision derives from classical liberalism: individuals deserve to be treated as persons, not as members of a caste or class. That right is embedded in the Fourteenth Amendment's declaration that no "person" shall be denied equal protection under law. The sin of segregation is that it robs blacks of their entitlement to personhood, their right to make basic life decisions free from the taint of group membership.

The great triumph of *Brown* may have been its capacity to persuade the nation that racial fairness can only be understood in these classically liberal terms. Yet *Brown* does not represent an inevitability. It marks a choice among contending visions of the good society and the place of blacks in that society. The tensions between individualism and communitarianism, between a commitment to equal treatment and a belief in the consequential reality of racial differences, are of long standing. These venerable ideas influenced policy before *Brown*, and they have persisted in the wake of that decision. Subsequent decades have not been characterized by a single vision of racial justice, and only in looking back can one appreciate just how fragile is the triumph marked by the *Brown* decree. The decision caps this century's era of good feelings, a time when the force of ideological disagreement, if not ideology itself, was thought to have been spent. Yet, in race as elsewhere, this expectation proved misplaced. New and contending understandings of racial justice have emerged, some of them tied to earlier themes, others the result of a seemingly ascendant liberalism, still others an apparent rejection of the premises of *Brown*. On the one side, universalism, redistribution, and black separatism have vied for recognition as the descendents of *Brown*, a decision whose meanings have multiplied like fruit flies. On the other side, those unhappy with such contemporary remedies for racial injustice as busing and preferential treatment have drawn support from the ideas of communitarianism and individual difference.

The history of racial justice in America recounts both an evolving idea and a social movement. The movement engaged in a form of symbolic politics, using ideas as weapons in the struggle for inclusion in the larger society. Debates over the meaning of racial fairness have been replayed in some form wherever minorities are a significant presence. The diverse positions were powerfully heard as each of the five Bay Area communities sought to develop its own race and schooling policy.

II

The fullest exposition of the classical liberal position with respect to race, a position *Brown* rendered into constitutional form, is found in Gunnar Myrdal's *An American Dilemma*.[1] For that reason, *An American Dilemma* provides entrée into the debate over racial justice and the attempt in *Brown* to resolve that debate. Contrasting the thesis of *An American Dilemma* with the then-current apologias for racial inequality clarifies the nature of the choice made in *Brown*.

In painstakingly depicting the parlous state of American race relations, Gunnar Myrdal sought at once to set forth and to resolve what he termed the "American dilemma." White America's treatment of blacks as a distinct caste, whose members were at best marginal participants in the political, economic, and cultural life of the republic, has never been more fully set forth; at this level, *An American Dilemma* remains a valuable historical source book on all aspects of the lives of blacks. This description was not offered as an end in itself, but as a preliminary to reforming what was being described.

Blacks were far worse off than whites in this society, and the actions of government had contributed significantly to that situation: the data marshaled in *An American Dilemma* were meant to speak for themselves. These were not mere facts, but facts transformed into revelation. They would serve, Myrdal wrote, as an "educational offensive against racial intolerance."[2] Like the trumpets sounded outside the walls of Jericho, the delineation of inequity would bring about its demise. In this sense *An American Dilemma*, although conceived on a grander scale and addressed to a broader audience, was supposed to do for racial equality what the Brandeis brief had earlier achieved in the struggle for decent working conditions. The facts of life in the black community were so sharply at odds with what Myrdal saw as the "American creed," and the creed itself so powerful, that the pressure for reform to reconcile social fact and value would prove irresistible.

Myrdal cast the racial problem in essentially moral terms: the rightness of the idea of equality would win out.[3] Even as he described the caste system that operated with special force in the South, Myrdal envisioned its disappearance. *An American Dilemma*, while not oblivious to the difficulties attendant on change, emphasizes the inevitability of reform. "In this country," states Myrdal, "political, social, and economic conditions gravitate toward equality. . . . Democratic institutions can no more tolerate dual political status than two standards of ethics or discrepant units of weight and measures."[4] Little attention is paid to *how* change will come about. The stress is instead on the predictable demise of structural racism and the emergence of a modern social order designed to promote equality of opportunity and equality of respect, the basic premises of a classical liberal society.

While *An American Dilemma* speaks centrally to racial issues, it raises broader societal dilemmas. As Myrdal notes in his introduction to the book: "The Negro problem is an integral part of, or a special phase of, the whole complex of problems in the larger American civilization. It cannot be treated in isolation."[5] The resolution of the racial issue that Myrdal urges is consistent with the hostility of a classical liberal society—a society that depends on organized social action to safeguard individual liberty of thought and action—toward systemic barriers to the realization of that liberty.

This belief in the power of a unifying liberal American vision, capable of undoing even the manifestations of caste, is of long standing. It marks the "new man" whom Crèvecoeur identified even before the American Revolution and became an explicitly voiced vision after the revolution.[6] The founders of the republic often spoke of a social system that could claim "to represent the way to ultimate progress and a true social happiness."[7] Here lay the distinctive genius of the new nation; there was, Madison wrote, "no model on the face of the globe" for such a society.[8]

Central to this emerging social order was the dignity of the individual, and his concomitant claim to evenhanded treatment by the government. Self-government, Jefferson declared, would open a "widespread field for the blessings of freedom and equal laws."[9]

In such a world, the ascribed characteristics based on caste that counted for so much in a Europe marked by its feudal past were inconsequential. Group membership also mattered little when compared with individual achievement. While Americans would surely form groups, membership in these groups was voluntary, not immutable; people would belong to groups without being defined by them. Creditors and manufacturers, not blacks or women, were the "factions" Madison had in mind in the *Federalist Papers*. The national government would blunt the power of such groups, not sanctify them.[10] This vision is universalistic in character. As Jefferson recognized, it depended on the speedy "amalgamation" of new and old settlers.[11]

Myrdal frames the same point in normative terms. "The more general valuations—those which refer to man as such and not to any particular group or temporary situation—are morally higher. . . . The other valuations—which refer to various smaller groups of mankind or to particular occasions—are commonly referred to as 'irrational' or 'prejudiced.' . . ."[12] Consensus is better than conflict, the whole better than any faction, the universal preferable to the particular.

This stress on liberal consensus was seized on by mid-twentieth-century historians as the overarching theme of our nation's history. *The Liberal Tradition in America*, as Louis Hartz described it, operated without serious rival.[13] Writing more recently of America as a distinctive "union of states and a nation of free individuals,"[14] Nathan Glazer reasserted this view and related it to race. Where Myrdal could only forecast the eventual triumph of the American Creed, Glazer purported to witness and report it. A national policy of nondiscrimination emerged during the 1950s and 1960s, marking the death of an officially sanctioned caste system and thus apparently confirming Myrdal's prediction.

The classical liberal view of race elaborated in *An American Dilemma* is embodied in *Brown* and the 1964 Civil Rights Act,[15] outlawing discrimination on the basis of race. Yet there persist other conceptions of race that stress consequential differences rather than universal bonds, the group rather than the individual. The history of the republic can be understood in terms of conflict as well as consensus.[16] Such an emphasis makes particular sense in the racial context, for race has been perhaps the nation's most divisive social fact, straining its very capacity for survival. When one surveys the wretched conditions historically visited upon blacks as a matter of law and social reality, it is tempting to dismiss any explanations as empty apologies. Yet to do so obscures a more complex truth. Belief in equality has warred from the founding of the nation with the conviction that blacks are inferior and hence deserve to be treated differently. Were it otherwise, there would have been little need for a *Brown* decision and no uproar over that decision.

Racial inferiority is a familiar theme in our history. To the first English settlers, that inferiority was rooted in religious belief. "Slavery was inseparable from the evil in man; it was God's punishment upon Ham's prurient disobedience. Enslavement was captivity, the loser's lot in a contest of power. Slaves were infidels or heathens. On every count Negroes qualified."[17] During the revolutionary war era, more enlightened Americans began to entertain the possibility that the supposed inferiority of blacks was not a reason for but rather the result of slavery, and that it was possible to change dramatically the circumstances of blacks. An "uneasy equalitarianism" is evident in Hamilton's declaration that blacks' "natural faculties are perhaps [later amended to "probably"] as good as ours."[18] Yet late in the eighteenth century equality between the races was hard to imagine, even for those opposed to slavery. The willingness of the founders to treat blacks as less than persons for purposes of allocating electoral votes among the states suggests that blacks were largely irrelevant to the earliest discussions of liberty in the republic. It was the community of white persons for whom the Constitution was framed, since only whites were regarded as equals.

The dream of an all-white republic, "where the full promise of equality could be realized because there was no black population to be relegated to a special and anomalous status,"[19] took shape during the revolutionary era and persisted throughout much of the nineteenth century. As late as the eve of the Civil War, blacks enjoyed no prospect of equal opportunity or equality before the law. Equality of esteem was an unheard-of notion. Blacks lived out their lives "on a different and lower plane"[20] than whites, in the North as in the South. "Race prejudice seems stronger in those states that have abolished slavery than in those where it still exists, and nowhere is it more intolerant than in those where slavery was never known," Tocqueville reported in *Democracy in America*.[21] An exaggeration perhaps, but Lincoln could speak of blacks as not the equal of whites, and even the abolitionists regarded black people as lacking the aggressiveness and intellectual talents of the white race.[22]

This widely held view was threatened but not undermined by emancipation. Because blacks were doubtless persons, they were entitled to basic constitutional protections. Equality, however, seemed to many a foolish notion. As a British observer wrote, it amounted to "putting the fools' cap on republican principle."[23] With the rapid demise of Reconstruction governments in the Southern states and the subsequent ascendency of regimes hostile to blacks, even the lip-service aspiration to equality was discarded. There was wishful thinking, born of Social Darwinism, that blacks would become extinct in the struggle for social existence. Proposals for mass deportation were also frequently heard.[24]

While believers in black inferiority, particularly in the antebellum South, had coupled their views with fantasies of recreating a feudal order in America,[25] one did not have to abandon the idea of the republic in order to insist on the relevance of racial differences. It was possible to reconcile this viewpoint with a commitment to equality of opportunity—for equals. That position maintained that "the Negro was a completely different species of mankind: undeveloped, 'child-like,' amoral, and much less endowed with intellectual capacities than the white man; he was meant by the Creator to be a servant forever; if kept in his 'place' he was useful or at least tolerable, and there he was happy; 'social equality' was unthinkable as it implied intermarriage which would destroy the white race and Anglo-Saxon civilization."[26]

Belief in racial inferiority, coupled with dedication to maintaining the integrity of the white community as a distinct entity, became tied to a whole philosophy of society and of human life.[27] That "benevolent internal colonialism"[28] sanctioned Jim Crow laws in the South. It lent respectability to such widespread Northern practices as whites-only job offerings and racial covenants.[29] This was no aberrant belief but a widely shared social perspective.

Racist convictions, however wrongheaded and reprehensible, cannot be wished or willed away. Was it possible for a court, even the Supreme Court, to undermine this tradition? Could "law-ways" change "folk-ways"?[30] More than a quarter century after *Brown*, such unalloyed racism has almost vanished. When *Brown* was decided, though, the perdurability of prejudice commanded respect and counseled political caution. President Eisenhower, declining to press for strong antidiscrimination legislation, described himself as "one of those people who has very little faith in the ability of statutory law to change the human heart, or eliminate prejudice."[31] Nor did liberals believe differently. "We must proceed gradually," Adlai

Stevenson declared, "not upsetting habits or traditions that are older than the Republic."[32] If the racial dilemma was truly as profound as Myrdal described it, perhaps it lay beyond the ambit of law—or so responsible political actors could argue even into the 1960s.[33]

The idea of a community defined in racial terms was also advanced by blacks themselves. Interest in creating a black society on American soil or in returning to Africa dates almost to the founding of the nation. While despair at never fully becoming part of the society motivated some of this interest, other efforts were animated by a powerful and positive vision of black culture. Late in the nineteenth century, blacks developed an interest in their own history "to give themselves a sense of dignity and pride of race to affect the inferiority doctrines of whites and to stimulate a group solidarity."[34]

Reflecting liberal tradition, *An American Dilemma* describes assimilation—Jefferson's "amalgamation"—and not separation as properly the norm. "We assume that it is to the advantage of American Negroes as individuals and as a group to become assimilated in American culture."[35] After all, blacks had little to lose. "In practically all its divergences, American Negro culture is . . . a distorted development, or a pathological condition, of the general American culture."[36] But "the new Negro," as W. E. B. DuBois labeled him, saw things differently. Blacks constituted "a distinct group with a distinct mission, yet part of the United States";[37] separatism was an opportunity, not a pathology. This second dissenting strand of argument is far less evident in the debates over racial policy preceding *Brown*. Racial separatism was urged mostly by whites, and *Brown* treats it as imposed on blacks, not preferred by them. Yet when separatism was proposed in the name of black power during the late 1960s, the idea could draw upon a considerable history.

Understood in the light of these diverse and competing views, the *Brown* decision acquires even greater significance. It does not merely ratify a certainty but denotes a preference consistent with the classical liberal vision. *Brown* changed the nation dramatically. For a sizable portion of the country, discrimination on the basis of race had been legally mandated. Now it was impermissible. Discrimination had also been a way of life, its rightness taken for granted. Now it had been decreed wrongful.

The *Brown* decree set in motion extraordinary changes. Yet it did not, indeed could not, still the conflict over racial justice; the opinion proved too vague, the device of a court order too weak, for that. Fear and resentment, frustration and impatience, puzzlement and perplexity have provoked continuing disagreement.

III

Like *An American Dilemma* before it, the *Brown* decision is clearer about the nature of the wrong than about the dimensions of the right. The idea of equality, while connected to the rights of the individual, is otherwise weakly specified. In light of the gross, massive, and officially sanctioned nature of then-prevailing inequity, greater clarity was not needed; in light of the persisting ambiguities surrounding equality, greater clarity may not have been possible. Whatever the explanation, the open-endedness of the entitlement has encouraged various interpretations of racial justice, each with its own view of what good policy means.

During the ten years between *Brown* and the passage of the Civil Rights Act, the evil condemned in *Brown* seemed clear enough. The American Creed was the governing premise. In the aftermath of a savage police assault on civil rights demonstrators, President Kennedy delivered an address that Myrdal might have written: "We are confronted primarily with a moral issue. It is as clear as the American Constitution. The heart of the question is whether all Americans are to be afforded equal rights and equal opportunities; whether we are going to treat our fellow Americans as we want to be treated." [38] Martin Luther King spoke similarly to a quarter of a million people gathered in Washington, D.C., to support civil rights legislation. "I have a dream that one day this nation will rise up and live out the true meaning of its creed." [39] In the Civil Rights Act of 1964, Congress finally acted, proscribing discrimination on the basis of race in publicly provided services, employment, and accommodations. Taken together with the Voting Rights Act, the Civil Rights Act recorded what had become the American norm.

Evil suffered patiently as inevitable, Tocqueville remarks in *The Old Regime and the French Revolution*, "seems unendurable as soon as the idea of escaping from it is conceived." [40] Certainly this was true of racial injustice, and the slow pace of change in the decade after *Brown* proved deeply frustrating. Not much had happened, except at the symbolic level; in the Deep South, fewer than 2 percent of all black children were attending desegregated schools. The National Association for the Advancement of Colored People (NAACP) had had to abandon its optimistic slogan, "Free by '63." What would the next decade bring?

In the interval, the problem itself was transformed. The black population, once largely Southern and rural, had moved North— almost half of America's blacks lived above the Mason-Dixon line—and was increasingly concentrated in the cities. Race had become a national, not a regional issue.[41] Perceptions had changed as well. No longer was it routinely presumed that the formal entitlements of *Brown* and the civil rights laws adequately addressed the issue. Was the right to be free from discrimination meaningful without the means to exercise that right? Just what did racial justice mean, as principle and social fact?

Taken together, *Brown*, the Civil Rights Act, and the Voting Rights Act join two different if related ideas of racial equality. The principle of equal opportunity announced in *Brown* speaks to life chances, to the possibility of economic and social mobility. The principle of equal respect, a core liberal idea, primarily concerns political capacity. These principles were taken to mean quite different things. To some, equal opportunity implied integration, reviving the Jeffersonian notion of amalgamation. To others, it was a command to redistribute social resources, whether in terms of money, jobs, or educational outcomes. The vote itself was conventionally thought a sufficient guarantor of respect, for it enabled the individual to participate in a pluralistic democratic society. To those who had become cynical about the prospects for pluralistic democracy, however, respect could be secured only in the context of racial solidarity, of black power. These several understandings of racial justice have shaped social initiatives, leading to such school-specific policies as compensatory education, affirmative action, and community control. Those policies in turn have evoked critical reactions, some recalling the original reading of *Brown*, others derived from the communitarian, ethnocentric tradition that *Brown* sought to overturn.

The integrationist view perceives equality as demanding an end to racial separation. It is not enough that the formal barriers to racial mixing have been removed. As long as blacks and whites remain separated in fact, justice has not been achieved, for the evil condemned in *Brown*, the harm to children (and by extension to all persons) has not been alleviated. As long as race is salient, it remains a divisive social reality. Segregation leads to conflict. It jeopardizes the possibility of a common culture and a truly democratic order.[42]

Although serious attempts to achieve integration in housing and jobs have been made, the integrationists have focused on the public schools. If the society as a whole cannot be integrated by law, it is thought, at least the schools can. Schools have also been regarded as a lever to more general social reform: integration in the schools just might catalyze wider change, brought about by a new and more tolerant generation.

In the context of education, *desegregation* and *integration* are often used synonymously, but the two terms can be usefully distinguished.[43] Desegregation means bringing together black and white students. Integration starts with racial mixing but implies a great deal more. It contemplates an environment in which students from diverse backgrounds with different expectations of school can benefit from an educational experience; it demands an understanding of diversity as a resource, not a disadvantage to be overcome. Small wonder, then, that integration is a very delicate, very difficult—and very vulnerable—enterprise.

Integration has been sought in the name of *Brown*, but the means used—including gerrymandered school district boundaries and deliberate racial mixing—go beyond the classical liberal insistence on color blindness. The integrationist's willingness to undo private- as well as state-created segregation raises the specter of governmental intrusiveness, and the desired end is not part of the familiar lexicon of nondiscrimination. The struggles over these matters, recounted in chapter 3 and in the case histories, result from attempts to work out the integrationist premise.[44]

The tension between classical liberalism and social welfare liberalism shaped this policy debate. Social welfare liberalism, a product of the New Deal, couples concern for individual liberty with attention to the well-being of the group; it blurs the distinction between equality of opportunity and equality of result. The differences between the two social philosophies determined how deliberate integration was regarded and also affected understandings of redistributive justice.

President Lyndon Johnson's 1966 Howard University commencement address reflects these uncertainties. "We seek not just freedom but opportunity—not just legal equity but human ability—not just equality as a right and a theory but equality as a fact and a result. For the task is to give twenty million Negroes the same chance as every other American . . . to pursue their individual happiness."[45] Two conceptions of the American ideal—equality as opportunity and equality as result—coexist here in imperfect harmony.

The redistributionist vision of racial justice speaks less to the hope of integrating black and white than to the sorry circumstances prevailing in the black community. Even as blacks' civil rights were being legally secured, several influential analyses contended that such entitlements were not enough. Kenneth Clark's *Dark Ghetto*,[46] Thomas Pettigrew's *The Negro in America*,[47] and Daniel Moynihan's report, *The Negro Family*,[48] concurred that things were getting worse, not better. Discrimination, prejudice, segregation, and the legacy of slavery had resulted in what Clark called a "tangle of pathology" in black communities: unemployment, poor education, unstable families, crime, drug addiction, frequent illness, and early death. Discrimination might lie at the source of this "disease," but since it had taken on a life of its own, ending the discrimination without doing more would not produce a cure.

These analysts called for massive government aid specifically focused on the black underclass. "Nothing short of a concerned and massive attack on the social, political, economic and cultural roots of the pathology is required if anything more than a daubing or a displacement of the symptoms is to be achieved."[49] The particulars of suggested governmental intervention varied with the importance assigned to family instability, unemployment, and under-education as causes of disadvantage, but major government aid was generally urged. The New Deal would come to the ghetto thirty years late, dressed up as the Great Society, bringing with it substantial resources that, it was hoped, would break the pathological circle of causality.[50]

Redistribution and integration were seen as compatible by their advocates, but in fact they pull in different directions. Integration is national and universalist in focus, redistribution localist and specifically aimed at aiding blacks. While the hope has frequently been voiced that, in the long run, a strengthened black community will welcome integration as equals, in reality the long run has come to seem very distant, the intervening tasks more important and harder to accomplish than once supposed. How might "the distribution of success and failure within one group be [made] roughly comparable to that within other groups?"[51] If nondiscrimination is insufficient because "discrimination in American life is so deeply imbedded in the minds and practices of individual Americans and their institutions,"[52] what will suffice?

The government's response was to offer aid to the poor through compensatory education, job training, housing development, and community-building efforts. Because of the disproportionately large number of poor blacks, much of this money went to blacks. As these programs too seemingly failed to arrest the "disease," more specifically racial aid has been authorized, in the form of legally mandated quotas for minority workers. While a certain policy logic is apparent—when what you've tried doesn't work, do more—the tie to classic understandings of racial justice has become increasingly attenuated. Racial specificity, once condemned as offensive to the rights of persons, was now said to be the only way of giving meaning to those very claims.[53] Equality, once an individual right, was now held to lodge in the group.[54] All this seems a long way from the conventional view of the teachings of *Brown*. At the least, it underscores the dynamic quality of equality.

A third approach to racial justice looks not to abolishing the ghetto but to securing the community's control over its institutions. In this view, set forth most fully in Stokeley Carmichael and Charles Hamilton's *Black Power*,[55] politically repressive America is seen as the problem, black power the key to equality. The existing structures of government are assailed as forces of oppression, agents of a malevolent paternalism that denies blacks the authority to act for themselves. Respect can come only from black solidarity.

Advocates of black power borrowed the description of ghetto pathology advanced by Clark and Moynihan to demonstrate white oppressiveness and black entitlement to redistributive aid. Resources alone, however, were not enough, for receiving aid without the authority to use it as the black community wished would only reinforce the pattern of dependency. The idea of redistribution was incorporated into black power; integration, in contrast, evoked scorn. The moral idealism of *Brown* was condemned as bankrupt, reinforcing "among both black and white the idea that 'white' is automatically superior and 'black' is by definition inferior. For this reason, 'integration' is a subterfuge for the maintenance of white supremacy."[56]

As a political diagnosis, black power seems riddled with ambiguities. If black power truly meant racial separation, it was hard to see how this might transpire in a country that has so thoroughly entangled the fates of the races. If on the other hand black power embodied no more than a black version of the new ethnic politics, an organizing strategy "necessary in a pluralistic society,"[57] where would it find its political allies? Even more than integration and redistribution, black power tested the elasticity of racial justice. The black estate was described as "a nation within a nation," but where *Brown* and the civil rights legislation were intended to undo that condition, black power meant to build on it.

Yet one idea, derived in part from black power, has powerfully influenced racial policy: racial justice necessarily entails black participation. Supporters of integration and to some extent of redistribution have sought to remove race from politics, turning it into a wholly normative question. But equality has an importantly political dimension as well. The core theme of black power is that racial justice has no meaning apart from people's expressed wants; it is ultimately rooted, not in idealism or resources, but in authority and respect. In diluted form, that notion became part of the War on Poverty. As David Greenstone and Paul Peterson observe, writing about this government effort: "Its content addressed the political relationship of black Americans to the American regime, not the economic relationships of poor people to the marketplace; its origins were rooted in a civil rights movement that focused on altering the country's political, not its socio-economic relationships; and its long-range impact has related to the political conditions of black Americans, not their economic status."[58] This conception of racial justice strains the credo of *Brown* that race is above politics.

Integration, redistribution, black power: although the ideas and their adherents have warred with each other, what they have in common also merits mention. Each strategy recognizes "that abolishing legal racism would not produce Negro equality,"[59] that an antidiscrimination strategy will not bring about a just society. Because each asks more fundamental questions of the social order, each is harder to achieve—harder even to contemplate in terms of what achievement might entail—than is simple nondiscrimination.

As long as racial justice could be contained in a unitary vision, it effectively monopolized political and intellectual discourse. Martin Luther King's dream had no real nay-sayers. But with the fissioning of the aspiration in the revelation of its multiple meanings and its growing national impact, resistance to "progress" in any of these forms became detectable.

That resistance has assumed two very different forms. On one side are those who see in black demands a threat to ethnically homogeneous white communities. Black power implied a kind of mutiny; redistribution gave resources to the undeserving and in the case of preferential treatment denied opportunities to needy whites. Integration was and remains the greatest source of unhappiness for these dissenters. It jeopardizes the cultural solidarity epitomized by neighborhood schools; it also exposes middle-class children to the "disease" of the ghetto, a disease that is thought to be contagious. In its attention to communitarianism and its recognition of racial differences, this critical viewpoint harkens back to pre-*Brown* understandings.[60]

The resisters also include those who base their objections to deliberate integration and racial preference not on grounds of self-interest and perceived personal threat but on principle. These critics assert their continuing fidelity to *Brown* and to classical liberalism, with its emphasis on individual merit. They believe that the Constitution forbids the singling out of racial groups for any purpose. Consequently, they oppose relying on race as a policy criterion, even for ostensibly good causes, especially where others who have committed no wrong are hurt.[61]

In the five Bay Area communities, the period between 1965 and 1970 was the stormiest—disagreements were most apparent, and political tensions highest. That has in some measure to do with the tenor of the broader debate over racial justice during this time.

IV

With respect to education as elsewhere in the society, no single conception of racial justice presently prevails. The earlier visions of integration, redistribution, and black power each endure in altered form and varying measure. Integration is still pursued, although generally with a less singleminded focus on racial mix and with greater attention to related issues of educational quality and institutional stability. Federal policy has remained redistributionist in character, although markedly less so under the Reagan administration. Policy debate focuses on the persistence of racial discrimination and more broadly on the relevance of race, as opposed to social class, as the mainspring of inequality.[62] The themes of black power, although not directly heard, find their analogues in the insistence of Third World groups on ethnically pluralist public policies.

Some progress toward equality between blacks and whites has been marked. Blacks are better off economically, more successful educationally, and stronger politically than they were a decade ago, although the movement has been uneven and has not kept pace with expectation. Of greater moment, the visions of just policy themselves have been transformed, in a manner at once the cause and the consequence of an altered policy climate. Race has a less central importance, and with respect to race, ideological argument is less frequently heard. This transformation, too, has affected the ways in which the Bay Area school districts continue the task of defining their mission with respect to nonwhite students.

The effort to bring about a universalist order through desegregation has persisted in public housing[63] and especially in public education. There is scarcely a city, Northern or Southern, that remains untouched by legal or political pressure to accomplish some racial mixing. Yet as this question has been pressed in predominantly black communities, the singleminded stress on numerical balance has come to seem inappropriate; there are just too few whites to go around. Partly for that reason, partly because simple numerical mixing has not had the desired social or educational consequences, integration now includes both student reassignment and policy reforms intended to improve the quality of instruction. These issues are taken up in greater detail in subsequent chapters. What matters here is that this apparently most straightforward of the conceptions of racial justice has grown increasingly complex and more closely linked to other policy concerns. Integration policy has been transformed into a racially driven *education* policy.

Redistribution was less talked about but more acted upon in the 1970s. The conflict-provoking community-action programs of the 1960s were succeeded by less controversial job programs and urban aid that actually committed more money to the black poor.[64] Affirmative action too became institutionalized, as Congress and the president fixed job quotas in some federally supported projects through statute and executive order.[65] Policy during the decade startlingly resembled what Daniel Moynihan, then counselor to President Nixon, urged in 1970 as "benign neglect . . . a period in which Negro progress continues and racial rhetoric fades."[66] This period may mark the high-water mark for redistributionist efforts, for such programs have been sharply trimmed by the Reagan administration.

Does benign neglect work? That question, which joins empirical and normative considerations, has no single, simple answer. Its economic and political components need to be disentangled; each brings its own dilemmas and confirms the complexity of the problem. Consider first the economic dimension. Looking at the earnings of blacks and whites in the aggregate yields a depressing finding: the ratio of black to white earnings actually declined between 1969 and 1978, from 61 percent to 59 percent. But this figure conceals deep splits within the black community. For male-headed households, the black-white ratio has increased from 72 percent to 80 percent; the exploding number of female-headed families brings down the overall figures.[67] The income of college-educated blacks has risen to near-parity with that of whites, and among all those employed full-time, the earnings gap has narrowed appreciably. For the bottom third of the black population, however, the story is grim. "The black underclass has evidenced higher unemployment rates, lower labor force participation rates, higher welfare rates, and, more recently, a sharply declining movement out of poverty."[68] Poor and middle-class blacks inhabit different economic worlds. Those differences seem to be both widening and becoming less readily surmountable.

What explains this pattern? For some, the familiar message bears retelling: discrimination remains, racism persists.[69] The unsubtle practices of the past have been supplanted by discrimination equally devastating in impact if harder to discern. This new racial oppression is detectable not in its forms but in its effect. Age, sex, location, marital status, industry, and occupation are held to count for less than race in explaining the economic marginality of blacks, and "something besides education seems to have made the critical difference."[70] That "something," it is believed, is discrimination, which can be remedied only by further redistributive efforts. Others view race as too narrow a focus and discrimination as an "incredible simplification"[71] of the causes of black-white inequality. They emphasize class and not race as the critical factor and urge assaults upon inequality "that go beyond the limits of ethnic and racial discrimination by directly confronting the pervasive and destructive features of class subordination."[72] Affirmative action is rejected by those who believe the policy only makes well-off blacks even better off, thus worsening stratification within the black population. That policy arouses principled as well as pragmatic opposition, for it is said to constitute "a radical and disturbing attack on the principles of justice and equal treatment"[73] that have historically been the basis of the liberal society.

These questions—specifically the issue of affirmative action—beget persisting controversies. The Supreme Court has confirmed the permissibility of taking race into account in university admissions, in hiring and promotion policies that a firm voluntarily adopts, and in federally funded projects.[74] Yet the divisions among the justices, as well as the hedged and tentative character of their opinions, reinforce rather than resolve the controversy.[75] Is it right to recreate group distinctions through preferential programs, and if so under what circumstances? Do these efforts have the effect of bringing blacks and whites closer together? With redistribution as with integration, puzzlement appears to yield puzzlement, and this is true in the realms of both fact and value.

The enhanced economic well-being of some blacks has not "significantly alleviated racial tensions in American society," William Julius Wilson argues, but rather focuses those tensions onto politics. Contemporary racial concerns center on the "struggle of power and privilege in the central cities," a "struggle over access to and control of decent housing and decent neighborhoods . . . access to and control of local public schools . . . [and] political control."[76]

This struggle is not new, of course. Black politicians have tried since emancipation to influence the course of politics, and the civil rights movement was aimed at opening up the political institutions of the society. In politics as in economics, some measurable successes have been marked. Proportionately, almost as many blacks as whites voted in the 1976 election; in 1960, blacks were only five-eighths as likely to turn out. Black registration in the South, proportionately less than half of white registration in 1960, nearly reached parity in 1976.[77] Over five thousand black officials held elective office in the United States in 1978, as compared with 103 in 1964; the number of black Congressmen and state legislators tripled during this period.[78] Community action of the 1960s begat interest group politics in the 1970s, as the pluralist system absorbed racial minorities, albeit imperfectly.[79] In debates over education black voices were likewise heard, if in numbers still disproportionately low, when an earlier generation of activists entered the system as participants. The black demand for inclusion in the system of governance has to some extent been answered, and with that achievement it has become possible for blacks and whites to bargain with one another. This circumstance poses its own dilemma: To what extent is racial justice a matter not of principle but of popular preference?

Blacks are not the only group to enjoy new political respect. The emergence of Third World—particularly Asian and Latino— groups as a potent force has prompted demands for ethnic pluralism, separatist in tone but without the sting of black power. The United States, it has been suggested, should become "a multicultural society in which the different ethnic groups live in a symbiotic relationship which enriches each other."[80] Although that language sounds conciliatory, the struggle over ethnicity in public policy, particularly with respect to bilingualism in voting and education and to the teaching of black English, has been fierce.[81] Government was previously asked to reallocate primary goods, money, and power. Now it is being called upon to make self-consciously particularistic cultural and racial value choices, again in the name of racial justice.

V

The problem of discrimination once seemed so self-evident as scarcely to require description, the solution so straightforward as not to demand elaboration. That has changed. Although consensus about the meaning of racial justice was always fragile and vulnerable, dilemmas have multiplied in truly dazzling fashion. There is disagreement about the meaning and continuing force of discrimination, as well as about the effectiveness and, differently, the legitimacy of strategies for combating discrimination. Concerning what is substantively right, and even the mechanisms for defining rightness, division is marked. No institution could resolve these disputes authoritatively, as the Supreme Court sought to do in *Brown*, for the national institutions themselves embody the tensions. Idiosyncrasy has prevailed out of necessity.

Decisions that bear on racial policy have to be, and are being, made. Even doing nothing marks a policy determination.[82] These choices are often made within the context of the public schools, for questions of racial justice and educational equity have come to be seen as closely interrelated. The larger debate over race has sometimes provided a setting for discussions about education. More typically, the debate itself has been waged in the educational arena, as racial fairness and educational equity merge. Race constitutes one key item in the policy equation. The Bermuda Triangle that is education represents the other, and for that reason the next chapter traces the evolution of equal educational opportunity. That discussion too has specific bearing on the experience of the five Bay Area towns. Throughout the period, their school boards and administrations have had repeatedly to consider what course of action is both racially and educationally defensible.

CHAPTER
3

Education: The Many Meanings
of Equal Opportunity

I

From the very beginnings of the republic, education has been
regarded as an "American religion,"[1] commanding extraordinary
public attention and allegiance. The vision of educational opportunity from that time to the present has been expressed in terms of
equality. The meaning of equality has evolved, but the language
has remained the same. America would provide common schools,
publicly supported, for the children of rich and poor alike: a revolutionary notion when contrasted with practice in eighteenth- and
nineteenth-century England.[2] And the aspiration of the earliest vi-
sionaries was equally revolutionary: an educational system that
would enable individuals to succeed on the basis of individual ability, unimpeded by the constraints of social class.

This understanding of educational opportunity complements
the liberal individualism that has been the dominant American political impulse. Success in schooling has been widely regarded as
the key to mobility in a fluid society, for it offers individuals the
chance to develop and be rewarded for their talents. The person
who benefits from an education is better off—and so too is the republic that nurtures the talents of its members. Education appears
to be at once a private good and a collective good, since everyone
seems to gain from its increased provision. For just these reasons,
Gunnar Myrdal identified education as the driving impulse of the
American Creed:

Education has always been the great hope for both individual and society.
In the American Creed it has been the main ground upon which "equality
of opportunity for the individual" and "free outlet for ability" could be

based. Education has also been considered the best way—and the way most compatible with American individualistic ideals—to improve society.[3]

In the debate over educational policy carried out in the five Bay Area communities, egalitarianism has been a recurring theme. Its symbolic power has often made education seem more vital and consequential than public works or social welfare.[4] Yet the aspiration to equalize educational opportunity has been subjected to severe stresses, and these too are germane. For one thing, equality is at most an aspiration, a goad to policy reform and not a present reality. For another thing, as with race, the meaning of equality in education appears various and fugitive. Just what is to be equalized, opportunity defined in terms of exposure or opportunity understood in terms of results? And how is responsibility for assuring equal opportunity to be apportioned between the state and the individual?[5]

The promise of equal opportunity is also uncertain. Throughout our history, equality in education has embraced a vision of common citizenship acquired through common schooling. That vision coexists uneasily with the fact of social and economic inequality, an inequality apparently too firmly entrenched to be overcome by the engine of education.[6] The liberal individualist character of equal opportunity denies this tension. It contemplates a gradual, almost effortless process of change on the part of persons and has nothing to say about groups or classes. Such an understanding of the dynamic of social change offers an incomplete response to the structural character of prevailing and persisting inequality.[7]

These doubts concerning the meaning and value of equal opportunity surfaced in the five Bay Area communities during disputes concerning the quality of instruction and alleged elitism in the schools. When tied to the matter of race, they acquired particular bite. Before the Supreme Court's decision in *Brown*, the interests of black children generally went unmentioned in discussions of equal educational opportunity. Until almost the turn of the present century, Southern blacks had no state-provided education, and elsewhere their opportunities were decidedly and deliberately inferior to those of whites. Neither the nineteenth-century advocates of common schooling nor the Progressive Era reformers spoke to the needs of black children.

Brown demanded a different way of thinking, not only about racial justice but also about equal opportunity in education. One abiding consequence of that decision has been to encourage a reconceptualization of equal opportunity that takes race centrally into account; after *Brown*, racial fairness and educational equity are tightly linked. The Supreme Court's opinion also offers an expansive understanding of educational opportunity, stressing the impact of schooling on life chances. "It is doubtful," the Court proclaims, "that any child may reasonably be expected to succeed in life if he is denied the opportunity of an education."[8] This emphasis on the saving powers of education is empirically questionable,[9] but it has nonetheless shaped discussions of educational opportunity ever since.

II

Fostering meritocracy, encouraging assimilation into a common culture, legitimating differentiation: these distinct understandings of educational opportunity recur throughout our history and remain salient today. While there are tensions among the themes, the persistent hope has been to reconcile them, to render education, as Horace Mann proclaimed, at once the "great equalizer" of individual circumstances, the "balance wheel of the social machinery," and the "creator of wealth undreamed of" for the nation.[10]

Equality in education was identified from the outset as furthering the aims of the new republic. Benjamin Rush, writing in 1786, asserted that education would "render the mass of people more homogeneous, and thereby fit them more easily for uniform government,"[11] and this pragmatic argument, rather than concern for the intrinsic benefits of learning, led half of the fourteen states that drafted constitutions before 1800 to guarantee some public aid to schooling. Homogeneity bore two distinct meanings: schools would make children more nearly equal and would also turn out individuals who shared cultural and political values.

Equality defined in this way was not the only reason to encourage public support of education. Such support, Thomas Jefferson asserted, would encourage a "natural aristocracy of talent." Primary schooling available to all would identify the ablest youngsters, those "worthy to receive and able to guard the sacred deposit of the rights and liberties of their fellow citizens."[12] A common education for the masses, further state-supported instruction for "twenty of the best geniuses . . . raked from the rubbish annually": this meritocratic order, which was Jefferson's hope, reappears, couched in less blunt rhetoric, in succeeding eras.

Both the potential and the bounded nature of equality are apparent in the common school movement of the nineteenth century. The schools themselves were free, uniform, and (by the last third of the century) compulsory. They brought together children from diverse backgrounds and exposed them to a common curricu-

lum, a "single educational ladder"[13] that all might climb. The new
school would, as New York education commissioner Henry Barnard wrote, be common "in the highest and best sense of the
word—common because it is good enough for the best, and cheap
enough for the poorest family in the community."[14] If, early in the
nineteenth century, education still had less effect on life chances
than did skills acquired elsewhere, the increasing specialization of
the labor market gave education a new practical importance. Literacy had value, not just because it buttressed the ideals of the republic but also because it served the emerging need for trained
professionals and clerks.

Common schools were also regarded as the vehicles of social
assimilation and development of a shared political culture. The
spread of common schools coincided with the first major wave of
immigration in the mid-nineteenth century, and was intended to
combat tendencies toward ethnic and religious divisiveness. That
concern underlay the pitched battles over state aid to parochial
schools during this period.[15] Public education would erase the taint
of differentness. The common schools, it was said, would train a
"homogeneous people, universally educated and imbued with the
principles of morality and virtue."[16]

Equality and assimilation were the themes emphasized,
but the educational system remained differentiated at its upper
reaches. Public support financed primary instruction, but only the
very brightest, who received scholarships, and the children of the
well-off could afford further education. Although job differentiation was still rudimentary and further education relevant to only a
handful of vocations, the link between unequal educational opportunities and life chances is apparent even at this time.

Fissures between the meanings of equality recur, although in
altered form, during the second great wave of educational change
instigated by the Progressives, beginning at the end of the nineteenth century. Progressivism defined equality of opportunity in
terms of a differentiated curriculum rather than as common instruction. It embraced two quite different notions of equality of citizenship, stressing variously cultural homogeneity and pluralism.[17]

By 1900, the hope of the common school advocates had become a reality. Almost all American youngsters received a primary
education, and most states compelled attendance at a public or
state-approved private school.[18] Yet even as universal primary instruction was achieved, its shortcomings commanded attention.

Common instruction worked well enough as long as the econ-

omy did not demand many highly trained workers. But an increasingly sophisticated industrial order called for a different kind
of work force: primary schooling without technical training was no
longer sufficient. Expanding the public school system to the secondary level served two quite different ends. It permitted schools
to give students "the preparation and training they required as future manual and industrial wageworkers."[19] It also undid the inequity inherent in the selective availability of high schools, which
until 1900 enrolled barely 8 percent of the eligible population. The
expanded secondary schools would both meet economic needs and
operate as "democracy's colleges."[20]

The new secondary school program propounded by the Progressives did not merely continue the pattern of common schooling but "transformed the nature of schooling itself."[21] What was
needed was not a curriculum classically academic in orientation
but one that, in John Dewey's terms, embraced "a new view of culture extending beyond traditional preoccupation with language
and literature to an inclusive concern with the whole vast pan-
orama of human affairs."[22] Life itself, not only the life of the mind,
properly formed the subject matter of education.

The language of aspiration remained genuinely egalitarian.
Progressivism envisioned a radically transformed social and political order, with schools functioning as "the educational correlates of
a democratic and progressive society."[23] This point of view dictated
that the curriculum vary with the child's needs and capabilities,
since only in that way might equality be served.

Dewey's criticism of classical education made the relevance of
the subject matter to the child's needs a primary consideration.
Others, starting from different premises, assailed the conventional
classical secondary curriculum as inappropriate for students who
would go not to college but to industry. Utilitarianism first, culture
later, the business community urged. In some cities business firms
set up their own schools, which taught practical skills; elsewhere
trade and manual training were brought into the public school
curriculum.

Not all children enrolled in the new secondary programs.
Those who appeared brightest continued to receive an academic
education; the advent of intelligence testing enabled educators
to distinguish them with considerable, if often misplaced, confidence.[24] So too did the sons and daughters of the well-to-do. During
the first two decades of the century, most immigrant children were
mustered into the work force directly after primary school. The educational system was thus stratified, and that differentiation was

also defended in terms of equality. Addressing the National Education Association in 1908, Dean James Russell of Columbia Teachers College asked, in terms reminiscent of Jefferson: "If the chief object of government be to promote civil order and social stability, how can we justify our practice in schooling the masses in precisely the same manner as we do those who are to be our leaders?"[25]

In insisting upon the inevitability of differentiation, Russell did not mean to abandon equality but to revitalize the concept, bringing schooling into harmony with the new society. The classical curriculum was itself seen as inegalitarian because it served the needs of only a minority. Without irony, Russell entitled his speech "Democracy and Education: Equal Opportunity for All." Differentiation betokened equality. "The idea inherent in the new [Progressive Era] secondary school curriculum," as James Coleman has subsequently noted, "appears to have been to take as given the diverse occupational paths into which adolescents will go after secondary school, and to say (implicitly): there is greater equality of educational opportunity for a boy who is not going to attend college if he has a specially designed curriculum than if he must take a curriculum designed for college entrance."[26]

This concept, in turn, altered the balance of responsibility between state and child:

Formerly, when the content and purposes of the school had been fairly well defined and commonly accepted, the burden of proof was on the student: he was told to perform up to standard or get out. Educational opportunity was the right of all who might profit from schooling to enjoy its benefits. Now, the "giver" of the equation was no longer the school with its well-defined content and purposes, but the children with their particular backgrounds and needs. And educational opportunity had become the right of all who attended school to receive something of meaning and value.[27]

How might "something of meaning and value" be offered to the diverse students who entered secondary school? Physical separation of students seemed too obviously undemocratic, too decisive a break with the practice of the common school. The comprehensive secondary school that housed varied instructional programs under one roof seemed to realize the best of both worlds, commonality and differentiation, and hence was thought to reconcile the tension between the meanings of equal opportunity. The high school attended to children's varied capabilities while continuing the common school tradition by bringing children of different backgrounds together in a single setting. As the National Education Association noted in an influential 1918 report, the secondary school "has a unique opportunity . . . because it includes in its membership representatives from all classes of society and consequently is able through social relationships to establish bonds of friendship and common understanding that cannot be furnished by other agencies."[28] Common citizenship and varied education would be fostered simultaneously.

The idea of common citizenship was itself strained by the substantial influx of new immigrants. Unlike earlier generations, many of whom were drawn from the British Isles, this cohort came increasingly from eastern and southern Europe and brought diverse customs and traditions to America. In educating immigrant youngsters, the preponderant Progressive hope was that "the many would be changed into one people, e pluribus unum."[29] Immigrants would be better off if differences were submerged—and so too would the society. "If the standard of living in the tenements is to be raised from that of the poorest classes in Italy and Russia to the American standard," wrote one urban school administrator, "it will be done through the teaching of home making in the public schools."[30] Exposure to American ways, through schooling, would make the difference.

This assimilationist approach contended for dominance with a pluralistic view, which offered a more capacious understanding of American citizenship. "For the enrichment of our national life as well as for the happiness and welfare of individuals," the U.S. commissioner of education argued in 1913, "we must respect [immigrants'] ideals and preserve and strengthen all the best of their Old World life they bring with them. We must not attempt to destroy and remake—we can only transform. Racial and national virtues must not be thoughtlessly exchanged for American vices."[31] In both approaches, transformation was the key. How it might be achieved and what form the new American citizenship would assume have remained key questions, confounding attempts to give equal opportunity a single meaning.

Progressivism dominated discussion of educational policy until mid-century. The elasticity of this school of thought, which enabled self-styled progressives to embrace simultaneously humane child-centeredness and the cult of the IQ test, meant that a great many nostrums could be passed off as progressive in origin and spirit. The life-adjustment movement, for example, which flowered after World War II, took the notion of educational breadth urged by Dewey and removed from it all traces of academic content or reformist sting. "Ethical and moral living" and "occupational adjustment" (preparing students to accept inherently alienating jobs) were what school should teach.[32] Revealingly, these objectives, too, were couched in egalitarian language, as a way of reaching students who could not cope with demanding academic or vocational training. Life adjustment "was the golden opportunity," a spokesman for the U.S. Office of Education declared, "to do something that would give to *all* American youths their educational heritage so long denied."[33]

A reaction to such excesses was predictable, for progressive education had begun to caricature itself. The form that the reaction took would have gladdened the hearts of those who promoted the common schools a century earlier. "Popular education," Arthur Bestor wrote in an influential critique of educational practice, "is designed to endow the people as a whole with precisely the kinds of intellectual power that have hitherto been monopolized by an aristocratic few."[34]

The burden of assuring this measure of equality rested squarely with the state:

The duty of the school is to make up, so far as it is able, the deficiencies of background which it finds in its students. Both in the short run and in the long, the democratic school must concentrate, as never before, upon the task of intellectual training. . . . The student who has been deprived of intellectual and cultural background at home must receive full restitution in the school.[35]

This hope was noble, if somewhat naive. Could all students really be expected to develop such intellectual skills? And how did this reinterpretation of the common school ideal square with the realities of the work place: Who would sweep the streets? This was precisely the rejoinder of conservative critic Hyman Rickover, whose proposals for schools that would develop the talents of the best and brightest recalled the urgings of Jefferson. "Unless we abandon false democratic clichés which interpret democracy as enthronement of the commonplace and obstruction of excellence, we may find that we have traded democratic freedom for a mess of pseudo-democratic mediocrity."[36]

Old tensions inherent in the idea of equality of opportunity had reemerged in a different setting. As in the Progressive era, resolution lay in comprehensive education. In *The American High School*, a widely hailed study, former Harvard University President James Conant rediscovered the virtues of the comprehensive school, an institution that undid all the "false antitheses" of American education. "At one and the same time," argued Conant, it "provides a good general education for all pupils as future citizens of a democracy, provides elective programs for the majority to develop useful skills, and educates adequately those with a talent for handling advanced academic subjects."[37] Equality of political citizenship could be coupled with educational differentiation, the compound embodying equality of opportunity. That approach recognized the needs both of a liberal meritocratic society and of the individual. "We can, through our schools, annually restore a great deal of fluidity to our social and economic life and in so doing make available for the national welfare reservoirs of potential professional talent now untapped."[38]

The American High School is a distinguished effort to weave together the several strands of equal opportunity. It embraces the consensual understanding of American political and social life that characterized the nation at the time. Yet the consensus that it asserts, quite like the earlier discussions of equality in education, does not speak to the plight of black schoolchildren and is thus radically incomplete.

The history of American education is in some measure an attempt to secure equal educational opportunity. The ideal, vague and protean to be sure, has suffused the process by which the educational system has grown and changed. That evolution has proceeded in rough accord with shifting perceptions of social justice. After *Brown*, those perceptions had to include the needs and wants of black Americans.

III

The drive for educational equality, like the larger campaign to bring about racial justice, bespoke blacks' desire for inclusion. If education is an American religion, blacks have long been among the most faithful worshippers. The promise of education has shone most brightly for blacks, even as they were denied full educational entitlement. The newly emancipated slaves, reported Booker T. Washington, were a "whole race trying to go to school,"[39] and education remained the primary focus in the legal and political drive to eradicate the lingering impress of slavery.

Throughout the country, blacks only belatedly and grudgingly received the benefits of publicly supported instruction.[40] Slaves in the antebellum South were legally forbidden to acquire an education. Because they attached an "almost redemptive meaning" to learning, blacks took extraordinary measures to foster literacy, including establishing clandestine schools and converting Sunday schools into ordinary classrooms.[41] Widespread public education did not come to the South until the beginning of this cen-

tury, although cities like New Orleans and Atlanta provided it earlier. When public schools were set up, blacks attended segregated
and woefully inferior institutions. Ten to fifteen times more money
was spent on each white student, such basic facilities as libraries
and laboratories were installed in white but not in black schools,
and the school year for black students was shortened to permit
them to do field labor. "Separate but equal," announced by the Supreme Court in 1896 as blacks' constitutional due, became a cruel
hoax.[42] Indeed, it was the failure of a South Carolina school district
even to provide a usable bus for its black students that ultimately
prompted the constitutional challenge to dual schools.[43]

Blacks in the North similarly valued education highly. "If we
ever expect to see the influence of prejudice decrease and ourselves
respected, it must be by the blessings of our enlightened education," a national black convention resolved in 1832.[44] Throughout
the first half of the nineteenth century, blacks attended separate
public schools; the common school was not open to them. Whites
feared that racial mixing would promote black migration, incite
violence, and prove fatal to the new system of public education.
The presumption of black inferiority also underlay insistence on
separate schools. Blacks "are not by nature equal to the whites and
their children cannot be made equal to my children, or those of my
constituents," a delegate to the 1857 Iowa state constitutional convention maintained.[45]

Blacks objected vehemently to this practice. Separate schools,
the *Colored American* charged in 1837, "so shackled the intellect of
colored youth," that an education acquired under such circumstances, was, comparatively, of little advantage; and blacks newly
arrived from the South were urged to boycott the separate schools
as "too self-degrading."[46] Black protest against segregated schools,
first voiced formally in Massachusetts, rehearsed arguments that
would be heard a century later in *Brown*. "It is the humanizing,
socializing influence of the school system which is its most important feature," stated a group of Boston blacks in an 1846 petition
for racially mixed schools. In a suit brought against the Boston
school committee, the black plaintiffs urged that separation sig-
nified inferiority. "Amalgamation is degradation," the school committee replied.[47]

While in Boston the court battle was lost,[48] the campaign for
desegregation persisted. "The point which we must aim at," Frederick Douglass wrote, "is to obtain admission for our children into
the nearest school house, and the best school house in our respective neighborhoods."[49] The Massachusetts legislature abolished

segregation in 1856, and following the Civil War this pattern was repeated in other Northern states. The commitment of blacks to education remained undiminished. At the turn of the century, black secondary school enrollment in the North was proportionately higher than immigrant (and in some cities native white) enrollment, despite the substantial obstacles placed in the path of blacks.[50]

Yet the tangible rewards of an education remained fewer, the connection between educational success and social mobility underlying the common school and Progressive movements far more remote, for blacks than for whites. The 1947 report of the President's Commission on Higher Education recognized this fact. "For the greatest majority of our boys and girls, the kind and amount of education they may hope to attain depends, not on their own abilities, but on the family or community into which they happen to be born or, worse still, on the color of their skin."[51] By expressly linking education and race, *Brown* was supposed to undo this pattern, to reconcile the treatment of blacks in the educational system with the promise of equal opportunity.

IV

Brown not only introduced race into discussions of equal opportunity but also altered the substance of those discussions. During both the common school and Progressive eras, attention centered on the ingredients of education, the availability of schooling at different grade levels, and the nature of the curriculum. Although these ingredients were thought to affect educational achievement and life success, outcomes did not provide a basis for judging the performance of the schools.

In stressing the impact of segregation on the life chances of black students, *Brown* began to shift the terms of discourse—even as resources were in fact being substantially equalized. Outcomes, not resources, have subsequently come to define equality. The development of sophisticated analytic techniques capable of relating inputs to outcomes has made it possible to judge schools against this new and more demanding test of equality. What policy reform might bring the new equality about: compensatory schooling? desegregation? community-controled schools? At no time in the history of the republic did the promise of education loom larger than during the twenty years after *Brown*. Yet how that promise might be realized, how equal educational opportunity might at last be made manifest, has remained an unanswered and perhaps an unanswerable question.

Beginning shortly after *Brown*, schooling provoked substantial interest on the part of the federal government. The hopes rang familiar. As in 1840 with the development of the common school and in 1900 with the emergence of the Progressive movement, education was to serve as the instrument of equalization, and in so doing to bring about the common political and economic citizenship that had proved stubbornly elusive. With *Brown*, though, education became a truly national cause. "The answer for all our national problems comes down to one single word: education," declared President Lyndon Johnson.[52]

The primary concern was with the children of the poor—especially, after the *Brown* decision and the civil rights struggles that followed, the black poor. This underclass, social scientists argued, differed from other urban villagers, for the "dark ghetto" exercised an especially tenacious hold on its members.[53] Ghetto poverty was not a transient state, a way station on the road to becoming Americanized, but was instead associated with a cultural pathology reaching every aspect of the lives of the black poor.[54] Ghetto families could not do much to help their children, since they were regarded as part of the problem.

The schools that served ghetto children reinforced this pathology. With few exceptions,[55] they offered a worse education than that available to the more advantaged and white students, and ghetto teachers' low expectations of their pupils only buttressed what psychologists described as a prevalent negative self-image.[56] The consequences for the children, continued marginal membership in the society, were bad enough. For the nation as a whole, they seemed worse. "Social dynamite" was how James Conant described ghetto schools in *Slums and Suburbs*.[57] None of this was exactly news—the Progressives had made similar observations about city life sixty years earlier—but the proposed cure, substantial federal assistance for compensatory schooling, was novel.

The federal government had previously offered little support to primary and secondary education, in part because liberal unwillingness to aid segregated schools had killed off earlier federal aid proposals.[58] That problem had been laid to rest with the passage of the 1964 Civil Rights Act, which required nondiscrimination as a condition of federal support.[59] To an administration committed to reducing inequality, education held obvious attractions. Reform through education would help the less well-off without inconveniencing the haves. It offered the prospect of reform through self-improvement, an idea with longstanding liberal appeal.

The Great Society shaped by Lyndon Johnson relied on a mixture of strategies to reduce poverty and improve the position of blacks. As some of these efforts, particularly community action, stirred up powerful political opposition, the administration turned increasingly toward less controversial reforms in education. Federally funded programs were designed to provide poor blacks with the skills needed to assure economic mobility. At the least, such measures would diminish discontent and reduce crime, no small concern in the aftermath of the riots in Harlem and Watts.

Since the New Deal, the federal government has often sought to achieve redistributive ends through social programs, in contrast to state and local governments, which have been primarily attentive to maintaining efficiency.[60] The Elementary and Secondary Education Act was conceived in this egalitarian tradition. Like the Progressive era policies, it was intended to refocus the energies of the schools on the needs of those who had been badly served. In part, this meant curricular redesign, which would involve "the whole child." More importantly, it implied eliminating educational disadvantage. The Head Start program, borrowing its name from the familiar metaphor of the foot race, was designed to provide special preschool help to overcome the depressing influence of home and community; Title I of the Elementary and Secondary Education Act, which financed special primary and secondary school programs, offered continuing special support.

By giving poor and black children something extra, the federal program went well beyond earlier undertakings. Head Start and Title I signaled more than a war on poverty. They also warred on the culture of the poor. While no one spoke openly of Americanizing blacks, the "mainstream" into which they were to enter was defined in white and middle-class terms.[61]

The compensatory education campaign assumed that the inferior quality of the schools attended by poor and black children seriously impaired their education. The notion that these schools were demonstrably worse institutions, and that spending more money on the education of the have-nots would enable them to do better, seemed intuitively obvious. Yet both suppositions proved wrong—or so the massive *Equal Educational Opportunity Survey*, popularly known as the Coleman Report, concluded.[62] The study relied on sophisticated methodologies able to probe the relationship between school resources and student outcomes in ways that had not previously been possible. What had been assumed now became the subject of inquiry.

The Coleman Report was supposed to give social science's benediction to the strategy of compensatory education. It set out to document the fact that school facilities were sharply unequal along racial lines and that this inequality caused differences in student achievement. The data did not support either conclusion. Differences in school facilities were small, and they had little or no apparent impact on student performance. If the Coleman Report's findings were to be credited, schools did not make a difference— more accurately, measured variation in physical plants, curricula, and teacher characteristics had little bearing on achievement.

Subsequent evaluations of Title I and Head Start programs appeared to confirm the conclusions of the *Equal Educational Opportunity Survey*. These extra efforts counted for very little in terms of achievement. Students enrolled in such programs made modest gains at best, and even these dissipated over time.[63] And it was achievement that mattered. As the chief author of the report writes: "The Report brought into the open what had been underlying all the concepts of equality of educational opportunity but had remained largely hidden . . . that the concept implied . . . equality in those elements that are effective for learning."[64] Reanalyses of the *Equal Educational Opportunity Survey* data further strengthened the report's central conclusion. School resources had been equalized—with no apparent impact on student performance.

Critics of the social system viewed these findings as evidence of the weaknesses of classical liberalism. To Christopher Jencks in *Inequality*, the Coleman Report stood as a vivid reminder of the extent to which differences based on race and class endure in this society, and the modest role of education in explaining those inequalities.[65] Far from being the cure-all so long imagined, schools were merely marginal institutions. Focus attention on education if you will, because better schools may make life more pleasant for eight-year-olds, but abandon the illusion that doing so will reshape the economic or political order. Despite the efforts of the social engineers, education seemed only to replicate preexisting social class distinctions, thus preserving inequality.

The conclusions of the Coleman Report and the reanalyses led some politicians to question the wisdom of "investing money where it really is going to accomplish very little if any good."[66] Yet increases in expenditure for schooling continued apace, far outstripping the rate of inflation, and parents and professionals generally discounted the gloomy portrait of education that the social scientists painted. This was particularly true of the civil rights movement, which reiterated its commitment to desegregated education. Blacks and liberal whites had not fought for equal educational opportunity only to learn that, for all that education mattered, they might as well have waged their battles over the desegregation of playgrounds and golf courses. Surveys confirmed that black parents still regarded success in education as essential for social survival. Desegregation brought blacks into the common school, and in that respect made it possible for them to realize the full benefits of education. As Christopher Lasch writes: "The struggle for desegregated schooling implied an attack not only on racial discrimination but on the proposition, long imbedded in the practice of the schools, that academic standards are inherently elitist and that universal education therefore requires the dilution of standards. . . . The demand for desegregation entailed more than a renewed commitment to equal opportunity; it also entailed a repudiation of cultural separatism and a belief that access to common cultural traditions remained the precondition of advancement for dispossessed groups."[67]

In an era that defined ideals of equality with reference to what was empirically possible, supporters of desegregation could find some support for their position in the Coleman Report. The single characteristic of a school that appeared to affect achievement was the one thing to which poor black children in segregated schools were denied access, namely white and wealthier classmates. A reanalysis of the Coleman Report data by the U.S. Civil Rights Commission, *Racial Isolation in the Public Schools*,[68] purported to substantiate this conclusion and placed the weight of social science behind desegregation.[69]

Throughout this period, desegregation carried a special and limited connotation outside the South, as an enterprise voluntary in nature, small in scope, and burdensome only to blacks willing to travel in order to reap its benefits. Such an approach was adopted by several of the Bay Area cities discussed in Part 2. While this effort generally worked well for participating students and had considerable symbolic importance, it could not begin to confront the question: What happens to those black children, the vast majority, who remain behind?

Racial mixing would occur neither naturally nor painlessly— demographic realities made that clear enough. The concentration of blacks in particular neighborhoods and in the urban cores of metropolitan areas, a continuing and increasing phenomenon, meant that students would have to be bused if desegregation were to occur. Racial mixing in those circumstances required massive rearrangements: not voluntarism but metropolitan school districts as big as Rhode Island were called for.

The common school historically attracted a diverse clientele, but that had been largely an artifact of low population density in the nineteenth century. With increased urbanization, such heterogeneity became rarer. Supporters of desegregation sought to revive the characterization of the common school as an institution drawing on students from different racial backgrounds, but efforts to bring this about by social engineering aroused passionate opposition. Even as the courts ordered the desegregation of Northern cities—a process that began in one of the Bay Area communities, San Francisco, in 1971[70]—popular unhappiness solidified. Polls reported that three-quarters of the citizenry embraced desegregation and opposed busing.[71] The simultaneously held belief in desegregation and unwillingness to do what was needed to bring it about tested principled understandings of equal opportunity.

Despite popular opposition, the effort to desegregate the schools, which emerged as a national and not just a Southern concern in the 1960s, continued and expanded during the 1970s.[72] Hardly any sizable Northern school district did not take some action regarding race. The character of the effort did, however, change. Where earlier the emphasis had been almost exclusively on racial mixing, interest in desegregation became fused with attention to the educational mission of the school; the drive for desegregation was thus transformed into a campaign to integrate the schools. In part, this marked a return to the historical interest of blacks in the quality of education. The stress on educational concerns was necessitated too by the need to achieve something more than a symbolic triumph in places where the white population was just too small to accomplish much racial mixing. Who, for instance, would benefit from a requirement that each of Washington, D.C.'s schools enroll 3 percent white students, the district-wide average, even under the improbable assumption that such an order would not drive the remaining whites elsewhere?

This reconceptualization also stemmed from the realization that bringing black and white children together only marked the beginning of the process of remaking schools in a manner consistent with the universalist vision. Questions of race and schooling touch upon almost all other issues of educational policy. They affect the allocation of district funds, the nature of school governance, the instructional regime, and the sensitivity of the institution to radically altered circumstances. These issues could not be ignored, either in the litigation designed to restore equal educational opportunity to black children or in school districts' continuing efforts to refine their educational mission. Such puzzles engaged each of the Bay Area communities, regardless of the approach taken to racial mixing. Yet there as elsewhere in the nation, effective policy answers have been hard to come by. What "works"—what promotes equally effective education—has remained unspecified.[73]

With respect to questions of racial justice in schools as with race generally, no single theme has dominated recent discussions. Redistribution and universalism have their educational analogues in compensatory education and integration. The community-control movement incorporates the precepts of black power.[74]

Arguments for community control of public schools were sometimes couched in educational terms. Children, it was said, could better control their own destiny (a factor that the Coleman Report had associated with achievement) in schools run by those who shared their values. But the process by which "fate control" might be enhanced was never specified, and this argument needs to be appreciated as the educational icing on a decidedly political cake.

Like black power generally, community control of schools was in part a reaction of blacks to liberal whites' failure to make good the promise of universalism.[75] Community control also embodied a positive political statement. Poor and black people were encouraged by federal law to engage in "maximum feasible participation" in the business of government. What better place to start than the schools, historically the most accessible of public services? Involvement of parents in running the schools, it was said, might revitalize dinosaurian school systems that had grown overcentralized and overbureaucratized, unable to adopt new strategies for coping with the variety of demands pressed upon them.

Community control offered a catchy label on which to focus attention. Taken literally, as a call for a transfer of power—Harlem or Watts likened to a new Caribbean nation winning its independence from an alien government—the movement came to nothing, since existing school systems refused to go out of business. In the five Bay Area towns, community control had little meaning except on the symbolic level. Yet community participation in school governance did significantly increase, and this too affected the idea of equal opportunity.

This change can in part be attributed to the federally imposed requirement of parental participation in planning programs for the educationally disadvantaged. The federal standard stressed consultation and advice giving, but in some school districts politically astute parents were able to gain more effective clout. The demographic factors that discouraged desegregation also led to a growing black political presence in the schools. An increasingly black electorate produced more black school board members, and blacks were also hired for positions of administrative responsibility.

These new black leaders were expected to be responsive in tangible ways to the needs of the black community. Their presence marked a subtle shift in the definition of equality. Proponents of compensatory education and integration each viewed equality largely as an externally shaped aspiration, fixed by constitutional norm or professional good judgment, that was general in character. In two respects this perception could be faulted. First, the constitutional command has not been expressed in uniform terms. The judiciary, as chapter 4 points out, has attended far more to local circumstance than has been conventionally supposed. Second, the plausibility of the professionals' claims to expertise, and consequently the legitimacy of leaving school decisions to experts, was diminished by the civil rights movement's assault on the schools. The findings of the Coleman Report undercut the professionals' credibility still further, for it now appeared that schoolmen who had promised to bring an end to poverty could do no such thing. Particularly where blacks made their presence felt politically, equality increasingly incorporated a political dimension. Equal opportunity now often implies satisfying the wants of the local community, shaping an educational system that matches the desires of its users within the bounds fixed by new fiscal constraints.

V

The idea of equal educational opportunity endures both as a hope and as a reflection of larger unresolved social issues. As David Nasaw writes after surveying the sweep of American educational history, "the public schools . . . remain 'contested' institutions with several agendas and different purposes." Although efforts to make them "into efficient agencies for social channeling and control" have failed, the schools will not be turned "into truly egalitarian educational institutions without at the same time effecting radical changes in the state and the society that support them." The public schools, Nasaw concludes, will "continue to be the social arena where the tension is reflected and the contest played out between the promise of democracy and the reality of class division."[76]

Introducing race into discussions of equal opportunity deepens this tension, for education at once reflects and is ideally supposed to overcome racial differences. The effort to bring about racial justice through education has only added to the puzzles, not yielded solutions. Is the sought-after end an educational environment that, as a consequence of effective integration, makes race less important, or is it instead one that overcomes racial differences by distributing extra resources to disadvantaged blacks? Is equal and indistinguishable treatment or separate but preferential treatment for minorities the appropriate guiding standard? Moreover, can either be achieved within the present limits of educational technology? And to what effect? What is the significance of bringing about even the most demanding of the understandings of equal opportunity, equalizing educational outcomes across racial lines, if such an accomplishment does not noticeably alter the prevailing pattern of social advantage? These questions have led some to question the premise of *Brown*, that equality in education is the key to social justice.

In making policy concerning both education and race, the meaning of equality has regularly been transformed even as some measure of equality was achieved. By the mid-1960s, America had made nondiscrimination with respect to race official policy and had largely equalized the distribution of schooling inputs. These milestones are best understood as marking way stations in the process of defining equality, not as end points. Process is the key, for it is in the transformation of meaning that an understanding of equality resides. That lesson is reinforced by examining the interrelationship between judicial decisions and political activity, and the interplay of legalism and politics within the structure of the decisions themselves. These processes endow social norms with concrete significance, for equality has assumed its varied meanings in different times and places through the course of policy implementation.

CHAPTER

4

The Interplay of
Legalism and Politics

I

How has race and schooling policy been shaped in this society? The prevailing view holds that, unlike most issues resolved in the give-and-take of pluralist politics, race is peculiarly the province of the judiciary. Similarly, while negotiation and compromise are said to characterize the normal process of policy resolution, racial questions are routinely defined in constitutional or ideological terms, with principle and precedent substituted for bargaining and brokering.[1]

These perceptions describe only a partial truth, for race and schooling is at once a judicial and a political concern. The federal courts have, of course, had a vital part in shaping the issue. It took a decision of the United States Supreme Court to place the matter squarely on the national agenda. Except for a brief interval during the mid-1960s, when the coordinate branches of the federal government acted in concert, the courts have remained a dominant influence ever since.[2] Yet race and schooling has also been a political concern. Even before *Brown v. Board of Education*,[3] nondiscrimination was required by statute in some Northern states.[4] Since that decision, a great many communities—including four of the five Bay Area towns—have voluntarily addressed existing segregation, molding an understanding of racial justice that fits the particular circumstances and needs of a place.

Outside the South, in communities that have taken some desegregation action, almost 60 percent of school districts with fewer than ten thousand students and more than 40 percent of districts with more than ten thousand have acted on their own initiative.

Litigation, while not uncommon (some three hundred desegregation court orders are in place nationally), still represents the exception.[5] The voluntary actions vary in their specifics. Some call for substantial busing, while others combine a lesser degree of racial mixing with additional changes—allocating new resources to predominantly nonwhite schools, for instance, or redesigning educational programs—desired by blacks and whites. Although these efforts have been influenced by constitutionally rooted norms or, more tangibly, by the threat of legal action, they represent the outcome of sustained political bargaining.

Even when a race and schooling dispute winds up in court, political concerns persist. Courts cannot unilaterally impose a workable remedy for the constitutional wrong of governmentally created racial separation. They necessarily depend on the collaboration—or at least the acquiescence—of a great many people inside and outside the school system if a remedy is to work. For that reason, judges have sought to shape decisions that can garner political and popular support within the bounds of the constitutionally acceptable and that are also pedagogically defensible. In doing so, courts have generally eschewed a narrowly legalist approach, preferring to manage a continuing negotiation among the interested and affected groups.[6] The law of these cases is not self-contained and rationalist, but a capacious net that ensnares fact and value alike. Whether a race and schooling issue is resolved in the courtroom or not, it retains both a political and a legal dimension. Through the interplay of politics and law, uniform constitutionally derived standards and idiosyncratic concerns, policy has been formed.[7]

The community histories included in Part 2 offer a detailed look at this process. This chapter examines the system of decision from three distinct vantage points. It first explores the evolution of Supreme Court doctrine, identifying the consistently mixed legal and political messages that the justices have sent to the lower courts since *Brown*. Next, it details the interchange at the local level between political institutions and the courts, noting how each influences the other's efforts to resolve an issue. Finally, it describes the joinder of law and politics within the confines of the judicial dispute. At each level, the pattern of interplay between legal and political institutions, and legal and political values, recurs. The effort to shape race and schooling policy does not embody a coherent strategy to effectuate unitary norms. It reflects instead a continuing struggle to identify resolutions at once politically palatable, educationally sensible, and constitutionally permissible, resolutions susceptible of evolving with changing understandings of the meaning of equality.

II

The Supreme Court's decision in *Brown v. Board of Education* stands as the most significant of this century—perhaps the most important in its ramifications for the larger society ever issued by the Court. The decision set in motion a social revolution that has fundamentally altered relationships between blacks and whites in this country. Even as it acted, the Court was necessarily concerned about the political implications of its decision. That concern influenced the way in which it identified the wrong and the scope of the remedy that it ordered. In this respect, the Supreme Court was at once principled and political.[8]

"No single decision has had more moral force than *Brown*; few struggles have been morally more significant than the one for racial integration of American life," writes J. Harvie Wilkinson III. "Yet school desegregation may be the most political item on the Court's agenda."[9] The ambiguities in *Brown* reveal this duality. Does segregation itself constitute the wrong, or just segregation mandated by law? Is segregation impermissible because it distinguishes on the basis of race or because it limits the educational futures of black children? While these are nominally matters of doctrine, the Supreme Court's lack of clarity in explicating doctrine has required a different reasoning process, which defines the wrong by inspecting what is required by way of remedy. Judicial decision making with respect to segregation is thus at its heart incremental. Wrong defines remedy, which in turn redefines wrong. The Court moves away from the evil to be undone, not toward some predetermined end. *Brown* sets in motion a decision-making strategy rather than resolving a problem.

For these reasons, the second *Brown* decision, which addresses the question of remedy, assumes special importance.[10] That opinion is, of course, best remembered for permitting desegregation to proceed with "all deliberate speed."[11] This standard subordinates the vindication of individual claims to the broader policy concern of securing general acceptance of the Court's edict through gradualism, and in so doing violates expectations of appropriate judicial behavior. In *Brown II*, the Supreme Court also leaves the pace and scope of the remedy to case-by-case determination, providing only the loosest of guidance; in that process, the specifics of the remedy reveal the constitutional evil to be undone. Remedy framing itself as conceived by the Court necessarily and properly takes into account concerns of policy and politics.

The particular factors regarded by the Court as pertinent in this calculus are themselves political in nature: "problems related to administration, arising from the physical condition of the school plant, the school transportation system, personnel, revision of school districts and attendance areas to achieve a system of determining admission to the public schools on a nonracial basis." Some of these are technical matters, hardly warranting postponing desegregation. Others—"the physical condition of the school plant," for example—suggest that, in the justices' eyes, white schoolchildren could not be expected to attend formerly black schools, despite protestations that black and white schools were in fact equal.[12] These issues were better resolved by political than by judicial initiative. "School authorities have the primary responsibility for elucidating, assessing, and solving these problems." Only if the political system defaulted should lower courts intervene. "Courts will have to consider whether the action of school authorities constitutes good faith implementation of the governing constitutional principles."[13]

In retrospect, such language sounds pious rather than plausible in its expectation that courts would act only in the face of political default. Between 1955 and 1968, however, this was essentially all the guidance that the Supreme Court offered on the matter. Only in the most exceptional circumstances—as with the outright challenge to the authority of the judiciary in Little Rock— was the Court roused to action.[14] Even in that instance, Justice Frankfurter was moved to plead for the cooperation of elected officials in achieving desegregation. Success in desegregation meant "working together . . . in a cooperative effort," not the imposition of judicial rule.[15] District court judges consequently enjoyed considerable discretion during this era. While somewhat constricted by the *Brown* opinions, the course of desegregation litigation varied enormously from court to court.

The generalities of *Brown*, coupled with deep political antagonism in the South and a hands-off attitude in Congress, provoked defiance rather than the willing implementation of desegregation that the Court hoped for. District court judges committed to *Brown* began substituting specific requirements for general guidelines. Bolstered by the passage of the 1964 Civil Rights Act,[16] which added Congressional support to the judicial arsenal, the Fifth Circuit—which encompasses the Deep South—developed a sophisticated and highly detailed remedial jurisprudence. In *Jefferson County*, that court ordered adoption of a freedom-of-choice plan larded with judicially imposed specifics.[17] The timing and form of the announcement to parents, the nature of equalization efforts among schools, the remedial programs, the location of new schools, the reassignment of faculty: each was spelled out in the decree. Concern with the pace of desegregation led the lower courts increasingly to direct their discretionary authority to the end of rapidly accomplishing desegregation.

Beginning with its 1968 decision in *Green v. County School Board*,[18] the Supreme Court confirmed and further hastened that endeavor. In *Green*, the Court cast considerable doubt on whether free choice was ever a constitutionally appropriate remedy; in *Alexander v. Holmes County Board of Education*,[19] it insisted upon immediate implementation of district-wide desegregation; and in *Swann v. Charlotte-Mecklenburg Board of Education*,[20] it approved a truly massive busing order. The language in those cases gave considerably more guidance to lower courts. *Green* demanded remedies that "promise realistically to work *now*"[21]—and by "work" the Court plainly meant achieve racial mixing. *Alexander* sought desegregation "at once."[22] Although these cases narrow the scope of trial court discretion, and hence the possibilities of a politically driven resolution of a desegregation suit, they still leave room for judicial maneuver. This persistence of ambiguity can be attributed to a willed lack of clarity in the opinions themselves.

Consider *Swann*, the most influential of the decisions and an opinion that is in some respects highly prescriptive. *Swann* notes the need for the Court to "amplify guidelines. . . . defin[ing] how far this remedial power extends."[23] With respect to student assignment, the Court identifies the circumstances under which one-race schools are permissible, the need for "frank—and sometimes drastic—gerrymandering of school districts and attendance zones,"[24] and the scope of permissible busing (limited only when "the time or distance of travel is so great as to either risk the health of the children or significantly impinge on the educational process").[25]

Even as it offers guidance, the Supreme Court creates new if more limited zones of discretion for district courts. How can a school district show that a one-race school is "genuinely nondiscriminatory"?[26] How does a court determine whether busing will "impinge on the educational process"? The Court chose not to address these questions. By leaving such matters to district courts, the *Swann* decision reaffirms the premise of *Brown II*. "Once a right and a violation have been shown the scope of a district court's equitable powers to remedy past wrongs is broad, for breadth and flexibility are inherent in equitable remedies."[27]

When they are so inclined, the justices can more tightly cabin the lower courts: a comparison of *Swann* with the reapportionment, criminal process, and abortion cases is instructive.[28] The counterpart of "one man, one vote" for desegregation would be racial ratios—and these the Court opted not to impose or even to permit. In choosing a different course, the Court could not have been unaware of the political ramifications of its action. *Swann* represents a bold judicial foray with respect to remedies for segregation, a high-water mark for judicial activism. It was bound to evoke controversy. Better, the Court apparently concluded, to leave such matters in the hands of lower courts, whose sense of nuance could be relied upon to lessen controversy. Although the Court demonstrated its impatience with the progress of desegregation in the South, it was never wholly willing to spearhead a second Reconstruction. Local values, reflected in the factual situations and remedial proposals presented to the lower courts, continued to count for something.[29]

The North was another story. Until 1973, the Supreme Court declined to review Northern desegregation disputes. When it did act in the Denver case, the Court resisted imposing a national standard with respect to desegregation, despite the apparent similarities between the Northern and Southern situations two decades after *Brown*. The holding in *Keyes v. School District No. 1, Denver*[30]—once deliberate segregation has been shown to exist in a significant portion of a Northern school district, a district-wide remedy should properly follow—was subsequently hedged by opinions attempting more precisely to link wrong and remedy.[31] These cases call upon courts to perform awesome mental experiments, imagining what the school district would be like if no illegal segregation had occurred; they systematically ignore the contribution of housing segregation to school segregation; and they restrict the capacity of courts to order remedies that cross district lines.

Keyes and its progeny do not bound but instead redirect the remedial flexibility of lower courts. In the second round of the Detroit litigation,[32] the Court approved a remedy that contemplated revising the student discipline code, creating vocational schools, mandating teacher retraining, and the like. That opinion appears to license lower court intervention in almost all of a school district's educational and administrative practices, for these touch upon the issue of race. While such remedies must be related to the wrong of racial discrimination, discrimination itself is understood to be diverse, multifaceted, amorphous, and immense. For that reason a district court judge's determination of the bounds of the remedy merits deference.[33]

From *Brown* to the present, the Supreme Court has eschewed a preemptive role. Although the Court has affirmed the necessity of accomplishing racial mixing,[34] this has not been its only theme. The Court treats the issue posed in the segregation cases as, in part, an educational problem calling for an educational solution.[35] It has also recognized the importantly political aspect of the issue. Supreme Court decisions of the past quarter-century "pleaded, mediated, mollified, or even withdrew";[36] only in the years between *Green* and *Keyes* can they be said to have imposed.

Taken as a whole, the Court's race cases teach "that competing moral claims" rooted in constitutional values "must be brokered and negotiated."[37] As political statements, these decisions reaffirm that the Constitution is not, as Justice Jackson put it, "a suicide pact; it does not require self-defeating acts."[38] Yet the decisions are more than political or educational statements. They ultimately derive whatever force they command from their constitutional underpinnings, their fidelity to the Fourteenth Amendment's aspiration to evenhanded treatment. Is it any surprise, then, that efforts to resolve the race and schooling issue through the political process have been deeply informed by constitutional values, or that in desegregation cases district court judges have found themselves with varied and complicated tasks to perform, obliged to be at once constitutional exegetes, political power brokers, and educational experts?

III

The lack of a fully elaborated constitutional doctrine encouraged the civil rights movement to regard the political and judicial processes as different means to a common end; both were heavily relied upon. In particular locales, race and schooling issues emerged as a political as well as a legal problem. The matter has usually first been broached as a political question. After an initial period of ideological stance-taking, the parties have attempted to reach some satisfactory resolution. When that negotiation succeeds, the issue never comes to court; only when bargaining breaks down does litigation ensue. Although the prevailing understanding presumes that legal sanctions are needed for policy reform, the facts are otherwise; in the North and West, changes in race and schooling policy have more frequently come about voluntarily than as the result of a court order.[39]

Even when the issue of race and schooling is resolved within a community, however, the possibility of recourse to the courts has affected the political dialogue.[40] The threat of a lawsuit is sometimes put forward to increase the bargaining strength of civil rights advocates; elsewhere, litigation is regarded as an indication of divisiveness inconsistent with the community's perception of itself. In either event, the law is salient. The substantial case-study literature does not reveal any school district that has confronted these questions without paying some heed to their constitutional dimension. Law and politics are routinely coupled, even when the issue is settled in the political arena.

Those who sought to address racial concerns in Northern school districts initially hoped for a political resolution. Beginning in the late 1950s, they attempted to convince school boards and school administrators that there existed a problem—racial isolation, as it was generally called, or more precisely the concentration of minority students in particular schools—that could be solved through voluntary action.

Civil rights proved to be a novel and disquieting matter for school officials. For almost half a century, educational policymaking had been largely removed from the political domain. The dominance of expertise over politics and school professionals over school board members was an enduring legacy of the Progressive era.[41] The rare exceptions, when political considerations prevailed, were roundly denounced as subverting good education.[42] Disputes over educational equality were thus initially thought to fall within the province of the professionals.

Many school administrators first responded to expressed concern about the quality of education received by black children by turning the issue into a familiar professional problem: What curriculum can best meet the needs of this group of students? Compensatory education offered an attractive answer, partly because it did not jeopardize professional hegemony. Demands that racial separation be treated as a problem requiring school district reaction were another thing entirely. These claims did not speak just to pedagogy. They were profoundly political in nature, having as much to do with the status of blacks in the schools and the social order as with the specifics of educational reform. For that reason, they could not be contained within the school administration. If such matters were to be addressed at all, the school board had to assume a central position.

Early school board responses to the plea that they "do something" about racial isolation varied from sympathetic attention, in such cities as New York and Providence, to hostility in Boston and Chicago. A few communities, among them Evanston and Berkeley, went so far as to restructure neighborhood school boundaries in order to accomplish desegregation. Others adopted policies permitting minority students to attend predominantly white schools outside their own neighborhoods.

The civil rights strategy was to stress the rightness of the cause. Particularly in the first stages of the struggle, when civil rights forces worked to place racial questions on the political agenda, the idea of racial justice embraced an essentially moral vision. Civil rights advocates challenged existing arrangements, and that challenge was proclaimed on behalf of a social movement, not an interest group.[43]

Before the late 1960s, the politics of race differed from the pluralist give-and-take that characterizes most issues. Pluralism assumes that nearly everyone can participate in politics, that those who feel strongly about an issue can readily make their views known and that they can expect to get some satisfaction from those in authority. This was not true of the civil rights crusade. The movement had been shut out of politics and lacked the usual forums for attracting attention. Because its message sounded threatening, the preponderant political reaction was hostile. Compromise appeared to interest neither side: winning was all.

Issues once resolved beget new issues. After civil rights groups persuaded school boards that their concerns deserved to be treated seriously—an endeavor that often involved the threat of litigation—concern shifted to the particulars of reform. This process continues in Northern cities; three out of five districts that have undertaken substantial desegregation did so after 1972.[44] As the effort to secure racial justice in the schools evolved from emphasis on symbolic demands to focus on concrete proposals, civil rights groups came to behave much more like interest groups. They located allies (notably supporters of better schools and increased teachers' salaries), made deals, and agreed to less than what they had initially demanded. Within the five Bay Area communities, pluralist and ideological politics were dominant at different times in each school district.

IV

Bringing a dispute over desegregation into the legal arena by filing a lawsuit signals a breakdown in the political process. Bargaining gives way to stance taking, interests harden into claims of rights.[45]

That transformation does not occur quickly, nor is it taken lightly. Most Northern desegregation suits were filed no earlier than the 1970s, whereas the issue of racial justice in the schools was framed at least a decade earlier.

Recourse to the courts marks not an end to politics but rather a new stage in the ongoing political process. The parties to the desegregation litigation are not strangers to one another. The issues over which they differ are familiar. Who is to blame for the extant segregation? What should be done about it? The forum is new, as is the introduction of an additional participant, the judge, with considerable formal authority. Because the court can render a legally authoritative decision resolving disputes among the parties, it exercises substantial potential power. That power can be used to order a particular outcome or to reshape relationships among the several parties to the dispute.

Judicial authority, although substantial, is also significantly constrained, for courts cannot guarantee a successful solution. Just as desegregation is an essentially political matter before litigation, so it remains a political matter after judicial resolution of a case. Although legal mandates affect the implementing of court-ordered remedies, that enterprise depends on mobilizing diverse community resources, including good will, to achieve the desired outcome. Where, as with desegregation, what may well be wanted is not a specifiable end but a process capable of adapting to the radical change of circumstances that desegregation brings, the subtler persuasive arts are likely to accomplish more than the brute force of decision.[46] Courts cannot run school systems.

Judges depend for the implementation of a remedy on the cooperation of the parties to the dispute. That dependency leads them to structure a political bargaining relationship designed to achieve agreement between the parties. Yet the bargaining process also differs significantly from run-of-the-mill politics. Permissible outcomes are bounded by the judge's understanding of what is constitutionally permissible. The court will approve, not any agreement, but only an agreement consistent with the teachings of *Brown* and its progeny. The judge himself may also hold views about the educational substance of a good outcome; if so, these are interjected into the bargaining process.

The desegregation cases reveal no single mode of judicial behavior but rather a range of judicial stances. The politically oriented judge stresses consensus as the primary concern, assuming a relatively passive role. The legalist judge, persuaded that the elaboration of authoritative principles in the context of a particular situation fully describes the judicial task, does not enter the political fray. For very different reasons, the judge motivated by particular educational concerns may behave similarly, looking to the parties primarily for after-the-fact support.

V

The vitally political nature of desegregation cases, and the consequently bounded authority of the judge, have long been clear to lower courts. More than a decade ago, the district judge in the Washington Parish, Louisiana, case described the work of courts as "an attempt by civic- and social-minded judges to add legal precepts to the force of moral, social and political principles in the effort of the responsible sectors of our society to eradicate the divisive and ruinous prejudices between the citizens of this nation."[47] The court's contribution is often understood as supplementary rather than primary, hortatory rather than directive. As the district court in the Lansing litigation declared, courts "cannot order people to be charitable to one another in their daily affairs. The law provides impetus, sets limits, corrects abuses—it is an external conscience. But the change of heart must come from within."[48]

This widely shared perception leads courts to urge compromise, in the belief that the real party at interest, the general populace, will be more likely to accept agreement than to respond to order. Urgings to "get something working," to "get people to reach a common ground," or to "collaborate"—very different from the language of adversarial relationships—are familiar; indeed, some judges regard adversarial behavior as inconsistent with the task at hand.[49] Even in courts that have been rebuked for overreaching their authority, the early stages of litigation are marked by attempts to mobilize support for a politically agreeable and constitutionally permissible plan. The insistence of the Pasadena district court judge that a racial remedy remain in effect for his lifetime was reversed by the Supreme Court, which used the occasion to limit the scope of the trial judge's remedial discretion.[50] Quite by contrast, the first remedial order in the Pasadena case was couched in general terms and was designed as a catalyst to spur a desegregation planning process already well underway within the school district.[51] In the annals of desegregation litigation, the decision to place South Boston High School in receivership is widely viewed as the most dramatic example of unilateral judicial action. Yet the Boston court relied first on the school district itself, then on a panel of masters chosen with an eye to their political astuteness, to devise a workable plan for the city.[52] In general, decisions do not speak of uncompromisable rights but rather concern themselves with divergence among interests, where some balancing is deemed both legitimate and appropriate.

In determining liability, the court fixes the constitutional rights and obligations of the parties. If one conceives of the initiation of a lawsuit as interrupting an ongoing political process, one can often see that process resuming in the course of putting together a remedy acceptable to the parties and to the court. It is in the remedial phase of litigation that courts are afforded the greatest scope for political maneuver.[53] Remedy framing involves the court and the litigant in a series of iterations.[54] The court issues an order, notes the responses of the parties (who have been urged by the judge to narrow the scope of their differences), then shapes a further and usually more precise subsequent order.

The court does not have in mind compliance with some pre-established remedy, the judge behaving much like a Socratically inclined law professor in leading the parties to embrace the "right" answer. To the contrary: within the constraints set by the law, there is no single right answer. Thus, in the context of a particular case as in the development of doctrine at the appellate level, the court's desire is to proceed incrementally, and this implies learning from the past. The trial court is less interested in achieving the best possible substantive outcome than in inaugurating a decision-making apparatus that will continue after an order is entered. It is in part for this reason that in desegregation cases district courts cede jurisdiction reluctantly: retaining formal control over a case permits the court to help maintain both the political and the constitutional integrity of decision making.

What has been described is only a mode of judicial behavior whose specifics are altered by circumstances. Where the parties are in essential agreement even before a lawsuit is filed, the gentle application of legal norms may suffice to prompt agreement. In some instances, school boards have depended on courts to order them to do what they would like to do, but lack the political will to accomplish on their own. In these cases, the nominally imposed remedy usually represents a solution agreed to by the parties and ratified by the court.[55]

Courts elsewhere have been more active. In Atlanta, the court relied first on a court-appointed citizens' committee and subsequently on the parties to promote a settlement, in both instances shielding delicate negotiations from public scrutiny.[56] The Dallas judge identified particular outside groups that in his judgment should aid in the remedy-framing effort; he thus helped bring into being, and relied on the recommendations of, a group that represented the diverse interests of the Dallas citizenry.[57] In each case, the court expressed its preference for negotiation over adversarial relations.

Judicial perception of the remedy as itself a process also enhances the likelihood of settlement. The trial judge in Denver noted that the remedy "won't be too final. . . . I think it's going to be temporary-final. . . . It doesn't look to me like we're going to wrap this up in one fell swoop."[58] In Las Vegas, the trial court permitted a one-year trial of a free-choice desegregation plan; only after it failed to achieve substantial desegregation was a more extensive plan put into effect. The court of appeals approved this step-by-step approach. "The present decree is the beginning, not the end, of the remedial process. No doubt it will be modified and adjusted in the light of process made in the elimination of the effect of segregation."[59]

Courts have relied primarily on remedies prepared by the district itself, and this too encourages compromise among the parties. The practice is somewhat unusual, for one does not normally ask the wrongdoer to set the terms of remedy. The standard explanation points to the special expertise of the school district, and the consequent appropriateness of drawing upon that expertise to provide practical guidance in solving the puzzles presented by remedy framing. That explanation makes some sense, since a school district should know better than anyone else how to promote racial mixing with least disruption of neighborhoods or which changes in pedagogical practice ought to accompany desegregation, but it is not fully persuasive. Where remedy framing demands change from standard operating procedures, the school district that put those procedures and practices into effect may be the worst agency to assume responsibility for the job. The district may know well how the system runs at present, but lack the perspective needed to determine how it should be run. Moreover, the district will probably seek to do as little as possible to satisfy the court.[60] Where this urge to minimize prevails, the plan that emerges in response to the court order will be less good, by the criterion of rationality, than what an outside expert might devise.

Other hidden benefits stem from dependence on the school district, and these help to justify the practice. Reliance on the district encourages negotiation between the parties. Sometimes such bargaining is expressly called for, as where plaintiffs are asked to participate jointly in planning; in any event, the fact that plaintiffs as well as the court will evaluate the district's proposal tacitly promotes the same end.

At this stage of the litigation, the district court may invite the participation of a number of outsiders—citizens' groups, intervenors with a thin claim to involvement, representatives of minority viewpoints—not represented in earlier phases of the suit. Their involvement turns the lawsuit into even more of a political forum. Because all of the parties to the process, including the judge, have something to gain from consensual resolution, a classic bargaining situation is set up.

In such instances, cooptation is what the court has in mind. A willing school board is far less likely to attempt to subvert or to manage grudgingly a remedy than one on which the remedial burden has been unilaterally foisted. Thus, trial courts have willingly accepted plans that are objectively worse—that is, less fully satisfy the *Swann* desegregation criteria—if such remedies meet the minimum constitutional obligation and are acceptable to the government agency obliged to implement them.

The remedies judges actually order also reveal the bargaining process at work. The orders differ widely from one city to the next, as one would expect of a political undertaking. The decisions seem responsive to variations among districts; community idiosyncrasies are honored in the opinions. And judges who decide several desegregation cases have reached quite different decisions. The judge who in St. Louis approved a consent decree involving no busing of students earlier ordered the merger of an all-black district with surrounding largely white districts; the judge who swiftly imposed desegregation in a rural Arkansas school district acted more reluctantly in Little Rock.

Of greater moment, the orders generally demand less in terms of racial mixing than a strict application of the prevailing Supreme Court standard might lead one to anticipate. The courts have consistently sought ways other than strict racial balance to achieve a "unitary" school system. The Coney Island court, responding to a proposal of the local school board, ordered a junior high school, the focus of the suit, converted into a school for the gifted. Reacting to school district suggestions, the Dallas court adopted magnet schools as the heart of its remedy. The Denver court attended to widely voiced community concerns about the demise of neighborhood by ordering that students be bused for only half a day (this aspect of the decision was reversed on appeal). The order in Boston left whole sections of the city untouched by busing.

The Memphis court ordered a plan that struck "a balance" between "practicalities" and "constitutional requirements"; in the face of the parties' "extreme opposite positions," the court attempted its own balancing.[61] The San Francisco decision permitted the school district to select its own plan, which promised less complete relief from racial isolation, rather than one proposed by the NAACP that offered more racial mixing at the price of less community involvement and support. Acceptability, not maximum racial mix, seems to matter most.

Bargaining does not always work. The process requires that the several parties to the dispute cooperate. Where this doesn't occur negotiations falter, for there cannot be a bargain without bargainers. While civil rights groups rarely if ever refuse to participate, school district or state agencies may opt out, either because their ideological beliefs are seen as absolute claims of right or because they resist the court's assuming responsibility for shaping the bargain.

Appellate review also limits the process of bargaining by permitting judicial second-guessing of the bargain itself. Even where the parties favor a consensual remedy to one imposed by the court, they may disagree on the terms of consensus. The school district may well prefer no remedy, and if it appeals the decision with this end in view, plaintiffs are likely to counter by promoting their original remedial suggestions. Alternatively, plaintiffs may seek appellate review in order to obtain a remedy more ambitious than that adopted by the trial court. In either scenario, the bargaining falls apart. The possibility that this may transpire reveals the fragility of bargaining. For it to succeed, all parties to the dispute must prefer implementation of the agreed-upon solution to *any* court order, whether that of the district or the appellate court.

Despite these caveats, bargaining has characterized much race and schooling litigation. Within the relatively broad discretionary range set by the Supreme Court's decisions, the outcomes of the cases have been quite varied. In good measure, that distinctiveness results from the workings of a constrained political process managed by the courts.

Despite the importance of bargaining over the terms of remedy, desegregation cases are not merely political events. The traditional legalist conception of litigation, which stresses the application of reason and precedent in developing and extending legal norms, powerfully influences thinking about how courts should and do behave. Whatever the actual bases of a judge's decision, this legalist refrain is routinely heard. And legalist concerns in fact delimit the scope of a trial court's actions, shaping the structure of a suit and the form of remedy.[62]

Law and politics are sharply distinguished in the conventional understanding. Law consists of authoritatively derived norms not subject to compromise between legal interests. Politics, in contrast, involves brokering among interested parties to reach a result that is not so much right as widely preferred. Law is a rational analytic enterprise in this conception, whereas politics honors the pragmatic. When judges take it upon themselves to engage in institutional reform,[63] they do so with evident reluctance. In *Hobson v. Hansen*, a race and schooling case that in the scope and particularity of judicial intervention serves as a model for this type of litigation, Judge J. Skelly Wright sought to reconcile the sweep of his opinion with a commitment to judicial restraint:

> It would be far better indeed for these great social and political problems to be resolved in the political arena by other branches of government. But these are social and political problems which seem at times to defy such resolution. In such situations, under our system, the judiciary must bear a hand and accept its responsibility to assist in the solution where Constitutional rights hang in the balance.[64]

That last phrase is the key. Courts, in Judge Wright's view, do not simply break political logjams. Only when there is a connection between political failure and constitutional rights do courts have license to intervene.

Yet the precise delineation of constitutional rights is not easily accomplished, especially where the legal source is a constitutional provision as designedly elastic as the Fourteenth Amendment. That amendment manifests a commitment to equality as powerful as it is vague, and judicial decisions elaborating and expanding upon its entitlement set in motion a train of further expectations. "Judicial activism feeds on itself. The public has come to expect the Court to intervene against gross abuses. And so the Court must intervene."[65]

This point is at once familiar and problematic. "Must" is rhetorical, for judges often enough intervene first and rationalize later. But something more than rationalization is involved. When they act in ways that seem quintessentially political, as in removing the headmaster of a Boston high school, or even suprapolitical, as in banning antibusing meetings in Denver, courts take great pains to relate what they are doing to a received tradition. This linkage to legal convention is vital. It matters that those affected by court opinions accept an essentially legalist view of the judiciary, for that makes support easier to come by; it is, after all, the process and not the outcome for which support is ultimately asked.

More than camouflage is involved in reliance on legalism. The court's perception of itself is also decidedly legalist, and that perception affects what the court will do. Deference to legal norms tells only part of the judicial story, but it is a significant part nonetheless. The limits imposed by law shape a lawsuit in a variety of ways.[66] They restrict the interests that courts will recognize as intervenors to those with a stake in the controversy whose point of view is inadequately represented by the original parties: intervention for political purposes, by those on either side of the controversy, is sharply discouraged.

Legalist concerns limit the scope of the questions that a court will entertain. In the midst of desegregation suits styled as disputes between black plaintiffs and the school district, other groups with distinct but assertedly related grievances have sought to participate in the litigation. Although an expansion of the scope of a desegregation suit has generally been permitted when the connection can persuasively be made—as when the would-be intervenors represent students with limited English, for whom desegregation is assertedly an inadequate remedy[67]—courts have not routinely permitted the suits to become forums for educational policy.

The significance of legalism is also manifest when legal questions and questions of educational policy, or legal and political questions, collide. The judge in the Little Rock suit, for instance, recognized that his opinion valued legalist over educational concerns:

The Court also realizes that the money that the District is going to spend for transportation will have to come out of funds that otherwise would be spent for increased salaries, educational supplies and materials, and for other conventional and desirable educational purposes. There is nothing that the Court can do about that. At this time at least the duty of the District to comply with the requirements of the Supreme Court, the Court of Appeals, and this Court in the matter of integration must take priority over ordinary educational considerations.[68]

Similarly, where political issues are explicitly broached, judicial affirmation of the primacy of constitutional values is commonplace. As Judge Doyle in Denver declared: "The shape of the Constitution is not dependent upon the way the people vote. . . . So I expect that the voice of the people is entitled to some consideration, but if it's in conflict with the Constitution of the United States, why, it's not going to carry any weight. It can't, in a court of law. The law is something else."[69]

The Wilmington litigation fully illustrates the impact of legalist concerns on the shaping of a lawsuit.[70] Because that case involved the creation of a metropolitan school district, it might be regarded as an adventure in judicial policymaking that exceeded the legally permissible. That was how the matter was perceived by those who sought the impeachment of the district court judge, arguing that "the likelihood of a revolutionary change in the Delaware public school system [brought about by the suit] has interfered with the function of that system."[71] Yet this perception misrepresented the facts. The task that the court set itself was a bounded, legalist task: "to order a remedy which will place the victims of the violation in substantially the position which they would have occupied had the violation not occurred."[72] Application of that standard led the court to insist on metropolitan-area relief. "The entire northern New Castle area must be treated as one community in terms of its population characteristics, because that is the way it was perceived and treated by the State and its citizenry."[73]

At each subsequent stage in the proceedings, legalist as distinguished from political concerns shaped the suit, minimizing the policymaking role of the court. The particular remedy proposed by the court serves as a case in point. One suggested approach involving urban-suburban school clusters was rejected because "fraught with complex problems unsuited for judicial determination." Another proposed plan had the regrettable consequence of "plac[ing] the Court in the ongoing position of general supervisor of education in New Castle County. In the event of disagreements over curriculum patterns or textbooks, the Court or a master would have to step in." Judicial creation of several new districts was resisted because there existed "little guidance from state or federal constitutional guarantees." The court did not mandate a county-wide district because that would have involved a "major shift in Delaware school policy."[74] The court's order was designed to intrude least upon the political workings of the system, and it explicitly permitted the state legislature to develop its own alternative plan.

While the influence of legalism varies from case to case, it is almost never insubstantial. Conversely, cases in which the legalist mode predominates cannot be understood as merely entailing the elaboration of a constitutional standard, wholly apart from political factors; the constitutional yardsticks are just too vague, the context too intrusive, for that. In a great many of the desegregation cases, concerns of law, politics, and educational policy coexist in interdependent fashion.

VII

Educational policy issues more or less intimately related to race also help set the course of race and schooling litigation. Until the 1970s, courts defined the scope of desegregation suits narrowly. The judiciary focused exclusively on factors influencing racial mix: pupil attendance zones, school construction and teacher assignment practices, and the like.[75] But racial balance alone has come to seem an imperfect remedy for the problems brought to light in a desegregation suit. The discrimination that the courts identified extended beyond purposeful discrimination to encompass substantive questions of curriculum, student discipline, and educational innovation; it also reached the structural apparatus of the system, the supposed racism of the educational institution itself.[76] In some instances, these concerns comprised part of a more complete remedy, one intended not just "to eliminate a 'violation' . . . but rather to remove the threat posed by the organization to the constitutional values."[77] Where an extraordinarily high proportion of black pupils makes racial mixing infeasible, attention to the substance and structure of the educational program may seem the only judicial response to extant discrimination that is not purely formalistic.

Once a trial court has undertaken to remedy racial discrimination, it makes little sense to confine that remedy to numerical balancing. For one thing, the wrong itself has deeper roots; for another, a remedy responsive to the linkage of educational and racial concerns is more likely to induce the kinds of reforms required to make nondiscrimination a reality. Even if the court views itself as hopelessly inept in matters of educational policy, it can at the least assure itself, as did the judge in Wilmington, that the school district is seriously attending to them; or it can recruit the kind of specialist help—a master or expert—that will enable it to speak effectively to questions joining racial justice and educational policy.[78] Most of the cases adopt one of these two courses. Yet on some occasions judges have regarded desegregation suits as affording a bully pulpit from which to excoriate present practices and propose new ones. They do so quite apart from the views of the parties to the dispute and with little heed to the connection between the policy issue being addressed and the nature of the constitutional wrong.

This behavior poses problems of both substance and form. To

be sure, the breadth of the educational policy issues that a desegregation dispute touches upon makes it difficult to bound remedy framing, since it is hard to think of an issue not affecting, and affected by, race. But if the courts are to be seen as something other than "school superintendents who enter office by a slightly different route," [79] attention needs to be paid to the limits of the court's inquiry. Failure to draw the parties into negotiation over the educational program poses a second source of concern. To these questions, there exists no single right answer. Choosing the "best" solution is largely a matter of strategy, and there is no reason to think that the courts have some special competence in this realm. To the contrary, insofar as the educational component of a remedy determines how well it will work in practice, there is every reason to leave such matters largely to the parties, who have a deeper sense of the practicalities. When that has not happened, the courts have introduced an extraneous element into the constitutionally constrained process of bargaining.

The Detroit case offers a classic illustration of a judge acting as an educationalist. After the Supreme Court rejected a remedy merging Detroit with the surrounding suburban communities, the trial court was ordered to devise a cure for the racial wrong involving Detroit alone. [80] Not just the scope of the remedy ordered distinguishes Detroit. Although the sweep of the court's mandate is impressive—including, as it does, provision of a new guidance program, an expanded student rights code, and an in-service training program, as well as establishment of an arm of the school bureaucracy to improve relations with the community, bilingual education, and a reform of the educational testing program—it is not unique. Other cities, among them Boston and Denver, have seen orders of similar breadth. What distinguishes Detroit is the way the judge went about the task.

The Detroit court undertook to mandate improved educational programs in lieu of greater racial mixing, voicing its unwillingness to treat "school children . . . as pigmented pawns to be shuffled about and counted solely to achieve an abstraction called 'racial mix.'" [81] In this effort, its concern was with educational benefits, not constitutional rights. This remedy did not emerge from negotiations between the parties. Although the judge shared the details of the plan with school district officials before releasing his opinion, it was his plan, not the board's. Indeed, the amount of racial mixing ordered was less than the school board itself had proposed, the educational policy changes far more extensive than those dreamed of by the parties. "The court was as enthusiastic

about revitalizing the educational process as it was reluctant to desegregate it." [82]

While the Boston court sought to draw the parties into the
remedy-framing task, its decision—particularly efforts to link the
school district to the area's universities, colleges, industries, and
cultural institutions—went well beyond what the parties had in
mind. That decision was intended as a prescription for excellence
in a district perceived as a shambles. "Both [the judge] and his experts apparently believed that the quality of instruction in Boston
Public Schools has been so poor for so long that a redistribution of
resources would not guarantee the plaintiff class the equal protection they were entitled to under the law. In order to provide equal
protection, the Judge and his experts believed it was necessary to
upgrade the entire system of education in Boston." [83]

The approach of these courts may have yielded a remedy similar to what a healthy political system would have adopted if left
to its own devices. The judges may well have acted as they did only
in the face of a bankrupt political order, hoping to restore a well-
functioning school district. But a court has little realistic chance of
achieving this objective. While the educational dilemmas are real
enough, they have not readily responded to other ministrations,
and there is no reason to think that a court alone—as distinguished
from a court acting in tandem with the parties—can do much better. Perhaps a court may best hope to influence educational reform
in a generally well-functioning district, where there is support for
policy change within the professional staff and consensus in the
political community. In a less fully professionalized or politically
more fractured system, a more modest judicial aspiration—limited perhaps to helping shape the rudimentary institutional structure—is more fitting. [84]

VIII

Politics and law: in the realm of race and schooling, each reshapes
the other. The political process, increasingly pluralist in character,
takes constitutional values into account. The judicial process, addressing an issue that has once and will again be deemed suitable
for local political resolution, typically eschews authoritative order
in favor of a search for agreement.

How well has this system functioned? Criticism of both the
process of decision making and the substance of decisions has been
severe and varied. Local politics, it is argued, has successfully
warded off the demand of racial minorities for inclusion, using the
appearance of pluralism to conceal paternalistic decision mak-

ing.[85] Courts are scored (by a different set of critics, to be sure) as threatening democratic decision making through opinions that impose detailed marching orders on such American public institutions as the schools.[86] The substance of determinations, the fit between the outcomes and our "public values,"[87] evokes at least as much disagreement. Localism itself, it is claimed, frustrates the larger concern for racial justice.[88] Supposed judicial fixation on racial balance is held to distract attention from more important educational matters.[89]

The critics perceive different worlds, and those differences provide further confirmation of the diverse and idiosyncratic character of the system of decision making. What one makes of that diversity depends both on an empirical understanding of the elements of variability, which the case studies in Part 2 further specify, and on a normative yardstick for appraisal, to which Part 3 speaks.

PART TWO

Race and Schooling: The Experience of Five Communities, 1955–1980

He who would do good to another,
must do it in Minute Particulars.

William Blake, *Jerusalem:*
The Emanation of the Giant Albion

CHAPTER
5

Contiguous Communities,
Disparate Histories

I

The Bay Area is not usually thought to typify the American land-scape. Quite the contrary: it is the exotic amid its more prosaic sur-roundings; the farthest out, and not just with reference to geo-graphic location. San Francisco may be, as the billboards declare, "America's favorite city," but it is not America's hometown. The icons of the region—Berkeley, its university synonymous with radi-calism; Marin County, that peacock-feathered pleasure palace; San Francisco itself, a Noah's Ark of divergent social types encased in a Victorian jewel box—summon to the popular mind not "America" but an image of what might as well be a foreign land or the embod-iment of *Future Shock*. The Bay Area is not, in any event, the ob-vious place to comprehend so quintessentially American a social policy problem as race and schooling.[1]

Voting and demographic data partly substantiate this percep-tion of distinctiveness. Treated as a whole, the Bay Area is politi-cally more liberal than the nation. Jimmy Carter, trounced na-tionally in 1980, prevailed there; George McGovern, who managed in 1972 to win only one of the fifty states, carried the region by 3 percent; and in 1968 Hubert Humphrey swamped Richard Nixon.[2] Democrats or liberal Republicans represent the area in Congress and the state legislature. While local elections are formally non-partisan, they frequently pit Democrats against one another. Resi-dents of the region are slightly better educated than the national average—the typical Bay Area adult attended school for more than twelve-and-a-half years, a half-year more than his counterpart elsewhere[3]—and are somewhat wealthier. The 1970 median income placed the Bay Area among the top 20 percent of standard metropolitan statistical areas.[4] Only one family in fourteen fell below the government's poverty level, in contrast with one in eight nationally.[5] Almost three-fifths of the Bay Area's work force holds white collar jobs, 10 percent higher than the national average.[6]

These indexes confirm that the Bay Area cannot routinely be treated as representative of the country. With respect to race, however, this liberal and well-off region shares fully the dilemmas that have confronted the North and West, and for that reason, its experience with race and schooling is instructive.

Blacks migrated to the Bay Area, mostly from the rural South, in increasing numbers beginning with the onset of World War II. They constituted just 1 percent of the region's population in 1940, a figure that climbed to 6 percent by 1950 and 11 percent in 1970.[7] Employment in wartime industries was the primary economic lure. Other and less tangible attractions also played a part, as a 1949 portrait of the black migrant reveals:

In California his children go to the same schools as other children. They go for nine months during the year. The buildings are new and warm and well lighted. He can ride on a bus without having to take a rear seat marked "colored." He can attend any movie and take any seat he likes; no climbin. the long flights of stairs to the uppermost stuffy balcony. He can walk down the street without having to move toward the curb when a white man passes. He isn't required, on perhaps pain of beating or arrest, to say "ma'am" to the women clerks in the stores.

He can vote by registering and going to the polls, and no nightshirt Klansmen are going to try to stop him. It isn't likely that he will be clubbed by bullying white policemen "just for the hell of it," thrown in jail and then charged with "disturbing the peace." When he works he knows that he will be paid in cash, get all that is coming to him. His children can use the library like any other children. He can join the local chapter of the NAACP or some unions or a local anti-discrimination committee without fear of violent reprisal at the hands of law and order.[8]

While California was not rural Alabama, it also proved to be a far cry from the promised land. By all the standard indicia, blacks have fared substantially less well than whites. Compared with the average for the Bay Area population as a whole, black families in 1970 earned two-thirds as much, proportionately three times as many black families had incomes below poverty level, and blacks were twice as likely to be unemployed. Blacks were also less well educated. They were 20 percent less likely to have completed high school; only one in eighteen had finished four years of college, compared with one in six for the entire population.[9] In each respect, these figures mirror national data.

Residential segregation is also the Bay Area norm. Four cities, which include 41 percent of the Bay Area's residents—San Francisco, Oakland, Berkeley, and Richmond—provide homes for 84 percent of the blacks. More striking still, ten neighborhoods, in which 9 percent of the region's population lives, house five-eighths of Bay Area blacks.[10] Standard indicia of racial isolation report the segregation of whites from nonwhites, and by this measure the Bay Area fares comparatively well. Two cities, Berkeley and San Francisco, were among the eight least segregated nationally in 1960, and the area had become markedly less segregated between 1940 and 1960.[11] As one regional agency noted, "nowhere in the San Francisco Bay Area do we find a teeming black ghetto comparable to Harlem or the Hough section of Cleveland."[12] But examining the segregation of whites from blacks, rather than all nonwhites, tells a very different story: throughout the area, the index of segregation in 1970 was thirteen to thirty-two points higher for blacks than for other races. The region's other nonwhite groups, Asians and Hispanics, have moved closer to whites, leaving blacks even more isolated.[13]

Voluntary segregation has presumably influenced residential patterns—although there is no reason to believe that blacks might be more anxious than, say, the Japanese to preserve their culture through separation. Discrimination informally codified into "rough custom"[14] was also at work, even in the area's most liberal communities. A test of housing discrimination, conducted in Marin County by the local Committee on Racial Discrimination in 1959, found qualified blacks turned away by realtors and builders in all but three of thirty-seven instances; six years later, a survey of 221 apartments revealed that 52 percent were not open to blacks (the owners were evasive in an additional 16 percent of the cases).[15] In Berkeley, a 1962 telephone survey found blacks barred from 80 percent of suitable and available apartments; the majority of the remaining 20 percent were located in predominantly black neighborhoods.[16] A 1966 study by the San Francisco Human Rights Commission reported that 45 percent of landlords polled declared that they would not rent to blacks, and another 15 percent fudged the question.[17] Discrimination in employment was similarly widespread. Not until the late 1950s, for example, did Bay Area school districts begin hiring blacks to teach in other than ghetto schools. During the early 1960s, discrimination against black salespeople by "automobile row" dealers and department stores became a target of civil rights activism.[18]

By the late 1960s, overt discrimination had diminished. As antidiscrimination laws became stiffer and knowledge of the requirements of law grew more widespread, some change in attitudes was reported. A poll of San Francisco landlords conducted in 1968 reveals the difference: 62 percent professed their willingness to rent to blacks, an increase of one-third in just two years.[19] In the wake of the Watts riots in Los Angeles and threatened blowups in San Francisco and Oakland, ghetto communities for the first time received their share of positive political attention.[20] Yet how much real change occurred? Writing about San Francisco, Tom Wolfe comments that "the bureaucrats at City Hall and in the Office of Economic Opportunity talked 'ghetto' all the time, but they didn't know any more about what was going on in the Western Addition, Hunter's Point, Potrero Hill, the Mission, Chinatown or south of Market Street than they did about Zanzibar."[21] An East Bay city councilman offered a more ominous appraisal of the long-term dimensions of the racial issue: "As long as it was a question of the Chinese and Japanese and the Mexicans we could expect them to get along fairly well, although none of them was ever fully accepted. But with the Negroes it is a different story. We haven't accepted them, and I don't see how we are going to."[22]

II

It was in this political and social climate that civil rights groups in San Francisco, Berkeley, Oakland, Sausalito, and Richmond set out to change the policies and practices of the public schools; the experiences of those communities are recounted in succeeding chapters.[23] The portents were mixed. On the one hand, San Francisco, Berkeley, and Sausalito were politically liberal, Oakland and Richmond not hopelessly conservative towns. The legacy of progressivism had left most of them free from machine control, in the hands of good government forces and professional managers.[24] The black population was relatively small—less than 20 percent in each town—and for that reason not especially threatening. Bay Area blacks were also politically sophisticated, and could count on liberal white allies in energizing a nascent civil rights movement.[25] If change could not occur here, some reasoned, it could not take place anywhere in the country. More positively, such cities as Berkeley saw themselves as models for the nation. On the other hand, the schools remained firmly in the hands of old-line professionals, who resisted interference from any quarter. The history of racial xenophobia (previously directed against San Francisco's Asian population) and the discrimination suffered by blacks in so many aspects of their lives belied the Panglossian notion that the public schools might easily accommodate claims premised on equal treatment of the races.

The social and political conditions of the Bay Area fixed the outer bounds of policy. Yet it is within each of the communities, rather than in the area as a whole, that the struggle over race actually took place. No single strategy animated the several civil rights campaigns. Although there was some interchange of ideas among NAACP and Congress of Racial Equality (CORE) leaders, and the more dramatic undertakings in one place evoked an understandable temptation to imitation elsewhere, civil rights groups in one city typically did not know the particulars of the proposals advanced by their counterparts in neighboring towns. Nor did school boards and school administrators respond with one voice to the issue. This fractionalized activity characterizes politics in a region that, despite sporadic attempts at collaboration among its cities, "has not grown together, but rather has grown apart."[26]

The recountings reveal commonalities as well as dissimilarities, with respect to both the substance and the process of decision. The dissimilarities are perhaps most evident, and confirm the extraordinary degree of differentness present in the Bay Area. Berkeley and Richmond, for instance, share little more than geographic proximity and a smoldering hostility. Although Oakland casts itself as San Francisco's rival, the two places do not have much in common. Consider the critical factors in the evolution of the race and schooling issue: *demography* (the size of the city, the nonwhite proportion of the population, the composition of the nonwhite community, and the change in racial composition over time); *political structure* (the importance of machine as distinguished from reform politics, the manner in which political business is conducted, the openness of the political process to participation by new groups, the general liberal or conservative ideological cast, and the degree to which school policy is politicized); *community culture* (the sophistication or parochialism of the city and the importance attached to conducting public business civilly); and *the organization of the schools* (the degree of professional control within the bureaucracy, the allocation of power between school board and bureaucracy, and the nature of the educational leadership exercised by these two groups). For each factor, the differences are at least as remarkable as the similarities.

Although the five Bay Area communities, taken together, are

not a representative sample, they do incorporate the spectrum of factors that have shaped race and schooling policy nationally. All of the actors in the national drama, from the Black Panthers to the Ku Klux Klan sympathizers, from the obstructionist mayor to the martyred liberal school superintendent, make at least cameo appearances. The racial composition of the school districts varies from 30 to more than 80 percent nonwhite. The several school systems are variously run by outsider professionals and insider loyalists, often in the same city at different times. Educational politics in some places manifests the persisting influence of progressivism, while elsewhere it is tied to the organized political machine. The courts decisively shaped the policy outcome in one city, had a hand in another, and were not directly involved in the remaining three communities. The race and schooling issue was handled peacefully in some places, evoked great tension elsewhere, and was everywhere as volatile as a grenade whose pin has been loosened. Some of the districts seem over time to offer better education to their students, while in others the system itself has deteriorated: the matter of race may have affected these outcomes.[27] Almost the only thing missing from the five cities' history is an instance of extreme and sustained violence centering on the schools. There is no Boston in the Bay Area.

These differences are of vital moment. They point to the importance of community character and the persisting force of idiosyncrasy. They confirm the variousness with which equality has been defined. Implicitly, they fix the limits of any uniform policy. Yet the common themes deserve comparable attention. Despite the lack of formal ties or even informal communication among communities, the evolution of the idea of racial justice traces a broadly similar pattern in each place. Race is placed on the policy agenda, often only after considerable struggle. The claim that racial separation be recognized as a school problem broadens into demands that efforts be made to bring blacks and whites together, even as the school system is modernized. The eventual frustration of that effort—attributable to different factors and assuming different forms in each place—leads to a redefinition of the driving aspiration. Most recently, there has been an apparent renewal of interest in old themes of racial equity, now framed in more pragmatic and less messianic terms. If racial equality remains elusive throughout this period, it continues to compel attention.

The ways decisions about race and schooling—and educational policy more generally—are reached have undergone a parallel transformation. Whatever the political character of a particular community, educational decisions were made by whites, for blacks, a quarter-century ago; for the most part these decisions were made by professionals, in order to further narrowly defined goals. No longer is this true. In almost all the communities, minorities have become active participants in educational decision making, and the process itself, if not routinely politicized, is susceptible to political control. Constitutional norms, unnoticed at the outset of this period, have also assumed greater importance. While racial concerns power these changes, their impact has extended beyond race, and that fact too has significance for policy. Uniformity and idiosyncrasy, participation and legalization: these themes set the terms of the case histories and specify the lessons to be drawn from them.

CHAPTER

6

San Francisco: Multitudes in the Valley of Indecision

I

The July 1971 federal district court decision in *Johnson v. San Francisco Unified School District*,[1] the first court-ordered desegregation of a large non-Southern city, climaxed one decade-long political struggle and triggered another that remains unresolved. The predecision struggle centered on the meaning of racial equality in the schools. Diverse groups, each with its own ideological stance and power base, jockeyed for dominance. Recourse to the court signaled the failure of this round of the political process and decisively altered the dimensions of the issue: with *Johnson*, desegregation in San Francisco became a constitutional as well as a political problem.

The *Johnson* decision imposed a legally authoritative definition of racial equality—one stressing racial mixing, or desegregation—upon a community unable to resolve the question politically. Although the decree was appealed and its wisdom is still questioned, San Francisco came generally to accept the court's view of equality. In this sense, the court's role was decisive.

The postdecision phase has involved giving meaning and content to the *Johnson* order through the actions of school board members, administrators, teachers, and community groups. These actions, undertaken largely outside the purview of the court, have been less than successful. While San Francisco's schools are substantially less segregated today than in 1971, some essentially one-race schools do remain and others are imbalanced. More important, the school district has done little to go beyond racial mixing to achieve an integrated environment; racial heterogeneity is seen as a legal requirement, not as a potential educational resource. This narrow reading of *Johnson*, consistent with the formal mandate but not with the implicit integrationist aspirations of the case, has been damagingly consequential.

Political negotiation over the racial issue did not cease with the *Johnson* order. On the contrary, both the process of framing a decree and the effort to implement it involved the kind of give and take among the affected parties that one associates with politics. Other political concerns, notably fiscal stability, have supplanted race on the policy agenda; in that sense, the intervention of the court has not had its intended effect. The 1978 implementation of a revised student assignment plan that excluded a largely black ghetto from the city-wide desegregation effort suggests the consequences of the diminishing significance of race. These political controversies have engaged the attention of minorities. The struggle over race and schooling brought blacks, Asians, and Latinos to political consciousness; that has been an important, if inadvertent, incident in the quest for racial justice.

Race and schooling policy remains unresolved. In 1981, as a decade earlier, San Francisco's racial practices have been challenged in federal court, in a case that promises to air fully the history of segregation in the city. While the outcome of the suit will not decisively settle the matter, it will formally oblige the school district to attend to matters that have gone largely ignored since the mid-1970s. Politics and law, intertwined throughout this history, will remain so for the foreseeable future.[2]

II

San Francisco prides itself on being different from—better than—most other American cities. It is not just the elegance of the place—the rare coupling of physical and man-made beauty, the machine *and* the garden—that distinguishes San Francisco, although the city trades shamelessly on its mystique. San Francisco thinks of itself as that rara avis, a politically progressive and tolerant community.[3] State Democratic politicians count on its votes to offset those of more conservative Southern California. Gay men and women have long regarded it as a haven and refuge. A host of ethnic groups, the arrived and politically dominant Western Europeans and the rapidly expanding, arriving groups of Asians and Latinos, decidedly unassimilated, enjoy both a community and a political life of their own. If these communities are ghettos, it is only an outsider's perspective that makes them so.

This image conceals recent, politically significant demographic changes. Although the effects have not been so serious or so visible, San Francisco has not been immune from the racial and ethnic conflicts that have beset other urban communities. San Francisco's population has declined in recent years—from 740,316 in 1960 to 678,794 in 1980—as former residents have moved to the surrounding suburbs, continuing to use the city as a workplace. The racial and ethnic composition of the city has changed notably: the city, 90 percent white in 1950, was 59 percent white in 1980.[4] The change is even more marked in the schools. Between 1965— the first year for which racial data are available—and 1979, the proportion of white students declined from 46.4 percent to 20.7 percent.[5]

Blacks currently constitute the largest single minority group, almost 15 percent of the population. Drawn to San Francisco by the promise of wartime employment in the 1940s, they found housing in Hunter's Point, the isolated southeastern corner of the city, and many have remained clustered there. Until recently, Asians rather than blacks were the city's have-not group. The traditional kinship ties of the Chinese and Japanese and the outright prejudice of San Franciscans encouraged both groups to withdraw into their own enclaves.[6] Since wartime internment, the Japanese community—about 1.3 percent of the population—has shrunk slightly. Other Third World groups, including the Chinese, Filipino, Vietnamese, and Samoan populations, grew rapidly following the liberalization of immigration laws in 1965; in 1980, about 11 percent of the population was of Chinese origin and about 5 percent was Filipino. In addition, some 8 percent of the city's population, concentrated in the center-city Mission District, was of Hispanic descent, primarily Mexican and Central American.

Beginning in the mid-1960s, these ethnic groups demanded from city government in general, and the public schools in particular, better jobs, better schools, and—perhaps most important—political recognition of their worth. The school desegregation issue was one important focus of this new politics.

During the 1950s, San Francisco schools epitomized the then-prevalent civic virtues. They were well and professionally run, and were largely detached from politics. The introduction of racial concerns altered the picture considerably.

From 1922 to 1972, the San Francisco Board of Education consisted of seven persons named by the mayor and ratified pro forma by the voters for four-year terms. In effect the board was appointed, an elite group whose members saw their obligation to be assuring that San Francisco maintained a reputation for public school excellence, which meant relying on able professional leadership.[7] Harold Spears, superintendent from 1955 to 1967, embraced the philosophy that school governance properly belongs to professionals and not to politicians or laypeople. In his view, schools serve a vital but narrowly conceived social purpose: they prepare the young to become productive citizens. The task of the school board is to obtain public support for the professional administration's policy, not to be armchair quarterbacks.

Superintendent Spears' attitude toward race and schooling reflected the classic liberal tradition of racial neutrality; institutional decisions should turn on individual attributes, not on the irrelevancies of racial or other group characteristics. Spears saw the longstanding neighborhood school policy as a splendid exemplification of that tradition. "We have all races in our schools," observed Spears. "Everyone living in a certain area, regardless of race, goes to the school in that area."[8] In 1960, Spears asserted to the United States Civil Rights Commission that racial discrimination was not a problem in San Francisco; the district was scrupulously color-blind in its student assignment and personnel policies.[9]

These avowals implied a denial that problems of racial injustice even existed in the schools, a view that was not shared by the local chapter of CORE and by the Council for Civic Unity, an umbrella organization representing several civil rights groups.[10] In January 1962, leaders of the two groups urged the board to recognize that the schools were de facto segregated, to declare that predominantly black schools were educationally undesirable, and to prepare a program for eliminating segregation. No specific alternative was offered. What was really being sought was an expression of official awareness and concern, a willingness to acknowledge the reality of the problem.

The civil rights groups had been encouraged to make their request by their earlier success in preserving one city high school as an academic, rather than a comprehensive, high school (academic excellence was, at least in 1961, perceived as a civil rights issue). The board had acceded to pressure by the civil rights group—an "unexpected surprise" for the advocates, who had not realized that they could be quite so effective—and reversed the superintendent's recommendation to convert the school into a comprehensive school.[11] With respect to desegregation, however, the board was politically more prudent. It deferred to the professional judgment of the superintendent, and asked him to report back on the matter.

Spears' mid-June report, entitled "The Proper Recognition of a Pupil's Racial Background," was not similarly prudent.[12] Because that report flatly rejected the accusation of de facto segregation, it became a focus of controversy. Spears insisted that providing adequate schooling for black children was a "highly complicated educational matter" that should be left to professional educators. The problem, however, stemmed not from the schools but from "disproportionate housing, indifferent parents, limited job opportunities for youth, and unresponsive pupils." Blunt words, indeed, and Spears' rejection of a racial census was even more blunt:

> We are now faced with the movement to emphasize differences in the color and races of pupils. . . . In some school systems, such records are now prepared annually. One asks for what purpose do we so label a child, and in turn, post a sign on his school indicating the racial makeup of the student body at the moment? If we are preparing to ship these children to various schools, in predetermined racial allotments, then such brands would serve the purpose they have been put to in handling livestock. But until somebody comes up with an educationally sound plan for such integration, then this racial accounting serves nothing but the dangers of putting it to ill use.

Spears recognized the symbolic importance of the question that had been put to him but he opposed using children as "tools" in a process of social change. Racial labeling was, in his judgment, a perversion of the schools' purpose, namely instruction in the pedagogical basics of "reading, writing, spelling, arithmetic, English, geography, history, civics, and so on." The upshot of Spears' position was to uphold the status quo: "I have no educationally sound program to suggest to the Board to eliminate the schools in which the children are predominantly of one race."

The superintendent's statement turned a debate over the meaning of equal educational opportunity into a battle between the school board and superintendent on the one side and the civil rights movement on the other. In September 1962, at the most stormy meeting in the history of San Francisco's public schools, 1,400 citizens appeared, variously to denounce and to defend Spears' position. Fifty-two speakers addressed the marathon session.[13] The civil rights groups demanded, in the words of NAACP spokesman Terry Francois, that the "racial composition of the schools become a matter of concern to this board and its administrators."

Francois and the other civil rights spokespersons were not urging wholesale changes in student assignment. To them as to the superintendent, it was important to retain "to the maximum ex-

tent possible . . . the basic character of the neighborhood schools.
. . . We have never advocated a particular percentage." That point
was reiterated by CORE and the Council for Civil Unity. In statements delivered to the board, both groups urged the board to take
race into account as a legitimate basis for decision making, to do so
voluntarily and not in response to a court order. Those criticizing
the civil rights organizations' position were established minorities—Italian, Irish, and German—fearful of the demise of neighborhood schools and indeed of their own neighborhoods. Other minority groups went unheard at the board meeting, for at this time
desegregation was perceived solely as a black-white problem.

The civil rights groups sought during the fall of 1962 to re-
pudiate the Spears report. They insisted upon a citizens' advisory
committee as the most likely vehicle for formulating and legitimating a policy that committed the school district to overcoming racial isolations.[14] The demand reflected distrust both of the board of
education and of the superintendent, a fact that the board itself
recognized. Some response to this rapidly escalating issue more
satisfactory than the superintendent's statement was called for, but
the board chose to appoint an ad hoc committee composed of its
own members rather than creating a citizens' group, in order to
keep the issue under its control.

The strategy did not satisfy the civil rights organizations.
CORE staged a sit-in following the meeting and threatened more
protests. The NAACP filed suit against the school district, charging that San Francisco had discriminated against black students
through pupil assignment and transfer policies, and seeking district-wide relief.[15] The civil rights groups saw both the sit-in and
the lawsuit as efforts to step up political pressure. What they really
hoped for was not a legal confrontation but a statement committing the district to work toward desegregation and the appointment of an administrator to handle individual grievances concerning discrimination.

The board's ad hoc committee provided such a resolution. Its
April 1963 report admitted that segregation, although not deliberately practiced by the school district, persisted nonetheless and
recommended that promoting desegregation be one criterion for
drawing attendance-zone boundaries.[16] That declaration, the appointment of a black human relations officer, and the reassignment
of several hundred minority students to predominantly white
schools could not "cure" the problems of racial segregation; nor
were they intended to. But these actions provided at least momentary satisfaction. The NAACP allowed the desegregation litigation

to lapse, praising the board's endorsement of a racial criterion as a "step forward."[17] The superintendent urged unity. The chairman of the Committee for Neighborhood Schools was soon to propose limited desegregation "experiments."[18] A process of mutual accommodation seemed to be working, as demonstrations and lawsuits became new tactics in the traditional political pattern of negotiation and compromise.

The resolution would be short-lived. During much of the 1963–64 school year, civil rights organizations did not continue to press the school system with specific demands. The focus of the movement shifted, although briefly, to employment, as the outright refusal of dealers on "automobile row" to hire blacks became the subject of primary attention.[19] The NAACP felt it appropriate to give William Cobb, the human relations officer, time to maneuver but soon realized that it had won an empty victory. Spears and his staff had taken no further steps, and Cobb, who had effectively been frozen out of the administration's decision making, appeared to be more concerned with educational standards than with civil rights issues.

Spears did take one action he thought would appease civil rights groups. He proposed a bond issue to build a new high school in a racially mixed area. But, not having raised the matter with the NAACP, he failed to reckon with the split within the black community. The NAACP, responding to pressure from its Hunter's Point constituency, reversed its earlier stand and insisted that new schools be built in the ghetto; the powerful Central Labor Council announced that it would recommend rejection of the bonds unless the NAACP supported the plan. With understandable bewilderment, Spears found himself negotiating a plan that included construction on sites he "would never have dreamed of asking for."[20] This accommodation was ultimately a costly one. Six years later, the plaintiffs in *Johnson* would point to the construction of ghetto schools as evidence of the school district's deliberate segregation of black students.

In order to apply new pressure to the board, civil rights organizations regrouped into the Coordinating Council for Integrated Schools; from the roster of member groups, it appeared that everyone supported desegregation. The council demanded a racial census of the school population in order to make plain the extent of segregation. Through picketing and persuasion, its demand prevailed.

The census, released in 1965, proved anticlimactic: while it revealed the existence of some predominantly one-race schools in

San Francisco, it also showed considerable desegregation.[21] There was substantially less segregation than in most other large school districts. The eight high schools had black enrollments ranging from 8 to 34 percent, and only two of the fifteen junior high schools were more than half black. Racial disproportion was greatest in the ninety-five elementary schools. Four schools were more than 90 percent white; seven were more than 90 percent black.[22]

Although the census prompted no further desegregation efforts, an important symbolic shift was occurring: racial isolation in San Francisco's schools was increasingly recognized as a problem worth studying. During the last years of the Spears era, studies were the order of the day. Beginning in 1966, the NAACP Education Committee undertook the thankless task of gathering data on school expenditures in an effort to demonstrate that low expenditures in predominantly black schools caused the low achievement-test scores of students in those schools. These data were intended to embarrass the board of education into action. The board also turned to research, contracting with the Stanford Research Institute (SRI) to conduct a preliminary study upon which a master plan for desegregation could be based. By commissioning a study, the board hoped both to buy time and to meet a desperate need for wisdom offered from the vantage point of detachment. At least the first objective was achieved. SRI's report was not made public until mid-1967, the waning days of Spears' administration, and the board postponed its response until Spears' successor could study and react to the document.[23]

In July 1967, Robert Jenkins was appointed as the new superintendent. Jenkins had survived ten years in Pasadena, California, a community that had undergone limited school desegregation. He was chosen for his talents both in innovating and in involving citizens' groups in his administration. To an increasingly desegregation-minded board (the three most recently appointed members had strong civil rights backgrounds), Jenkins appeared capable of leading San Francisco into the new era. His ultimate failure evidenced the complex and treacherous political environment within which desegregation had to be sought.

The board gave Superintendent Jenkins six months to study and respond to the SRI report, *Improving Racial Balance in the Public Schools*, before making its own recommendations. The SRI study was technically commendable and offered a dozen alternative ways for San Francisco to desegregate.[24] Yet it showed little awareness either of the diversity of San Francisco's ethnic groups and neighborhoods or of pedagogical and administrative issues involved in desegregation. In several San Francisco neighborhoods, including the racially mixed southwestern corner (comprising the Ocean View, Merced Heights, and Ingleside neighborhoods) known as OMI and Hunter's Point, local groups organized to address the problems—including the racial problems—of their schools.

OMI obtained funding from the U.S. Department of Health, Education and Welfare (HEW) in 1966 to attack housing and school problems that local groups had identified as causes of neighborhood deterioration and white flight.[25] Funds from the HEW grant were distributed to the five elementary schools in the OMI area, and each school chose projects it regarded as essential. The overall objective was to enhance the schools' effectiveness and to entice middle-class whites to remain in the area.[26] The organization envisioned a future in which desegregated schools would be the natural by-product of a genuinely desegregated residential area.

A second grass-roots organization was emerging in the Hunter's Point–Bayview district,[27] an almost all-black neighborhood. Concern did not focus on desegregation, for distance and white unease made that idea infeasible. The community group sought instead to improve its own schools, obtaining federal funds for community aides and parent-teacher councils at each primary school.[28]

Neither OMI nor the Hunter's Point project interested or involved the central school administration. The SRI study and the superintendent's reaction mattered far more, for they would fix the course of the district's racial policy.

Superintendent Jenkins' response altered the terms of the policy debate. Whereas SRI's study focused specifically on desegregation, Jenkins emphasized "educational equality/quality," an ambiguous phrase that was to inform San Francisco's planning efforts for the next three years. The shift was more than semantic. SRI's primary concern lay with such mundane matters as restructuring school attendance patterns and devising a transportation system to facilitate city-wide desegregation. Jenkins argued that a commitment to educational quality as well as equality required "ways to achieve a better racial and ethnic balance in the schools, ways that are consistent with the maintenance and extension of high educational standards for all students."[29] Desegregation, he asserted, should be coupled with ambitious (and costly) new educational ventures, so attractive that they would make racial mixing something that both white and black parents would actively want.

Jenkins proposed a number of new educational options, among them an "Educational Park . . . a bold and dramatic approach to the pursuit of excellence for urban areas." The result would link increased desegregation with pedagogical innovation. The superintendent suggested that the board solicit community reaction to his ideas, as well as those of SRI, but community forums held in response to this recommendation produced only conflict. For the first time, attention in San Francisco was focused on the possibility of busing children to promote desegregation.

The superintendent and the board, unprepared to take decisive action, sought to defuse the hostility. They appointed a citizens' advisory committee whose members included a cross section of community sentiment. The committee was charged with reviewing the "equality/quality" proposals and the ideas that had surfaced at the community forums, and with drafting recommendations. In its June 1968 charge to the committee, the board committed itself for the first time to "improvement of quality education through the orderly integration of its schools." The commitment was hedged round with qualifications—"due regard" would be paid to "sound education approaches and the unique problems of San Francisco," and only "practical plans that are feasible and acceptable" would warrant board consideration[30]—but it was the strongest statement that had thus far been put forward.

The committee report, submitted in February 1969, embraced desegregation in a markedly limited sense.[31] It proposed desegregated "School Complexes," subdistricts within the city, in two preponderantly middle-class neighborhoods, Richmond and Park South. The two neighborhoods had been carefully chosen for ease of school desegregation. Both were residentially integrated to some degree and had stable student populations. Black and white students living in these neighborhoods would have to be bused only short distances. Speedy implementation was urged. "Every additional day of delay will only further reduce what faith remains in the School District's willingness to move ahead."

Before approving this recommendation, the superintendent solicited the views of the parents, teachers, and administrators whose schools were to become part of the new complexes. The response was generally enthusiastic. Substantial numbers of parents became intimately involved in the enterprise and advanced a host of new ideas. That reaction encouraged the board of education— most of whose members were personal friends of and continuing collaborators with the civil rights movement—to approve implementation of the complexes, beginning in September 1970.

A decade-long campaign by civil rights advocates had at last produced a tangible administrative response, a compromise tailored to the political realities of San Francisco, a victory for the NAACP in its continuing battle to secure desegregation. Many sections of the city remained unaffected by the proposal. OMI and Hunter's Point were progressing with plans for community renewal and control over their neighborhood schools. Few Spanish-speaking people were involved in the complexes themselves, but by participating in the citizens' advisory committee, Hispanic community leaders had generated some support for the concept of bilingual education. The Chinese Big Six Companies, which informally ran Chinatown, had also used the citizens' advisory committee as a forum to press for improvements in the instruction of Chinese immigrant children who were unable to speak English. These communities continued to seek greater administrative responsiveness, and some regarded the complexes as a hopeful sign, indicating new openness and willingness to embark on community-initiated ventures.

Prospects for the venture seemed remarkably good. Considerable support for the complexes existed, both in the affected neighborhoods and city wide. The planning process had produced a plan that aspired to do more than mix racial groups.[32] It was tacitly understood that if the two complexes succeeded the model might eventually be adopted throughout the city. The board president called them "pilot programs: if they work we can apply the idea elsewhere in San Francisco."[33] Thus, at the beginning of 1970 it seemed that a peaceful revolution, achieved through the political process, was at hand. Even cutting back the plan to just one complex, in the Richmond area, for financial reasons did not much allay the prevailing optimism.

It was the unanticipated political crisis that proved crucial. Joseph Alioto, mayor since 1967, had declined to involve himself publicly throughout the desegregation controversy, correctly pointing out that the board of education had exclusive responsibility for school policy.[34] Yet early in 1970, to the surprise and consternation of the civil rights groups, he chose to become the focal point for political opposition to the proposed complexes. Alioto had built his reputation in good part on his capacity for working with the black community.[35] The mayor's seeming inconsistency on the desegregation issue was partly an act of political calculation. No one had emerged to speak forcefully for the city's ethnic backbone, fearful of efforts to alter the traditional neighborhood school system; there was political capital to be gained from the issue.

Alioto's position was also consistent with views he had held since he was retained by the board in the 1962 NAACP litigation. He favored limited desegregation, including voluntary busing of students. He believed that school attendance boundaries should be gerrymandered to reduce racial isolation. He had appointed outspoken liberals to the board of education. But at mandatory elementary school busing, even to the limited extent necessary to desegregate schools within the complexes, he drew the line. In his view, seven-year-old children should not have to ride a bus in order to affirm a principle.[36]

Alioto's position produced political shock waves. He was promptly joined in his fight by conservative Supervisor John Barbagelata, who proposed a ballot measure to poll voters' attitudes toward mandatory busing. Although the referendum was advisory in nature, it heated up the controversy. The strongest response came from Charles Belle, president of the local NAACP chapter: "I am sick and tired and ashamed of the segregated school situation in San Francisco. We know white racists want to keep segregated white and black schools here."[37]

In June, by a margin of nearly three to one, voters declared that the board of education should not be permitted to bus or reassign elementary school children to schools outside their neighborhoods without parental consent. The referendum did not sway the school board, which pursued its planning for the complex. Mayor Alioto recognized that he had lost this round of the political battle. He urged those who agreed with his position to file a lawsuit seeking to halt the implementation of the Richmond Complex.

Suit was duly filed in the California Supreme Court,[38] but it was not the most important case to be filed that month. Alioto's statements had persuaded NAACP President Belle that the educators' concern for "quality" was irrelevant and that a suit to compel district-wide desegregation could wait no longer. As Belle told Superintendent Jenkins: "I had hoped that we might avoid this, but the mayor has turned desegregation into a political and emotional battleground. We'll get an instant solution in federal court."[39] The advent of *Johnson v. San Francisco School District* represented at least a momentary failure of political bargaining and moved the dispute into a different arena. Decisions concerning desegregation policy were no longer exclusively the board's responsibility.

III

The NAACP brought legal action because, in the end, it felt that it had to. Mayor Alioto had raised the political ante to a point where some response was necessary. A lawsuit, always regarded as a vital tactic in the struggle to improve opportunities, had become the appropriate symbolic response to what was viewed as the white community's attempt to frustrate black aspirations. More pragmatically, because the constitutional meaning of de jure segregation had expanded markedly since the NAACP filed its first complaint in 1962, a favorable court ruling could reasonably be expected.

The complaint, filed on June 24, 1970, asked for complete student and faculty desegregation in the elementary schools. It also sought a temporary restraining order assuring that the district would proceed with plans for the Richmond Complex; the board's wavering on that issue had left the NAACP uneasy.[40] The scope of the suit was deliberately limited to the elementary schools because the NAACP leadership believed that desegregation during the early years of schooling, before children's racial attitudes hardened, was crucial. Time constraints also forced the limitation; it was felt that deliberate segregation could be more easily and quickly demonstrated with respect to elementary schools.

The complaint in *Johnson*, drafted by a young solo practitioner, Arthur Brunwasser, was consciously patterned after recently concluded litigation in Pontiac, Michigan, which had stretched the meaning of de jure segregation further than had any other federal court decision.[41] To establish that San Francisco was de jure segregated, the plaintiffs' case cited school district data revealing increases in racial segregation between 1964–65 and 1969–70. The decade-long history of discussion and investigation of racial injustice in San Francisco's schools was reiterated in order to show the district's awareness of segregation. Relying on the Pontiac case, plaintiffs claimed that legal culpability should attach to its failure to rectify that segregation. Particular emphasis was placed on ten schools built during the past decade that allegedly had increased segregation. Ironically, among them were several neighborhood schools in largely black Hunter's Point that the NAACP had earlier insisted upon as the price for its support of a school bond issue. Plaintiffs also attacked the OMI and Hunter's Point projects, not for their aspirations but for their failure to reduce segregation.

Two depositions were critical in proving the district's culpability. William Cobb, the district's human relations officer, noted that he had advised the superintendent that several contemplated construction projects would increase racial imbalance. Building had proceeded nonetheless because other factors, such as availability of land and accessibility, were treated as controlling. Board member Laurel Glass corroborated Brunwasser's assertions that a neighborhood school policy actively "discourages the achievement of racial integration" and that little had been done to improve racial balance. Conspicuously absent from the plaintiffs' case were some of the characteristic elements of de jure segregation suits, such as detailed accounts of gerrymandering school boundaries in order to maintain racial separation, busing black children past white schools to attend predominantly black schools, and assigning black teachers to black schools. Such evidence either was not available or had not been located.

The plaintiffs' argument did not rest in this recital of wrongdoing but in the claim that segregation, whether deliberate or unintended, was harmful to black children. Brunwasser relied on the SRI report and the nationally known Coleman Report as authoritative sources for the proposition.[42] The plaintiffs' case thus combined the two strands of prevalent legal argument, a thinly argued claim of de jure segregation and a strong emphasis on the hurtfulness of segregation.

Although the board of education lodged a defense, it generally accepted the plaintiffs' arguments. The board believed in the rightness of desegregation.[43] Its membership had become markedly liberal since the mid-1960s: a majority were closely associated with the NAACP and viewed the educational complexes as a possible prelude to more far-reaching desegregation efforts. But the board lacked the political will to achieve city-wide desegregation. This tension was reflected in its decision not to retain experienced outside counsel, as it had in the 1962 litigation, but to rely instead on the city attorney's office. The *Johnson* case marked Assistant City Attorney George Krueger's first federal court appearance. Krueger regarded the plaintiffs as legally obliged to demonstrate specific acts of de jure segregation if they were to prevail. The district's case was straightforward. Krueger argued that the district had no duty to correct racial imbalance and that "the best refutation of the de jure charge was the history of voluntary efforts to integrate."[44] Thus, plaintiffs and defendants found themselves relying largely on the same record; the difference lay in its interpretation. To plaintiffs, the record revealed a decade of evasion and delay. To defendants, it demonstrated the district's good will in trying to desegregate.

Plaintiffs and defendants were not the only parties or would-be parties to the litigation, and the introduction of other intense and divergent views confirmed that desegregation retained its political dimensions. A modest attempt by a black legal services lawyer to use *Johnson* as a vehicle for bringing about community-controlled black schools was quickly thwarted by the court.[45] Concerned Parents, a group of Richmond neighborhood parents, sought more vigorously to oppose the NAACP's efforts. The members of the group had filed their own suit in state court, charging that the Richmond Complex plan violated federal and state constitutional and statutory rights. When they found themselves upstaged by *Johnson*, a case seeking far broader relief than the plan they were resisting, they were permitted to intervene in that case. Although Concerned Parents was not opposed to "natural integration," its essential aims were to stop the Richmond Complex and to halt district efforts to uproot the neighborhood school, neither directly relevant to the *Johnson* suit. Concerned Parents' attorneys also made a broader argument that existing segregation in San Francisco was not unconstitutional, but they were denied full opportunity to demonstrate it because the court restricted their participation in the critical fact-finding stage of the inquiry.

The multiplicity of positions advanced in *Johnson* could have proved troubling to a less firm judge. But Judge Stanley A. Weigel was able to control the proceedings closely—all too closely, in the judgment of the intervenors and his outside critics. From the very first day of the proceedings, Weigel had a clear command of both the record and the issues. His stated desire to "flush out every point of view"[46] was belied on occasion by his actions. Weigel's questions, particularly those addressed to the defendants, were pointed and sometimes barbed. There was no trial in the case, and little testimony was taken orally at preliminary injunction hearings. The district's own data, the depositions, and the briefs were the bases upon which argument proceeded.

Weigel's approach, although expeditious, had serious costs. In his desire to hasten the adjudicative process, the judge quickly cut off arguments he viewed as extraneous, and consequently many of the plaintiffs' factual allegations concerning the causes of segregation in San Francisco were never tested by the time-honored process of cross-examination. Nor did Judge Weigel ever make clear during oral argument the constitutional standard he was applying. He posed a critical question: "Does not a school board, which for ten years has known of the existence of serious racial imbalance, have a positive duty to do everything it can to act effectively in the interest of eliminating that imbalance?" Insofar as the question suggests that segregation is unconstitutional whatever its cause, that position was of questionable validity in 1970.

Throughout the hearings, Judge Weigel urged a settlement: "I still very much prefer . . . to have the Board . . . come up with a specific plan for the provision of equal educational opportunity, including meaningful correction of the racial imbalance."[47] On September 22, 1970, he postponed decision in the case until the Supreme Court decided *Swann v. Charlotte-Mecklenburg Board of Education*,[48] a suit that was expected to define the duties of school authorities and the powers of federal courts with respect to desegregation. The order was also expressly cast as an invitation to the district to plan for eventual desegregation: "If . . . the Board of Education works out details for maximum changes based upon the assumption that the Supreme Court will require them, the Board will then be able to act effectively, in case of need, without causing confusion and with a minimum of unnecessary dislocation."[49] In one respect, Weigel's request was wholly reasonable, for he was simply asking the district to undertake contingency planning. Yet if Weigel wanted the *Swann* decision in hand before issuing an opinion, did not San Francisco also need that decision to determine what, if anything, it would be obliged to do?

The fact-finding stage of the litigation had been concluded quickly—perhaps too quickly. Conflicting viewpoints had been aired but not fully explored. The merits of the charge that San Francisco had deliberately segregated its schools consequently were not thoroughly examined.

Every year during the past decade has witnessed a "crisis" in American education. For San Francisco, the 1970–71 school term was worse than most. The district found itself faced with a bewildering assortment of problems, few of them directly linked to desegregation. The year included, among other events, a protracted teachers' strike, a report that sixty-two schools were vulnerable to earthquake damage and would imminently have to be reconstructed or closed, student strikes over asserted administrative recalcitrance and demonstrably wretched conditions, a protest against busing in the Richmond Complex, suits filed by the Chinese- and Mexican-American communities alleging that their children's educational needs had been ignored, a demand that a $500,000 black studies program be created in an inner-city high school, approval of a student-drafted "bill of rights," and the district's first financial "crisis" in recent history—a reported $6.7 million deficit.[50] In that strained atmosphere, every district activity was converted into a marginal enterprise. Small wonder, then, that planning for desegregation was not assigned high priority.

Administrative leadership was also in turmoil.[51] Superintendent Jenkins resigned suddenly in June 1970, leaving the board little time to search for a successor. Thomas Shaheen, previously superintendent in Rockford, Illinois, convinced board members that he was totally committed to desegregated education and that he saw no need to incorporate "quality" components to make the concept workable. Shaheen's reputed aggressiveness was perceived as essential in coping with the prevailing politically charged climate. The new superintendent did not live up to his billings.

Shaheen "communicated" endlessly with top administrative staff, teachers, and political groups, bringing to all of them a vaguely messianic message of change. But communicating is not the same thing as administering, and very little of the latter was done under Shaheen. Instructional programs, the heart of Superintendent Spears' concerns, were left to the discretion of site administrators and staff, as the central administration simply ignored the schools' educational mission. With respect to a host of activities—community-based educational ventures in the residentially integrated OMI section of the city and in the predominantly black Hunter's Point neighborhood, an emerging demand for bilingual education, more mundane problems of building maintenance, class-size reduction, and the like—there existed no consensus on the district's obligations and little money for institutional expansion.

The budget was a shambles. Jenkins had bought peace with the teachers' organizations by agreeing in 1968 to hire 900 additional teachers over a three-year period, despite steadily declining enrollments. As a result of this and other acts of largesse, per pupil expenditures had risen by almost 50 percent in just four years. The district had to cut back. But where? With no one attempting to set priorities, building maintenance, curriculum, counseling and guidance, music, and athletics—all areas once contained in a hierarchy of activities and services whose raison d'être was pupil performance—could all claim shares of the education dollar. And who could argue that their claims were invalid?

In addition to problems caused by his weak administering, Shaheen became personally identified with an effort to demote 125 white administrators in order to increase efficiency and to enlarge the number of nonwhite administrators. Those scheduled for demotion successfully challenged the action in court as discrimination in reverse.[52] The demotion fiasco further eroded Shaheen's authority with his staff and made it harder for him to convince hostile San Franciscans to embrace city-wide desegregation.

The Richmond Complex, San Francisco's attempt to wed

quality with desegregation, was also afflicted by this failure of leadership. The experiment was beset with struggles for autonomy and for internal control. The complex did demonstrate that desegregation within a relatively homogeneous extended neighborhood could work and permitted teachers to try out new instructional styles and materials. Neither was a trivial achievement. But the complex did not meet the expectations of its creators. Like numerous other district programs, it was an organizational prodigy deserving of support. But the district's inability to establish priorities made special attention to the program impossible.

In this tumultuous environment, the district considered how to respond to Judge Weigel's September order.[53] No action was taken until January 1971, when Superintendent Shaheen appointed three committees to consider city-wide desegregation. The citizens' advisory committee, originally intended to review the efforts of two committees comprising district personnel, wound up doing most of the work. Neither the board nor the top-echelon bureaucrats wanted anything to do with the issue. An offer of help from the California Education Department's Bureau of Intergroup Relations was rebuffed. "No one in San Francisco thought that the court was for real," the state consultant concluded.[54]

Each of the committees sought a rational, computer-aided method of sorting students on the bases of race, proximity, socioeconomic background, and academic achievement. Yet, as they soon learned, the district's antique record-keeping system rendered that expectation infeasible.[55] The hoped-for creative programming turned into a less exciting and less successful effort to dig out basic information, and in April the citizens' committee reported that planning could not begin until early summer. In a memorandum to the superintendent, several senior administrators asserted that desegregation could not be accomplished before September 1972, unless San Francisco chose to disregard all "we have learned about efforts toward orderly desegregation."[56] The hope of "orderly desegregation" was shortly to be dashed by the district court.

On April 20, 1971, the Supreme Court announced its long-awaited decision in the *Swann* case.[57] Rather than adopting nationwide constitutional standards, *Swann* addressed itself exclusively to school systems that prior to the 1954 *Brown* decision had been segregated by law. The Supreme Court did, however, set down guidelines concerning what was required "to eliminate from the public schools all vestiges of state-imposed segregation,"[58] and Judge Weigel could rely upon those, at least by analogy, in developing a remedy for San Francisco.

Although it did not insist on precise racial balance, *Swann* did permit judges to use data concerning imbalance "as a starting point in the process of shaping a remedy."[59] More significantly, the district-wide busing scheme that it approved for Charlotte, North Carolina, was truly massive.

One week after the *Swann* opinion was issued, Weigel ordered the desegregation of San Francisco's elementary schools in September 1971. That order confined its discussion of the legal and factual issues to a footnote in which Weigel accepted all arguments advanced by plaintiffs, even those for which evidence was at best scanty or contradictory.[60] The court found de jure segregation on the bases of both action and inaction. For example, the opinion concluded that school construction policies had "perpetuated and exacerbated" racial imbalance, ignoring the many racially neutral factors that led to those construction decisions. It also found discrimination in the drawing of unspecified attendance zones, failing to assess the legitimacy of the district's concern for a neighborhood-based school system.

Supplementary findings issued in June were constitutionally somewhat more persuasive.[61] The court noted, for example, the discrimination implicit in the district's disproportionate assignment of minority teachers to identifiably black schools.[62] But these findings also treated plaintiffs' claims generously, and the district's rejoinders went undiscussed. Taken as a whole, the findings suggest that the court embraced an extremely expansive definition of unlawful desegregation, one that almost obliterated the distinction between de jure and de facto.

Resolving the legal dispute proved a difficult matter. For one thing, the Concerned Parents group reappeared, fortified by new counsel and eager to reopen the issue of legal wrong. For another, intervenors representing the Chinese community suddenly emerged to object to its inclusion in any desegregation plan. Finally, members of the board of education could not accept the conclusion that they or their predecessors had acted illegally. These parties moved to upset the orderly sequence of planning that Weigel anticipated.

The court's order posed a difficult dilemma for the board. The desegregation of San Francisco's elementary schools was not in the abstract an unpleasant prospect, but several factors militated against compliance. The six-week planning period the judge had allowed seemed impossibly short. Some board members were unconvinced by the court's conclusion that San Francisco had engaged in de jure segregation; others had changed their views on the wisdom of city-wide desegregation. The board was also faced with the possibility of political extinction, and that may have influenced its judgment. A proposition inspired by antidesegregation sentiment and calling for the creation of a popularly elected board to replace the appointed body was to appear on the November 1971 ballot, and a showing of resistance to the court order may well have been thought politically prudent. By a vote of four to three, the board committed itself to appealing the decision.

Concerned Parents faced no such dilemmas. The intervenors' lawyers eloquently and sometimes wittily expressed their opposition to the court's conclusion that San Francisco had acted improperly with respect to race. When Concerned Parents argued that the district was not legally to blame for its segregated schools since it had not caused the segregation, their words echoed those of Superintendent Spears ten years earlier: "There is nothing whatsoever in either *Brown* or *Swann* which requires that justice be blind to the effects of the institutional racism implicit in the notions that children are fungible commodities and that Negro children must be in the company of white children before they may improve their achievement."[63] The intervenors and the district both sought a stay of Weigel's September 1971 desegregation deadline, pending the outcome of an appeal. On June 4, after a brief hearing, Weigel denied the motion, an action consistent with a decade of federal district court responses to similar motions. The case would go forward on schedule.

In devising a remedy consistent with *Swann*, Judge Weigel enlisted the district and, to its surprise, the NAACP. Each was ordered to prepare, within six weeks, a plan assuring that "the ratio of black children to white children will be . . . substantially the same in each school."[64] Largely because of the time pressures, both the district and the NAACP focused on busing students to achieve a greater racial mix. They produced desegregation, not integration, plans.

The district's plan was put together by the citizens' advisory committee almost by default: the board lacked the inclination and the staff lacked the time for the task.[65] The committee's schedule left little opportunity for educational dreaming. The committee did consider such educational issues as the fit between desegregation and bilingual education, the need for greater choice among educational alternatives, and the involvement of parents in school policymaking, but the primary focus was on racial mixing. The committee quickly dismissed the possibility of incorporating minor boundary adjustments, preservation of already desegregated schools, and voluntary busing arrangements into its scheme. Although such an ad hoc approach might well have generated a solution tailored to San Francisco's needs, it was rejected both because it seemed unlikely to satisfy the court's ambiguous mandate and because the detailed evidence needed to evaluate such schemes was not at hand. In lieu of particularistic analysis, the committee relied on the formula of the California state guidelines for racial balance: the proportion of a given ethnic group in a racially balanced school must deviate no more than fifteen percentage points from that group's proportion of the school-age population.[66] Since, for example, 28.7 percent of the children in San Francisco's elementary schools were black, a school enrolling between 13.7 percent and 43.7 percent black children would be racially balanced with respect to blacks; a similar calculation was required to determine if the school was balanced with respect to white, Chinese, Hispanic, and other major population groups. Although this formula was admittedly arbitrary, it had already obtained official blessing. Any other formula could be—and was—attacked as equally arbitrary.

Within this broad framework, debate focused on two different approaches, "zone" and "city-wide." The zone approach, building upon the experience of the complexes, would divide the city into extended neighborhoods, minimizing busing distances because the "neighborhoods" would be contiguous. This approach tried to preserve "political integrity," implying something akin to neighborhood schools, to diminish white unhappiness and lessen any consequent flight to the suburbs. Under a zone concept, the California guidelines represented the maximum of politically tolerable desegregation. In contrast, the city-wide approach treated the state guidelines as setting the minimum permissible desegregation. Its advocates were less concerned with white acceptance of the plan or the preservation of neighborhoods than with the greatest possible socioeconomic and racial desegregation.

The citizens' advisory committee converted these broad notions into plans that could be put into effect during the coming year. The committee recommended Horseshoe, a plan that divided the district into seven zones, left the Richmond Complex and the prospective Park South Complex largely intact, and barely satisfied the California 15-percent guidelines. The leading "city-wide" alternative was ranked fourth among seven plans. Proposals concerning questions not directly related to numerical desegregation were consigned to appendixes in the committee report. The board of education quickly approved Horseshoe and submitted it to the court. A decade of public discussion and a court order had culminated in a desegregation plan hastily created by a small group of citizens and staff working far from public purview. The board and Superintendent Shaheen, faced with other dilemmas, could not devote time to the planning process.

The NAACP was even less prepared than the district to undertake desegregation planning.[67] The outside consultants the NAACP retained were able to spend only forty-eight hours in San Francisco. Their Freedom Plan, completed in three weeks, resembled the citizens' committee's city-wide plan in many ways. It created six attendance areas, several of which were not contiguous. One of its zones required busing students between the northeast and southwest corners of the city, a substantial distance even given the compactness of San Francisco. Boundaries were drawn to provide not only for racial balance but also for socioeconomic and achievement-level mixing, insofar as the skimpy data available permitted such calculations. With respect to education-specific issues, the hastily drawn Freedom Plan was virtually silent. There had not been time for serious consideration of anything other than student placement.

Both the NAACP's Freedom Plan and the district's Horseshoe Plan were submitted to the court on June 10, meeting the court's deadline and drawing the judge's praise. Weigel sought the help of all counsel in choosing the plan "which will meet the requirement of the law with minimum inconvenience to . . . the children and parents affected." Yet new intervenors were to upset the enterprise.

In May 1971, the Chinese Big Six Companies, the lineage-based private political and social organization that unofficially governs Chinatown, chose to become involved in the desegregation case.[68] They realized that what they had viewed as a squabble between blacks and whites might well disrupt their community-based public schools. To the Six Companies, desegregation was a disaster. It threatened their tenuous hold on the new immigrant population, and constituted an assault on the Chinese people's ethnic identity. What lay outside Chinatown—the *bok gooi* and *hok gooi* ("white devils" and "black devils"), schools less orderly and less concerned about achievement than their own—was unpromising.

The Six Companies organized a noisy protest against the citizens' advisory committee's plans, which stunned that group but otherwise had no effect. Neither did the appearance at the June 3 board meeting of what the press termed 600 "booing, footstomping . . . shouting . . . Chinese-American parents—half the audience."[69] The Horseshoe Plan that was approved preserved most of Chinatown as part of a single zone but required the busing of many students into and out of Chinatown. The Six Companies decided to intervene directly in the litigation. They turned to Quentin Kopp, an attorney for the original Concerned Parents intervenors.

Kopp tried to bring this new group into the case literally days before a final decision concerning a desegregation remedy was anticipated. His "complaint of plaintiffs in intervention," filed on June 18, was explosive. The Chinese had an independent right to be heard, Kopp claimed. Although no one represented their interests, they were to be unwitting parties to court-ordered relief. Kopp attacked the *Johnson* suit as collusive: "The findings of fact and conclusions of law were obtained by negligence, acts of omission and obvious failure to present material evidence."[70] The Chinese community, Kopp declared, "should not without hearing be subjected to a 'cure' they neither need nor want." Even if posed at an awkwardly late moment, the argument that Chinese-Americans were entitled to special consideration was not without legal plausibility. But responding to that argument would almost necessarily have meant delaying desegregation, and that Weigel was unwilling to do. On June 30, the motion to intervene was denied and each of its arguments dismissed. Kopp, by no means finished, filed a motion for a stay of the court's order, reargued the issue before Weigel in August, and appeared before the Ninth Circuit when the case was heard on appeal. Meanwhile, he launched a successful campaign for a seat on the board of supervisors from the steps of Chinatown's Commodore Stockton School, turning the case to his political advantage.

Judge Weigel faced a difficult choice of remedy. Reflecting then-prevailing judicial practice, his concern focused on the degree of racial mixing that could properly be ordered, not on integration measures. But within that realm, should he adopt the NAACP plan, which promised substantially more racial mixing of students, or the board's proposal, which represented the wishes of a community whose choices concerning desegregation policy were constitutionally constrained? Weigel scheduled an informal session in chambers, "to help the Court to fully understand the plans which have been submitted" and to get the "unguarded cooperation" of all concerned.[71]

Most of the in-chambers session was devoted to a detailed review of the two plans submitted. Judge Weigel repeatedly expressed his unhappiness with the board "for having done very little until, on, or after April 28 . . . to get ready for the various contingencies that were . . . plainly foreseeable last September." Yet Weigel felt that he could not undo deficiencies in the district's planning. The judge did not focus on remedial issues other than racial balance, for until recently, judges had viewed broader educational policy questions linked to race as beyond the competency of the court. Weigel's opinion treated these matters as the responsibility of the district, noting only that the stress on desegregation did not "de-emphasize quality education."[72] He did urge, however, that Horseshoe be reshaped to minimize racial and ethnic imbalances, and after the in-chambers session the district undertook some modification.

Substantially less time was devoted to discussion of the NAACP's Freedom Plan. The proposal had certain advantages. It provided for significantly more socioeconomic and racial desegregation, and it kept the residentially integrated OMI community intact. To the NAACP, the plan's authorship "by complete outsiders, who have no particular axes to grind," was also an advantage. The board had "been just too interested in community participation." Action, not discussion, was what the NAACP wanted: "You go ahead and [desegregate] . . . and don't worry about selling it to the community."[73]

The court thought otherwise. In its view, the fatal defect of the NAACP Freedom Plan was the absence of even symbolic community involvement. That the NAACP's plan did a better job of reducing segregation was clearly apparent to the judge, but precisely because it was the NAACP's plan and not the board of education's it was less likely to gain community acceptance and hence to be fully implemented.

This difference was vital to a judge who recognized the controversial nature of any system-wide desegregation order and the importance of securing public acquiescence in, if not support for, this action. For this phase of the task, it was essential that he have some backing from the board of education. The primacy of that objective led Judge Weigel to approve both plans, leaving the final choice with the board.[74] The judge recognized that more than reassigning students was at issue. "It is essential to have the good willed, open-minded and genuine cooperation of school administrators, teachers, other school personnel, parents and the community at large."[75] Weigel was self-consciously speaking to those who would be most affected by the decision, the citizens of San Francisco. How they would react remained uncertain.

The *Johnson* case was far from over. During July and August of 1971, the Chinatown intervenors sought unsuccessfully on several occasions to stay Judge Weigel's order until the Court of Appeals heard the case. The effort to postpone the inevitable came to an end when Supreme Court Justice William Douglas rejected Kopp's last request for a stay: "*Brown* . . . was not written for blacks alone. . . . The theme of our school desegregation cases extends to all racial minorities treated invidiously by a State or any of its agencies."[76]

The Ninth Circuit tarried almost three years before deciding the *Johnson* case. In the interval, plaintiffs' counsel Brunwasser pressed the district court to modify its order, in order to address problems in implementing system-wide desegregation and to extend desegregation to the junior high schools. Weigel's only response was to order the district to report annually "all action taken to comply with the judgment, and to show plans for implementation in compliance with the letter and spirit of the decision."[77] The judge subsequenty denied a motion to consolidate the *Johnson* case with *O'Neill v. San Francisco Unified School District*,[78] a suit brought by the NAACP to desegregate San Francisco's junior and senior high schools. Any further trial court action would await the appellate ruling.

On June 22, 1974, the Ninth Circuit Court of Appeals delivered its opinion in *Johnson*.[79] The 1973 Supreme Court decision in *Keyes v. School District No. 1, Denver*,[80] had set guidelines for judicial inquiry in non-Southern desegregation cases. As the circuit court stated, *Keyes* required a finding of "segregation intent" to establish de jure segregation, which the district court had not made in *Johnson*. Hence the case was remanded "to afford [the trial court] an opportunity to reexamine the record on the issue of intent."[81]

Had the Ninth Circuit opinion been issued more expeditiously, it might well have proved consequential. The Concerned Parents intervenors were prepared with a host of demands for data that in their judgment would have demolished the conclusion that

San Francisco had practiced de jure segregation. In 1974, however, neither the Concerned Parents nor the district was disposed to re-open what then seemed a stale issue.

IV

To announce a decision concerning segregation is one thing, to secure its implementation altogether different and more difficult. The court's order was framed in terms of racial ratios. It was a desegregation order, calling for balance as a remedy. The opinion, however, aspired beyond desegregation, reaching into the more nebulous terrain of integration.

As a direct result of the *Johnson* case, San Francisco's schools became more desegregated. In the narrow sense, the decree succeeded. Even here, however, success was imperfect, since at least 20 percent of the district's schools remained imbalanced according to the Horseshoe formula. Integration involves more than just racial mixing. It touches upon almost all the policies and practices of a school district. For that reason, integration requires the support of those inside the system—including the school board, administration, and professional staff—as well as the sustained involvement of the outsiders who brought the suit. Neither insider support nor outsider involvement has been evident in San Francisco, and as a result integration has not been tried much on a system-wide basis. Other concerns, rooted in race and ethnicity but not addressed to the consequences of racial mixing, have assumed greater importance, as has the crisis brought on by a precipitous decline in the district's budget.

Desegregation has increased, although not to the extent envisioned by the framers of Horseshoe. Before the decision, eighty of the ninety-six schools in San Francisco were imbalanced in terms of the 15-percent standard. Horseshoe lessened but did not eliminate this imbalance. In 1971–72, one-third of the elementary schools were imbalanced with respect to one or more racial groups. By 1975–76, that number had climbed to almost one-half, but of these only seven schools were more than half black.[82] This partial failure could have been predicted from an examination of Horseshoe itself. Several schools and, more seriously, several entire zones had been within a whisker of being racially imbalanced when the plan was adopted.

The loss of white students coincident with desegregation was one cause of the post-*Johnson* imbalance. For some years, the proportion of white students had fallen as white families moved to the suburbs. Between 1965 and 1970, the year preceding *Johnson*, the percentage of white elementary-school students in the district declined from 42.8 percent to 34.5 percent; the average annual decline was 1.7 percentage points. During 1971, the first year of Horseshoe's implementation, the percentage of white students dropped an additional 4.1 points; whites now constituted 30.1 percent of the student population. But such "flight," if that is the proper term, occurred only during this initial year. Between 1971 and the present, the average rate of decline has been 1.6 percentage points, slightly lower than in the years preceding Horseshoe. Yet one should not underestimate what such changes, coupled with an absolute decline in enrollment of more than one-third during the decade, mean in terms of actual numbers of students; there are only about 40 percent as many whites attending elementary school in San Francisco in 1981 as in 1970.

District policies also contributed to racial imbalance. As a protest against the *Johnson* decree, approximately one thousand Chinese-American students enrolled in private "Freedom Schools," named ironically for the schools established in the South as part of the fight for desegregation. While these schools offered only a short-term solution for the Chinese community, the district reacted with alarm. In wooing students back into the system, San Francisco tacitly exempted them from participation in the desegregation plan.[83]

The vehicle for this exemption was an administrative device known as the temporary attendance permit (more recently dubbed the optional enrollment request, or OER). In theory, OERs were to be used for students with particular instructional needs that could not be met in the school to which they had been assigned or for health problems that would be exacerbated by busing. As the program was operated, OERs were distributed willy-nilly to hundreds of students claiming motion sickness, foot ailments, and maternal attachments; as many as one-third of the students obtained OERs.

Other district practices have discouraged desegregation. As a result of special programs, resegregation has occurred in classrooms within nominally desegregated schools. Classes for the gifted, hastily expanded with desegregation, have a white enrollment proportionally higher and a black enrollment correspondingly lower than the district-wide average. Blacks, who number 27.6 percent of the district's students, made up as much as three-fifths of the enrollment in classes for the educable mentally retarded and educationally handicapped, traditional dumping grounds for difficult-to-manage or slow-learning pupils.[84] These racially disproportionate enrollments run counter to the *Johnson* opinion's prohibition of "educational techniques or innovations" that re-create segregation.[85]

San Francisco undertook voluntarily to desegregate its junior and senior high schools, but that process did not proceed smoothly. Although in May 1972 the NAACP filed suit demanding immediate secondary school desegregation,[86] the case was not pursued vigorously, and was ultimately dismissed in August 1976 by the consent of the parties. Because the district hewed to the boundaries set by Horseshoe in drafting attendance zones for the junior and senior high schools, racial imbalances were predictable, and have been exacerbated by the practice of routinely granting OERs to those who request them. The effects in terms of racial mix parallel those at the primary school level. Although there has been less desegregation than the district's plan contemplated, every secondary school has become more desegregated.

If one looks beyond the numbers, the picture appears more bleak. In implementing *Johnson*, the district made few efforts to couple desegregation with any educational programs designed to promote integration. Except for the Richmond and Park South complexes, the zone boundaries did not allow for ongoing educational enterprises. The attempts to develop a school-based program that would help keep the OMI area residentially mixed collapsed when Horseshoe divided its schools between two zones. The largely black Hunter's Point region, which had begun to devise new techniques for instructing minority-group children and for involving parents, was also separated into two zones. A bilingual program sought by the Latino organizations was abandoned for lack of district money. The district's "educational lighthouse" school, which before *Johnson* had been staffed by teachers and students from San Francisco State College and had drawn a racially mixed student body from the entire city, disappeared in the wake of desegregation when it was absorbed into the regular system.

There are San Francisco public schools that, either by reputation or in terms of achievement-test scores, are "good," but the district can take little credit for encouraging this excellence. Some of these schools are small "alternative public schools" set up at parental instigation and constantly struggling for survival. In other schools, highly motivated principals and superb teachers have produced good results despite central office indifference. The *San Francisco Chronicle*'s education reporter, who spent three weeks observing fourteen elementary schools shortly after desegregation, concluded: "There are no longer good and bad schools . . . only good and bad classrooms . . . it all depends on the teacher."[87] The same remains true today.

These outcomes can be traced to sustained indifference on the part of the school board and administration and inattention to the issue of integration by civil rights groups. The issue has steadily diminished in importance through lack of concern; in the process, legal literal-mindedness has been substituted for thoughtful innovation.

Superintendent Shaheen tried unsuccessfully to use the advent of desegregation as a vehicle for shaking up the administration. Shaheen saw himself as a "facilitator," but he offered even staff loyalists little support. He embraced too many new ideas at once and consequently gave all of them short shrift. His distrust of San Francisco's old-line administrators heightened tensions in the central office; he alienated the teachers' organizations by choosing encounter groups and public meetings over face-to-face bargaining; and he upset the board by proposing to take a vacation during the first two weeks of desegregation.[88]

"Shaheenigans" and desegregation were central issues in the 1971 mayoral campaign. Both Alioto and his conservative opponent urged Shaheen's replacement; both endorsed a charter amendment calling for an elected (and presumably less liberal) school board. The mayor won a smashing victory; Quentin Kopp, lawyer for the Chinatown intervenors, was elected to the board of supervisors; the charter amendment was approved; and the soon-to-be-dissolved appointed board began to ease Shaheen out.

The board of education elected in June 1972, after a campaign largely centered on busing, was more conservative than its predecessor; only two strong supporters of desegregation were among the seven winners.[89] But the problem that had persisted since Spears' retirement remained: Could anyone intelligently run the schools? The departure of Shaheen in August 1972 did not dramatically improve the quality of school administration. His successor, Steven Morena, tried and failed to reduce bureaucratic infighting. In 1975, Morena reported that he was unable to manage the district because of the board's incessant interference with and injection of political considerations into educational administration.

Morena's successor, Robert Alioto (no kin to the former mayor) has had better luck than his predecessors in reasserting administrative control. He was aided in that task by the efforts of the San Francisco Public Schools Commission, an august citizens' group appointed by State Superintendent of Public Instruction Wilson

Riles to sort through the administrative nightmare that San Francisco's schools had reputedly become. From the first, the commission saw its primary task to be aiding the administration, restoring to professional hands the authority that since the Spears years had been assumed by the school board. The chairman of the commission publicly condemned the board's "meddling in administration," a call taken up by the *San Francisco Chronicle*, which editorialized that "the San Francisco schools are not working because the superintendent has no authority." [90]

This criticism, coupled with an election in which board usurpation of the superintendent's prerogatives was an issue, gave Superintendent Alioto some room to maneuver. With respect to desegregation, he has used that leeway to junk the Horseshoe Plan, substituting a more flexible and educationally more ambitious plan termed the Educational Redesign. [91]

The Educational Redesign, which went into effect in the 1978–79 school year, abandoned both the zone concept and the racial-balance formula of Horseshoe. The grade structure, in which the primary and secondary years were divided into four three-year units, was replaced by a primary school–middle school–high school arrangement, with students spending four years at each level. Under the new formula, no school may enroll more than 45 percent of any single ethnic group, and at least four ethnic groups out of the nine for which the district keeps records are assigned to all schools. The multi-ethnic city—in which blacks and whites, excluding Hispanic students, together number less than 50 percent of the student body—maintains multi-ethnic schools, in which no single minority is to be a majority. Attendance areas for each school are constructed with an eye to preserving residentially integrated neighborhoods; natural "balance" has not been disturbed by the assignment plans. Taken together, these elements of the Educational Redesign have permitted the district to bus fewer than half as many students as under Horseshoe. And the district has issued far fewer OERs: 1,250 in 1980, as compared with almost twenty thousand three years earlier.

The Educational Redesign coupled these changes with educational innovations, notably an expansion of the alternative public schools, which could draw from the entire city; it also closed twenty schools because of declining enrollment. The hope was to revive the "quality" elements of the late 1960s complexes, which had disappeared with *Johnson*. During 1977, the proposed plan was aired at community meetings, attended by more than three thousand citizens around the city. Criticism focused partly on process: the meetings, it was charged, were window dressing; the plan's contours had been set without involving teachers and parents. School closing produced understandable antagonism. The policy was favored—as long as it affected someone else's schools. Concern about desegregation was heard as well. On one side, the abandonment of the Horseshoe standard was scored as "racist and divisive," and the NAACP described the new plan as "clearly and blatantly unconstitutional";[92] that proportionately more blacks would be bused also evoked unhappiness. Board members, some of whom would have preferred more racial mixing, found themselves uneasy allies of the administration.[93] On the other side, opponents of busing made their presence felt in demonstrations at the school board and letters to the *San Francisco Examiner.* Wrote one parent, "the school board should abandon the cause of social reform and begin to educate, not eradicate [presumably through encouraging white flight] the children of our city."[94]

The most substantial racial issue involved the three primary schools of Hunter's Point. Horseshoe had fared least well in that geographically isolated part of the city, and to remedy the situation the superintendent initially called for the pairing of schools in Hunter's Point and Treasure Island, a naval base whose schools had long enjoyed considerable autonomy. Spokesmen for both communities resisted the proposal. Naval officers threatened to pull their children out of school. Hunter's Point parents urged the school district to "leave us alone. We'll educate our own children. Just give us the money and everyone else get out of here." A fourth-grade student from Hunter's Point, appearing at the community meeting held there, asked: "Why should we be bused to other schools when we have good schools here? Why should we be bused to your schools while none of your kids are bused here to ours?"[95]

The Hunter's Point situation was even more confusing than the public reactions suggest. While there was some evidence that families there were interested in desegregation—when polled, 30 to 40 percent said that they wished to join in a racially mixed open enrollment plan—far fewer actually participated. Linking Hunter's Point with Treasure Island was a singularly inapt—and for a politically astute superintendent a surprisingly inept—match, so obviously doomed to failure at the outset that one can only speculate whether this might not have been the intention of the administration. After the public hearings, the merger was abandoned. Superintendent Alioto declared, "whether for reasons of educational quality, safety, . . . or racism . . . we have not been able to racially balance schools in Hunter's Point."[96] The three Hunter's Point schools are consequently almost entirely black.

In June 1978, plaintiffs in the *Johnson* case challenged the Educational Redesign in federal court, reopening the case in the process. The local NAACP was willing to acquiesce in the change, but the national organization—fearing what would be regarded as a symbolic defeat in the first major Northern city to experience desegregation—assumed control of the case. Judge Weigel refused to rule on the matter, dismissing the *Johnson* suit instead.[97] Inaction on the part of both sides was the primary reason Weigel advanced for dismissal. As he noted, "circumstances have changed significantly since this Court's judgment in 1971" with respect to "the racial mix of the district, the governance and administration of the schools, and the operant legal standard." For those reasons, dismissal seemed appropriate to the court.

The NAACP promptly filed a new suit, but the interesting question is whether anyone still cares. The supposed beneficiary of the case, the black community (especially the Hunter's Point neighborhood), has demonstrated no enthusiasm for the litigation: the pending case is a battle between lawyers, not a popular cause. Demographics has diminished the possibility of meaningful desegregation, for at present fewer than one in five students in the San Francisco public schools are white. Even Zuretti Goosby, longtime member of the school board and ardent supporter of desegregation, expresses doubts about the wisdom of the suit. "There is no longer a constituency for desegregation."[98] That is not the most hospitable climate for judicial intervention.

In the years since *Johnson*, issues other than desegregation have aroused more concern among the various groups—civil rights supporters, blacks, and other ethnic groups—that were directly or tangentially connected with the case. This shift partly reflects changing perceptions of the value of the struggle, especially in communities where the population is preponderantly nonwhite. Many white civil rights supporters lost their abiding commitment to desegregation in San Francisco. Some moved on to new issues, whereas others were simply worn down.

Blacks were never directly involved in substantial numbers in the *Johnson* litigation. Like most other desegregation suits, it was pressed by an elite. Black parents have lived with a decision that in important respects has not improved their children's lives. A 1974 survey of San Francisco pupil and teacher attitudes suggests the depth of the problem. In the argot of this survey, black and Spanish-speaking children remained negative in their self-concepts and in their attitudes toward school, and scored higher on measures of school anxiety than did their white or Asian counterparts. Black and white students had little to do with one another. While teachers' attitudes toward multi-ethnic schools were generally positive, their expectations for Asian and white children remained higher than for black and Spanish-speaking students.[99]

Black students have also not fared well in more readily measurable terms. Their basic skills test scores have improved slightly over time but remain well below the norm. At the sixth-grade level, for instance, the average black is a year and a half behind. Moreover, blacks have fallen farther behind white students and other minorities, including Hispanics, a gap that widened by the equivalent of two months between 1976 and 1978. By far the worst scores are reported for students in the Hunter's Point schools.

This is familiar, if dreary, stuff: reports of dramatic improvement in black achievement scores would astonish. But what is there to do? Superintendent Alioto expressed his willingness to "pump money into Hunter's Point."[100] Hunter's Point schools have been granted extra resources—compensation, perhaps, for not being included within the Educational Redesign. At a time when staff was being cut back elsewhere, the school district added twenty additional teachers to the Hunter's Point schools and, with the aid of a local foundation and San Francisco State University, a substantial basic skills tutoring program, drawing in parents and college students, has been mounted. San Francisco has returned a decade later to educational ideas that were swept aside in the effort to achieve racial balance.

In the other ethnic communities, notably Asian and Latino, there has been an awakening of interest in the public schools. Emerging ethnic pride, diligent efforts to overcome factionalism and to present a more united political front, and the availability of federal funds for bilingual education encouraged this strong interest in the schools. The desegregation order also triggered these groups' concern for equality of opportunity with blacks and whites. A turning point was the Supreme Court's 1974 decision in *Lau v. Nichols*, which specifically ordered San Francisco to provide Chinese students who did not speak English a "meaningful opportunity to participate in the public educational program."[101] To the foreign-language-speaking communities of San Francisco, *Lau* was an invitation to press demands for bilingual-bicultural education.

Following *Lau*, Superintendent Morena appointed a Citizens'

Bilingual Task Force to shape a bilingual program. During the 1960s, civil rights organizations had equated equal opportunity with desegregation, assuming that this remedy would produce an equal distribution of educational resources and would help overcome the psychological harm of racial isolation. The bilingual task force held a decidedly different view:

The burden should be on the school to adapt its educational approach so that the culture, language and learning style of all children in the school (not just those of Anglo middle-class background) are accepted and valued. Children should not be penalized for culture and linguistic differences, nor should they bear a burden to conform to a school-sanctioned culture by abandoning their own.[102]

It called for the creation of four language-based school complexes, enrolling Chinese, Latino, Filipino, and Japanese students. The district resisted the "positive" or "affirmative" segregation implied in this proposal; as a pragmatic matter, it lacked the resources to make such a commitment. Instead, San Francisco agreed to offer "a meaningful opportunity to participate in the public educational program" to each limited-English-speaking child.

The school district has given specificity to this amorphous commitment. The bilingual education budget for 1978–79 was almost 30 percent higher than that for the previous year, even though the total school budget became considerably smaller; when the school district was obliged to lay off teachers, it exempted bilingual instructors. The ethnic groups remain active, on occasion warring with one another for school district support. Asians and Latinos, largely excluded from the *Johnson* litigation, have become full participants in the struggle for political recognition in the schools.

The new ethnic politics is played out in the context of ever-diminishing resources. The school board's agenda is now largely determined by the district's financial crisis: laying off and firing teachers, terminating programs, and closing schools. The drop in enrollment and the corresponding reduction in state aid calculated on a per pupil basis has contributed to this situation, as has the budgetary shortsightedness of past boards (which, for example, spent district funds on earthquake-safety measures for schools that were closed shortly thereafter). The major cause is the limitation on property tax rates imposed by Proposition 13.

Between 1975 and the present, the school budget, adjusted for inflation, has shrunk considerably. The teaching staff is 25 percent smaller than in 1975—the age of the average professional employee is now well over forty—and the administrative staff has been so drastically trimmed that even one-time critics of the bureaucracy now wish for a bit more central office support. The Educational Redesign, approved just months before Proposition 13, lost a number of its more innovative programs. The redesign, coupled with the cutbacks, forced substantial dislocation both of teachers and programs; what is offered in any particular school changes from one year to the next, and the school environment generally lacks stability. A prolonged teachers' strike in the fall of 1979 soured relationships among teachers, administrators, and the larger community.

It is hard enough to attend to questions of education when the predictability of the enterprise is constantly in jeopardy, harder yet for an institution that regards itself as in decline to devote much attention to educational reform. "Retrenchment, uncertainty, keeping the system going—*that* is what preoccupies the board," reports its president.[103] San Francisco can only hope that from the modestly expanded alternative school program, other features of the Education Redesign, the stirrings in the minority communities, or the new round of desegregation litigation there can emerge an institutional renascence linking race to the instructional mission of the schools.

Richmond: Busing, Backlash,
and Beyond

I

In Richmond as in San Francisco, a political solution to the issue
of race and schooling encompassing substantial desegregation
seemed at one point to be achievable.[1] A riven board governing the
schools of Richmond—an aggregation of urban and suburban East
Bay communities located just north of Berkeley—voted in 1969 to
adopt a district-wide desegregation plan. Because the board knew
that its decision might be overturned by the electorate, it collaborated with the local legal services office to secure a state court decree insulating desegregation from the vagaries of politics. "The future of the district lies in the courts," the liberal board president
declared.[2]

Voluntary district-wide desegregation was aberrant, almost
revolutionary, in predominantly working-class and conservative
Richmond. The decision to undertake such action represented an
act of conscience on the part of elected officials, a willingness to do
what was perceived as morally right even at the price of political
survival. It also imposed a vision of racial justice sharply at odds
with prevailing community values.

Popular reaction to the board's action was swift and unequivocal. Three weeks after the desegregation plan was adopted, a
coalition whose spontaneous and widespread appeal stamped it as
a genuine movement swept the liberals from office. The turnout,
two-thirds of Richmond's registered voters, was among the largest
in Richmond local election history. "The parents have regained
control of their schools," one partisan asserted.[3] Events bore out
this point of view. The liberals' reliance on the courts to protect

district-wide desegregation from democratic political reversal proved misplaced, as the judicial decree turned out to be less authoritative than anticipated. Fragmentation within the black and liberal white neighborhoods of Richmond effectively precluded the mobilization of serious political opposition to the new conservative board's policies. The aberrant act was undone. The prospect of district-wide desegregation, as envisioned a decade ago, now seems remote.

The liberal position was rejected by Richmond, but concern for the fair treatment of black students has not wholly disappeared. Just after assuming office, the conservative school board adopted the so-called Richmond Integration Plan, under which volunteering students could transfer from one school to another, with the effect of promoting a greater racial mix; the district bore the cost of busing those students. During the past decade, open enrollment has been institutionalized. The plan has permitted self-reliant, resourceful, and upwardly mobile blacks—at present, approximately one in six black elementary schoolchildren—to swap neighborhood ghetto schools for desegregated schools.[4] Open enrollment, coupled with the quietly achieved gerrymandering of secondary school attendance boundaries to promote "reasonable racial balance,"[5] has converted many of Richmond's schools into genuinely racially mixed institutions—no mean feat in a residentially highly segregated city. Even when, because of fiscal pressures generated by Proposition 13, the district ceased to pay for student transportation, black families continued to support open enrollment.

The Richmond Integration Plan was reluctantly adopted by a school board whose members viewed it as "the lesser of two evils."[6] If over time voluntary desegregation has been accepted, it arouses no great enthusiasm among conservative board members; the 1978 busing cutback revealed limited political support for desegregation. Despite this, a measure of racial justice has come to Richmond. The system has not resolved its racial problems, for blacks who remain in ghetto schools receive a worse education than that available in the predominantly white schools and perform worse than any other comparable group of Bay Area students. But Richmond's maintenance of a stable voluntary desegregation plan is a considerable achievement, particularly when contrasted with the experience of other cities. Liberal ideals of racial equality stemming from the civil rights movement, tempered by the realities of the social and political environment, have not entirely vanished.

II

Communities reveal much through their aspirations. Consider the Bay Area cities. San Francisco's conceit was to envision itself as the Athens of the West. Oakland, the "All-American City," likened itself to everywhere, whereas Berkeley, decidedly different, would be like no place else. Richmond, in the eyes of its boosters, saw itself as the West's Pittsburgh.[7]

This aspiration went unrealized until the advent of World War II. New shipyards attracted thousands of workers; in less than a decade, Richmond's population quadrupled to more than one hundred thousand. The new migrants also altered the racial composition of the city: a community that had been 1 percent black in 1940 became 13 percent black ten years later.

Whites began abandoning Richmond in the 1950s. The more affluent settled in the hill communities of El Cerrito and Kensington; working-class whites moved to the new bedroom towns of Pinole and El Sobrante to the north and east. Although the industrial base remained stable, the population of the city proper had by 1975 declined to 70,023, and the proportion of blacks had grown to 41.4.[8] Money and energy have gone into the suburbs, where, for example, an imposing new shopping complex has been constructed. Downtown Richmond is a kind of urban wasteland.

As a result, Richmond differs notably from the surrounding Contra Costa County communities. Richmond itself, like its small but predominantly white neighbor San Pablo, is a factory workers' town. The city's blacks, concentrated in what is popularly known as the "Black Crescent," a swath cut across the city's western flatlands, are primarily employed in private industry.[9] One step up the social ladder are the development communities, Pinole and El Sobrante. El Cerrito and Kensington, preponderantly professional, are indistinguishable from the adjacent Berkeley hills. Historically, these towns have had little to do with one another. But because the five communities were fused as a single school district in 1964, they were obliged to adopt a single race and schooling policy.

For half a century, from 1899 to 1949, the Richmond schools were presided over by one man, Walter Helms.[10] This remarkable reign shaped the character of the system as one run by professionals, not by the lay board. The public schools were in all significant respects autonomous, the authority of the superintendent unquestioned. The elected school board members, drawn from the professional and business community of Richmond, nominally exercised stewardship over the system. In fact, the board deferred to the superintendent's wishes, while Richmond residents passively embraced whatever the schools provided. Board members served many terms and were returned to office in low-turnout elections. Board meetings were sparsely attended and focused on trivial concerns.

Helms exercised tight personal control over policy and administrative affairs. Decisions concerning school sites, building needs, budget, and personnel were all reached internally. When something was brought to public attention, it was merely for legally required ratification. Such autonomy could be maintained in part because, as Helms observed, "the people I dealt with were all my boys." [11] Equally important, Helms' perception of the school system's needs corresponded with the wishes of the business leadership, which sought to keep taxes low in order to encourage new industry.[12] But Helms also maintained Richmond's school operating expenses at state minimum levels. Supplementary programs— school bands, drama, and the like—were supported by the city's fraternal organizations and the Parents and Teachers Association (PTA), not through taxes.

The influx of newcomers during the war years greatly expanded Richmond's student population. Between 1940 and 1945, elementary enrollment increased fivefold. With no outside support for new school construction and longtime residents unwilling to burden themselves in order to help the newcomers, the system was put to severe strain, revealing hostility among factions within the community.[13] The expansion of the Richmond school system also disclosed the limits of one-man rule. After Helms' retirement in 1949, the administration was converted into a modern bureaucracy, capable of managing a large and heterogeneous student population. The community tensions first apparent in the war years did not, however, disappear. They reemerged in different form in the late 1950s, when explicit attention began to be paid to questions of race.

III

As Richmond's population growth slowed following the war, the school district was able to provide generally better schools for the newcomers as well as the longtime residents. Yet racial problems, concealed during wartime, began to emerge. In earlier times, such antagonisms might have been defused by the administration, but by the late 1950s a somewhat more cosmopolitan school board began gingerly to take independent action, stressing equity-rooted concerns. In so doing, the board collided both with its own administration and eventually with a community more parochial than its elected leaders.

The struggle over district-wide desegregation late in the 1960s reveals these differences in full bloom. They are prefigured in controversies concerning comprehensive secondary schools and the merging of Richmond with the surrounding suburban districts. Richmond's black students were historically concentrated in a single high school, a fact that concerned the local NAACP chapter. In March 1958, as the district was considering modifying secondary school boundaries, the NAACP urged that race be explicitly taken into account. "High school boundaries running east and west across the city would help integration both with regard to economic and racial background." [14]

The school board agreed that east-west boundaries would be preferable—but not for racial reasons. "Race was not talked about. We wanted to equalize education offerings, and thus make each school truly comprehensive," recalled one of the board members. [15] The board's position echoed the Progressive view of secondary education, which had recently been taken up by James Conant in his inquiry into American high schools. [16] The administration, which saw comprehensive education as inefficient, proposed providing specialized programs in the two schools: vocational education in the poor and significantly black school, academic programs in the white school. While in the past the administration's position would routinely have been adopted, this was a different type of issue posed at a different time.

The board's decision represented a pioneering effort, marking one of the first occasions on which an American school district acted to equalize whites' and blacks' schooling conditions by bringing the two races together. The voters were displeased. A recall effort, unprecedented in Richmond, was mounted, and although it failed a board-proposed tax increase was turned down at the polls. [17] For the first but by no means the last time, the Richmond school board would entertain a social vision at odds with that of its constituency.

After this venture, the school board reverted to a more familiar deferential stance. The adoption of a comprehensive high school plan modestly allayed but could not resolve the racial dilemmas confronting the district. Within the comprehensive high schools, segregation along social-class and racial lines persisted. The increasing concentration of blacks in particular neighborhoods, coupled with the growing proportion of black children in the school system, produced more predominantly black primary schools. Only a solution encompassing more than Richmond itself could adequately confront those concerns. Unification of Richmond with the surrounding Contra Costa County suburbs provided the occasion to test that possibility.

Separate boards governed the secondary and primary schools in the Richmond area until 1964. While a single high school district encompassed Richmond's secondary schools (including those of Kensington and El Cerrito), as well as schools in the adjacent towns and unincorporated areas of San Pablo, Sheldon, and Pinole-Hercules, each of the communities had its own elementary school board. The districts had cooperated with one another, but unification had not seriously been considered, since the richer Richmond district would suffer financially, substantial administrative changes would be necessary, and the virtues of smallness would be lost.[18]

Passage of a state statute offering a financial incentive for merging districts eased the fiscal concern.[19] The idea of a merger had considerable appeal to the increasingly liberal, desegregation-minded Richmond board. Because the surrounding towns had almost no black students, the merged district would have proportionately fewer blacks than Richmond, and desegregation would consequently be easier to achieve. The Richmond board was not unaware of this. As one member subsequently stated: "It's one thing to integrate schools with a 25 percent black population, another when the blacks are 40 percent and rising."[20]

Because proposing unification as a means of achieving desegregation would only have assured its defeat, other equity-based arguments for consolidation were offered instead. Resources in the greater Richmond area would be more fairly distributed, the board claimed, and students throughout the district would be more uniformly prepared for secondary education.[21] The Richmond administration had opposed a merger in the past, seeing it as a drain on city revenues, but the district's new and progressive outsider superintendent, James Merrihew, shared the board's enthusiasm for unification.[22]

Consolidation was approved by 54 percent of the voters in 1964.[23] Only in the outlying areas of Pinole and Hercules did voters reject the proposal. That efficiency, not possible desegregation, was what the voters thought they had endorsed is clear from the vote on an anti-fair-housing initiative also appearing on the 1964 ballot. Every community in the new unified Richmond district except

Kensington supported that segregation-promoting measure. Even Richmond proper voted 55 to 45 percent against open housing.[24]

The new school board, four of whose five members came from the former Richmond elementary school district, had a view of its mandate different from that expressed in the fair housing vote. The board was unconcerned that it did not mirror the composition of the enlarged district. It perceived itself as a group of civic-minded, nonpartisan citizens who, together with a professional administration, would govern the schools on behalf of a passive working-class constituency. This was the established pattern in Richmond, but it had depended for its success on a harmony of interests among board, administration, and citizenry that no longer existed.

This difference was not taken into account by the school board. Following the 1958 contretemps over secondary school redistricting, the Richmond board had stepped back from the fray. After the 1965 postunification election, a new and confident board pushed forward in its efforts to advance the civil rights of blacks, whose interests it saw as too long neglected.

Primary schools in the new Richmond Unified School District were almost completely segregated. While blacks constituted only 22 percent of the 24,161 elementary school population, they were concentrated in ten of the district's forty-six elementary schools, six of which were more than 95 percent black.[25]

Richmond's blacks had long taken this situation for granted, for those who settled in Richmond during the war were accustomed to the Southern segregationist tradition.[26] The generation that had grown up in Richmond, however, had a less passive attitude. With respect to matters of school policy, they were encouraged by school board member Maurice Barusch, familiar with problems in the Black Crescent through association with a neighborhood house there, to press their concerns before the board.

The local CORE chapter presented the board in September 1965 with a detailed report describing the extent of elementary segregation.[27] Introduction of the segregation issue by a civil rights group demanding that something be done was typically how race got onto the agendas of school boards in the mid-1960s. What was unusual in Richmond was the fact that the board had tacitly initiated the confrontation and was favorably predisposed to CORE's position. The obstacles confronting the board, including insufficient revenue to undertake any new ventures and an administration uninterested in civil rights issues, were, however, formidable.

The Richmond board immediately acknowledged "the need for racial balance in our schools and for improved understanding of the related problems"—an acknowledgment that only bitter struggles could secure in Oakland and San Francisco.[28] It appointed a citizens' advisory committee, predominantly liberal in outlook, six of whose nineteen members were black.[29] The committee was provided staff assistance and given a year to produce a report and recommendations. If the committee embraced the then-prevailing conventional liberal wisdom, it could be anticipated to urge district-wide desegregation. The committee's real if hidden function was "to legitimize the process of desegregation."[30] Because it was a nominally representative citizen's group, that recommendation could be seen as having popular support, thus easing the board's task in implementing it—or at least so the board hoped. The school board was attentive to the national reexamination of racial policies, as well as to parallel undertakings in such nearby towns as Berkeley and Sausalito. It was determined to lead Richmond into the mainstream of schooling reform with respect to race.

This resolve on the board's part was remarkable. Board members had long been drawn from community affairs, business, and professional backgrounds. Yet those who ran for office in the mid-1960s were a different breed, cosmopolitans and not locals. Their concern for the plight of the black community derived from a national frame of reference that stressed equalizing opportunity and eliminating racial barriers.

The school board was willing to pursue programs that would specifically benefit blacks, among them concentrating new federal education monies in the predominantly black schools and spending Economic Opportunity Act funds to employ black community members in black schools.[31] Its primary interest, however, was in desegregation. The possibility of desegregation was discussed in meetings run by the advisory committee, arousing considerable concern among white residents who realized for the first time that the school board might actually consider reassigning students in order to remedy segregation.[32] By May 1966, a hastily formed group, the Citizens' Committee for Neighborhood Schools (CCNS), had gathered 10,500 signatures on a petition opposing reassignment and "forced busing."[33] Black groups such as CORE, fearful that Richmond would let the racial issue die, demanded immediate desegregation and threatened to organize a boycott at two predominantly black junior high schools.[34]

The board refused to commit itself to any policy position in advance of the committee's report. Throughout the 1965–66 school year, however, its general concern for equitable treatment was manifested in recommendations that teacher talent be more fairly distributed, that secondary schools be open to all district students regardless of where in the district they resided, and that greater efforts be made to equalize instructional programs.[35] These board initiatives disquieted an administration unaccustomed to taking policy direction from the board. Sensing the strains, Superintendent Merrihew submitted his resignation.[36] The board's desire to treat blacks equitably had to be addressed within the context of scarce resources, a racially polarizing community, and a leaderless administration.

The Richmond board attempted to cope with this unprecedented situation in a variety of ways. It replaced a retiring board member with a prominent black attorney, the former chairman of the local NAACP education committee and the first black to serve on the board.[37] That act, combined with an open enrollment plan for 600 junior high school students, was designed to assuage the black community. The board saw its other difficulties in psychological terms, as constituting a problem in human relations. In searching for a new superintendent, the board sought someone committed to establishing harmonious relations within the school community. To promote interracial understanding, it established "communications skills" workshops. Through its example and with the direction of a sympathetic administrator, it hoped that staff and students of different races would learn to relate as equals, and that learning could serve as prelude to and predicate for desegregation.

This humane approach reflected the board's faith in the power of moral suasion and its resistance to the notion of inherently conflicting political interests. Board members imagined that their own sense of civic virtue could be cultivated throughout the school community, that blacks and whites could be brought together despite enormous differences in background. The aspiration was lofty, but the chosen tactics were insufficient to test the vision. Communications skills workshops were attended only by the already convinced. School administrators were unpersuaded that they should undergo therapeutic treatment for attitudes that had served them well and that by all accounts reflected community sentiments.[38] The new superintendent, Denzil Widel, similarly failed to meet the board's expectations. Confronted almost imme-

diately upon assuming his post with a strike by the nonadministra-
tive staff, Widel's opposition earned him a reputation as the board's
lackey rather than the administration's leader.[39] Instead of harmo-
nizing staff relations and easing tensions, the superintendent generated antagonisms. The administrative staff thought him a moral
do-gooder and an inept administrator. Consequently, the Richmond administration became in effect two separate administrations. Widel hired his own staff with newly available federal funds.
Meanwhile, veteran Richmond administrators turned to Deputy
Superintendent Woodrow Snodgrass, one of former Superintendent Helms' "boys," whose experience in the schools had earned
him their respect and whose disappointment at not being chosen
superintendent cast him as adversary to the liberal board.

The surprise element in the citizens' advisory committee report, released in March 1967, lay in what was *not* recommended,
namely elementary desegregation. Instead, the report urged a
change in grade structure. Educational programs in smaller, kin-
dergarten-through-grade-four neighborhood schools were to be
improved; fifth and sixth graders would be reassigned to more racially and socioeconomically heterogeneous intermediate schools;
programs in the high schools would be substantially equalized. Although proposing a new grade structure was intended to accommodate divergent viewpoints, it succeeded only in antagonizing
the partisans. Liberals were upset because elementary schools
would remain racially isolated. Conservatives disliked the disruption of the status quo, and feared that racial balance for all grades
was an inevitable next step.

The committee report also encouraged resistance to the
board's view of racial justice. The report pointed out the practical
impediments to district-wide housing, and hence could be used
to argue against such an arrangement. Rather than providing a
source of objective judgment, the advisory committee offered a target for the anger of those whose views were clearly antagonistic.
Its report enabled the CCNS, formed when the advisory committee
was first appointed, to turn itself into a political organization. Two
CCNS founders, Goy Fuller and Virgil Gay, were nominated to
challenge incumbent school board members in the April 1967
election.

Through the vehicle of the advisory committee, the liberal
school board had sought community legitimation of its concerns. It
did not impose its views of racial justice but rather treated these
vexed questions as properly the province of public discussion. Although the effect of this strategy was not to win consensus but to

arouse a resistant community, it is not clear that the board could have behaved otherwise. As a board, its powers to implement reform were inherently limited. Because the school administration, which normally carries out policy, was hostile to the board's views, an end run on the administration by appointing a citizens' committee to secure popular support made considerable political sense. Although the strategy boomeranged, this is always a risk of exposing policy issues to public scrutiny. Similarly, the stress on "communication" within the school community was a hoped-for means of reforming administrative attitudes. That the approach failed may have had as much to do with the unexpected difficulties that robbed the new superintendent of staff respect before he could fully assume office as with the wisdom of the strategy itself.

The board's efforts altered the way decisions were reached in Richmond. Up to this point, Richmond had been managed by an elite leadership. Desegregation foreshadowed the emergence of a mass political movement stressing traditional and insular values, unconnected to established political or economic structures, which would remake the Richmond educational system.

During the early discussions of desegregation, dissenting views rarely reached the Richmond school board. Board members shared generally similar views on the matter. Community concern about "forced busing," preservation of neighborhood schools, and the like was primarily directed at the citizens' committee, not the board. The April 1967 election, which added two CCNS members to the board, changed this situation. The board became obliged constantly to confront the racial question in an increasingly acrimonious environment.

Prior to the election, the board was not worried about the 1967 CCNS challenge. The incumbents, including the black appointee, had the blessing of business interests; given Richmond's historical acceptance of the leadership endorsed by those interests, reelection seemed a certainty. The incumbents were unwilling to turn the election into a referendum on desegregation. One reported: "The question most frequently asked was—are you for or against integrated or neighborhood schools. I refused to answer."[40] For its part, CCNS saw the election not as a way to win board seats but as a forum for airing its views. But because liberals split their votes between the two incumbents and an unequivocal advocate of desegregation, the CCNA candidates won with only plurality support.

The election marked the breakdown of board consensus on

gradual progress toward desegregation and turned board meetings into forums for argument over racial policies. After his defeat, the black board member proposed that elementary desegregation be begun. No one would second the motion. "How could we, in the face of growing opposition?" one member asked.[41] Member-elect Fuller called on the board to declare that it would not propose the busing of white as well as black students in order to remedy racial imbalance. The board refused to take this position either, preferring instead to keep options open.[42]

Modest desegregation efforts remained possible. With the support of white parents in Point Richmond, a well-to-do liberal enclave on the city's waterfront, the board adopted a "model" desegregation plan. The all-white Washington School enrolled 120 blacks previously attending overcrowded Nystrom School, and the district paid for the costs of busing. Because the plan was voluntary and acceptable to parents at both schools, conservatives as well as liberals could embrace it.[43]

This harmonious episode was, however, the exception, for the conflict was real enough. Liberal board members were urging a "practical" desegregation policy,[44] but this did not assuage the conservatives, who continued urging a no-busing policy. "If it is not done, there will be a mass exodus. . . . Richmond will become Berkeley."[45] For their part, black and white civil rights leaders began to grow impatient with the board. At almost every board meeting, they began demanding more than symbolic support and what they saw as token action.[46] In response, in November 1967 the board charged the superintendent with developing guidelines— not plans—to improve racial balance.[47] These guidelines aroused conservative opposition: race was to serve as a "primary criterion for all building plans and site selection" and for allocating such resources as "teachers, school supplies and curriculum designs."[48] Of more immediate relevance, conservatives massed against a plan to bus blacks from an overcrowded black school to empty classrooms at a nearby white working-class neighborhood elementary school.[49]

Both opponents and proponents of district-wide desegregation found the situation intolerable and began taking steps to alter it. In spring 1968 a conservative group, the Save Our Schools Committee (SOS), launched a recall campaign against board chairman Maurice Barusch. Although the effort failed,[50] it marked the beginning of an ultimately more effective campaign to give the antibusing forces control over the board. The recall drive provoked an analogous effort on the part of the black and liberal white community to achieve its goals. Whereas the conservatives turned to the political process, the liberals considered seeking desegregation through the courts.[51]

Board meetings had degenerated into shouting matches by the end of the 1967–68 school year. Polarized, paralyzed, and besieged from without, the board could neither sustain the initiative nor accommodate the partisans. The vacuum of power at the center encouraged more militant groups to assume leadership. Conservatives anticipated the next board election. Liberals looked to the judiciary. The attempt to use the political system in a small working-class city as a vehicle for implementing the liberal vision of racial justice had failed. The struggle over racial policy was no longer controlled by the board, which had become the arena for and not the agent behind events.

IV

It had become clear by spring 1968 that the Richmond school board would be unable to desegregate the district. To the cadre of committed civil rights supporters, an alternative strategy, recourse to the courts, was called for. What could not be accomplished politically would be mandated judicially: or so the civil rights groups, and eventually the board majority, hoped.

The Contra Costa Neighborhood Legal Services Foundation, a federally funded legal services office in Richmond, assumed responsibility for the case.[52] Its suit, filed in state court in October 1968, focused on segregation in a single Richmond school, the Verde School. The complaint asserted both the existence of deliberate, or de jure, segregation and the impermissibility of even adventitious, or de facto, segregation. It demanded that construction be halted on an addition to Verde and that Verde itself be desegregated.[53]

The legal services lawyers had little experience in civil litigation. None had ever worked on, let alone put together, a major case. This inexperience led them to reach policy decisions that, although plausible at the time, proved ultimately fatal: bringing suit in state, not federal, court and focusing on a single school, rather than challenging district-wide segregation.

The decision to file in state court was defensible. Despite the fact that the overwhelming majority of desegregation cases have been brought in federal courts, the prevailing federal constitutional standard against which to judge the permissibility of segregation had not been established in 1968. If it was necessary to show that desegregation in Richmond was "deliberate," the lawyering job would be formidable. In contrast, the California Supreme Court had some years earlier indicated that the fact of segregation, not its cause, offended the California state constitution.[54] Since the existence of segregation was undoubted in Richmond, the burden that the lawyers would have to bear in a state court suit would be considerably lighter.

Most desegregation suits have sought district-wide relief rather than focusing on a particular school. Plaintiffs' attorneys, however, rejected this approach and concentrated their energies on one elementary school, Verde, an extremely congested North Richmond school whose enrollment was 99 percent black. Several factors influenced this decision. For one thing, if proof of intentional segregation was required, it was most easily made with respect to Verde. The decision to build and then to enlarge Verde in the face of community opposition to desegregation seemed to the legal services attorneys clear evidence of intentional segregation.[55] The Verde suit was also viewed as a "trial balloon," the first in a series of attacks on Richmond segregation. The lawyers intended to use the judicial finding of de jure desegregation they won in the Verde suit to prevent the district from reopening the matter in suits concerning other segregated schools. If for some reason the Verde suit failed, a different legal strategy—most likely a district-wide case—would be pursued.

The suit was hardly an adversary proceeding in the usual sense. The liberal board majority had discussed the case with legal services before it was filed. The board liberals accepted the allegations and embraced the proposed remedy.[56] Before 3,000 people, probably the largest crowd ever to attend a public meeting in Richmond, the majority announced that it would not oppose the case.[57] The board also proposed preparing three remedies, each involving the desegregation of Verde and two neighboring schools, leaving the choice to the court.

This action liberated the liberals. They could now abandon any pretense of persuasion and were free to devote themselves to aiding the district-wide desegregation that they hoped would be brought about by court action. "We knew we were right," said board president Barusch. "We were on God's side."[58] "Two-Way School Busing Looms," announced the *Richmond Independent*.[59] Other Bay Area newspapers carried the story, noting that the board chairman had asserted that "the time has come for everyone's good to integrate the [Richmond] schools."[60] The conservative board minority reacted angrily. "[We have] endeavored to arouse the public and to make them aware of the deception practiced by three people who don't care what the residents of the district think, who don't care about the children, who have said repeatedly that there would not be two-way busing, and now it is being planned and will destroy the district."[61]

Contra Costa County Superior Court Judge Richard Arnason subsequently ruled that, since there was no dispute between the nominal adversaries over the appropriateness of *a* desegregation plan, the board and not the court would select a plan.[62] The board majority did so, after amicable negotiations with the legal services attorneys. The proposed settlement reached beyond the circumstances of the suit to embrace the entire district. Desegregation would be phased in, beginning with the Verde pairing and reaching the Kensington and El Cerrito hills three years later. The hope was that gradual implementation of the desegregation plan would lead to its eventual acceptance by the community. The impending court order was to serve as a mantle of authority for the board's desegregation effort.

The January 1969 court order turned out to be far less encompassing than anticipated. The terse opinion[63] treated the school district's refusal to admit or deny the facts as legal services had pleaded them as an admission of those facts. Although such an admission would normally mean that the plaintiffs' rights had been violated and that some remedy was appropriate, the fact that the district seemed predisposed voluntarily to provide just such a remedy worked against it. The court noted that "a plan to desegregate . . . has become a fait accompli." It treated that action not in constitutional terms but rather as a "legislative decision," for which the court would assume no responsibility. The lack of real controversy between the parties had rendered the issue wholly political, effectively depriving the judiciary of any legitimate role.[64]

Although disturbed by the ruling, legal services could not readily assert through appeal that it had somehow lost an uncontested case. The lawyers and the liberal school board members attempted instead to proceed as if they had unequivocally won. The board majority, acting with rare decisiveness, focused its energies on implementing a desegregation plan during its remaining months in office. Generating this political commitment, not summoning the moral authority of the courts, was what the legal strategy accomplished. By 1968, however, the commitment to desegregation in Richmond was unavailing. Three years after district unification had first made desegregation possible, a strategy undertaken by three members of a school board lacking a constituency, incapable of fully controlling the administration, and unable to address the opposition tactic of mass politics, could not and did not succeed.

V

Desegregation dominated the 1969 school board election in Richmond, as it would dominate school politics for the next several years. The prospect of eventual desegregation had been sufficiently threatening to elevate two political unknowns to the board two years earlier, upsetting the historical pattern of elite governance. In 1969, with desegregation more than a remote possibility, a traditionalist and communitarian movement created an entirely new politics in Richmond.

As the board majority was acquiescing in the Verde suit, a new antidesegregation umbrella organization, United School Parents (USP), was being organized. USP members met with parents who shared their concerns and formed units in school after school, sometimes taking over existing PTAs. An estimated ten thousand Richmond residents belonged to the organization.[65] The group's membership was diverse, ranging from those with Ku Klux Klan sympathies—one member vowed to loud applause that he would "put on a white robe and take a gun in hand before they'll bus my kids"[66]—to more thoughtful conservatives from the Kensington hills. Financial support came from parents' contributions, fundraising events, and small donations from local businessmen and realtors' associations. Opposition to city-wide desegregation was strong enough to unify this group in its effort to win the election of a new and more responsive school board.

Parents' meetings, attended by as many as four hundred people and focusing on violence and imminent busing, were the central activity of USP. Parents also discovered a common unhappiness with other ventures initiated by the liberal school board and Superintendent Widel. A "family life education" course, for instance, was said to include a description of the human reproductive processes that was "obscene . . . a communist conspiracy to undermine family life."[67] The hiring of twenty-five teachers' aides, some of whom had criminal records, as part of a Model Cities program also provoked outrage. Richmond was beginning to resemble neighboring Berkeley, to the manifest unhappiness of the conservative community. Taxes too were a source of concern for traditional-ist parents, a sizable constituency in Richmond and its post-war suburbs. Far from being a financial bonanza, unification had cost the school district money. Taxpayers were ill disposed to contrib-ute more; as a result, financial crisis—cutbacks in basic services, even early school closing—seemed likely.

In preparing for the election, the liberals lacked both a sub-stantial constituency and an organization. Moreover, liberal groups had almost as little trust for one another as for USP. While the Black Caucus was able to rally around one candidate, the whites were splintered. Eleven liberals entered the race, each endorsing some variant of a desegregation policy. The last-minute formation of a liberal "unity" slate had little effect.

The liberals' chances, weak even at the outset of the cam-paign, were not improved by school board efforts with respect to desegregation. The board's plan involved the affluent hill areas only in the third year of operation, and that made some supporters of desegregation unhappy. They urged the board to include one grouping of hill and inner-city schools during the initial phase of desegregation, thus demonstrating the district's commitment to a comprehensive solution and removing the entire initial burden of desegregation from working-class San Pablo parents. Just two weeks before the election, the board did so. This action, intended to aid the liberal cause, had the opposite effect. Hill parents unpre-pared for the development were unhappy. Others grew increas-ingly anxious. If the desegregation plan could be expanded in April, might not a new liberal board undertake district-wide de-segregation not in phases but all at once? The board also proposed a huge tax increase. New money was doubtless needed—teachers' salaries, for example, were among the lowest in the Bay Area—but the timing was not propitious. A "big spenders" label could only hurt the liberals' effort.

The conservative campaign, which enjoyed both a clear tar-get in the board's desegregation efforts and solid grass-roots sup-port, was managed superbly. The USP campaign played on the very real anxieties of Richmond residents. Its flyers urged "Educa-tion, NOT Transportation" and "Stop the Buses." In the April 1969 elections, 67 percent of the eligible voters, more than twice the average school election turnout, gave the USP slate a better than two-to-one victory over the combined votes of all the other candi-dates.[68] Only in Kensington did the liberals win, and there the mar-gin was less than 4 percent; including Kensington in the first phase of desegregation had doubtless influenced the vote. The proposed tax increase was also rejected by a vote of three to two. The board's actions had fostered the emergence of a grass-roots social movement, which proclaimed in victory that "the parents have regained control of their schools."

In some respects, the 1969 election results heralded the restoration of the *status quo ante*. Old-line administrators once again assumed leadership over the school system. They shared the views of the new board and the voters and could readily turn the "no forced busing" sentiment into a working mandate.

At the very first meeting of the new board, the triumph of the old-line group within the administrative staff was confirmed. Superintendent Widel was rendered a figurehead, all his powers transferred to insider Woodrow Snodgrass, who was appointed to the new position of associate superintendent. Snodgrass called upon the new board not to revoke the desegregation plan previously adopted, an action that would merely invite judicial intervention, but rather to modify the plan.[69] The "modification" that Snodgrass presented was an open enrollment plan, the Richmond Integration Plan, on which the veteran staff had been secretly working for months. The plan designated clusters of schools, each containing one predominantly black and several white schools. Within each cluster, students from the black school could choose one of the white schools and students attending one of the white schools could opt for the black school. The district, which otherwise did not bus students, provided transportation for volunteers.

The Richmond Integration Plan attracted wide support. It was consistent with the April 1969 mandate, which had turned down "forced busing," while at least leaving open the possibility of individually chosen desegregation. As board member Virgil Gay declared: "The board and the community are united on this issue. It fulfills our campaign promises, and this board keeps its promises."[70] The *Richmond Independent* also approved. "The basis of the new plan is free choice of parents and pupils,"[71] and that was preferable to coercion. Although unhappy liberals saw the plan as "a facade for integration . . . controlled tokenism" and urged that parents boycott the effort,[72] the administration was committed to making it work. White hill children were recruited for a much upgraded center-city school, and the deadline for enrolling in the voluntary plan was extended. In 1969–70, the first year of the plan's operation, 553 elementary-school-age pupils (all but five black) volunteered, about 9 percent of the 6,330 black elementary pupils in the district.[73] The inner-city schools remained largely black, but black students became a substantial presence in a number of schools that had previously been almost entirely white. Whereas twenty-seven of the forty-eight elementary schools had enrolled fewer than 10 percent black students in 1967–68, a year later only sixteen schools were thus concentrated; the number of "balanced" schools—that is, schools whose black population was within 5 percent of the district average—rose from one in 1968 to eight in 1969. That is precisely what the initial phase of the two-way busing plan would have achieved.

The administration was understandably pleased, claiming "the best record in the state" in terms of the number of pupils attending desegregated schools.[74] The plan did not upset educational programs in any of the "receiving" schools, which on the average enrolled only twenty-two minority students. Transportation costs were modest. Overcrowding in the inner-city schools was relieved. The success of the venture confirmed the school board's faith in the administration. The community's confidence in the school system was reflected in voter approval of an increase in the tax rate, smaller than what the liberals had urged but still the first such hike to be approved since unification.[75]

The administration exercised its renewed authority to encourage desegregation at the secondary level. When in 1970 a boundary change involving two of Richmond's high schools was necessitated by school rebuilding, the administration issued guidelines for boundary adjustments and then announced assignment changes, which the board promptly ratified. Declared Superintendent Snodgrass, "The new guideline best meets the needs of the district, upsets the least number of people, and meets the official constraints of school capacity, proximity of home to school, and reasonable racial balance."[76]

Without any fanfare, "reasonable racial balance" had become an administrative criterion. When the two high schools reopened, they were substantially more desegregated as a result of the boundary changes.[77] Where it was administratively feasible and prudent to do so, blacks would be dispersed among the inner-city schools, even if some gerrymandering was required. That policy, initiated by the administration, was accepted by the board. The era of lay political domination had come to an end. Although the board did concern itself with certain matters that had troubled its supporters prior to the election, among them sex education, the old-line school administration achieved a modus vivendi with the new board that gave the staff substantial control over the running of the schools.

VI

The liberal board's attempt to use the Richmond lawsuit to persuade the citizenry to embrace its district-wide desegregation plan had resulted instead in the election of a board bent on undoing what it saw as the liberals' mischief. The liberals hoped that the courts would protect and secure what the board had begun. As outgoing board president Barusch noted in his farewell address: "The future of the district lies in the courts. . . . The new board will be forced to implement what we've done. We have here a fait accompli. We have changed the school boundaries to reflect an integrated district, and any attempt to change it back will wind up in a lawsuit." [78] While a lawsuit did in fact take place, the strategic errors of the legal services attorneys undermined liberal expectations. Although the desegregation suit would hang over the Richmond school district until 1974, the district proceeded as if political and educational considerations, not constitutional ones, were paramount.

Immediately following the conservative board's approval of the Richmond Integration Plan in July 1969, legal services sought to bar the district from implementing this modification of the liberals' phased venture. A new trial judge issued the second decision in the Richmond case: Richmond would have one year to prove that its voluntary plan could work. [79] The decision was puzzling on several counts. For one thing, the court expressly declared that "the freedom of choice or open enrollment plans are not effective to accomplish racial balance" but gave the district an opportunity to prove it wrong. For another, a remedy was imposed despite no finding of legal wrong. Richmond had a duty to achieve racial balance even though the court had determined that the district had "at no time . . . indicated any desire to perpetuate racial imbalance or to continue segregated education."

The analytic weaknesses of this decision, like its predecessor opinion, may be due in part to the judge's lack of familiarity with constitutional issues. Unlike federal district courts, in state courts arguments based on the equal protection clause are infrequently heard. Political considerations were also relevant. The trial court fully appreciated the strength of popular local support for the voluntary desegregation plan, for state courts do not enjoy the degree of insulation from localism that is the prerogative of the federal bench. In giving the school district a chance to operate a voluntary plan, the court was acting with political prudence.

Having exhausted state court channels, the legal services attorneys focused their attention on the federal courts. In December 1969, they filed a new suit in federal district court relying on asserted de jure segregation as the basis for district-wide desegregation.[80] But the federal court, noting that the California court retained jurisdiction over the Verde School case, abstained until that suit was resolved.[81] Legal services, thwarted again, decided to focus on the still-pending state court case. A conclusive state court ruling would either oblige the school district to desegregate or permit revival of the federal court action.

Richmond's opposition to court-ordered city-wide desegregation remained strong. Buttressed by private counsel, it was prepared to reopen the case. In January 1971, the district moved for permission to file an amended answer denying the allegations of the original 1968 complaint.[82] When, astonishingly, the motion was granted,[83] the school district contended that the district had committed no constitutional violations and was therefore under no obligation whatsoever to desegregate.[84] The effect of this essentially political action was to grant the district a new trial and the prospect of a different judgment.

The trial began two years rather than the originally projected one year after the new school board had altered the desegregation plan. The two conservative board members first elected in 1967 had been returned to office without serious challenge. Popular unhappiness with mandatory busing had not diminished. Just before the trial date, all of the local superior court judges requested that the case be heard by someone from outside the county. The reason for this remarkable request reveals the extent to which state court judges anticipate and try to evade political pressures. "The action," wrote the presiding judge, "is one with substantial local political overtones."[85] Although a local jurist had granted Richmond's motion for a retrial on the merits, no one wanted to preside over that trial. The California Judicial Council selected Judge Raymond Sherwin from neighboring Solano County.

The Verde School case should have been relatively straightforward, but the two-month trial was neither tightly conducted nor closely managed. The inexperience of the legal services attorneys marred the proceedings. Witnesses were called upon to discuss not only Verde School but also the neighboring schools, the history of school construction, and boundary changes. They were asked about district-wide racial patterns, socioeconomic conditions, student achievement, attitudes towards the open enrollment plan, and similar matters, despite the attorneys' inability to bring any of this evidence to bear on the question of segregation at Verde.

Whereas other judges might have insisted on a more sharply focused and shorter proceeding, Judge Sherwin was lax. By questioning witnesses himself, allowing leading questions, and relaxing the rules of evidence, the judge gave the legal services lawyers every chance to prove their case. In the process, Judge Sherwin permitted the scope of the trial to encompass more than the Verde situation. By tolerating the inclusion of evidence concerning district racial attitudes, policies, and practices, the judge converted a conventional trial proceeding into an expanded review of the Richmond school district.

Desegregation disputes demand broad review, for they are in good part disputes over policy, and in this respect the judge's permissiveness was appropriate. Yet in the process of managing the case, Judge Sherwin strayed too far from the role of impartial decider. During the hearings, for instance, he became annoyed at the school district witnesses for what he saw as their evasiveness. In responding to a criticism voiced by the district's counsel concerning the snail's pace with which plaintiffs' counsel questioned Superintendent Snodgrass, Sherwin declared, "If the witness would not equivocate, that would avoid the necessity of this kind of recapitulation."[86] Sherwin also took offense at what he considered patently racist implications of the responses of current school board members. The judge subsequently reported that the testimony of school officials caused him to lose his sense of objectivity. "I came into the case impartial, but I got absorbed and lost a good part of the separation."[87]

The school district offered a vigorous defense. The Richmond Integration Plan, the district declared, revealed its lack of segregatory intent. The weak academic performance of blacks, regarded by plaintiffs as establishing the inferiority of the schools to which they were assigned, was in the district's view a socioeconomic and not a racial phenomenon, which could best be addressed through compensatory education programs. The mandatory busing of the first phase of the rejected liberal board plan was described as too costly and lacking in community support.

Throughout the trial, the participants seemed preoccupied with making ideological points rather than with establishing the legal rightness of their positions. Lawyers' statements resembled political orations and their questions were criticized by Judge Sherwin as "stump speeches."[88] Plaintiffs' attorneys were sarcastic in their inquiries, prompting frequent admonitions from the bench. The spectators at the trial behaved like rooting sections, offering encouragement to their favorite advocates. The court's opinion was consistent in tone with the proceedings. It addressed not only the legal question, the permissibility of segregation at Verde, but also the larger social issue and context out of which it emerged. The opinion begins: "This case has been publicized as a school busing case. In fact, it has little to do with busing. Rather, it concerns the tragic absurdity of racial segregation and discrimination and the resistance to measures designed to remedy such conditions."[89] A long excerpt from board member Fuller's testimony designed to display that racism provides the opinion's introduction.[90] The judge's conclusion was made of judicially more familiar stuff. The court found the Richmond school district to have discriminated against black pupils and rejected the open enrollment plan as inadequate. Because of the way in which the suit was framed, the remedy was necessarily limited to the Verde School. The school district was ordered to produce a plan for the desegregation of Verde, to be implemented the following September.

Had this order gone into effect pending review, as happened in San Francisco after the trial court decision, the course of events in Richmond would have been very different. But California state courts, unlike the federal courts, routinely grant stays in civil rights litigation, and in Richmond the stay effectively preserved the status quo pending appeal. It seemed nonetheless that the legal services strategy had worked after all. A state court had found segregation in a single school. With this decision serving as "collateral estoppel," a case could now be made against the other schools.

More than two years elapsed between Judge Sherwin's ruling and appellate review. During this time, the USP school board slate was again reelected, and the school administration maintained the open enrollment program. Although the Richmond school district had apparently lost its case in court, the decision had no perceptible effect on the community or on the management of the schools.

The appeal presented some of the same difficulties as had the original trial. The plaintiffs' briefs were disorganized, poorly documented, and weakly argued. As at the trial, their argument lacked specific focus on the Verde situation. The school district's attorneys, in contrast, prepared competently written and well-researched briefs, asserting the permissibility of the district's actions.

The appellate court issued two consecutive opinions. In both, the trial court was criticized for making findings and conclusions with respect to the district as a whole, rather than limiting its attention to Verde School. The plaintiffs' treatment of the evidence was castigated as "deplorable . . . and inexcusable upon the part of any lawyer."[91] The first appellate opinion upheld the portion of Sherwin's opinion ordering desegregation of Verde, concluding that that school had been shown to be de facto segregated. In its second opinion, issued in response to a request for clarification by the school district's attorneys, the appellate court reversed itself and remanded the entire case for a new trial.[92] References in the lower court opinion to events not linked to Verde had irretrievably contaminated the proceeding, the appellate court now concluded. Future litigants could point to those findings as establishing the illegality of segregation throughout Richmond, and that was held inappropriate. The appellate court opinions were legally as problematic as were the trial court efforts. The issuance of a "clarification" that amounts to a reversal, without new briefing or argument, is unusual; the rationale for ordering a new trial with respect to Verde is at best strained.

Six years after the original complaint was filed, in August 1974, the California Supreme Court decided not to hear the case—a wise decision, given the ungainly legal history of the dispute. Although a new pretrial order was issued, interest in the suit had subsided. Legal services was unwilling to take further action without minority community support, and an inquiry undertaken by the Justice Department did not lead to federal intervention. The legal strategy has in effect been abandoned.

That strategy was flawed from the outset. The use of the courtroom for exclusively political purposes, as in the Richmond trial, threatens the legitimacy of the judicial process. All public law cases are of course political to some extent, but they are generally rooted in legal analytics, and this was entirely absent in the Richmond suit. The trail of badly conceived decisions in the Richmond case is due in part to the fact that in its early stages the suit was a dispute in name only and that the quality of lawyering was appalling. In all its stages, the lawsuit also reveals the vulnerability of the state courts to political suasion: the unwillingness of local judges to hear the dispute; the disjunction between wrong and remedy in the first phases of the case; the trial, itself excessively ideological in character; and the unpersuasive appellate opinions.

Judicial ineptitude, a harsh but accurate characterization, is apparent throughout. It is no exaggeration to suggest that not one of the opinions handed down in the case is adequately reasoned. The contrast between the case record in the Richmond suit and the history of almost any federal court desegregation case (including the San Francisco litigation) serves as a reminder that the claims of greater independence and competency that are supposed to justify a federal trial court system do not lack basis in fact.

VII

Since the ouster of the liberal board and the restoration of the administration's hegemony, Richmond's public school system has demonstrated remarkable stability. The administrative personnel have remained much the same; retiring Superintendent Snodgrass handpicked as his successor his former deputy, Richard Lovette. The administration continues to be preoccupied with the maintenance of its own authority and with such administratively familiar priorities as economy—a heightened concern in the wake of Proposition 13—and ease of management. The board, its composition largely unchanged, has deferred routinely to an administration that demonstrated its responsiveness to the wishes of a working-class and traditionalist constituency. Judging from present appearances, it would seem that neither the era of liberal domination nor the court order requiring desegregation of the Verde School had ever happened in Richmond.

This stability has evoked varied reactions. To the dominant conservative community, it has been cause for celebration. In a 1974 testimonial dinner honoring Superintendent Snodgrass as "Contra Costa County Man of the Year," supporters noted: "We have a good system here. It has survived because the present superintendent . . . knows how to run a school system."[93] Richmond liberals were less pleased. Beginning in the early 1970s, they sought unsuccessfully to build a unified political base for the election of a reformist school board. In the 1971 and 1973 school board elections, the conservative candidates won ready reelection. Voter turnout was less than half what it had been in 1969. Familiar patterns of community acquiescence had reasserted themselves.

Richmond's school board members during this period all lived in the newer suburbs of El Sobrante and Pinole. The liberals felt this guaranteed their unresponsiveness to the needs of inner-city Richmond. There was an element of historical irony in this concern, since between 1965 and 1967 the board had been dominated by Richmond and Kensington residents, while residents of the outlying areas had little say in matters of school policy. Now that the liberals had become the victims, they proposed abandoning district-wide representation and dividing the district into five electoral wards. Conservatives were displeased by this suggestion, not least because the conservative incumbents lived in just one of the proposed wards. USP sought to turn the redistricting issue into a referendum over busing. The reformers treated the question in terms of political representation, declaring that ward elections provided a "buffer against the tyranny of the majority."[94] Reformers also linked ward elections and better schooling, arguing that ward representation embodied "the last chance to improve the Richmond schools."[95] The spirited campaign brought a majority of district voters to the polls. Ward elections lost by less than 5 percent. The status quo had been endorsed, but not overwhelmingly. Representation and the concomitant possibility of diversity within the district was apparently of some interest.

A liberal candidate, Eddis Harrison, finally won a seat on the school board in 1977, replacing a retiring incumbent; surprisingly, Harrison was the top vote-getter in the election.[96] Her victory led some to hope for greater board responsiveness to the heretofore unrepresented black and liberal groups, but this has not happened. Board member Harrison has been a dissenter, not a policymaker. On a wide range of matters that in other places have been in the public domain and consequently the source of public controversy, policy has remained an administrative prerogative. Decisions on school closings, for instance, have been made by the staff and not the board.[97] The stable order prevails, and will for the foreseeable future.

The Richmond Integration Plan was enacted in 1969 by a school board that had just been elected on an antibusing platform. Its adoption revealed no principled commitment to desegregation but rather a pragmatic recognition that unless some affirmative measures were voluntarily adopted the state judiciary might well insist upon more.

By the mid-1970s, desegregation was no longer a significant political rallying cry in Richmond, and the effort to impose desegregation through judicial decree had failed. Although under such circumstances one might have imagined that open enrollment would be allowed to die a quiet death, this did not happen. Quite the contrary: until 1978–79, participation in the plan gradually but steadily increased. What little public opposition had initially been expressed in the white suburban schools quieted down, although violence flared briefly in 1980. With declining enrollments, principals of white neighborhood schools had an incentive to attract black students and the school dollars that came with them.

Voluntary desegregation, devised in defiance of the liberals' legal strategy and derided at the time as a sham undertaking, became institutionalized as it was implemented. To Superintendent Lovette, "this is a program for the nation to observe—desegregation without busing can work."[98] Yet the district never made voluntary integration a central concern. In the wake of budgetary cutbacks necessitated by Proposition 13, Richmond stopped transporting students wishing to attend racially mixed schools, with predictable adverse effects on open enrollment.

The number of students participating in the open enrollment program more than doubled over the years. One in five black students participated in the elementary plan in 1977–78, the high-water mark of the program. The elimination of free transportation cut back but did not destroy the enterprise. In 1979–80, one-sixth of the black students chose a more desegregated school.[99]

Open enrollment reaches only those students whose families believe that desegregation offers an escape from the low expectations and low pupil achievement characteristic of the inner-city schools. It places the burden on those desiring a racially mixed education, a continuing sore point among black community leaders, who have noted that no whites participate in the venture. Open enrollment also benefits only those who want to be helped in this way, rather than securing a desegregated education for all children, as would a plan oriented to racial balance.

At the elementary level, the open enrollment plan has increased both the number of desegregated schools and the number of predominantly black schools. If one focuses on "racially balanced" schools, those in which the racial mix is within 5 percent of the district average, and "imbalanced" schools, which have proportionately more black or white students, the number of balanced schools increased from one (in the year preceding the open enrollment plan) to eight in 1978–79; the number of schools with disproportionately low black enrollment decreased from thirty-seven to twenty-seven. However, the number of schools with disproportionately high black enrollment also increased, from ten to fourteen. In "imbalanced" schools enrolling more whites than the district average, the racial mix is substantially greater today than prior to open enrollment. In 1968, twenty-nine schools were 10 percent or less black; a decade later, just four schools had such a small proportion of blacks. Even Richmond's "imbalanced" and predominantly white schools have a substantial black enrollment. The same is not true of predominantly black schools, which are somewhat more segregated today than before the inception of open enrollment. There were five schools with more than 90 percent black students in 1968, compared with seven a decade later. The absolute enrollment decline, coupled with the departure of approximately one out of five students formerly assigned to the inner-city schools, has also substantially reduced their enrollment.

At the secondary level, open enrollment somewhat lessened racial separation. While five of the thirteen junior and senior high schools were "balanced" prior to open enrollment, the range in proportion of blacks was considerable: in 1968, three secondary schools were less than 4 percent black, while one was 75 percent. Open enrollment, coupled with boundary changes designed to further "reasonable racial balance," reduced this range. Although only one of the fifteen secondary schools was "balanced" in 1978, none were less than 13 percent or more than 67 percent black. In the Richmond district as a whole, the percentage of blacks attending predominantly black schools dropped slightly between 1968 and 1978, from 55 percent to 50 percent, even as the proportion of black students in the district increased from 25 to 38 percent. This is not an unimpressive shift, particularly when contrasted with the experiences of other Northern cities.

For participants in the open enrollment program, the experience is said to have been a good one. Because the incoming students generally had high academic aspirations, the predominantly white schools did not alter their essential educational mission even when they became desegregated, and that has benefited both whites and blacks. As black community leader Billie Alexander, a past unsuccessful school board candidate, observed: "We know for a fact that the curriculum in the white schools offers a better chance for a successful education."[100]

To a traditionalist administration in a community that has consistently spent relatively little on education (1979–80 per pupil expenditures were approximately one-third lower than San Francisco's and Berkeley's), subsidizing desegregation was less important than providing an education. When Richmond had to trim some 11 percent from its budget after the passage of Proposition 13 in 1978, the half-million dollars expended on busing students in order to promote racial mixing was a tempting target. Busing was eliminated. Student choice was expanded to include any school in the district other than the one to which a student was assigned, if the choice improved the racial balance of the school. Students would, however, have to find their own way to the school, and in a large district with meager public transportation this made it far harder for black parents to send their children to racially mixed schools.[101]

The school district defended its action as a cost-efficient choice. As one board member put it: "Eliminating busing saved a substantial amount of money [approximately 8 percent of the total cutback] without impairing the education of children. It was not a racial decision."[102] Similarly, Superintendent Lovette noted that, in choosing between busing and "program," the former simply counted for less.[103]

This rationale can be faulted on several counts. For one thing, distinguishing between desegregation and "program" reveals that little value was placed on the educational benefits enjoyed by those who chose to participate in the Richmond Integration Plan. Subsidized busing was a low priority precisely because it was seen as not especially beneficial; that is clearly a racial judgment. As board president Virgil Gay observed: "Busing doesn't work: it doesn't help anyone achieve better, it is wasting money which could be better used elsewhere, and it does not bring about the social utopia which liberals envisioned."[104] Neighboring Berkeley, faced with more stringent budget cuts, did not even consider eliminating its busing program, a fact that bears out the substantial differences between the two communities. For another thing, the budgetary necessity of eliminating busing may be questioned. Even in the face of declining enrollments—there are 25 percent fewer students attending Richmond's schools today than there were a decade ago—the district continues to build new schools,[105] and as a result money that might be used to pay for student transportation is expended on almost-empty buildings. Moreover, the district's budget surplus would more than pay for busing. Finally, as black community spokesman Billie Alexander argued, budget cuts "should have been across the board, not focused on entire programs—busing and child care—which mostly affect blacks."[106]

The board's decision to end the busing program provoked a demonstration, a rare occurrence in Richmond since the 1960s. Some seventy-five parents picketed the school administration building on the first day of classes, and a complaint was lodged with the Office of Civil Rights, demanding that federal funds to the district be cut off. What has astonished many people, including board members, is the fact that many parents have found some way to continue taking advantage of open enrollment. "There is no question in my mind," said one board member, "that many parents care a great deal about the open enrollment program."[107] To them, desegregation remains a goal worth making sacrifices for.

Viewed as a whole, the Richmond district remains preponderantly white. In a real sense, open enrollment helped create two separate school systems in Richmond, one desegregated and one black.[108] The former appears to be working reasonably well. The latter, in which most of Richmond's black students are enrolled, is in serious trouble.

In schools that enroll 90 percent or more black students, the average sixth grader scores in the sixteenth percentile in reading on a state-wide test; test scores in these schools are the lowest in the Bay Area. The district's sixth-grade average is substantially higher, in the forty-third percentile, whereas sixth graders in schools that enroll 90 percent or more whites are, on the average, in the sixty-third percentile. School officials attribute this disparity to socioeconomic factors over which they have no control. Virgil Gay goes somewhat further. "I wish people would get off the race problem. It is a family problem, poor people do badly all over. Liberals promise the world, but it just doesn't work."[109] Black spokesmen hold a different view. They assert that the data reveal Richmond's indifference to the inner-city schools. They note, for instance, the district's reluctance to hire substantial numbers of black teachers (in 1979 only 12.8 percent of the teaching staff and 14.5 percent of the administration were black);[110] the sharp cutback of a federally funded teacher's aide program, which had flourished under the liberal regime; and alleged mismanagement of the federal Title I, Elementary and Secondary Education Act (ESEA) program, designed to benefit poor and educationally disadvantaged children. At the symbolic level, indifference to black concerns is also detected. Richmond is, for example, the only Bay Area school district not to commemorate Martin Luther King's birthday.[111] Open enrollment, which reduced overcrowding in the inner-city schools, has deprived those institutions of their natural student leaders. Although increasing amounts of money are spent in the inner-city schools, it is unlikely that without strong educational leadership or parental involvement money alone will make much of a difference.

But what is there to do? At a time when desegregation is no longer routinely seen as the only measure of racial justice in the schools, it is not clear that closing the inner-city schools would be the wisest course. Consider the case of Verde School, the segregated school on which the unsuccessful legal strategy focused. Enrollment in Verde has declined to less than one hundred, and its students have the worst achievement record of any Richmond school, but when in 1977 school district officials discussed closing the building, community spokesmen rushed to its defense. A black minister from North Richmond declared to the board that Verde is "a sort of sweetheart . . . loved by the people there."[112] Can that sentiment be harnessed to promote effective action with respect to the inner-city schools? Can Richmond be as successful with these students as it has been in the other schools in the district? If the past is any sort of guide, the prognosis is pessimistic. Then again, the educational prognosis for any American city with a sizable concentration of poor and nonwhite students is also pessimistic.

The limited open enrollment plan in Richmond, coupled with scant support for black schools, reflects both the potential and the limits of racial politics in a predominantly working-class and racially mixed school district. Writing in 1972, Lillian Rubin observed that "Richmond is in many ways America in microcosm, and its agony reflects the pain in the land today."[113] Richmond remains a microcosm, but in a different sense. At a time when visions were clearer, the avowed parochialism of such a community was seen as impeding racial justice; then, the liberals could be criticized for not imposing district-wide desegregation, including busing, while they had the authority to do so. Yet in terms of numerical desegregation and community reaction, Richmond has done better than many supposedly more enlightened places. More generally, as the meaning of racial justice proves more elusive, reliance on self-interest within a constitutional framework may become almost as acceptable a basis for social policy as it traditionally has been for economic policy.[114]

CHAPTER
8

Berkeley:
"Schools Worthy of Imitation"?

Sing a little song of integration
Berkeley will be watched by the whole nation
When you and I make a date
To integrate . . . in sixty-eight.
                                        "Integration Calypso"

I

On September 10, 1968, Berkeley, California, became the first American city with a population larger than 100,000 and a sizable black community to completely desegregate its schools.[1] That event completed a process begun four years earlier with the desegregation of the junior high schools (high school students historically attended a single city-wide school). It was a joyous occasion and a much recorded one.[2] Congratulatory wires were sent by the U.S. commissioner of education, civil rights spokesmen, and national business and labor leaders. At the end of the day, Superintendent Neil Sullivan was understandably exultant. "You could sense the exhilaration throughout the city. Where was this dread of busing, this great specter of fear? Vanished into the clear September air of that beautiful first day."[3]

Seen from the vantage of 1968, Berkeley's actions marked the triumph of liberal ideals with respect to racial justice and schooling. Berkeley had acted not because, as in San Francisco, a federal judge required it to, but because racial mixing was thought to be right. Its actions did not represent the decision of an elite imposed upon a resistant community, as in Richmond, but a biracial political consensus—or as close as one can come to such a consensus in this divided society. Some years later, the outlook was decidedly more gloomy. In a 1976 report, the school district observed: "Busing and realignment of attendance boundaries have balanced the racial mix of the school community. But a subtler and more serious form of isolation has thereby surfaced. It is isolation expressed in the distance in academic achievement between white vs. nonwhite students."⁴ School board president Marc Monheimer scored the early 1970s as a time of "chaos and moral disarray."⁵ Only in the past few years has Berkeley, struggling now to make do with less money, sought seriously to confront again the dilemmas of integration.

What happened after 1968? Berkeley failed to move beyond racial balance toward an integrated educational setting that consciously undertook to relate race to broader concerns of educational purpose. Instead the school district became fragmented in purpose, seemingly rudderless. A mere three years after desegregation, the district was touting choice and diversity in an experimental schools program that enrolled three out of every ten Berkeley students. In Berkeley, experimentation and not integration became the goal of policy. Other factors also contributed to fragmentation in the district, including forays by the school board into antiwar politics, mischievous efforts to address racism by denigrating whites, and job politicking that brought substantial numbers of less qualified, and less integration-minded, minority staff into the school district.

To treat Berkeley as a struggle between the pre-1968 forces of racial enlightenment and the post-1968 temptations of radical and racial politics is an oversimplification. For one thing, the historical separation between the eras is not so sharp; the germ of Berkeley's difficulties significantly predates 1968. For another thing, in stressing the national significance of what it was about, Berkeley may have undermined its prospects for successful integration. National attention is drawn to such dramatic policy initiatives as voluntary district-wide busing, not to the more mundane task of implementing an integration plan. Berkeley acted partly to attract this attention. If the school district was to remain in the national limelight, it always had to be doing something new. Moreover, with willingness to change direction—whether by introducing "impact teams" in the elementary schools or by establishing experimental schools in the system—came the outside money on which Berkeley grew increasingly dependent. Innovation was rewarded by recognition and resources, but steady, unspectacular performance was not. Seen in this light, the commitment to integration in Berkeley was simply not powerful enough to override the countervailing forces.

Between the mid 1960s and the mid 1970s, the Berkeley school district saw itself as in the vanguard of social change. The educational institution would remake itself and then fulfill George Count's half-century-old dream of remaking the social order.⁶ The aspiration to revolution was present at least rhetorically. Many of the circumstances were apparently right for radical change: the character of the town, the nature of the population, the commitment of institutional leadership. That Berkeley has abandoned its revolutionary mission to share the more prosaic struggles of urban school districts for survival at a time of fiscal retrenchment, and for a sense of purposiveness in the enterprise of schooling, indicates the ultimately limited malleability of institutions of mass public education.

II

Berserkeley.   That play on the city's name summons up the most widely held image of the place. Beginning in the early 1960s, what was new in politics was forged in Berkeley, to be taken up elsewhere by the ideologically committed or fashion conscious. The city was an "American symbol," as one journalist put it, "carefully monitored by reporters, the FBI, social scientists, and urban strategists eager for a glimpse of the future."[7]

Berkeley's strategic positioning on the knife-edge of change in an era characterized by near-constant change aroused differing reactions. To Martin Luther King, "Berkeley has stirred the conscience . . . of America."[8] The city saw itself in even more grandiose terms. One self-evaluation referred to Berkeley as "the conscience of the white western world. It was, whatever else was thought of it, the intellectual epicenter of the United States as well."[9] "Whatever else was thought of it": the parenthetical phrase embodied an acknowledgment that to some, among them conservative politicians in neighboring Richmond and Oakland, Berkeley's political and social awakening was a nightmare, not a vision.

The city had not always aroused such controversy. Throughout much of its history, it was a sleepy suburb and resort town, home of a good but not especially distinguished university. Town-gown relationships were peaceable, for the university did not upset the calm of the place. Although Berkeley elected a socialist mayor in 1912, that was a decided aberration. Until the late 1950s, Berkeley was politically conservative, economically self-sufficient, and culturally ingrown. Both the nine-member city council, which administers Berkeley in tandem with a city manager, and the five-member board of education were dominated by Republicans. In 1953, a former University of California "all-American" won a seat on the school board by campaigning against an incumbent who had voted to permit Paul Robeson to perform at the high school auditorium. "It takes an All-American to beat an un-American," was his campaign slogan.[10] Even as late as 1963, Berkeley's voters turned down a fair housing ordinance for the city.

By the early 1960s, however, the political and social character of Berkeley had dramatically altered. The changes were largely due to two factors: the coming of age of the University of California, and the emergence of a sizable and politically astute black community.

In the years following World War II, the university grew in size and began aspiring to international status. If it was not yet the multiversity, neither was it the placid place of prewar years. This change necessarily affected the city, for although Berkeley is not just a university town—there is, for example, a fair amount of small light industry and a sizable white-collar work force—the university is the single most important influence. Its 25,000 students constitute nearly one-quarter of Berkeley's residents and its 11,000 employees represent a similar proportion of the work force. The university's impress is also felt in subtler ways. A fair proportion of the town's political leadership is routinely drawn from the faculty and, to a lesser extent, the students. Issues first aired on campus quickly reach the town, among them concern over limitations on speech, sustained and militant opposition to the Vietnam War, and support for the farmworkers' union. City reforms—including restrictions on auto traffic, efforts to reshape police-community relations by bringing patrolmen into close contact with neighborhoods and by establishing a review board, and assurance of free medical care in city-run clinics—represented responses to a progressive, if sometimes oddly focused, impulse that had its roots both in the university and in those whom it attracted to the community.

As the style of campus politics changed during this period, emerging, in the view of the 1970 Presidential Commission on Campus Unrest, as 'an authentic political invention—a new and complex mixture of issues, tactics, emotions, and setting—that became the prototype for student protest throughout the decade,"[11] it drew to the city a new breed of settler. The politically active saw Berkeley as an alternative to suburban stagnation or urban helplessness. The flower children were attracted to the anything-is-possible permissiveness of the place; their remnants—the runaways and drifters and junkies—hang on in the shadow of the campus. These diverse newcomers in turn helped to reshape the political and cultural life of the town. The fact that the experimental schools movement became so significant, and so deeply im-

bedded in public institutions, is but one example of the indirect
influence on Berkeley of the university and of those whom it
attracted.

The growth of Berkeley's black community constitutes the
second noteworthy change of the postwar years. Before World War
II, only 4 percent of the city's population was black. In Berkeley as
in the rest of the Bay Area, blacks were attracted in substantial
numbers by the shipbuilding industry. By 1950, the black proportion of the population had nearly tripled, to 11.7 percent; today,
blacks, Asians, and Latinos together constitute one-third of Berkeley's 103,000 residents.[12]

In a compact town, the impact of this demographic change
was readily apparent. To be sure, in Berkeley as elsewhere blacks
and whites live in geographic near-isolation. Professionals, aca-
demics, and businessmen who commute to San Francisco across
the bay cluster in the hills, where old mission-style and sleekly
contemporary homes command magnificent views of the San
Francisco skyline. The city's flats house a more heterogeneous population: students, skilled white workers, and nonwhites. But what
distinguishes Berkeley from its neighbors is a commitment, beginning in the 1950s, to linking the economic and political destinies of
the two Berkeleys, hills and flats, black and white.

The 1952 presidential campaign brought a new generation of
liberal whites into politics.[13] When that campaign ended, they undertook to revitalize the moribund local Democratic party organization. In this effort, they sought alliance with black leaders, who
had come to Berkeley during the 1940s and displayed considerable
political acumen in opening up employment opportunities for
black workers and professionals, especially in the schools and city
agencies. The black community itself was special. Compared with
blacks nationally, Berkeley blacks were better educated and had
"fewer persons at the bottom of the social scale, more in the middle, and a few more at the top."[14]

The black and white communities together produced in
Berkeley a rare and politically portentous demographic combination: a well-educated lower class, a sizable well-to-do and well-
educated upper class, and a relatively small middle class. As Mary
Metz observes:

[Berkeley] is not like many suburban areas or cities centered around universities and other "intellectual" industries because it has a really sizeable
minority with low education and low status occupations. At the same time
it does not share with many core cities, which still have large numbers of
white persons, the presence of a large proportion of persons with middle

education and middle status jobs who tend to cling fiercely to the educational and racial status quo.[15]

In short, the composition of the community enhanced prospects for liberal political gains.

Beginning in the late 1950s, blacks and whites joined forces in order to bolster the voting power of their respective communities. By 1961, when the city council and the school board each had their first black member, both parties to the coalition were reaping the benefits of the strategy. The liberal Democratic coalition supplanted conservative business leadership as the dominant force in Berkeley politics, enduring until the mid-sixties. Berkeley voters imposed upon themselves the highest tax rate in the state during this period, and were thus able to secure a cornucopia of public services, of which a disproportionate share was allocated to the flats.[16]

Bitter disputes over the rightness of the American presence in Vietnam characteristically came to Berkeley earlier than to other places, and splintered the prevailing liberal alliance. In 1966, the incumbent congressman, a Democrat, was a "War on Poverty" liberal. He was also a resolute supporter of the war, and that dissatisfied a growing band of radicals, drawn into politics as a means of demonstrating their moral commitment. A 1966 primary challenge was unsuccessful, but a 1968 challenge was not. Self-styled radicals also began campaigning for local office; although they never constituted a majority of either the school board or the city council, their triumphs further splintered the Democratic Party.

The impact of this political change on the black community and on black-white relations was substantial. No longer was there an organization that could with some legitimacy claim to speak for Berkeley's blacks, and consequently the black-white liberal coalition collapsed. The blacks who were chosen by the radicals to run for office were newcomers to town, who bought and bullied their way onto the ticket. They spoke for no constituency. Not that this much disturbed the radicals, who were less interested in grassroots politics than in movement politics, less concerned about the fate of Berkeley itself than with Berkeley as symbol for a different future. "If there is revolutionary change inside the mother country," Tom Hayden stated in 1970, "it will originate in the Berkeleys—a vanguard unit of utopian levelling revolution."[17]

The school system was not immune to the impact of these changes in the university, and in the demographics and politics of the town. Beginning in the 1950s, school reform in Berkeley was a centerpiece of the liberal coalition. The liberals' greatest triumph was the desegregation of the public schools. The emergent political and cultural radicalism was also felt, both symbolically—in official gestures of opposition to the Vietnam War, for instance—and instrumentally—in assaults on the deadening hand of uniform public education, and eventually in the substitution of diversity for integration as the paramount goal of the public schools. The Berkeley public school system was very much a child of its place and time, attentive to the nuances of racism, responsive to liberal and radical criticism. Quite self-consciously, it set out first to reform and then to revolutionize the social order.

III

The character of a community can often be detected from the nature of the schooling that it provides. In Berkeley, the conservative and efficiently run town of 1950 maintained a school system similarly conservative in outlook, hierarchical in organization, and Scotch in matters financial. Alterations in community character were also embodied in the school system. The changing demography of the town and the emerging liberal black-white political alignment decisively influenced the schools, particularly in the way they addressed the newly relevant issue of race.

Berkeley effectively maintained two school systems under Superintendent Thomas Nelson.[18] For students keen on a university education, the district offered superb instruction at all levels. Elite elementary schools directed students to a junior high school that, in its sense of tradition, resembled an eastern preparatory school. For the rest, a bare-bones education sufficed. In that way, Berkeley could keep the costs of schooling down, thus satisfying the pocketbook concerns of an electorate that approved only two of eleven school bond elections between 1926 and 1965. Those who wanted a better education than Berkeley could provide sent their children to private schools; one Berkeley child in nine was educated outside the public school system.

The citizenry was evidently satisfied with this arrangement. It chose board members from the cadre of conservative Republican businessmen that generally ran the city's affairs (occasionally, a businessman's wife would serve). The board in turn deferred to the superintendent for professional management. Board meetings were short and humdrum affairs.

New teachers suffered under this system. Close supervision weeded out talent that was stubbornly individualistic. Starting teachers' salaries were low, and each year 20 percent of the teaching staff left for financially more attractive positions. Teachers' unhappiness produced the first serious challenge to the conservative regime. In 1956, having been denied more than a token salary increase by a board unwilling to raise the property tax rate, the teachers collected sufficient signatures to put a tax levy on the ballot. Because increased salaries alone could not command popular support, the teachers joined forces with those concerned about the quality of schooling. The campaign for the tax increase united parents interested in reducing class sizes with teachers interested in improving their economic position. Their claim that the schools were "substandard" and miserly in their treatment of teachers carried the day: 57 percent of Berkeley's voters supported the tax hike. Emboldened by this success, the parents' and teachers' groups joined with the Democrats and with civil rights organizations to elect the first liberal, Paul Sanazaro, to the school board.[19]

Sanazaro sought substantial changes in Berkeley's schools: new school buildings, overhaul of the curriculum, and general upgrading of the quality of the system by spending more money. As long as Superintendent Nelson ran the schools, however, significant reform was unlikely; one liberal was just a dissenting voice. Nelson's retirement in 1958 offered Berkeley a choice. The district could either maintain the status quo by selecting an insider for the post or it could risk shifting its course by hiring an outsider. Division among board members precluded the selection of someone in the administration and led the board to hire C. H. Wennerberg, a superintendent from Southern California who had presided over a rapidly expanding school district and so knew a great deal about launching school-building programs.[20]

The new superintendent revamped the administration, removing the most conservative holdover administrators from the center of power and replacing almost every school principal. He cut the district's traditional ties with the business community almost completely, preferring instead to reach out to the new parent groups and to teachers and administrators who wanted to reform the schools. Berkeley's problems appeared legion, and included "stress at the high school level only upon academic classes, an isolated school organization . . . where hidden agendas are a way of life, and school plants that due to economy measures aren't able to meet standards of safety."[21] The era of consensus was over. School politics in Berkeley was now a matter of coalition politics—and, concomitantly, of "hidden agendas." Wennerberg relied on the board's two liberal members, a second having been elected in 1959, as well as on nascent community groups, to support his efforts. These new voices urged Berkeley to respond positively to black requests, first advanced in the late 1950s, that the district recognize the relevance of race for policy.

In the mid- and late-1960s, Berkeley's liberalism with respect to race commanded attention. When the subject was first broached a decade earlier, however, the instinct of the school board and the administration was to skirt the question. The evolution of Berkeley's stance toward race was both shaped by and a confirmation of the altered political character of the community.

"We are here to learn how we can help." So stated the NAACP, in formally bringing the topic to the attention of the school board in January 1958. "We have heard of the Springfield Plan, the St. Louis Plan, the Washington Plan. What is the Berkeley Plan?"[22] The NAACP called for an inquiry into broad "areas of concern" touching on race, among them ways of "distributing minority group teachers" and "presenting and executing a program involving integration techniques and procedures."[23]

Although the NAACP presentation marked the first time that race was publicly discussed in Berkeley, the issue had been simmering for some years. The black student population had grown from an estimated 5 percent in 1939–40 to 23 percent in 1955–56; it would reach 30 percent before the end of the decade.[24] Yet the district continued to behave as if this change had not occurred. It hired relatively few black teachers (5.9 percent of all staff was black in 1958) and assigned those it did hire exclusively to schools in the flats. As late as 1954, Superintendent Nelson stated that he would never assign a black to the high school, and although he eventually changed his mind, it was to appoint a nontenured black man to teach retarded youngsters.[25]

Such treatment, which had been endured by Berkeley's old-line blacks, was unacceptable to the generation of black residents who had come to Berkeley during and after the war. Like those who were pushing for an upgraded curriculum and new schools, they wanted more and better schooling than the conservative leadership of the district was willing to offer. In that respect, they were linked to other reformist groups.

The board majority was prepared to treat the NAACP's presentation as if it had not happened. Only the persistent intervention of liberal board member Sanazaro led the board to agree to consider what action might be taken. The administration, caucusing after the session, concluded that the issues the NAACP had raised were beyond the purview of the schools.[26] That apparent evasion did not sit well with the NAACP, which asked that a citizen's committee be appointed. The board reluctantly acquiesced, noting that there were "certain racial problems" worth studying and leaving to the administration the task of formulating an agenda.

The agenda of the citizens' committee, as shaped by the school administration, did not speak of reassigning teachers or desegregating students but dealt instead with school-community "liaison," "behavior problems," and training programs designed to make teachers more sensitive to "the psychology and culture of various minority groups." Although Superintendent Nelson knew that he would not be in office to receive the committee's report, he did what he could to jettison and, failing that, to severely limit the enterprise.

New Superintendent Wennerberg was far more enthusiastic about the citizens' committee, seeing it as a way to break down the self-imposed isolation of the system. The committee's report, issued in October 1959, was consistent with Wennerberg's views.[27] While no mention was made of desegregating the schools—a prospect not seriously contemplated by anyone at the time—the school district was urged to hire more minority teachers and to distribute them fairly throughout the system, to guard against counselors' directing blacks to dead-end programs, to address discrimination within the high school, to offer in-service programs to teachers, and to strengthen ties with community groups outside the business community. Most interesting, perhaps, was the general stance of the report. How, it was asked, could prejudice persist in such an enlightened community as Berkeley? In so framing the issue, the committee hinted at the obligations that followed from political enlightenment.

Under Superintendent Nelson, the Berkeley schools had maintained their distance from most segments of the community. Wennerberg undid this pattern, weakening traditions of hierarchy within the administration and forging alliances with all manner of groups outside the system.[28] That change made further attention to racial issues inevitable.

The new order was apparent in the style of administration. Wennerberg introduced annual retreats, at which administrators were free to let their hair down. The retreats were voluntary, but most staff members felt obliged to attend. At each school, similar efforts to foster informality among teachers and to overcome racial distinctions through professional "rap sessions" were instituted.

These efforts were planned by a small group of newcomers lodged within the central office. Over time, they became expert in all manner of race-related questions. They also formed a cadre committed to desegregation, ready to press for it when the time was ripe. The administration was not wholly successful in its desire to encourage staff development, but its actions nonetheless constituted a significant departure from past practice. And Wennerberg's initiative had real effect on teachers who wanted to involve themselves in policymaking outside their own classrooms. During the tax-hike election of 1956, such teachers had gone outside the schools into the political arena. Now they became participants in study committees, group leaders, and the like. The system had become accessible to them.

The teaching staff changed in another significant way. Between 1958 and 1962, the number of black teachers more than doubled, to seventy-five, and thirty Asians were hired. Although most of these teachers were assigned to schools in the flats, a predominantly white grade school had a black principal for the first time, and ten of the fourteen primary schools had black teachers.[29]

With respect to employment practices, staff development, and curricular innovation, the Wennerberg administration departed from previous courses of action. Opening the schools to widespread community involvement marked the greatest and perhaps the most significant reform. Wennerberg used the report of the citizens' committee as the basis for a series of meetings involving the myriad civic, church, and social organizations that functioned in Berkeley. He hoped that such town meetings, involving over one hundred of these organizations, would generate the ideas and the commitment needed to address the knotty problems of race discussed by the committee.

Openness in Berkeley had all of the charm of novelty. Suggestions about teacher recruitment and placement, curriculum, and guidance poured in. The inquiry was extended beyond the boundaries of schools, to examine the effects of housing and employment discrimination; seemingly, nothing touching on race was irrelevant or off limits.[30] Once inaugurated, openness is an approach to policy not readily reversed. Berkeley's inquiry aroused hope among civil rights groups that more than frank talk about racial problems could be achieved. The apparent ease with which changes were occurring in the schools raised new expectations that the school district had to confront.

Berkeley had made "giant accomplishments" with respect to race, declared the CORE in a May 1962 presentation to the Berkeley school board. But far more needed to be done. The district should recognize that its schools were segregated, commit itself to ending segregation, and appoint a citizens' committee charged with producing a plan to achieve that goal.[31]

Four years earlier, when the NAACP had made more modest demands of the board, the reaction was chilly. A new superintendent and a board that since 1961 had had a liberal majority were more receptive to the CORE position. Within the school administration, however, powerful voices counseled rejecting the CORE position. "Why should we surrender to CORE?"; "Look at all we have done—what do they want, busing?"[32] For its part, CORE threatened to hold a sit-in and to go to court if the district rejected its demands. That proved unnecessary. Dissension was not aired publicly, in part because of the bureaucratic astuteness of the "intergroup education" cadre. On the superintendent's recommendation, the board appointed a thirty-six-member committee, the second outside body to inquire into race and schooling issues. This group had a broader charge than its predecessor: to determine the extent and effects of de facto segregation and to make policy recommendations to the board.

The existence of segregation was undeniable. Two of the district's elementary schools were more than 90 percent black, and eight enrolled more than 95 percent white students; one of the three junior high schools was three-quarters black, and another was 99 percent white.[33] What, if anything, to do about that segregation was far less clear. "The [initial] prevailing view" on the committee, reports longtime school board member Carol Sibley, "was that some plan embracing compensatory education and open enrollment would be offered, 'topped off by a stream of platitudes.'"[34] Things turned out very differently. The more deeply the committee probed, the more seriously it took the issue. From all accounts that the committee received, segregation caused problems; something stronger than platitudes was required. That was very much the position of the superintendent, who, during the year the committee labored, stepped up minority hiring, in-service training (110 of the district's 700 teachers participated), and community involvement, bringing black and white parents together to talk about common problems and to air antagonisms.

The citizens' committee recommended in November 1963 that Berkeley adopt a policy of "color consciousness" and that "specific plans for integration be carried out."[35] Its own "specific plans" startled the city. They included limited elementary school redistricting and more radical shifts in the boundaries of the racially imbalanced junior high schools to produce a better racial mix, open enrollment, compensatory education efforts from kindergarten through high school, summer school to provide cultural enrichment, and an end to the elaborate secondary school tracking system.

The committee report thus linked pedagogical change and pupil reassignment. Public attention, however, focused on reassignment. Although the proponents of desegregation dominated heavily attended board meetings,[36] a poll conducted by the *Berkeley Gazette* found that four-fifths of the citizenry surveyed opposed the report's recommendations. Those meetings also produced suggestions for changes in the specifics of the redistricting plan. One proposal—to divide all of Berkeley's seventh and eighth graders between the two predominantly white junior high schools, while assigning all ninth graders to the flatlands school—seemed preferable to the committee's plan. With respect to the wisdom of redistricting, however, the board was reluctant to commit itself but instead turned the matter over to the administration to determine what was "educationally desirable and practically feasible."[37]

The staff report that Wennerberg brought to the board in May 1964 supported redistricting. Opponents of desegregation within the administration, sensing the view of both the superintendent and the board, did not lodge strong dissent. The report itself argued for desegregation at all levels, including school pairing at the primary level, largely on normative grounds. "It is morally right, basic to a democratic society, socially inevitable, and educationally sound." Berkeley had to act, not only to bring racial justice to one American town but also for symbolic reasons: "What we do, and the spirit in which we approach the problems of segregation in our schools, is important to the future of our country and of the world."[38] Berkeley was looking beyond its own circumstances to take into account national perceptions, and beyond the nation to the court of international opinion.

This was heady stuff for a community that just a few years earlier had counted on its "good Negroes" to calm any racial tempests that might arise.[39] In the main, the superintendent's argument persuaded the board. But the liberal school board was politically more cautious than the administration. Its concern with "feasibility" included taking into account the predictable political consequences of its actions. For that reason, the board decided to table indefinitely any plans for elementary desegregation. Board members hoped that limiting desegregation to the junior high schools would appease conservative opposition. They were far less confident that Berkeley was ready to embrace elementary desegregation and hence postponed that question. Eventual system-wide desegregation was, however, clearly possible. The board's decision to name Neil Sullivan, who previously had run a school system in Prince County, Virginia, for black children locked out of the public schools, to replace retiring Superintendent Wennerberg revealed to the observant that total desegregation was probably just a matter of time.

Conservatives thought otherwise. The Parents Association for Neighborhood Schools (PANS) sought and eventually obtained sufficient signatures to give voters the opportunity to recall the desegregation-minded board. Because two of the four liberals on the board were forced by circumstances to resign—one to accept a pulpit in the East, the other because of his appointment to a judgeship—the struggle was over two board seats.[40] Liberals—including the teachers' and students' organizations—believed they had grasped the reins of the future. The conservatives, led by the newly retired principal of the all-white elite junior high school, imagined they saw the sacrifice of the junior high schools for an untested social theory; abandonment of meritocratic tracking, which could only impede the ablest; and the ultimate subversion of the neighborhood schools. The conservative *Berkeley Gazette* made the recall cause its own. "The board is destroying a city to test a theory," stated a typical story.[41]

The liberals ultimately prevailed, by a larger margin than anticipated: 57 percent of the voters opposed the recall effort, in an election that drew a heavy turnout. Their triumph was repeated in spring 1965, when by a three-to-two margin the liberal slate defeated the PANS-endorsed candidates. With that, the dispute was largely won, at least in the political arena. The conservative faction did not strenuously attempt to reopen the issue of desegregation; for the most part, the remaining issues concerned when, not if, system-wide racial mixing would occur.

Neil Sullivan came to Berkeley in 1964 with an overriding mission: to bring about the complete desegregation of the schools and to move beyond racial mixing to an integrated educational system. In his first message to the staff, he called for "new directions toward schools worthy of imitation."[42] By doing itself proud, Berkeley would become a beacon district. By that metric, success conjoined instrumental change and symbolic message.

District-wide desegregation was some time off. Berkeley had first to get on with the task of revamping the junior high schools in the scant few months between board-decreed desegregation and the reassignment of students, and resolving a wide range of pedagogical problems in the primary schools.

The desegregation experience varied markedly between the junior high schools. The all-ninth-grade West Campus made the transition relatively painlessly, for there conditions for the change were right. A racially mixed group of teachers had taught together for some years; the principal provided stable leadership; and the flatlands community had strongly supported the change. Perhaps because the shared attitude was that the school was now "part of the whole city" and not a ghetto backwater, it fared far better than did Garfield, the formerly elite school. There, none of the preconditions for success existed. Teachers who had spent forty years providing what amounted to a private school education to Berkeley's best and brightest now found themselves facing students who were ill-prepared for serious academic work. They were decidedly unenthusiastic about the new task they faced. As Superintendent Sullivan wrote: "Gandhi himself could have learned some passive resistance techniques from some of the old-school teachers."[43] There was little administrative leadership to speak of. The principal was new, his predecessor having retired to campaign against desegregation, and unknown to the staff. Students of both races also contributed to the uneasiness. Reports Sullivan:

Some Negro boys and girls pushed and shoved and pulled hair, threatened and chased and shook down white youths for coveted possessions. White boys and girls tended to take out their hostility in caustic wounding words or in isolating themselves from classroom or social contact with their Negro fellow students.[44]

The Garfield school had undergone a social revolution. The transformation encompassed not only the color of the students, but also the very mission of the institution. Garfield knew how to instruct the most talented and highly motivated. It did not know what to make of a decidedly more heterogeneous student body. Nor did it receive much help from the school district, since by the mid-1960s even to air such issues was to risk the label "racist."

Discouragement with the consequences of introducing desegregation to students whose early experiences had been shaped in segregated schools led the school district to emphasize programs at the elementary level. Better preparing younger pupils for inter-racial education might make a difference, it was thought. Berkeley had sponsored experimental compensatory education programs in four predominantly black elementary schools since 1962. Pupils in those schools ranked in the lowest tenth percentile of achievement among California students (hill schools' pupils ranked in the upper tenth). With the aid of Ford Foundation money, the district reduced class size, developed new teaching materials, and provided tutor-ing.[45] It also created a sizable parent aid program by 1967; sixty-four parents participated in an effort that, whatever its other vir-tues, secured money and jobs for the black community. "You name it, we've tried it or are trying it," Superintendent Sullivan in-formed the U.S. Commission on Civil Rights in response to inqui-ries about Berkeley's efforts to expand educational opportunities for minorities.[46]

But to what avail? In 1965, fifth-grade pupils who had been exposed to the panoply of compensatory help demonstrated no higher achievement than had fifth graders enrolled at the same schools three years earlier. Nor had the gap in fifth-grade reading level between students in the black schools and those in the hills schools been reduced. "High hopes have reaped an insignificant harvest. . . . The mass of minority children remain in desperate iso-lation . . . destined to adult failure,"[47] Sullivan asserted.

The remedy, as the superintendent saw it, was desegregation. Although in 1964 desegregation at the elementary school level had been tabled indefinitely, this did not keep the district from testing the waters in 1966. After scrupulous preparation—"PTA meetings in black and white schools, joint meetings, inter-school meetings, workshops for teachers"[48]—Berkeley bused 238 students from the four black schools to schools in the hills. The program was not billed as a desegregation effort, but rather was said to relieve "overcrowding in ghetto schools." It was carefully managed to in-sure its success. Only students who were selected by the district and whose parents consented participated, and those students were sent only to schools whose PTAs gave their blessing to the venture. The hills schools remained overwhelmingly white, and thus could operate much as they always had. The pilot desegrega-tion experiment was generally regarded as a success. There was even modest improvement in achievement scores of black students assigned to the hills schools. This venture was not unique. Neigh-boring Oakland, a far more conservative community, had done much the same thing at the same time and with less fanfare. But to Sullivan, the Berkeley experiment was just a beginning. "This tokenism was a demonstration to speed up that day of [district-wide] integration."[49]

Berkeley citizens generally endorsed what was happening in their schools. In 1966, by a three-to-two margin, the voters approved a 50 percent hike in the tax rate. The campaign had emphasized "smaller class sizes, a librarian in every school, more books, reading specialists . . . tripling the High Potential Program and support for a science camp."[50] Berkeley, a district that ten years earlier had been one of the most frugal in the region, was now among the most lavishly endowed.

Between 1964 and 1966, the city of Berkeley became a hot-house germinating the new radical politics. Campus confrontations involving the Free Speech Movement and emergent opposition to American participation in the Vietnam War absorbed community energies and inevitably touched the school district. The schools generated their own brand of excitement. Despite—or perhaps because of—all its unresolved issues, Berkeley resembled a system that seemingly managed change without chaos and that could thus come to terms with what seemed an incipient revolution.

Superintendent Sullivan declared in the aftermath of the 1966 tax hike vote, "We could call it a vote for integration,"[51] and it seemed a propitious time to plan the desegregation of the primary schools. The opposition had to all appearances withdrawn after the failure of recall. Although antidesegregation candidates ran for the school board in 1967, the liberal incumbents trounced them by three-to-one margins. The superintendent took every opportunity to speak of the virtues of desegregation, and the board was consistently unanimous in its support. Divisions within the administration had largely healed, partly through adroit management and partly through the departure of the dissidents. Parents involved in the pilot busing effort were, in the main, pleased with the outcome. Yet neither the board nor the superintendent broached the subject until spring 1967, when for the third time in Berkeley's history a largely black community group demanded desegregation.

"Delay is the deadliest form of denial," a black parents group, the Committee on Quality Education, argued before the board in April 1967.[52] The board's response was wholly sympathetic. "We don't want anyone in this community to get the idea that this board . . . is at all satisfied, or even patient with the progress we have made," declared black board member Reverend Hazaiah Williams. "Our impatience is of the highest order."[53] Other board members voiced similar sentiments. Attaching specifics to the sentiments was more difficult.

System-wide desegregation was what was wanted, at least by Superintendent Sullivan, who pronounced open enrollment plans a "dismal failure" where they had been tried.[54] But immediate desegregation was out of the question. It was essential in the administration's judgment that a year be devoted to planning before the event, in order to guard against a repetition of the Garfield Junior High School experience. Without staff involvement in the particulars of desegregation, that school remained plagued with "high staff turnover and considerable student misconduct."[55] The board agreed, and voted to "affirm its general commitment to the principle of eliminating de facto segregation . . . within the context of quality education . . . not later than September 1968."[56]

Because Berkeley is a compact community with relatively few schools, the logistics of desegregation were comparatively simple. There were nonetheless serious questions to be sorted out. Some involved student assignment. What plan could achieve the greatest racial mixing with the least time spent on the school bus? Which children would spend what portion of their school lives attending school outside of the neighborhood? Others were essentially pedagogical. What should be the grade structure of the primary schools? How could special programs—Title I, ESEA, designed to aid the educationally disadvantaged, for example—be provided for a dispersed clientele? Crucial too was the political need to coopt those, especially teachers and parents, who would be involved in desegregation. The planning that was carried out kept each of those concerns in mind.

Teachers groups, PTA chapters, individuals: everyone was drawn into the act of planning.[57] The proffered proposals developed variations on two basic configurations: either maintaining kindergarten-through-grade-six (K-6) schools, altering existing boundaries and busing students to achieve balance; or establishing separate primary (K-3) and middle (4-6) schools, with all children being bused for half their schooling careers. The K-6 plan required less tinkering with student assignments, but since it involved more busing of blacks than whites and hence imposed what was thought to be an unfair burden on blacks, the superintendent preferred the K-3/4-6 plan. Because the youngest blacks were required to ride the buses under this arrangement, it could be said that this plan too treated blacks inequitably, but to that argument,

Berkeley had a pedagogically rooted rejoinder. The hill schools were smaller and hence provided a more intimate environment appropriate for the youngest students; the larger flatlands schools were better equipped to handle fourth through sixth graders.

Superintendent Sullivan's recommendation to the school board in October 1967, that the K-3/4-6 plan be adopted, flushed out the opposition forces in the school district. For one last time, they marshaled arguments against desegregation, but to each argument the district offered a strong rejoinder. Whites would flee Berkeley, the conservatives argued. Not so, countered the district, noting that between 1963, just prior to junior high school desegregation, and 1967 the proportion of whites had declined by only 4 percent (from 54 to 50 percent).

Academic standards will fall, the critics asserted. In response, the district could point to the 1966 tax increase as well as to the increasing availability of federal and foundation funding, which had enabled Berkeley to reduce class size, raise teacher salaries, and develop new special programs. One of the particularly attractive features of being the first sizable city voluntarily to undertake the task of desegregation was the eagerly awaited windfall of new money that would come to Berkeley. The anticipated half-million-dollar cost of desegregation in 1968–69 (a figure including a good many one-time expenditures, and hence expected to drop appreciably in succeeding years) would reap an anticipated $2.5 million in new money.[58] By doing good, Berkeley would be able to do very well for itself.

The citizenry is opposed to desegregation, the conservatives argued, calling attention to a petition signed by 2,800 parents urging a vote on elementary desegregation. The several school board elections in which antidesegregation candidates had been trounced, coupled with the tax increase, offered some evidence that the majority of the Berkeley citizenry in fact supported desegregation. The board, confident that it would prevail, asserted that head counting was inappropriate because the rightness of desegregation did not depend upon the views of the majority. The school board that had decided for political reasons not to desegregate the elementary schools in 1964 behaved by the beginning of 1968 as if such politics were irrelevant. "Boards of education are elected to make policy, not to conduct polls," said one board member.[59] The board unanimously approved the recommended plan for implementation the following September.

Opposition still simmered. In spring 1968, another recall campaign was threatened if the desegregation decision was not submitted to popular vote, but that threat went unfulfilled. For all practical purposes, the January 1968 action marked the end of the debate over whether to desegregate Berkeley's schools. The conservative *Berkeley Gazette*, which had vigorously opposed the "social engineers" who favored desegregation, editorialized: "It's time to bind up the wounds of dissension and pull together for implementation of the program elected officials and the school administration believe is best."[60] The fact that elected officials had reached a decision was apparently decisive. Unlike other cities, where political decision making seems only to escalate such disputes, in Berkeley the board's vote was accepted as conclusive. Also unlike other cities, which evaded the matter of desegregation entirely, thus removing it from the overtly political realm, because of fears of community unrest, Berkeley seized the day. What had transpired was an almost textbook-perfect triumph of pluralist politics.

Between January and September 1968, administrative and teaching staffs were deeply engaged in working out the details of desegregation.[61] Because Berkeley was first, it needed to invent all the transition strategies. At that, it succeeded splendidly. With "the world" perceived as watching, things had to go well—at least in the first days. Determining which students would attend which schools marked only the beginning of the undertaking. Because of the small size of the district, assignments could be planned with particular concerns in mind—neighborhood self-identity, street crossings, and the like—while still achieving a racial mix in each school of approximately 50 percent white, 40 percent black, and 10 percent "other" (mostly Asian) students.

In the semester preceding desegregation, teachers observed and taught at schools whose racial composition differed substantially from their own. When new teaching assignments (partly based on teacher preference) were determined, months before they would go into effect, meetings of the staff were organized. Curriculum revision was undertaken in the hope of addressing the substantial black-white reading gap. Students were involved through youth councils, day trips for all fifth graders, joint meetings between children who would be paired in flats and hills schools, and attempts to deal with racial concerns as they emerged within the classroom.

These efforts made the transition to a desegregated school system easier and served the commendable political purpose of uniting a diverse community behind the undertaking. What had begun under Superintendent Wennerberg in the early 1960s—the breaking down of barriers between school and community, the creation of new linkages between staff and citizenry—culminated under Sullivan, as Berkeley created a consensus concerning the rightness of desegregation specifically as well as generally.

That the first day of desegregation was carried off without a hitch, permitting Berkeley to become in fact the national symbol that it had long imagined itself to be, seems in retrospect an almost inevitable culmination of this process. How could it have been otherwise? Almost all of the forces shaping the Berkeley school system in 1968 pointed to success: the depth of moral commitment, the belief in pedagogical benefits of desegregation, the anticipation of financial reward and national attention that would accompany the occasion. The community had almost persuaded itself that it had nothing to lose and everything to gain from its own transformation.

Berkeley's experience since 1968 has been far less heady. Many factors combine to explain that change, including concern about diminishing resources, new ideological agendas, the splintering of the liberal coalition, and an administration with a different sense of the district's future. The unity of purpose that made desegregation possible splintered, and in that process the district lost a sense of direction. These changes did not occur overnight. If one reexamines the period preceding desegregation, trace elements of the disrupting factors can be detected. Berkeley's difficulties before and especially since 1968 tell a complicated and critically important story about the fragility of the liberal idea of racial justice.

IV

The aspiration genuinely to integrate Berkeley's schools ceased to enjoy pride of place on the agenda of the school system some time after 1968. This transformation was due in part to a changing ideological climate, which affected not only Berkeley but the nation as well. As black school board member Hazaiah Williams bluntly stated: "Martin Luther King's dream is dead."[62] But Berkeley was not the passive victim of circumstance. It determined its own fate.

Several aspirations supplanted integration, among them the hope of limitless educational choice, the empowerment of the minority community, the assurance of financial stability, and the deliberate institutional destabilization of the district. At no time was the possibility of formally dismantling Berkeley's desegregation program aired, for that would have done violence to the symbol. Yet in attempting to do well by everyone, honoring all the aspirations at once, integration was effectively forgotten. Because of the immense demands that a change in institutional character as profound as integration creates, the sustained and imaginative attention of all participants in the enterprise is required for its achievement. If more than racial mixing is to occcur more has to be wanted, and that was not clearly the case in Berkeley.

Institutions as organizationally complex and as deeply imbedded in their political contexts as school systems do not transform themselves overnight. In Berkeley, one can trace uneasiness with integration to factors whose force within and without the school system had been slighted or overlooked in the process of constructing a consensus for desegregation.

Traditional pockets of opposition to racial mixing existed in Berkeley. The support of Berkeley's teachers, for example, was known to be tenuous. The teachers' organizations did embrace the desegregation plan, and teachers' responses to an attitude survey revealed that on the whole they were not resistant to desegregation. Yet individual teachers' strong interests in career advancement and working conditions produced grumblings over reassignments, the disruption of school facilities, stepped-up affirmative action, and in-service training, made compulsory in 1968. White parents were to all appearances acquiescent, but it was nonetheless feared that those who had opposed desegregation might move to the nearby suburbs or send their children to private schools.[63]

While these potential antagonists, familiar in all desegregation histories, counted for less in Berkeley than almost anywhere else in the country, other and subtler factors, of at least equal potential disruptive significance, were also at work. Returning to Berkeley from a national conference of black educators one month before the initiation of desegregation, one administrator was moved to wonder whether Berkeley's desegregation was the wave of the future or the last gasp of the past. The gradual erosion of the national liberal consensus on race and the emergence of black separatism were already noticeable in Berkeley. As Superintendent Sullivan recognized:

Berkeley is not an island, immune to militant black power to the south in Oakland, to the north in Richmond and west across the Bay in San Francisco. Black Power grows in Berkeley—in the black student union [at the University of California], the Black Muslims who seek to lead separate, superior Negro education, and the militant Black Panthers.[64]

The case for desegregation of Berkeley's schools had been placed on high moral ground. "We must integrate now, not because Negro achievement is helped, but because our survival depends on it."[65] But academic achievement remained the primary concern of the schools, and for that reason the substantial disparity between the performance of blacks and whites spelled potential trouble. Although school-by-school data were not revealed prior to desegregation, analysis of reading achievement in the elementary schools ranked Berkeley students well above the state-wide average.[66] That admirable record was traceable not to the performance of students in the middle ranges but to the exceptionally high scores achieved by the ablest students. Upper quartile first graders were six months ahead of the average California first grader; upper quartile sixth graders were a year and a half ahead of the state-wide average. At the opposite end of the academic spectrum, the school district reported, "our slower students are holding their own when compared with the slower students of the state." In that context, "slow" was a euphemism for "black." Would the achievement of these students improve dramatically with the advent of desegregation? The record of black tenth graders who by 1967 had spent their junior high school years in desegregated schools was discouraging. The relative performance of these students was no better than that of black sixth graders who had attended only segregated schools.

Berkeley focused on this gap when it concentrated its energies and its federal funds on the educationally disadvantaged, but the distressing results of those efforts only fueled the argument for desegregation. In the desegregated high school, black students who saw themselves as the have-nots of the institution were increasingly disruptive and disrespectful of the teaching staff. Their behavior prompted unhappy faculty to invite the California Teachers Association (CTA) to study the "verbal and physical abuse of teachers."[67] Something clearly had to be done. In spring 1968, Superintendent Sullivan, confronted with a critical CTA report, appointed a staff committee charged with "discovering the causes of growing tensions among students . . . and increasing alienation between students and staff."[68]

The staff committee was deluged by student complaints concerning the rigidity of the high school. Its specific recommendations reached into the grab bag of then-popular innovative ideas, including a "vital and relevant" curriculum, increased flexibility in scheduling, and student involvement in governance. Of greater moment was the general thrust of the committee report.[69] Minority students, it concluded, were alienated by the oppressive structure of the school, and required a curriculum more responsive to felt needs. This recommendation marked a subtle shift in Berkeley's thinking. Previously, the thrust had been to further integration by extending the same opportunities to all, as in undoing the rigid secondary school tracking system. The staff committee argued that racial equality could better be achieved by providing an array of opportunities to everyone, that integration could be achieved not by insisting on sameness but by fostering experimentation in the schools and by providing choice for students.

Although choice did not necessarily imply racial differentiation, race became a relevant criterion. The Black Students Union seized on this aspect of the staff report. In the fall of 1968, it demanded that culturally "appropriate" choices be offered, among them an expanded black studies curriculum, new black counselors, soul food in the cafeteria, and the firing of all "racist" teachers. Over the vigorous protests of some of the high school teachers, all the recommendations except that concerning racist teachers were approved. For their part, teachers were required to attend a sensitivity training course designed to expose them to minority cultures.[70] The call for a separate black school was a logical next step, had anyone in the district been thinking ahead at the time. The blacks' success energized other ethnic groups. One month later, the Brown Berets were urging the board to expand its bilingual program in order to accommodate the Latino population.

Minorities were not the only ones interested in widening the range of educational choices available in the high school.[71] A 1967 summer arts program at Berkeley High School, which linked the study of dance, drama, and art with student-initiated projects, blossomed two years later into Community High, a small, culture-oriented school-within-a-school, which became predominantly white. The old Continuation High School, historically a place to which students were banished to complete their formal schooling, was renamed East Campus in 1967 and transformed by a new principal and energetic staff into a mecca for alienated white and black students. Herb Kohl, whose work with students in Harlem had earned him something of a national reputation, opened Other Ways, an alternative school within the Berkeley school system, part happening and part genuine educational ferment. Like Community High, it appealed especially to whites, particularly in its early years.

Educational experimentation had aroused the interest of the school district by 1968. It seemed to represent innovation and thus was consistent with the district's self-image. As Superintendent Sullivan had observed, some time earlier: "We do not favor change for change's sake. However, . . . to stand still in the sixties is to fall behind. We must be ready to implement those innovations which careful study shows to be advantageous."[72] Experimentation also seemed one promising strategy to promote integration, as the East Campus experience indicated. That it might be inconsistent with integration was less fully appreciated.

Taken together, these factors—the disgruntlement among some white teachers and parents, the comparatively weak achievement record of blacks, the emergence of black militancy and white enthusiasm for alternatives to the common school experience—confirmed that the success of integration could not be taken for granted but rather required substantial work. "Nurturance" was needed, as Superintendent Sullivan subsequently said,[73] but Sullivan chose not to oversee that process. One day after school opened in 1968, the superintendent announced his resignation; he had been appointed Massachusetts' Commissioner of Education. "My job in Berkeley was done," Sullivan recalled. "And besides, I was ambitious."[74]

The board was in a turmoil. It had relied on Sullivan both for planning desegregation and for taking political leadership in reconciling the interests of the many small emergent factions in Berkeley. Board members believed that Sullivan's charisma was critical to the success of desegregation, and the special nature of his role as superintendent make this belief plausible. The superintendent had been encouraged by a united board to speak out, to take political and policy leadership in the community and the schools. Selection of a successor who could carry Sullivan's efforts to fruition was thus a particularly important decision. For that reason, the board looked beyond the capable administrative staff for an outsider of stature, who could "keep Berkeley together" while sustaining a grandeur of vision for Berkeley's schools.[75]

Sullivan's successor, Richard Foster, who had headed the nearby San Ramon district, was perceived by the board to be "a 'teacher's superintendent,' an innovator dedicated to integrated education and willing to work in unconventional ways to accomplish desirable educational ends."[76] Foster was appointed with a mandate to achieve "true integration," while also exploring "options for learning" in the school system.[77]

Things worked out differently, in good part because the new superintendent's unstated agenda was different. Foster was an experimenter, not an implementer. Experimentation made possible greater choices for students, provoked the radical systemic change that Foster thought necessary, and—not incidentally—enhanced the superintendent's own reputation, just as effectuating desegregation had enhanced the reputation of his predecessor. To be sure, no single individual can remake a school system. Foster was able to impose his agenda largely by capitalizing on the nascent forces resistant to the integrationist consensus. The effect of this new vision on the Berkeley schools was profound.

Desegregation in Berkeley embodied the triumph of the liberal vision of racial justice in the schools. Altough the busing plan was color-conscious in assigning students to secure racial balance, the ultimate goal was to render color irrelevant, to admit blacks and whites to full participation in the educational system as individuals and not as members of a class. With the nominal attainment of the vision, fissures began to appear in the broad coalition supporting desegregation. The liberal ideology that had informed the desegregation movement could not provide adequate philosophical support for the agendas of emerging radical white and militant black groups. The former wanted educational alternatives, new institutional structures. The latter sought to create black enclaves that would provide both opportunities for "strategic withdrawal"[78] on the part of students who would be resegregated by choice and new positions for black professionals who were, by and large, hostile to the ideal of integration.

These ideas were not wholly new to Berkeley. What was new was the enthusiasm with which they were embraced by the central administration. A district that had previously adhered to an understanding of the necessity of change linked to "careful study" and subordinated reform to the ultimate goal of integration now became a place that, as school board member Louise Stoll stated, provided "instant gratification of everyone's wishes."[79] From a means, experimentation was converted into an end. Rather than attempting to develop support for a common educational mission, the effectuation of integration, the school system placated diverse groups by providing each of them with what they wanted.

This regime collapsed by 1974. The organizational structure of the school system could not stand the strain of near-constant change. Radical whites and militant blacks found that they had not achieved what they sought. Eventually, the realities of budgetary constraints, overlooked in the heady years following desegregation, forcibly turned the district's attention to its own survival. In the meantime the liberal ideal of integration was almost forgotten.

The transformation of Berkeley in the late 1960s involved a host of factors, including the agenda of Superintendent Foster, the emerging black consciousness, divisions within the school board, the influence of such external issues as the Vietnam War, and the politics of jobs. The multiplicity of relevant factors, and the inter-relationships among them, make this history especially difficult to recount. Of central importance to the transformation was the stress on experimentation, culminating with the Experimental Schools Project (ESP). Although that program drew partly on familiar ideas, it also brought new money, a new organizational framework, and a new agenda to Berkeley; it is an appropriate starting point for assessing post-1968 events.

"Creat[ing] options for learning" had been one of the charges given by the board to Richard Foster when he assumed the superintendency in 1969. From the outset this objective was treated as of central importance, dwarfing integration. "Schools-within-schools" became the theme at Berkeley High School. Community High, the arts school that had started as a summer institute, was installed as an alternative to the regular high school. Within two years, several other subschools, variously stressing Third World culture and history and skills acquisition, were flourishing, supported in part by a grant from the Ford Foundation.

Similar experiments were occurring at other grade levels. One middle school operated an "environmental studies" program designed to get students to explore the community; another was open, unstructured and ungraded. An entire primary school was divided into three subschools—one stressing multicultural instruction, the second adhering to a traditional approach, the third adopting an individualized learning style—to appeal to a range of interests. A new junior high school was opened by parents and teachers concerned about the impersonality of the existing institutions and eager to offer a more intimate alternative. By 1971, ten alternatives, covering kindergarten through high school, had been set up and were vying for students.[80]

Enrollment in the alternative schools was based not on assignment, as in the regular schools, but on choice. For those concerned about maintaining racial balance as a prerequisite for integration, this proved troubling. Some of the new schools achieved a racial mix. That was not, however, the case in Community High.[81] Despite the school's diligent efforts to recruit blacks, it acquired a reputation as a haven for upper-class white hippies. Blacks who did enroll in Community High found themselves disaffected, intimidated by the verbal quickness of the professors' children. Led by a black teacher, they retreated to a black "tribe" within the school. When even that arrangement seemed too confining, they petitioned the school board for approval of a separate institution, Black House.

The rationale for Black House embodied a frontal attack on the premises of integration. The mere mixing of black and white students, it was said, was not only insufficient but in some cases actually hindered blacks' educational opportunities. What was called for, black board member Reverend Hazaiah Williams vehemently argued, was a "strategic disengagement"—the military metaphor suggesting that blacks lived in a constant state of war with the larger society. Some black students needed isolation in a supportive environment in which they could learn about their own cultural heritage and work on mastering basic academic skills. That isolation would be only temporary, for after blacks acquired rudimentary psychological and intellectual self-confidence, they would be better equipped to participate as equals in integrated classrooms. Black House, as its founder said, would serve as a "fort to strengthen and endow black youth mentally and morally." [82]

Superintendent Foster supported the Black House proposal. It was compatible with his belief that experimentation was critical to the solution of the problems of urban education and consistent with his paramount concern for black students. Shortly after becoming superintendent, Foster had stated that he was chiefly interested in discovering "what wipes out black kids in our school system." The frustrations attendant on desegregation represented one possible answer. More pragmatically, Foster realized that the only way he could build black support for his emerging program of widespread experimentation was by supporting in turn any experimental efforts proposed by blacks.

The school board's reaction was less enthusiastic. With great moral fanfare, Berkeley had just desegregated its schools. Was not segregation wrongheaded, whether voluntarily pursued or imposed? Board member Sam Markowitz derided the idea as a "throwback." [83] Carol Sibley recalls that "the Board's first reaction to this new and in some ways 'dangerous' concept ['separatism' again] was mixed, as was the reaction of the black community— some giving it all-out support, some feeling strongly that it was a reversal of all it had been struggling for." [84] Despite these concerns, Black House received unanimous approval. Board members advanced a number of reasons for their decision. [85] The school would be small, enrolling no more than one hundred students. It was a temporary response to the plight of students who had thus far experienced only a segregated education. It was supported by the superintendent, to whom the board continued to look for leadership, and by the board's one black member, who presumably spoke for the concerns of his constituency. Most important, racial separation could be seen as a "reasonable experiment."

It is difficult to see how at the time the board could have done anything but endorse the Black House experiment. Approval had, after all, been given to other experiments that appealed more to white students than to black students; that Black House was expressly limited to blacks seemed a distinction without a difference. This fact reveals how unselfconsciously and how far the school district had moved from its unequivocal support of integration. Reverend Williams made it clear that approval of Black House betokened a perception of racial justice different from that animating the 1968 desegregation efforts. "The old civil rights mentality died about the same time that Martin Luther King died . . . the dream did die."[86]

By early 1971, Berkeley's first financial crisis—a projected deficit of $2.6 million—threatened to curb further experiments. At just that moment the Office of Education providentially announced its intention to support districts interested in producing "comprehensive experimental change."[87] The new federal program was tailor-made for Berkeley's ambitions. Never mind that system-wide integration might be thought change enough to preoccupy the district for the decade. Berkeley could demonstrate its proclivity for continuing innovation by pointing to the alternative schools already in existence, and the superintendent had demonstrated his talent for fostering creativity. The Office of Education was readily persuaded that Berkeley desired yet again to refashion its schools.

There were some who worried about the long-term effects of sizable federal support on Berkeley's fiscal stability, but they were a tiny minority. As board member Carol Sibley wrote: "Berkeley had demonstrated its willingness to try new ways . . . citizen pressure for long overdue changes in school approaches . . . produced a commitment on the part of the district to educate *all* of its children."[88] The ESP would presumably make realization of that commitment possible. To Superintendent Foster, the ESP grant came as a godsend. It was the vehicle for revolutionizing the school system. Using language reminiscent of Professor Harold Hill in "The Music Man," he commented: "I sell alternative schools as one of a half dozen strategies to change a system. Just providing alternatives for kids is not where my head is."[89] Foster subsequently expanded on the point:

In a sense, every system wants to become entropic rather than changing. It wants to go back because everybody's comfortable that way. You've got to think of experimental money to prevent the system from dying. . . . It wants to atrophy. The amoeba wants to go back to its original position . . . of no motion. . . . You've got to create motion. That motion has to come out of experimental money.[90]

Seemingly overnight, the ESP proposal was put together.[91] "The gold rush was on," commented board member Mary Jane Johnson.[92] Some of the alternative schools were already operating or scheduled to open in the fall; others had long been thought through; still others were on-the-spot inventions, responses to administrative dictates that an experimental school be instantly conjured up. In retrospect, even Superintendent Foster felt that the schools should have been clearer in their aspirations.[93] Once set in motion, however, Berkeley's funding proposal acquired its own dynamic. Gone was the stress on community participation that had characterized the Sullivan era. In the press of events, the creation of new ideas was more the product of administrative fiat than joint community-professional planning. Schools were invented to satisfy Washington guidelines, which called for a range of schools covering all grade levels, not to satisfy community needs.

The alternatives that survived administrative screening promised to undo all the perceived evils of the day: systemic racism, undemocratic organization, incapacity to teach basic literacy and arithmetic, and failure to involve parents in the instructional enterprise. Choice was the key. As the proposal's writers put it: "The richest life is filled with choices."[94] What any of this meant was decidedly unclear. As an outside evaluation of the ESP program in Berkeley noted:

The problems were racism, class bias, bureaucracy, and the prevalent failure of the schools to educate. The solution is options. It is difficult to perceive the efficacious correlation between the problems, which seem so complex, and the solutions, which seem disarmingly simple. Unless, that is, the options were posed as follows: we will give you a choice between racist and non-racist schools, between class-biased and non-class-biased schools, between bureaucratic and non-bureaucratic schools, between schools that do not educate and schools that do. Then, presumably, the overwhelming majority of parents and children would, in their wisdom, choose all the second alternatives in that series, and the racist, class-biased, bureaucratic, and non-educative schools would shrivel away. That our scenario is, on the face of it, sheer fantasy already indicates the problem of options as the solution.[95]

No questions were asked by a school board that did little more than rubber-stamp the administration's plan. Berkeley was awarded $6.1 million over a five-year period, extending to 1976.[96] While that grant represented only 3.7 percent of the school district's total income and less than one-quarter of all federal funds allocated to the district during those years, the significance of ESP was far greater. As many as 30 percent of all Berkeley students were enrolled in ESP programs and much of the district's energy was concentrated on them. The ESP did produce the "motion" that Foster sought. It also confirmed the fact that experimentation, not integration, had become the district's primary concern. The two goals were to prove irreconcilable.

Many of the ESP schools that received approval appealed to two distinct groups, white hippies and racial minorities. In the common schools, these students were mixed. Not so in ESP, as the evaluators reported: "Within [the ESP], there is a dual tracking system for the 'new, hippy youth' who choose highly diverse options, and another tracking system for 'turned off' minority students who are referred to remedial schools for work in basic skills, or for ethnic awareness within a framework of 'survival skills.'"[97] Several of these schools, among them Black House and Casa de la Raza, a school designed for Chicano students, were explicitly racial in orientation. As the director of Black House said in response to a question posed by the Senate Select Committee on Equal Educational Opportunity: "The qualifications [for admission to Black House] are that the students must be black."[98] Others appealed covertly to the same ethnic groups through references to "cultural heritage," "basic survival skills," and the like. Schools that focused their energies on high-potential students or on the creative arts attracted an overwhelmingly white clientele, even when special efforts were made to recruit minorities.

It is easy to understand why this situation occurred. A journalist who visited Community High (rechristened Genesis) wrote:

Far out. The high school . . . for white freaks. (There was not a black face in the Genesis class I saw.) . . . Genesis seems perfectly typified by the white boy with long hair and a vest sitting in class barefoot balancing a red, white, and blue beachball on his toe. But the students were enthusiastic about classes . . . and not terribly worried about their exclusiveness. Several students explained that if blacks wanted to come to Genesis they could take a course on the black experience.[99]

The racial and ethnic separatism apparent on the face of the ESP proposal produced the first serious controversy over the program and the first marked division on the board in almost a decade.[100] Louise Stoll, a newly elected board member, posed the issue of racial isolation in the context of developing guidelines for the new program. Stoll was unhappy about Black House and Casa de la Raza, but felt it was too late to rescind their mandate. She urged that these schools be treated in the ESP guidelines as exceptions, not as models for other schools to emulate. Stoll's proposed guidelines called for the board to "reaffirm the existing policy of total integration of *all* Berkeley schools, including Experimental Schools," even as it acknowledged the "essential need" for the two controversial alternatives. Superintendent Foster countered with language that, while appearing innocuous, stripped the commitment to integration of any significance:

The Board reaffirms its policy of quality integration and acknowledges the ethnic diversity in the school population as a valuable condition and an educational resource. Further the Board endorses for the District an educational plan that reflects the needs of a pluralistic school community.

Around those guidelines, battle among board members and the superintendent raged. Foster spoke of integration as a flexible process, "and in that process it was going to be an ever-evolving thing. . . . What might facilitate the pluralism of the 1960s would not do in the seventies and eighties." Sam Markowitz, a board member who had actively promoted desegregation, found this position troubling. "It may be that we're just rationalizing a type of change, by using 'times have changed' as a rationalization. As someone who believes in integrated schools, I want to know why suddenly the principle is not openly good." Stoll was even more abrupt: "The trend in the proposed experimental schools divides students by race. Not by kind of education, not by approach to education, not by how we will teach reading or writing or arithmetic, but clearly and simply a division by race. . . . It's Orwellian to say that we integrate by separating."

The rejoinders offered by Superintendent Foster and board member Hazaiah Williams were equally blunt in minimizing, even denigrating, what had been accomplished in the name of racial mixing. Said Foster, "Berkeley, as every city that moves into desegregation, just put its feet into the water." Williams referred to desegregation as the "preliminary integration schema," whose value was "to allow us to see, for the first time, the inside workings of the racist system." To him, Black House was not an exceptional case. "For you to define me as an exception is a racist response to me. . . . You whites have always owned the power to make that kind of determination over us. We are now saying that we have come of age."

The board was unable to write guidelines concerning race policy, but the subject did not disappear from its agenda. At the very next meeting, the director of Casa de la Raza, angry at the board for allegedly not providing sufficient staff positions for his school, introduced a new and troubling element into the equation.[101] "Is it going to take the whole Berkeley Chicano community to come up here and burn this goddamn building down, for you people to respond?" That attack gave Reverend Williams a chance to push the board still further. He walked out of the meeting to "see if we can organize the black and Chicano communities to come in here and tell you this kind of irresponsible stuff has got to stop." The board eventually approved the additional staff for Casa and one week later authorized another alternative school designed for Asians. Berkeley's rejection of integration as an overriding policy goal, apparent in actions that the district had taken, had become a matter of public record.

Throughout its five-year existence, ESP continued to be dogged by questions of race. The racial exclusivity of Black House and Casa de la Raza, duly reported to the Senate Select Committee on Equal Educational Opportunity in 1971, aroused the interest of Arkansas Senator John McClellan, who wondered whether the "new ground rules for resegregation" should not be "made known to the entire American public."[102] As in the years preceding desegregation, Berkeley acquired a national reputation, but this time the circumstances were altogether less happy. Protracted negotiations between the Office of Civil Rights (OCR) and the district followed McClellan's query. Two years after the question had first been aired, in June 1973, OCR finally concluded that the two schools' policy of racial exclusivity violated Title VI of the 1964 Civil Rights Act. OCR took the occasion to make new civil rights policy: "No student may be permitted to attend a one-race or racially-isolated class for greater than twenty-five percent of any school day." With that determination—and the threat that, if the schools were not shut down, the school district would lose the balance of its ESP grant—Berkeley capitulated. Black House and Casa de la Raza quietly disappeared, their students and staff absorbed for the most part into other ethnically identifiable schools.

Student enrollment in ESP schools continued to divide generally along racial lines, particularly in the secondary programs. Schools that appealed especially to whites felt obliged to broaden their appeal in order to attract minorities. In so doing, they often lost the distinctiveness that had made them genuine alternatives in the first place. Community High became a second-rate institution. Herb Kohl's Other Ways "evolved" into Marcus Garvey Institute, a black school, and that in turn became U.N. West when, as the site director reported, "Superintendent Foster told us to change from black to multi-cultural." The ESP director characterized U.N. West's faculty as "thugs off the streets who acted as pseudo-militants."[103] An outside evaluation noted one effect of these pressures. Only one-quarter of the ESP schools were found to be "diverse" or innovative in curriculum, teaching styles, or structures.[104] Schools oriented toward nonwhites felt no compunction to desegregate and remained predominantly nonwhite in enrollment. Taken as a whole, ESP existed as a parallel and largely segregated school system within the Berkeley schools, too sizable to be merely an anomaly in a district whose common schools continued to adhere to the goal of integration.

The ESP program also became a vehicle for substantially increasing the number of black teachers in the school system. ESP schools—funded with "soft money, unconstrained credentialling requirements, encouraged by Foster to be innovative in their hiring practices"—took the opportunity to hire minorities on an overtly racial basis.[105] Foster saw this commitment to affirmative action as vital if racial parity within the system was to be achieved. The district as a whole had for some years diligently recruited nonwhites. Between 1968 and 1972, the proportion of nonwhite professionals had increased from less than one-quarter to almost 40 percent. Because the faculty was growing, this nearly doubled the minority professional complement. The minority proportion was far higher in the ESP program. More than two-thirds of ESP professionals were nonwhite, even though ESP schools had been directed to look first within the common schools for new recruits.[106] ESP not only gave black students their own schools but also served as an important source of patronage for their elders.

Because of the number of students that it enrolled, the number of professionals that it hired, and the amount of district attention that it commanded, ESP affected race policy in many ways. From ideological politics to patronage politics, nothing having to do with race went untouched by ESP. The evolving racial consciousness of which Superintendent Foster had spoken also directly affected the common schools.

"White racism is essentially responsible for the explosive mixture which has been accumulating in our cities since the end of World War II."[107] That sweeping diagnosis of America's racial maladies, offered by the Kerner Commission to explain the race riots of the 1960s, was enthusiastically embraced by Berkeley as describing not only the nation but also Berkeley itself. By inculcating middle-class values, the school district asserted, "education has fulfilled the expectations of racist society and has become itself a racist institution," and the "structural organization of the school system . . . provides a major overt example of institutional racism." Even the common school was said to be "outmoded," because it "reflects historic tendencies toward racism in American culture."[108] Every issue was redefined in racial terms. As board member Sam Markowitz remarked: "This district is obsessed with race and racism: it's the prime factor in every decision."[109]

The asserted ubiquity of white racism made white liberals in Berkeley hesitant to speak out against any black point of view, even to resist the antiwhite sentiments and the physical abuse of whites that was widespread at the time, since to do so was to risk being called a white racist. For their part, blacks, unprepared for the demands placed upon them, were pushed into positions of leadership, caught up by national tides of minority assertiveness. That some would overplay their hand seems, in retrospect, inevitable. As a result of the understandable failures of blacks and white liberals, reverse racism became a killing weed in the integrationist garden.

The intent of the school board was, of course, far different. Consider, for example, the black studies program, inaugurated at almost precisely the same time as desegregation.[110] Proponents argued that courses in black history, culture, and literature would strengthen black students' self-image, and would thus provide them with the psychological resources to improve academic performance. They also asserted that black studies courses would afford whites the chance to enrich their understanding of blacks, helping more firmly to link the races. The case for black studies in Berkeley was clear enough. Indeed, it is hard to imagine how a school district could offer a meaningful integrated education without paying some attention to the cultures of minority students. Yet what happened differed from what was intended. Having decided that something should be done about black studies, the district lacked a sense of what the job involved. The school administration, unprepared to heed the advice of its veteran black teachers, who had been reared on a literary diet of Frederick Douglass and W. E. B. DuBois, relied instead on younger and more militant blacks, who presumably brought a more "relevant" perspective to the task. These teachers were given free rein to develop and export the black studies curriculum.

The results of this venture might be comical, if one had both a sense of humor and some perspective. The new curriculum was often ungrammatical and inaccurate to the point of outlandishness (one tale referred to Christopher Columbus as getting permission "to exploit the underdeveloped lands" from "the King of Europe"; another described the founding fathers as "nearly all slave-holders"). It also repeated itself from grade to grade. "Who's this Crispus Attucks that keeps getting killed off every semester?" ran one joke.

Frequently, though, the work of the black studies teachers was decidedly unfunny. The program meant different things from school to school, but reverse racism—or at least insensitivity—was widely apparent. The orientation at the high school was divisive and antiwhite; horror stories about "what the man has done to us," not analysis, predominated.[111] At some of the lower schools, a resilient faculty functioned as a counterforce to black studies extremism. Elsewhere, however, the impact of black studies was disturbing, nowhere more so than at the 4-6 Longfellow School.

Longfellow's principal received the backing of Superintendent Foster and board member Hazaiah Williams in the "blackening" of the school's curriculum. His declared intention was to eliminate, within two years, "the racial achievement disparity that exists between Black, Asian, and White students." The prescription was breathtakingly simple:

What we have here is a curriculum designed for the middle class white child, shaped to his mode, manner and style of living, his background and his history. A program that has parity is one that says to black kids too: "You're part of this system." Until blackness is brought into the instructional program, black kids are not part of the system.

Curricular "parity" would involve black studies courses, taught by blacks with the requisite "sophistication and commitment to the program."[112]

Berkeley liberals might find that formulation improbable but not objectionable. In operation, however, black studies at Longfellow degenerated into an antiwhite venture, affecting both teachers—who were pressured to hold racially separate staff meetings—and, especially, students. One teacher informed his fourth-grade class that whites had invented birth control to further their genocidal plans for the black race. Another ordered all "dumb blondes" out of her class in order to show white children how it felt to be the object of thoughtless discrimination. Blacks were encouraged to write "hate whitey" essays, which were posted on the school's bulletin board.

"Kill whitey" appeared on more than one white teacher's blackboard. In a 1971 assembly observing Martin Luther King's birthday, a local junior college drama class presented a play concerning the coming black revolution. Actors depicting black revolutionaries screamed "kill the pigs," "kill whitey," and "kill your mother." The final scene of the play depicted the hero of the drama embracing the revolutionary spirit, killing his Aunt Jemimah mother, who insisted on working as a domestic.[113]

Some white parents vainly protested this treatment. Black studies teachers would not permit them to visit their classrooms. Principals pleaded powerlessness. One board member reported that black studies was still an experimental venture; if some whites suffered in the interim, that was regrettable but unavoidable. Superintendent Foster said: "We will make more mistakes in delivering skills to minorities . . . we can only try not to make the [same] mistake again." Concern about "racism" precluded any other response. As board member Louise Stoll stated: "Many white parents who were dedicated workers felt that their children now were being discriminated against in an ugly way. And they protested it. And we didn't do anything about it because we were afraid that we might possibly be called by that nasty word, racist."[114]

Liberal uncertainty kept the school board from responding strongly to other antiwhite gestures, both symbolic and tangible. When in July 1972 the principal of the Lincoln School urged that its name be changed to Malcolm X School, the board approved the suggestion over the objection of those who thought that singling out the Lincoln School—rather than, say, Cragmont—was gratuitously insulting. The name change, the principal declared, "will produce an esprit de corps." Said board member Stoll, "renaming the school does not necessarily denigrate its former name," although it was unclear what other construction could be put on the action. Superintendent Foster added: "Maybe we should change the names of schools every three, four, five or ten years."[115]

Six months later, the board had the more serious issue of violence in the schools on its hands. The mere two-day suspension of students who brutally beat a high school mathematics teacher aroused widespread ire, particularly because this was not a unique episode. The high school principal reported that violence in the school was increasing. The PTA demanded an inquiry, but the board did not know how to respond. Because the violence had primarily been perpetrated by blacks, any policy concerning violence in the schools could be seen as an antiblack policy; discipline itself had become racist. A month later, the board merely reiterated existing policy, called for parent volunteers (rather than police) to help enforce it, and retired from the fray.[116]

Under other circumstances, teachers who had struggled for desegregation could have been expected to introduce a healthily critical perspective on these issues, because black studies was undermining desegregation. Although to some extent this did occur, teachers—especially white teachers—felt decidedly on the defensive by the early 1970s. They distrusted the superintendent because he belittled their ability. They were disappointed with a school board, itself apparently the captive of current political fashion, whose notion of democratization in the schools involved opening faculty toilets to students, and whose ideological fixations led it to require teachers to lecture on the evils of the Vietnam War.[117]

Berkeley had become a deeply riven district. Race, the issue with which it was "obsessed," was the chief but by no means the exclusive source of divisiveness. Superintendent Foster had hoped that the ESP would help reform the traditional bureaucracy, but instead that program was uncomfortably lodged within the existing structure, arousing the jealousies of the common schools and a sense of powerlessness and fragmentation within the alternatives themselves.[118] The flexibility that the superintendent promised— "My door is open to everyone"—now seemed a mask for manipulation and favoritism, particularly when racially differentiated treatment of black and white administrators came to light. Foster's inconsistent behavior, once taken as the sign of a man impatient of bureaucratic rigidity, increasingly engendered distrust among teachers; in a 1972 poll, more than 90 percent of the teachers declared their lack of confidence in the superintendent. Early in his term, the superintendent talked almost mystically about the future of schooling; later on his favorite phrase became "I never promised you a rose garden."

The board was divided between the majority, led by Hazaiah Williams and supporting Superintendent Foster, and a vocal minority, critical of Williams' black power stance and uneasy about the reemergence of racism under that "skilled weathervane," Foster.[119] ("Whatever happened to you?" Louise Stoll once asked Williams. "We used to look to you for guidance.") In April 1972, with two years to go on his contract and in the midst of unremitting discord, the superintendent publicly "resigned," only to stay on at the behest of the majority. Reverend Williams assailed Foster's two board opponents as white racists who had "eroded the leadership image of a district that . . . has tried . . . to deliver significantly to blacks," and declared that Foster's precipitate departure would "turn back the clock."[120] Although Foster did not leave until the end of his term, his gesture only confirmed the split on the board and in the community.

V

Money had built the Foster administration: money spent in the service of nominally pluralistic ideology and less intangibly to guarantee power and jobs for militant blacks and radical whites. Money was to produce "motion," as Foster put it. As long as outside money flowed into Berkeley, this strategy of supporting seemingly everyone could work. As Foster described his approach: "I understand the concept [of priorities]. It wasn't a concept we worked on. I worked on the other approach: if it's a good idea, where's the place to market it. I don't think we ought to be the one that places internal proposals against each other; our job is to see if we can get them funded."[121]

Only when the money stopped coming did the real cost of Superintendent Foster's approach become apparent. In spring 1975, less than a year after Foster's departure, Berkeley discovered that it was literally bankrupt, more than three million dollars in debt. Suddenly, Berkeley was the New York City of school districts. That circumstance forcibly turned the district away from experimentation to the harsh reality of maneuvering for survival. In the process, Berkeley schools have become far more conventional and mundane, far less "worthy of imitation" than either Neil Sullivan or Richard Foster had envisioned. They have also begun again to confront the delicate issues of integration.

In the heady years following desegregation, budgetary matters were not of particular concern. Berkeley believed that good works, first integration and later experimentation, would attract money like a magnet. Worrying about financial matters would only drain energy needed in the service of innovation. "Fiscal concern was not an issue at that time," said the then business manager of the district. "The big push was to develop new ideas and the idea was that someone would find the dollars somehow."[122]

Money was in apparent abundance during the period. Per pupil expenditures more than doubled between 1967 and 1974, placing Berkeley at the highest level in California. Berkeley residents paid for this munificance by imposing on themselves the stiffest school tax rate in the state, but even as early as 1970 it was clear that local money alone would be insufficient. The district's salary account was overdrawn by $850,000, and a payroll had to be "slipped" into the following year. By the beginning of 1971, Berkeley was facing its first fiscal crisis, an anticipated $2.6 million deficit. In that context, "the [$6.1 million of ESP] grant money arrived in time to bail the school district out of a sticky financial situation."[123]

From the outset some recognized that this short-term rescue might well have disastrous long-term financial consequences. The chairman of the Citizens' Budget and Finance Committee went before the school board in April 1971, urging it not to rush into the new federal program.

If the board approves the proposal, it will be making a major policy commitment and programmatic decision binding the new board members and covering the five year duration of the grant. Approval of the proposal will represent the high water mark in a sustained pattern of nonmanagement and nonplanning, which seems to characterize the Berkeley schools' top administration.[124]

The board did not heed the warning. Only later did it learn that, as an accountant hired to sort out the fiscal mess commented, "grants cost money."[125]

Much of the ESP money went to hire staff to teach in the alternative schools. Because state law forbade Berkeley from employing professionals on a temporary basis, more than one hundred new employees acquired tenure after spending three years in Berkeley. When the grant lapsed, these professionals had somehow to be absorbed into the regular system. What they would do was far from clear. By 1974–75, fully half of the district's certificated employees were out of the classroom, acting as skills specialists, curriculum writers, and assorted other things. "What does a school district do with 20 'videotape experts' when the grant for 'videotaping for evaluation' runs out and the people are tenured?"[126] Business practices in the district grew lax. When the assistant superintendent complained, he was removed from supervising the process, and the business manager reported directly to Superintendent Foster.

By the time the ESP grant ran out, new federal moneys were not so readily available. Had Berkeley been able to continue raising its tax rate, it might well have honored its commitments, but the passage of a state school finance reform act in 1973 linked revenue to enrollment and placed a ceiling on the number of dollars that could be raised for each student. Berkeley was a high-spending, high-taxing school district with a declining enrollment, and its revenue-raising capacity could not keep pace with its operational costs. The school board compounded the problem by using general revenues to replace departing staff in order to fill "critical" classroom vacancies, producing a budget that was scored for being "mindless." As board member Louise Stoll summarized the problem: "The combination of hiring permanent personnel with soft money, declining federal grants, new state funding laws and declining enrollment, inflation, and unforgivable business practices, led—quite predictably—to an incredible financial crunch." [127]

Foster saw things differently. "There was money to be had in Washington, but the board restraints limited my ability to get it." [128] A California Department of Education management team had informed Berkeley of impending disaster at the outset of 1974, but the board majority ignored the warning. Laval Wilson, who succeeded Foster as superintendent in 1974, was instructed by the board to straighten out the financial situation—by then an impossible task. One year later, disaster arrived. Berkeley's budgetary deficit, first estimated at $800,000, grew during the spring to $1.5 million. In June 1975, an embarrassed business manager who confessed to "overoptimism" about revenues predicted that the actual deficit would run between $2.5 and $3.5 million. The latter figure amounted to 10 percent of the district's entire budget.

What was to be done? The district's calculations were by now so widely distrusted that a Citizens' Fiscal Analysis Committee was appointed and given free rein to review the books. Its conclusion confirmed the existence of a deficit at least as large as had been projected. "In blunt terms," the committee concluded, "the district is both technically bankrupt and in violation of law." [129] That finding finally forced the board, which had grown more attentive to budgetary matters with the resignation of Hazaiah Williams and the election of a fiscally more conservative member, to take drastic action. Unable because of state law to lay off personnel without six months' notice and legally required to produce a balanced budget, the board resorted to every financial gimmick in the books, but was still obliged to trim salaries and benefits and to relax class-size limits. This action provoked a prolonged strike in fall 1975 and substantial community bitterness, directed first against a school board that had let this unhappy circumstance come to pass and then against the teachers, when the strike dragged on for five weeks. [130]

Beginning with the 1975 strike, Berkeley abandoned its pretensions to greatness through extravagance. Robert Frost's question "What to make of a diminished thing?" has become the district's guiding concern. The selection of Laval Wilson, a black administrator with a reputation for industry and a concern for curriculum reform within the context of a desegregated system, as superintendent confirmed the end of radical dominance over Berkeley's school affairs. This transformation was due in part to the contrasting styles and viewpoints of Foster and Wilson. Foster believed in limitless innovation; Wilson felt that Berkeley should "try to make sense of all these things we've got going."[131] Foster was a politician; Wilson was straightforward, occasionally politically inept. Foster's administrative structure defied the best efforts of organization-chart makers; under Wilson, the administration was rebureaucratized. Foster distrusted research and data gathering, preferring to innovate willy-nilly; Wilson devoted a substantial portion of his energies to collecting baseline data on all manner of district activities. Foster described himself as "assertive, not aggressive; enabling; unwilling to be had by any faction; someone who enjoys being his own person, who understands change, and creativity." Wilson's self-description focused on his capacities as a manager.[132]

Berkeley's transformation was also in good measure the inevitable concomitant of financial reality. The 1975 budget measures did not solve the district's problems but merely provided a year's grace. In 1976, faced with a persisting deficit, Berkeley hired no new personnel and laid off eighty-two professional employees. This pattern has continued: in 1978, some fifty more professionals were dismissed for budgetary reasons. A sizable number of nonprofessional staff has also been discharged. The certified staff, which numbered almost twelve hundred at one point, had been cut by more than four hundred in 1979.

The layoff process confirmed the nexus between racial ideology and racial patronage in Berkeley. In 1971, on the eve of the first financial crisis, Hazaiah Williams persuaded the school board not to fire teachers on the basis of seniority. "If we fire only nontenured teachers we wipe out all the gains in minority hiring made during the last two years," he said. Those gains afforded a significant source of power and patronage for the black community. Maintaining a substantial proportion of nonwhite professionals was also held to benefit minority students. "Our primary task at this hour is to deliver the basic skills for black and Chicano students,"[133] stated Williams, who, together with the superintendent and the board majority, assumed that task could be achieved best by nonwhite, and presumably more empathetic, teachers.

The board's position flouted the law, which mandates that seniority rights be respected when reducing staff. When Berkeley actually had to issue layoff notices in 1976, 70 percent went to nonwhite staff hired during the preceding few years. Those who supported the cutbacks as the only feasible measure open to the district were publicly attacked as racist pigs. Board member James Guthrie described the experience as "sitting in the trenches and absorbing the shells."[134] The first personnel cuts were made by a bitterly divided board. Over the years, however, the election of a new, fiscally minded board, coupled with the realization that to trim a school budget by some five million dollars in three years requires staff cutbacks, has brought a return of the consensus politics that prevailed before desegregation. More recent staff cuts were undertaken by a unanimous board. The board's concern for prudent management led it to vote against renewing Laval Wilson's contract, which expired in June 1980. "A lack of administrative skills," inefficiency in the business office and in data processing, and a refusal to substitute analysis for hunch were the factors cited by the board majority.[135]

Energies have been concentrated on shrinking the school district's scope and reducing its ambitions in order to keep the budget balanced. But race and schooling issues have not been ignored in the process: indeed, the district is more attentive to integrationist concerns now than under Foster. The firing of Wilson, as board member Melinda Robinson declared, "in no way diminishes our commitment to make integration work." Throughout the Foster era, the busing program remained intact. Even during the worst days of the financial crisis, no one proposed terminating it, even though ending busing would have made it possible for the district to avoid salary cuts. As board member James Guthrie declared: "Integration had become an article of such overpowering faith in Berkeley that it was inviolate."[136]

Busing alone would not produce integration: on that, the district had been clear from the outset. By the mid-1970s, black parents were asserting that basic reading and math skills, not cultural awareness, mattered most. The gap between black and white achievement in Berkeley had not been appreciably affected by busing or by the ESP, whose students performed indistinguishably from common school students. The district noted in 1973 that "the growth rate of black and Chicano students is below average, while that of whites and Asians is above.[137] Prior to desegregation, the average white student in the lowest quartile of whites was nevertheless reading at exactly the national norm, and that remained true after desegregation. In 1973, after six years of desegregated schooling, the black student in the highest quartile of Berkeley's black students was still below that norm.

Superintendent Wilson made basic skills acquisition the priority in Berkeley. Applying for Emergency School Assistance Act Funds in 1976, the district noted the "isolation expressed in the distance in academic achievement between white vs. nonwhite students. This academic isolation gives rise to and is aggravated by . . . separatism in the classroom and on the playground."[138] The commitment of the administration to black achievement has had some apparent payoff. Achievement-test scores reveal modest improvement in black performance each year since 1975, particularly in the early grades. Because white test scores have improved even more, the racial gap has widened.

Improvement in black achievement did not, of course, result from administrative fiat, although the administration did make clear its interest in the issue. Schools serving grades four through six, generally regarded as weak institutions, were thoroughly revamped. All of the principals were replaced. New money, including federal funds, was spent to reduce teacher-pupil ratios even as these were being increased at other grade levels, to hire more aides, to spruce up the physical facilities, and to deploy "impact teams." Instruction was individualized to a greater extent, incorporating a "Reading Management System."[139] The schools were divided into racially mixed mini-schools to promote a more intimate environment, with students assigned to a single mini-school for continuity of instruction. David Tansey, who succeeded Wilson as superintendent, has continued to stress academic proficiency, with "high expectancy levels set . . . [for] all kids."[140] These efforts do not much differ from what had been begun in the district a decade earlier, before experimentation and black separatism assumed paramount importance. Integration had again become a goal worthy of pursuit in Berkeley.

The initiatives of the Wilson administration also affected whites. Since desegregation, the Berkeley schools had been in delicate racial balance, with almost precisely as many whites as blacks. First the excesses of experimentation, then the teachers' strike, began making whites uneasy. In 1970, for the first time blacks outnumbered whites. Nothing approaching white flight ever occurred in Berkeley, but some saw it as a likely possibility. After the 1975 strike, board member James Guthrie stated that "already, several of Berkeley's once integrated schools have now 'tipped' in favor of non-whites."[141] More recently, this pattern has reversed itself. The proportion of whites, 45 percent in 1980, is as high as at any time since 1968, and although the relative changes in population distribution have been slight, this trend suggests that Berkeley is likely to remain stable and balanced.

Changes within the school system, begun under Wilson and continuing under Tansey, have encouraged white as well as black parents in the belief that Berkeley is finally coming to terms, in a less self-conscious and less self-congratulatory way, with the integrationist mandate of 1968. It is at least possible that Berkeley's schools, under conditions that are in many ways less auspicious than those prevailing a decade ago, will become the integrated institutions it was hoped they might some day be.

VI

Seen from the vantage of the late 1960s, Berkeley embodied the realization of the liberal idea of race and schooling. Blacks and whites were mixed on terms that burdened the one race no more than the other, and genuine integration was widely thought achievable. "We will not fail here," Superintendent Sullivan asserted. "Where else would there be hope of success if there was failure here in Berkeley?"[142]

Yet almost at the moment of system-wide desegregation, the liberal vision ceased to sustain the Berkeley schools. The rapid demise of the integrationist vision is traceable to many factors. Some of these—the aspirations of the superintendent, for instance—are idiosyncratic. Other factors, especially those touching on ideology and the relationship between ideology and power, can more readily be generalized. What they reveal is both the fragility of liberalism and, perversely, the enduring strength of liberal ideals, even when arrayed against aspirations more tangible and immediate in nature.

Between 1958, when the NAACP first appealed to the school board to attend to the consequences of racial separation, and the complete desegregation of the schools a decade later, the relationship between racial mixing and racial justice was clear. Eloquent black leadership, an articulate superintendent, and impassioned school board members all sounded the same litany. In doing so, they spoke as the voice of progress, contending with those seeking to preserve an iniquitous status quo. Yet once the ideal had been achieved, the forces that had promoted it ceased, for the most part, to contribute to the making of policy.

The task of implementing integration by deliberately bringing together two disparate cultures involves less the reassertion of

ideals than the managing of a volatile process. It depends upon the
arts of compromise and common sense and the capacity to manage
predictable crisis, not skill in the bully pulpit; in Berkeley those
traits were in short supply. Implementation also proved less exciting than the vision that preceded it. Necessarily so, for as Lionel
Trilling has written, "It is one of the tendencies of liberalism to
simplify. . . . The ideas that can . . . be passed on to agencies and
bureaus and technicians incline to be ideas of a certain kind and a
certain simplicity: they give up something of their largeness and
modulation and complexity in order to survive."[143] A new black
leadership and a new superintendent were also questioning the necessity of linking racial mixing and racial justice, urging that other
routes existed to the same end. To adhere to the necessity of racial
mixing in the face of such assertions was to risk denying blacks the
very equality that racial justice betokened, and in so doing to engage in a new form of racism. Or so it was asserted, in a dynamic
that proved irresistible.

Berkeley was not the only community to flirt with separatism,
as the Sausalito history, recounted in chapter 9, confirms. The evolution of racial politics in Berkeley during this period mirrored, although in exaggerated form, changes in race relations throughout
urban America. What is more remarkable is Berkeley's capacity to
reassert ideals of racial equality that had seemingly been buried in
the late 1960s. This transformation was easier to accomplish because most blacks and whites attended racially mixed schools even
during the experimental era. Pertinent too has been the declining
significance of racial ideology.

Not that Berkeley has restored the old liberalism in toto:
there no longer exists the sense of mission, the single-minded commitment to an idea whose moral rightness and educational ef-
ficaciousness is beyond dispute. The Berkeley school district has to
assure its institutional stability and solvency. Then it can get on
with the business of integration, because integration still seems of
value to those caught up in the process.

CHAPTER
9

Sausalito:
Sense and Sentimentality

I

The history of race and schooling in Sausalito and Berkeley is similar in many respects. Both communities were pioneers of a sort. Sausalito—a small, wealthy, politically liberal San Francisco suburb—voluntarily desegregated its public schools in 1965.[1] The school district, which included the racially and economically heterogeneous area surrounding the town proper, was the first in California and one of the first in the nation to take this step. Its decision was voluntary, prompted by a widely shared belief in the rightness of desegregation, not by threatened litigation or sustained political pressure. Community enthusiasm for desegregation made this social experiment a likely candidate for success.

The evolution from desegregation to integration was a problematic enterprise, the process even more turbulent in Sausalito than in Berkeley. A 1970 grand jury report observed that "what began as a beautiful dream of a fully integrated educational institution where children, regardless of social background, might mingle, work, play and learn together, has turned into a nightmare."[2] Separatist black power politics, initially encouraged by the very liberals who had pursued desegregation, drove moderates out of the public schools in the late 1960s. Student enrollment in the Sausalito system, which offers kindergarten through eighth-grade instruction, declined by more than one-third, and the proportion of whites in the upper grade school, where black power politics corroded the educational curriculum, fell from 60 percent to 38 percent.[3] The professional staff was beset by turnover and turmoil. In a deeply divisive election, two members of the school board that had permitted this state of affairs to transpire were recalled by the voters. Prospects for successful desegregation seemed remote. The hoped-for integration to be achieved by linking racial and educational concerns appeared merely romantic.

Yet out of the chaos of this period Sausalito has managed to build a school system that takes integration seriously. A new board of education and an energetic superintendent, himself a veteran of San Francisco's efforts to desegregate, moved beyond the old controversies to resume neglected tasks of leadership and administration. Student achievement substantially improved as the instructional program acquired both diversity and quality. Whites, whose mass departure threatened to turn Sausalito into a predominantly black district, have been attracted back into the public schools, which are again 60 percent white. Sausalito has reversed the seemingly irreversible process of degeneration. The district's energies are now focused on ways of encouraging instructional excellence for both blacks and whites, rather than on the more abstract and turbulent issue of racial justice.

The history of race and schooling in Sausalito is thus one of dramatic policy shifts: from consensual desegregation to destructive racial divisiveness to a less ideologically laden integration. In Sausalito as in Berkeley, the politics of racial justice were at different times ideological and pluralist in character, and this political transformation paralleled shifts between sense and sentimentality as a basis for political decision making. Factors tending to promote stability in Sausalito's schools also deserve attention. That Sausalito was able to remake its school district is due to the possibility of cohesiveness inhering in smallness, the availability of abundant resources, the healing effects of time, and, most vitally, the durability of parental concern, irrespective of race, for the education of their children. In a very real sense, Sausalito has reclaimed its schools for the wider community.

II

Sausalito is a tiny school district. At no point since desegregation has it enrolled more than one thousand children, and in 1979–80 it enrolled fewer than five hundred.[4] Despite its size, the district's population is extraordinarily varied. Its students come from Sausalito, a wealthy community whose population numbers 7,090;[5] from houseboats docked in the Sausalito marina; from the families of military personnel stationed at three nearby forts; and from Marin City, an unincorporated area adjacent to Sausalito with an all-black population of some fifteen hundred. Apart from Marin City, the district is overwhelmingly white. This diversity of background imposes special demands on Sausalito, for the backgrounds, wants, and educational needs of students are distinct.

Because they are transients, military families have had little to do with school district policymaking. The same has been true of houseboat families, whose political energies have focused on their struggle against developers planning a permanent, high-rent houseboat marina. The racial issue has been played out in Sausalito proper and Marin City, so these communities need to be understood in somewhat greater detail.

The extraordinary beauty of Sausalito gives the town its special character. The natural site, a commanding position on the bay with spectacular views of San Francisco, has been embellished by tasteful commercial ventures, shops and restaurants at the water's edge, and architecturally noteworthy homes hugging the cliffs. The place defines charm, and only in the last ten years have modern apartments and tourist shops begun to mar the landscape. The community's elegance, coupled with its proximity to San Francisco, is reflected in the escalating price of housing; even a modest home costs $200,000. The city is politically more liberal than its Marin County neighbors, as party registration and state and national elections reveal, but it is not a politically energetic community. As one former mayor noted: "It's more of a bedroom community; people come for a party or to sleep"[6]—not, presumably, to run things.

As the cost of housing in Sausalito has skyrocketed, families with young children have been discouraged from moving into the town. Over time, Sausalito has become increasingly a home for singles, and consequently fewer children attend the public schools. This prospect was apparent more than a decade ago, when a report made to the Sausalito Board of Education observed:

There is little evidence to support the prospect that the city of Sausalito will entice families with elementary children to take up residence in the community. . . . The city appears to be moving in the direction of apartment residence, of relatively high cost, serving other than families with children. Its easy accessibility to downtown San Francisco, its investment in recreation and art interests and the restrictions of the terrain do not give encouragement to extensive family type residency.[7]

The houseboat population, historically comprising aging hippies with squatters' rights to the piers, is changing as commercial developers raise the price of docking space. This change will bring more single individuals and small families to the houseboats. The larger group of apartment dwellers is predominantly composed of single residents: in January 1976, the average housing unit in Sausalito was occupied by fewer than two persons.

Like Sausalito, adjacent Marin City is magnificently situated in a valley between the bluffs and the bay, but there the similarity ends.[8] Marin City is an anomaly, a largely black enclave in preponderantly white Marin County (its 1,500 residents constitute 40 percent of the county's black population), a predominantly low-income community in one of the nation's wealthiest suburban areas. Although geographically proximate, Marin City is physically separate from Sausalito. That separation is marked by a chain-link fence that ostensibly protects Marin City youngsters from freeway traffic but also underscores the symbolic distance between the two communities. The juxtaposition of these two radically different neighbors, Marin City and Sausalito, gives the Sausalito school district its special character.

Marin City residents have been politically active—they had to be, in order to assure the community's survival. The town, originally built on federally owned land to house the families of shipyard workers during World War II, was then substantially larger and residentially integrated. After the war, however, most of the whites departed. The government's quiet hope was that, having outlived its usefulness, Marin City would simply wither away. The buildings were allowed to deteriorate, and in 1952 the federal government moved to declare the land surplus as a first step toward selling it. Angry black residents protested that were the land developed commercially they would be driven out of the county, for there was no other low-income housing. Marin County was persuaded to purchase the land, which was then developed as federally subsidized low-income housing.

Marin City's residences—a handsome mix of high-rise apartments, rental town houses, cooperatives, and privately owned homes, substantially lower in density than the wartime buildings—serve as a testament to what public housing at its best can achieve. The community is a ghetto only in the sense that its population is now largely black, since almost all the remaining whites moved out during the redevelopment. It reveals little of the social disorder common in urban ghettos. Yet Marin City is a poor community.[9] Its median income is only one-third of the county-wide average, and almost one-third of its residents are unemployed.

The school-age population in Marin City has also been declining. Black families who originally thought of Marin City as a transitional home have become locked into its subsidized public housing by the unavailability of affordable private housing in the area, and there has consequently been less opportunity for families with young children to move in. Since 1964, Marin City's school enrollment dropped from 470 to fewer than two hundred.

Sausalito residents appreciate the virtue of smallness. Twice during the 1950s and 1960s they voted down proposals that the school district merge with neighboring Mill Valley, a slightly larger and almost all-white town. Merger would have substantially reduced the proportion of blacks in the district, an appealing result for some,[10] but also would have cost Sausalito residents money, for the existing district is rich. Sausalito has a substantial property tax base and has received a sizable federal Impact Aid Grant, based on the number of military families' children; Title I, ESEA support for the "educationally disadvantaged"; and state compensatory education money. Nearly one-sixth of the district's budget comes from such special sources. These dollar advantages convert into tangible and visible resources. One teacher is employed for every nineteen Sausalito students, a ratio many colleges would dearly love to emulate and 15 percent lower than the county-wide average. Per pupil expenditures are even higher than Berkeley's, almost one and a half times those of Richmond.

Until the advent of desegregation, the school district, like its Bay Area neighbors, was a politically peaceful place. The five-member board of trustees, elected for staggered four-year terms, was dominated by wealthy, often conservative Sausalito residents—housewives, professionals, businessmen. Since the 1950s, the board has consistently had one black member, a Marin City resident. At its semimonthly meetings, much of the board's time was spent reviewing minor personnel and budgetary items. It generally deferred to its superintendent on more substantial questions.

The school district did not, however, enjoy complete political autonomy. In 1966, when its student population fell below 900, Sausalito came under the supervision of the county superintendent of schools, an arrangement dictated by state law. This oversight has in the main been delicately exercised. Although the county acts as auditor and treasurer for the district and county officials have filled interim terms as Sausalito superintendent at the district's request, only during the crisis of 1970 did the county assume a more activist role.

Before the advent of the racial issue, Sausalito had the kind of public school system that its voters wanted. The quality of that system's offering, defined in terms of reputation or measured student achievement, was another matter. Little public attention was paid to instructional issues, and when the board talked about curriculum at all, it was in the broad terms of educational philosophy, not in programmatic specifics. The high proportion of Sausalito children attending private schools—40 percent in 1970, four times higher than the county-wide average—provides the beginnings of an explanation for this apparent indifference. Well-to-do parents showed their lack of confidence in the public schools by voting with their feet. Issues of educational quality had not been resolved when the question of race and schooling first emerged in 1963. On the contrary, concentrating on that issue permitted the district to avoid questions of quality for almost another decade.

III

More rapidly and amicably than neighboring communities, Sausalito concluded that racial separation in its four public schools constituted a problem and undertook to do something about it by desegregating the schools.

A single school had served all sixth- through eighth-grade students in the Sausalito school district since 1946 and was thus formally desegregated. But because students were grouped on the basis of tested ability, they were effectively resegregated, blacks predominating in the bottom track. Since a sizable number of whites withdrew their children from the Sausalito public schools at sixth grade, the school had a substantially higher percentage of black students than the district-wide average. Attendance boundaries for schools serving the lower grades coincided with the district's segregated housing patterns. The Marin City school enrolled 93 percent black students, whereas its Sausalito counterparts were almost all-white.

The sharp demarcation between Marin City and Sausalito had long troubled the quintessentially liberal community. A commission studying the district's schools in 1951 stated: "Democracy prospers most when amalgamation of different races and those of different social and economic levels is accomplished. Marin City is a challenge in practical democratic action to the Sausalito School District, and if permitted to operate in this community environment, schools of Sausalito School District can make an important contribution to democratic living and to improved citizenship for the citizens within the District." [11] A quarter-century later, a black Marin City citizens' group bluntly spelled out the continuing character of that "challenge." "Government endorsement of housing discrimination during the first half of this century helped create Marin County and Marin City, and while white Americans have talked of integration in school and residential areas, the practice in Marin County has remained racist and fostered segregation."[12]

The issue of desegregation became politically salient by the early 1960s, with the local chapter of CORE acting as a catalyst in the process. CORE itself was an integrated group. Its chairman was a black Marin City resident; a white Sausalito housewife and the wife of a white school board member headed its education committee. When CORE's initial emphasis on expanding integrated housing in Marin County stumbled over the hard rock of economic reality, the organization turned its attention to the schools.

CORE brought the issue of desegregation before the Sausalito Board of Education in September 1963. The board responded by seeking help from the California Commission on Equal Opportunity in Education, the state agency charged with providing technical assistance to communities concerned about integration. When nothing more happened throughout the school year, CORE organized a one-day school boycott on May 18, 1964, in observance of the tenth anniversary of the Supreme Court's decision in *Brown v. Board of Education*.[13] The symbolic linkage between the segregation that *Brown* had condemned and racial separation in Sausalito did not pass unnoticed.

In a letter sent to parents soliciting support for the boycott, CORE stressed the nexus between segregation and educational quality.[14] Black children who had received "inadequate preschool preparation" and were thus "less able [than whites] to learn to read" got "baby-sitting," not preschool instruction, in the school district's child care center. The Marin City school was criticized for offering a "second class education," inferior to that available in the white primary school. Ability grouping in the upper grades "does not operate . . . to stimulate the supposedly integrated Negro children to stronger efforts or greater achievements. The vicious circle goes on and on." The boycott itself reflected the racial divisions within the community. Only one-third of the Marin City students were in attendance at the lower school, almost all of them white, and slightly more than half of the students at the desegregated upper school honored the boycott. At the predominantly white school, attendance was normal.

The July 1964 report of the state commission treated the CORE grievances as factual findings.[15] "A condition of racial imbalance exists in the Sausalito School District, which has legal, social, ethical and educational implications." Although neither the segregation nor the inequities were viewed as deliberate, that fact was perceived as irrelevant. The "deterioration in school-community relations . . . which contributed to the alienation of the schools from substantial segments of the communities within the district" had to be arrested. As in other reports of the state commission, no particular desegregation plan received official backing. The report instead recommended that the Sausalito school board create a citizens' advisory committee to study equal educational opportunity, considering school building needs, school finance, and compensatory education as well as segregation. That committee, the state body suggested, should examine the child care program and assess the wisdom of consolidation with neighboring Mill Valley as a means of promoting desegregation.

The influence of the California Commission on Equal Opportunity in Education varied from one Bay Area community to another. In San Francisco, the help of the commission was accepted grudgingly and its advice largely ignored; in Oakland, the state had a more significant role in defining the policy agenda but was ultimately ineffective in securing significant policy change. The commission was taken seriously, almost literally, in Sausalito. Following its recommendation, the board appointed an eighteen-member citizens' advisory committee. Although the formal charge to the committee did not explicitly mention "integration," "desegregation," or "racial balance," the board was definitely moving in that direction. The committee included the black member of the school board and a black shop owner from Marin City, as well as two military parents and Sausalito housewives, businessmen, and professionals.

By the time the committee finished its work in June 1965, the board had become even more supportive of desegregation. Three new members were elected in April 1965, and although desegregation went largely unaddressed in the campaign, CORE used its considerable influence in Marin City to insure the selection of a school board that would act rapidly. David Freedheim, a young Sausalito businessman, was one of the candidates backed by CORE. Freedheim was not a member of the organization, and was regarded by his Sausalito neighbors as a sensible businessman, certainly no threat to conservatives in the white community. "My friends in Marin City told me, 'Don't do a damn thing in this campaign except smoke your fat cigar,'" Freedheim said, recalling the election. "And that's what I did."[16]

The report of the citizens' advisory committee contributed to

the momentum by urging desegregation in the interest "of furthering morality and law."[17] The citizens' group concluded that an
"ideal" mix, 75 percent white and 25 percent black,[18] could be
achieved only by expanding the district's boundaries, and for that
reason, recommended unification with neighboring Mill Valley. In
the interim, however, it was imperative that Sausalito act. Professional advice on the specifics of desegregation was provided by Marin County school superintendent Virgil Hollis and two colleagues
(one of them Richard Foster, who would become Berkeley's school
superintendent in 1968), who recommended immediate desegregation of all grades in the district. The substance of their desegregation proposal responded to CORE's initial grievances. All
kindergarten children would attend the Marin City school, while
lower-school children would be enrolled in two Sausalito schools.
A single school would continue to serve grades six through eight,
but the district was to phase out ability grouping. One hundred
thousand dollars in district funds would be spent refurbishing one
Marin City site, doubling the number of volumes in the public
school libraries, and purchasing audiovisual equipment. The preschool program would be turned into something more than a
baby-sitting service through hiring a dozen professionals, including a speech therapist and a guidance consultant.

Not a single opponent spoke out at the July 1965 board meeting called to hear and comment on these proposals. The political
liberalism of the community made opposition difficult to express,
and whites unhappy about desegregation could opt out of the system. As one woman actively involved in the desegregation effort
later observed: "We were a group of what you would call Stevenson
liberals. During the sixties the big excitement was integration. We
saw ourselves as part of history—not down South but right here in
our own backyard, we're integrating."[19]

Other factors also eased the implementation of policy change.
Because the district was relatively wealthy, it was able to couple
desegregation with at least cosmetic improvements in the educational program, and hence could assert that everyone would be
better off. The district's teachers strongly supported desegregation.
A survey conducted earlier that year found that twenty-nine of
thirty-seven teachers favored desegregating district schools from
preschool through eighth grade, while only three expressed opposition. Desegregation, the teachers said, was "inevitable and
necessary and perhaps the only 'moral' answer."[20] Although implementation proceeded on an extremely tight schedule, the pos-

sibility of desegregation had been discussed for several years both in Sausalito and Marin City; the work of the citizens' advisory committee and the interviewing done by Hollis and his associates had kept the citizenry involved and informed. Because of the small size of the district, no student would be transported a long way to school. The district's hilly terrain had historically made student busing necessary, and for that reason busing students to achieve desegregation did not become a rallying point for controversy. "White flight," assertedly detectable in other communities during the first year of desegregation, was conspicuously absent: 934 students, 3 more than in the previous year, enrolled in 1965, and the district's racial ratio remained unchanged.

Sausalito's efforts had substantial symbolic significance. The town had apparently made Martin Luther King's dream come true in one small corner of the republic. For that reason, desegregation in Sausalito drew attention and praise all out of proportion to the numbers of students involved.

Events in the months following desegregation appeared to bear out these optimistic sentiments. Instructional programs underwent subtle modifications. In the upper grades, clusters for specific academic subjects replaced a single ability-grouping assignment for all subjects, and as a result classes were desegregated. Enrichment programs in reading and mathematics financed by federal compensatory education funds were undertaken in the lower grades; consultants from nearby universities were brought into Sausalito for the first time to aid teachers unfamiliar with instructing "educationally deprived" youngsters. Persisting community enthusiasm was evident in the formation of the interracial Sausalito Parents Club, the holding of community suppers in Marin City churches, and the sponsoring of race relations workshops by both the newly merged Sausalito and Marin City PTA and CORE.

Despite the goodwill and the new programs, nagging educational problems persisted. Marin City students continued to perform badly, and with desegregation the performance gap between black and white became highly visible. A sizable number of inept teachers impeded instructional reform. These problems led to the resignation of Sausalito's superintendent after just one year on the job. His successor, Philip Schneider, appointed because of his presumed commitment to desegregation, would take the district down a very different path. As in Berkeley, the choice of a superintendent in the years following desegregation proved critical.

IV

The task facing Sausalito seemed clear enough, even if the formula for its achievement was not: maintain desegregation while improving the district's instructional program. In Superintendent Schneider's hands, however, this mandate was dramatically altered. Instead of worrying about specifically educational concerns, the district attended to new demands for black power, attempting to relate those demands to ongoing desegregation. Just as Sausalito was ahead of its time in undertaking desegregation, so too would it respond to a militant black consciousness well before most other American communities.

The shift from desegregation to black power as a focus of attention was not made suddenly, but was rather the cumulative result of numerous decisions by the superintendent and a compliant board. The evolution of Sausalito policy began innocently enough in 1968–69 when Sausalito's teachers, all but four of whom were white, were urged to attend encounter groups led by San Francisco psychologist Price Cobbs, coauthor of *Black Rage*.[21] Individual and group counseling with the district's black psychologist followed the encounter sessions. Schneider defended these efforts as jolting white teachers into awareness of the needs of their new clientele.

The 1968 hiring of James Toliver, a black power advocate, to work in the upper-grade school (renamed the Martin Luther King School after King's assassination) could similarly be regarded as a prod to school district consciousness, but Toliver's role proved far more significant and disturbing. Although some of his efforts—for example, persuading the school board to adopt as a goal for staff hiring a racial mix consistent with the district's—seem unexceptionable today, others suggest the attempted radicalization of the school district.

The King School became Toliver's fiefdom.[22] He formed a black studies committee that taught Afro-American history and culture at the guidance center, previously used to help students with academic problems. Soul music was played during lunch and recess breaks. The traditional February assembly honoring Abraham Lincoln and George Washington became in 1969 "black martyrs day" assembly at King.

Toliver also had close ties with the Black Panthers, whose involvement in school affairs speeded the radicalization process. The Panthers, based in nearby Oakland, began organizing a cadre of unemployed and angry young blacks in Marin City in the late

1960s. Their rhetoric was far more militant than that of the local CORE chapter, and the Panthers excluded whites. Panther posters depicting policemen as pigs were hung in King School classrooms. Toliver took several classes of seventh- and eighth-grade children on a field trip to Black Panther Party offices in San Francisco's black Fillmore District. In spring 1969, the Black Panthers began a school breakfast program at the King School. The *Independent Journal*, a Marin County newspaper, reported: "One young man clearing [the breakfast] tables led about a dozen children briefly in chants of 'free Huey' and 'power to the people,' accompanied by a clenched fist Panther salute."[23] The Panthers made their presence forcibly felt in other ways. One teacher at King School, subsequently elected to the board of education, recalls: "A little boy selling the Black Panther newspaper came into class. I told him I didn't want him to interrupt the class and he threw a knife at me."[24]

Any empire builder needs allies within the system, and Toliver was no exception. At Toliver's suggestion, the district began recruiting avowedly militant blacks in the winter of 1969, advertising in such publications as the *Berkeley Barb* and the Black Panther newspaper. Black community organizers, including Panther Party members, were hired as consultants. William Bradley—referred to as Chaka, after a powerful Zulu warrior—was retained, nominally as a teacher's assistant in a math class but in fact as a black separatist propagandist. White teachers also began to feel the pressure. The district's French instructor resigned in May 1969, unhappy about the constant friction between black and white students. "The black students will relate better to a black teacher," she said.[25]

Some Sausalito parents were aware of and profoundly upset by the changes occurring in their schools. A great many chose to leave. Between 1965 and 1969 enrollment dropped from 934 to 660, and in the year Toliver began to assert his power, enrollment declined by 19 percent. A disproportionate number of the departing children were enrolled in the upper grades of the King School, where the black power influence was strongest: by 1970–71, the proportion of whites there had fallen to 38 percent. White families either moved farther north in Marin County or sent their children to nearby parochial or private day schools. Others complained to the school board, but to no avail. The contretemps over the Black Panther breakfasts brought 175 persons to the board, mostly to criticize, but the board approved continuation of the program.

The hiring of Sidney Walton as principal of the King School

proved to be the beginning of the end for Schneider and the board's most radical members. Walton was referred to as the "man with a gun," because his book, *The Black Curriculum*, featured a full-page photograph of the bearded administrator with a rifle pointed in the air, a knife on his hip, a second rifle and ammunition casually propped in the foreground, and the inscription "Liberation, then peace, Sid Walton." The text was at least as inflammatory.

Organize the Black Community, Black students, Black faculty members and your worries are over and "Chuck's" worries begin. The rest is simple if you address yourself to the concept of "by any means necessary." . . . Let the establishment members know that you are willing to die to get what you want and you ask them, "who is willing to die to stop you."[26]

Walton urged black youngsters to attend school, not to obtain a traditional education but to "develop the necessary skills which will enable us to carve out a nation state out of this honkies' stolen land or out of his stealing ass." None of this kept Superintendent Schneider from nominating Walton for the King post or the board from hiring him. Walton's race was his primary qualification. CORE leaders pressured school trustees to make the selection, and the board acceded to their demands.

A liberal school board and superintendent, early and ardent desegregation enthusiasts, found themselves unable to say no to anything that the cadre of black spokesmen demanded, even if what they sought was inconsistent both with desegregation and with sensible educational practice. In the process, the board and superintendent were inadvertently but nonetheless decisively radicalized. Encounter groups, Black Panther propaganda, and a gun-wielding principal were a far cry from integration as it had been envisioned a scant three years earlier. One white supporter of the policy shifts tried to explain her enthusiasm: "I think the Sausalito schools are attempting to reach black children in a way that no other district has tried, and I feel I and my children can deal with black militancy."[27]

Even Walton initially seemed reasonable. In a September 1969 letter to parents, he wrote: "Let me . . . reassure you that my major concern at MLK School is to see that the entire faculty at the school dedicate its efforts to providing all children the kinds of humanistic experiences coupled with quality education that will prepare them to be socially responsible citizens fully capable of loving and respecting each other in a dignified manner."

A great many parents were unpersuaded. Some turned for help to county superintendent Virgil Hollis, whose office exercised supervisory authority over the district. Hollis handled the situation delicately. Rather than intervene directly as he was empowered to do, Hollis referred parents to the Marin County grand jury's education committee. Grand juries in California have broad discretionary authority to review government programs, and schools are a common focus of interest. After receiving several complaints from parents of King School children, the grand jury began reviewing allegations of reverse racism.

The February 1970 grand jury report sided with those who had resisted the transformation of Sausalito's schools into black separatist institutions. Its critique was caustic. "The majority of the [Sausalito] board," the grand jury stated, "were so consumed with the complexities of society that were evidently beyond them, that it evidently escaped their attention that they were elected to fulfill the basic charge of educating little children." As a consequence, the report declared, the board had lost the support of "parents and a majority of the community," which it had enjoyed at the onset of desegregation. "The misuse of that same community . . . by school personnel involving them in the support or promotion of political causes and/or philosophy is to be deplored," the grand jury asserted.[28] Moreover, the report declared, student achievement had noticeably declined with the transformation of the King School into a separatist-oriented institution. King had become the only school in Marin County falling below state and national medians—this despite lavish expenditures, double the per pupil average in other county elementary districts.

The grand jury's recommendations were sweeping and harsh. "Until such time as attendance can be rebuilt," the report declared, the district should be run by the Marin County superintendent; in this context, rebuilding attendance could only mean attracting back white families. In the meantime, it urged an investigation by the U.S. Department of Health, Education and Welfare "into discrimination against children by the militants in the Sausalito School District." The report called on the district to "hire an inexperienced, credentialed principal for each school dedicated to teaching writing, reading and mathematics and the enforcement of reasonable discipline," a clear gibe at Walton, and "eliminate racially biased overtones" in the curriculum.

Although the grand jury recommendations were not legally enforceable,[29] they became the focus for debate in a community increasingly polarized into pro- and anti-school board camps. Unhappy white parents organized for the first time as Citizens for Excellence in Integrated Education (CEIE) to press for the sorts of policies proposed by the grand jury. The all-white CEIE took its cue from the final page of the grand jury report, which stated in capital letters: "The ultimate responsibility for the correction of the abhorrent condition partially described in this report rests upon the voting public."

Whites who regarded "deal[ing] with black militancy" as a virtue continued to applaud the board's efforts. Marin City blacks were also split between those organized by the Black Panthers, who spoke out on behalf of the King School regime, and the more moderate if less vocal majority, who began to fret about inattention to instructional issues. Board meetings, once mundane affairs, now ran into the wee hours of the morning. They were dominated not by educational policy discussions but by debates over contending ideologies.

Superintendent Schneider unsurprisingly defended the district's policies against the grand jury attack. The report, he declared, "demonstrates at a very deep level the fears of white people and their inability to meet black people as equals."[30] Yet Schneider too had begun to doubt the wisdom of hiring Walton as principal of the King School. The two skirmished publicly over symbolic issues. Walton lowered the American flag to half-staff at Martin Luther King School in memory of the youths killed in Vietnam, and when Schneider ordered that the flag be raised, Walton refused. At a deeper level, Schneider had come to conclude that Walton's politics were undermining the educational program at the King School.

Schneider's turnabout prompted similar soul-searching on the part of the school board. The pressure on the board to do something had mounted since the release of the grand jury report. CEIE called upon county superintendent Hollis to assume control of the Sausalito district and organized a campaign to recall the two white members of the Sausalito board most supportive of Schneider-era policy. Walton, a primary target of these efforts, was predictably bitter. "They seem to think they found a nigger to do the dirty work and now that I'm out on a limb they're going to cut me loose."[31]

The Sausalito school board meeting of May 4, 1970, called to consider firing Walton as King's principal, was one of the most remarkable sessions in the annals of such occasions. Having lost Superintendent Schneider's support, Walton was vulnerable, but he was hardly without allies, most prominently the Black Panthers, who demonstrated the meaning of militant action. One board member stayed away from the meeting, intimidated by unidentified callers who vowed to harm her family if she voted to dismiss Walton. The only black board member, Nat Johnson, was also threatened. It was rumored that his car had been wired with a dynamite charge while he was attending the board meeting, only to be unwired before he emerged, since he cast the sole vote in favor of retaining Walton.

At the meeting, Panthers carrying steel staves and accompanied by guard dogs ringed the room. After the motion to fire Walton had been introduced, Walton and Toliver spoke passionately in Walton's defense. When the motion carried three to one, one of their supporters rushed to the board members' seats, in the process throwing a crippled board member onto the floor. Nat Johnson then led "all you brothers who care about education" out of the meeting; his intention, Johnson subsequently reported, was to forestall violence. The strategy worked. Nearly all the blacks in the audience departed with Johnson; when they felt that it was safe to do so, the remaining board members decamped.[32] The next day, the board member who had been threatened resigned, stating that she could not "function in the atmosphere of rage which fills the district at this time and makes every decision a choice between unacceptable alternatives."[33]

The board's decision to fire Walton exacerbated the crisis atmosphere. Black students in King School staged a boycott in support of their fired principal, which provoked interracial violence. The district, unable to bring the situation under control, closed the school indefinitely. In a joint statement, the trustees, Schneider, and Hollis postponed all further board meetings until after the recall election. Fearing that recall would succeed, Superintendent Schneider abruptly resigned before the election. "If the board was recalled," stated Schneider, "I wasn't going to stay. Life is tough enough without having to fight a board that wanted to go backwards into the twentieth century."[34] Defenders of the board rued the polarization that in their view had been introduced into the school district by CEIE. The ex-president of the Sausalito Parents' Club, which in 1965 had aided the orderly implementation of desegregation, declared:

The school board is trying to meet head-on the massive problems of our society. We recognize that errors have occurred but we don't think the quality of education has been sacrificed. I don't think the people who have organized the recall election intend it to be destructive but that would be the result. It would tell the people of Marin City that the course of integration has failed . . . a great idea is now dead.[35]

The CEIE chairman was equally upset about polarization but held a different view of its origins. "The sad thing is that it's becoming a black and white issue. If we educate these kids properly, we turn out good black leaders and teachers."[36]

Where recall had failed in Berkeley and earlier in Richmond, the campaign succeeded in Sausalito. Sixty-three percent of the voters, a remarkably high proportion for a school board election, turned out to oust the two challenged board members. The margin was narrow: both liberal incumbents carried the two Marin City precincts and lost overall by less than 6 percent. The remaining three board members promptly quit; only after considerable persuasion did Nat Johnson rescind his resignation, providing the token black representation that would give the new school board some credibility to its Marin City constituency.[37]

The recall vote was not only an expression of no confidence in two board members. It also represented a rejection by the electorate of policies that had been pursued since 1968. In attending to issues of race and schooling, Sausalito would have to begin anew.

V

The fortunes of the Sausalito school district appeared bleak in 1970. The district was polarized around racial issues. Its schools were in chaos. It lacked a superintendent, had a demoralized teaching staff, and was threatened with the continued loss of white students. That Sausalito was able subsequently to develop an educational program that could command the commitment of white and black families makes the counterrevolution in Sausalito an extraordinary event.

Despite the fears of the ousted group, the new board dominated by CEIE members did not attempt to dismantle desegregation, but tried instead to bring some sense out of the shambles it had inherited. The district needed to hire a superintendent and to replace several staff members, including two principals who had resigned.[38] Something had to be done about the Panther presence. And it was vital to stem the exodus of students from the school district.

The Black Panther issue proved easiest to deal with. The district's acting superintendent ended the free breakfast program, removed party posters, and fired some of the community aides with close ties to the Panther organization. The declining power of the Panthers nationally doubtless eased the task. The party was on the defensive by 1971, its leaders more frequently in court than organizing black neighborhoods.

With respect to other matters, success came harder. In an attempt to retain white students, the board reversed the traditional practice of routinely approving interdistrict transfer requests: parents who wanted out would now have to move or to send their children to private schools. Despite this change, average daily attendance in 1970–71 was 562, one-sixth less than the previous year; since the initiation of desegregation five years earlier, attendance in Sausalito had almost halved. Although this decline could be partly attributed to the demographic trends already noted, the state of the schools also undoubtedly played a part.

The new board and administration could not develop an educational program that satisfied their diverse constituencies, and this contributed to the continuing exodus. CEIE board members fought for the adoption of what they termed a traditional education, but a sizable group of white parents, including many who had been most enthusiastic about desegregation, found this instructional emphasis unpalatable. They proposed creating an upgraded open-classroom alternative school within the public schools system, but the traditionalists on the school board would not permit such deviation.

The white dissenters hoped for black support in their efforts, only to discover that blacks had a very different educational agenda. Black parents wanted the schools to teach skills to children unable to read or do sums, not to offer "open" education, something that came as a surprise to the whites. "For eight years we had been fighting on the blacks' side politically, but we had never discussed educational goals," the leader of the white parents' group noted.[39]

The two groups went their separate ways, each forming private schools in 1971. The fates of the black-run and white-run alternative educational ventures were instructively different. The all-black Marin City Learning Center, which opened with fifty-five students, was doomed by financial instability and survived for just one year. Money was not a serious problem at the alternative North Bay School, which enrolled twenty-six children, for the parents could afford sizable tuition payments. The school's population was almost all white from the outset, partly because of the split over educational philosophy and partly because of economics. Unlike

similar schools in other towns, North Bay never provided scholarships to enable poor Marin City youngsters to attend. While the
Marin City Learning Center collapsed, North Bay prospered.

The school board came to realize that "traditional" education
was not a panacea. It contracted in 1971 with a consulting firm to
provide special reading instruction for twenty middle- and upper-
level students. The board also tried to run the district more economically, closing two of the district's four schools. To some extent,
these efforts paid off. In 1972, pupil enrollment in Sausalito
schools increased from 482 to 547 with the return of the Marin City
Learning Center students, the first enrollment rise since the initiation of desegregation. The racial balance in the student population
also shifted; for the first time, Sausalito public schools were more
than half black.

Although the CEIE-dominated board had begun rebuilding
the Sausalito school system, the antagonisms generated in the
1970 campaign did not dissipate. The traditionalist educational
views of CEIE members were a constant source of friction, as was
the leadership style of the CEIE-backed school board chairman.
Board meetings were conducted with a sharpness that accentuated
conflict even over minor matters, and consequently an adversarial
atmosphere persisted in the district. CEIE had reversed Sausalito's
separatist policies but could not substitute an agenda that would
command community consensus.

A change in the board's composition in 1972 made restoration
of civility possible. The CEIE members resigned for personal reasons, as did Johnson, the board's only black member. Those who
replaced them had no ties to either the revolution or the counterrevolution in Sausalito. They ran on platforms that emphasized
educational not racial issues, and did not view school politics in
ideological terms. It had been nearly a decade since educational
problems had been foremost in Sausalito school policymaking.
The 1960s concern over low-achieving blacks, the diverse educational needs of the district's children, and the problem of incompe-
tent teachers remained unresolved.

A shift in professional leadership powerfully spurred the district's recovery. Donald Johnson, the superintendent whom the
new board hired in 1973, had a history of concern with both desegregation and instructional quality. Johnson was deeply involved in
planning and implementing the desegregation plan that San Francisco had legally been obliged to adopt. He had fought within the
San Francisco central administration against efforts to undermine
the desegregation effort; since coming to Sausalito, he has been a

consultant to other communities undergoing desegregation. Johnson's years as an elementary school principal had given him a reputation for tough-minded leadership. His mandate was to upgrade the educational program while maintaining desegregation.

One worry, declining student enrollment, had eased. By 1973, enrollment in Sausalito was nearly stable, parents upset with the condition of the district's schools having already departed. Student enrollment stood at just over 500, with black students slightly outnumbering whites. The instructional problem, Johnson soon discovered, was largely a personnel problem. Approximately ten teachers, a sizable number in a district with only thirty-seven teachers altogether, taught badly. Because of California's tough teacher-tenure laws, Johnson was unable to dismiss them, but he could and did transfer the least capable to nonteaching positions and introduce teachers' aides into the classrooms of those who remained as teachers. Johnson sought to remedy the educational situation in other ways. Most notably, he aggressively pursued federal and state categorical funding, securing resources with which to purchase goods and services that in other districts would be thought unobtainable luxuries.

The tangible effect of these changes is perceptible only now. Achievement test scores have improved considerably since the turbulent early 1970s. At that time, sixth graders were almost two years behind grade level; by 1979, they were performing nearly at grade level, and third graders' scores equaled the statewide average. This accomplishment becomes even more impressive when contrasted with other California districts with a comparable demographic distribution—Richmond, for one. Sausalito's students are doing far better than their counterparts there and in similar districts.[40]

The superintendent's dealings with the one-time supporters of desegregation who founded the private North Bay School illustrate the change in political and educational climate that has occurred in Sausalito. Those parents had left the district in 1971, not because of the racial crisis but because of the school board's unwillingness to support nontraditional instruction. Johnson and the new board wanted them to return and were willing to permit the alternative school to operate within the public system. The education for which these parents had been paying $1,700 in tuition would now be publicly subsidized, an attractive prospect to the parents. Student desegregation, however, had to be maintained. For that reason, Johnson insisted that the school recruit black students so that its racial mix would approximate that of the district.[41] The parents concurred, and in 1977 the thirty white young-sters then enrolled in North Bay returned to the Sausalito school district. To confirm its change in character, the school was moved to Marin City, where it occupies the site of the former public school. North Bay's enrollment is almost half black, and there is a waiting list for both black and white students.

Sausalito has reversed the familiar pattern by which school districts are transformed from predominantly white to predominantly black. It has proportionately more whites than at any time since the turmoil of the late 1960s and early 1970s. As the North Bay School's experience suggests, more than racial ratios is at stake in Sausalito. Those involved in the venture have struggled to relate the distinct educational interests of the school's black and white students within the framework of desegregation. This is no easy task. In Sausalito as elsewhere some assert that it is an impossible task, that the differences—whether described in terms of background, need, or wants—are just too great to permit a common school program that makes sense to anyone. If North Bay and the regular schools in the district do succeed, they will have moved a long way toward providing a genuinely integrated education. Veterans of the desegregation battles are unsure exactly what they have accomplished. But for those whose children were not yet attending school during the turbulent era, desegregation is not problematic but taken for granted. That is a noteworthy change.

VI

The Sausalito school district differs in many respects from most communities that have addressed questions of race and schooling. It is very small and has resisted the allure of consolidation. Its population is bifurcated, incorporating economic and social extremes but almost wholly lacking a middle class. It is wealthy. These distinctive features, which partly shape Sausalito's experience with desegregation, also restrict the generalizability of that experience.

The events in Sausalito—the peaceful progress of desegregation, the slide to black militancy, and the renewal of interest in integrated schooling—are not, however, merely idiosyncratic. They starkly reveal some of the prominent ideological dimensions of the struggle to define racial justice and to relate that concept to the mission of the public schools. Most vitally, Sausalito's history makes plainer the dilemmas of black militancy and liberalism in this society.

The black power rhetoric of the late 1960s sounded like revolution, and for that reason almost invariably aroused anxiety and concern among whites. At the time, the threatened chaos seemed real enough: Harlem and Watts and Detroit stood as examples of what could happen. At least to the tacticians of the movement, however, the rhetoric had more strategic uses. It was meant to make blacks starkly visible and to render credible their demands for greater economic and political resources. In retrospect, the tacticians of the movement were not so different in their aspirations from other ethnic groups who sought to make a pluralist political system work for them.

The difficulty with such an approach is that it demands exquisite finesse in execution, a finesse often lacking among the soldiers of the movement, whose fatal error was to confuse rhetoric and reality. The tactician knows just how far to prod. In Sausalito, a measured demonstration of black assertiveness would have reminded the liberal school board that blacks too deserved a significant hand in managing schools that were half black. But the militants went substantially beyond this. The physically violent school board confrontation over Walton's firing represented just the last in a series of intolerable acts. When that happened, the Sausalito school district pulled itself together to oust a group that in its extremism represented almost no one in the community. That community, composed of blacks and whites whose predominant world view was hardly revolutionary, could ultimately only reject militancy. In Sausalito as elsewhere, blacks have subsequently acted in a more pragmatic, less confrontationist manner. Whether that approach will succeed where militancy failed in bringing about the sought-after redistribution of resources and power remains to be seen. Former Superintendent Schneider is skeptical. "It's easy for people with wealth and power to move out and go in another direction, while the blacks are stuck with what's left."[42]

In the special receptivity of the Sausalito school board and administration to black militant demands, one can see manifestations of "radical chic" at its worst.[43] Yet the Sausalito group significantly differed from the socialites toasting the Panthers at Leonard Bernstein's famous cocktail party. By sending their children to increasingly hostile school environments, they accepted the personal consequences of their actions. That children were expected to "deal with black militancy," as one white parent declared, may seem foolish today, but at the time it demonstrated a perverse form of moral courage.

The whites' position in Sausalito, similar in many respects to the view prevalent in Berkeley after the 1968 desegregation, is better understood as revealing the fragility of liberal values with respect to race. Desegregation came easier to Sausalito than to most places because of the pronounced liberalism of most of the town's politically active residents. The members of the citizens' committee that proposed desegregation supported a principle of racial justice central to the liberal creed: the entitlement of all individuals, regardless of color, to equal opportunity. That entitlement, it was thought, could best be realized in the school setting by bringing black and white schoolchildren together, thus making color-based distinctions harder to maintain and eventually irrelevant.

Although policy is not infrequently premised on norms of right conduct, knowing what is right is a difficult business. Who is to say that formal equality, which is all that the classical liberal principle guarantees, is enough—or even relevant? It takes a powerfully held conviction to adhere to this principle in the face of arguments that liberalism amounted to paternalism, or worse.

In this context white responsiveness to black demands late in the 1960s—in Sausalito, Berkeley, and elsewhere—becomes comprehensible. To speak of the era as turbulent offers both a truism and a truth. The black voices were forceful. Their demands, if taken singly, were often not unreasonable. The legacy of white guilt played upon by blacks muted doubters. Looking back, what impresses most is the terribly small distance between realism and romanticism, sense and sentimentality, as the basis upon which to base educational policy.

Sausalito's current stance has grown out of these experiences. Although history does not constitute proof, familiarity with past crises and their causes should strengthen the resolve of those committed to a framework of shared values, to fraternity rather than divisiveness as the basis of racial justice. The agenda of this new undertaking remains nebulous. What programs will emerge and how these will shape black-white relations in the future is largely unknown. One prediction can be made with some confidence, however. The ideological component of race relations is unlikely ever again to loom as large as it did in certain communities, among them Sausalito, at a time that only seems long ago.

10

Oakland:
Interest Politics Regnant

I

In Oakland as in the other Bay Area communities, pressure during the 1960s to desegregate the schools was strong.[1] The movement for desegregation in Oakland had its symbol, a new high school intended to serve an almost all-white section of the community and derided for that reason as a "bastion of bigotry." Civil rights leaders could muster considerable local support among diverse constituencies in both the black and liberal white Oakland communities and could also count on the blessing, if not the active involvement, of such national organizations as the NAACP, committed to the same end.

It was not inconceivable that desegregation in Oakland would be achieved through the political process. Although neither the board of education nor the school administration was enthusiastic about the prospect, they were not adamant in their opposition. Principled defenses of color blindness calculated to remove the question from the arena of discussion were not forthcoming; temporizing was the typical response, and that reaction preserved the prospects for settlement. In any event, recourse to the courts for an order compelling desegregation was always a possibility. The threat of judicial action was frequently voiced during this period.

Despite these circumstances, substantial desegregation never came to Oakland. The school district did take steps to bring black and white students together, but these reached no more than 3 percent of the student population. Of greater moment, desegregation was no longer of much interest to anyone in the city after 1970. Changing demography rendered the prospects for desegregation remote: the student population of approximately sixty thousand, almost one-half white in the early 1960s, was more than 85 percent nonwhite in 1979. Changing black ideologies and political agendas have also made desegregation seem less attractive than an educational system designed by and for blacks. As a prominent Oakland black activist observed in 1968 when this shift in concern was becoming increasingly evident: "Why hurry? Oakland will be ours."[2]

Both ideological and legal strands of the race and schooling issue, dominant in other Bay Area communities, are present in Oakland. They are, however, subordinated to quintessentially political concerns; not the politics of symbols[3] but pluralist struggles over who gets what, when, and how much. Oakland confirms that disputes over such volatile issues as race can evolve into matters capable of being addressed in terms of conventional interest politics.[4]

II

During the mid-1960s, Oakland was viewed by federal and state officials and by the press as a "racial tinderbox," a community that might well be engulfed in a riot on the scale of Watts or Detroit. This prediction demanded very little imagination. Oakland shared with those communities the problems of economic stagnation, overcrowded housing, an underfinanced educational system, and high unemployment, especially among young blacks.[5] The city's highly visible contrasts—between rich and poor, hills and flatlands, whites and nonwhites—only dramatized the inequities associated with American urban life. Its population peaked in 1950; ever since, white and middle-class families have been moving to the surrounding suburbs, while nonwhite and poor families have used Oakland as a port of entry to the region.

Until World War II, the population of Oakland was almost entirely white. Blacks first arrived in large numbers to work at the naval base and in wartime industry. After the war, the number of black residents steadily increased. Between 1950 and 1980, the city's black population grew from 47,562 to 159,234; the Mexican-American community expanded in the same period from 16,500 to 32,491; and the Asian population grew from 6,781 to 26,341. Together, these three groups constitute more than three-fifths of Oakland's residents.[6]

Demographic changes of this magnitude would have considerable impact anywhere, for such newcomers make novel and substantive demands on the economic and political resources of the city. In some respects, Oakland was even less prepared than other cities to respond to these demands. As a community, Oakland still suffers the sting of Gertrude Stein's jibe about her hometown: "There's no *there* there." It is a city searching for its identity, very much in the shadow of San Francisco across the bay.

The political system in Oakland is in good part a legacy of the Progressive era and as such was naturally resistant to the new-comers' goals.[7] Politics in the Progressive model was to be efficient and forward-looking, not parochial. To that end, the city aban-doned a ward-based council system some fifty years ago in favor of city-wide council and mayoral elections. Political legitimacy de-rived in good part from conformity to procedures rather than from measures of performance. Of greater moment, the political sys-tem was a far less significant force in shaping Oakland than were the professionals, the city manager and the governmental agency heads, who administered the city.[8] Although Oakland has charac-teristically been perceived as a conservative town, run by powerful business concerns—notably the *Oakland Tribune* (owned for many years by the Knowland family), the Bechtel Corporation, and Kai-ser Industries—for their own benefit,[9] that rendering tells at most a partial truth. Business interests have significantly influenced electoral politics, but the city's administration has a significant life and impetus of its own. Although the city has preferred economic growth to economic redistribution as a basis for policy, this fact hardly distinguishes Oakland from other places. The preference for growth is largely administrative, rooted in Progressive beliefs about the general benefits of community prosperity. It does not constitute evidence of an effective power elite.

This pattern of stewardship was challenged during the 1950s and early 1960s. City administrators began to perceive that the newcomers were hostile to the rationale underlying how benefits were distributed. "A people problem," the city manager termed this gap between city programs and neighborhood values; together with other agency officials, he established a variety of programs designed to socialize residents to prevailing values.[10] Most note-worthy was a network of district councils established to encourage citizen participation in city affairs.

Participation in the late 1950s was expected to bring citizens' values into line with prevailing norms of governance. However, participation has a way of producing unanticipated consequences, as those who made "maximum feasible participation" of the poor a national policy slogan would learn a decade later.[11] Out of the dis-trict councils and, subsequently, the Ford Foundation-funded Grey Areas program and the Oakland Economic Development Council of the 1960s emerged a cadre of articulate black leaders to express what they saw as the interests of their particular community. This new leadership forced a reexamination of how the city did its political business. It had a particular impact on the affairs of the schools, where race became a central concern early in the 1960s. Black leadership and an altered political-administrative environment brought about a reassessment of racial policies.

III

Until race became an issue in Oakland, school politics was a humdrum affair.[12] School board meetings were brief, sparsely attended, and noncontroversial in character. Power both to make and to carry out policy resided primarily with the professional administration, led by long-term Superintendent Selmar Berg; the board preferred it that way.

The seven-member board was elected, but through the device of appointing successors to retiring members and supporting their subsequent candidacies as incumbents it functioned as a self-perpetuating institution; in forty-eight contests over a forty-year period, only five nonincumbents were chosen. This insularity was reflected in its membership, which was almost entirely conservative, Republican, drawn from the business and legal communities, and white. The board did not mirror the polyglot character of the city. Not until 1958, when Barney Hilburn, a Republican lawyer, was chosen by board members to fill a vacancy, did a black serve; another decade would pass before a second black, also a Republican, was elected.[13]

The issue that in 1961 first prompted racial controversy was the attendance zone drawn for Skyline High, a new secondary school located in the Oakland hills, for the choice of boundaries would promote or retard racial mixing.[14] Historically, the attendance zones of Oakland's five existing high schools extended from the flatlands into the hills. Those boundaries, although based on neighborhood considerations not on race, had the significant incidental effect of creating racially and socially heterogeneous student bodies in the secondary schools. The proposed Skyline High boundaries were drawn very differently. The proposed attendance zone stretched ten miles across Oakland's hills and brought into a single attendance area the one overwhelmingly white and wealthy section of Oakland. The student body of Skyline High School was therefore almost entirely white, whereas each of the other high schools became substantially more nonwhite. Whether by inadvertence or by design, the Skyline boundaries created substantial seg-regation in Oakland's secondary schools.

Questions concerning racial justice often have a significant ideological component and, like so many ideological questions, de-pend upon symbols for their political momentum. The establish-ment of an identifiable white school created the instrument of pro-test. The symbol of a white school—a "bastion of bigotry," as one of its detractors labeled it—commanded attention in the early 1960s.

It was the NAACP that first drew attention to the new bound-aries, as it was the NAACP that would play a major role in keeping attention focused on desegregation until the mid-1960s. That orga-nization was never representative of the black community in Oak-land. No single organization, neither the churches nor the neigh-borhood associations nor the political coalitions that came and went during the period, could claim to speak for Oakland's blacks. This factionalism within the black community was evident in other political domains, notably the city's poverty program. With respect to race and schooling, however, the NAACP, energetically led by a young black lawyer, Donald McCullum, assumed a posi-tion of leadership unchallenged during the early years of struggle; that was enough to assure it at least a hearing before the board of education.

The opportunity for a hearing, however, does not guarantee serious consideration. In January 1961, McCullum urged the Oak-land Board of Education to reject the Skyline boundaries on the grounds that they would diminish the prospect for desegregation. The proposed boundaries created "a private prep school supported by public funds," McCullum observed. A group of liberal parents living in the hills argued before the board that maintenance of an almost all-white school would deprive their children of the oppor-tunity to be schooled with black youngsters, and, for that reason, was harmful. Superintendent Berg rejected these pleas. He did not dispute the value of desegregation but held that the Skyline neigh-borhood would eventually be socially heterogeneous, "judging by the developments at the other high schools"; in the meantime, Berg asserted, any differently drawn attendance zone would wreak havoc with other attendance arrangements. Berg's response satis-fied the board, which voted six to one in favor of the proposed Sky-line boundaries; only Hilburn, the black board member, dissented.

There matters stood for over a year. In spring 1961, William Nolan, a liberal Democrat, upset the predicted succession by beat-ing the Republican board nominee. Although Nolan immediately began criticizing the quality of education in Oakland, tying his concerns to the question of desegregation, the board's vote on Skyline's boundaries meant that there was no particular policy issue on which to focus attention.

The board of education was preoccupied with selecting a successor to Superintendent Berg, who early in 1962 announced his intention to retire. The board was divided over the type of successor to appoint: an outsider, who would be likely to make substantial changes in the management of the schools, or an insider, who might reasonably be expected to maintain prevailing practices.[15] The insider, Assistant Superintendent Stewart Phillips, won out, over the vehement opposition of Nolan and Hilburn.

The selection of Phillips constituted a defeat for the politically inexperienced and fragile coalition of blacks and white liberals that had begun to concern itself with desegregation and educational quality. It led to a renewed assault on Skyline and, more generally, to a focus on racial separation in Oakland's schools. What the civil rights group wanted at this time was not substantial desegregation, but some indication that its view of what racial justice entailed would be taken seriously. In spring 1962, board member Nolan proposed that Oakland consider either adopting an open enrollment plan or redrawing attendance boundaries to encourage racial mixing. McCullum, president of the NAACP, demanded that the school district reassign substantial numbers of blacks to predominantly white schools, thus raising the "silk curtain" of segregation. McCullum threatened to bring suit, challenging the district's student assignment practices, if the political approach failed.

Some five hundred people, an enormous crowd in the annals of Oakland school politics, assembled to hear these issues debated at a May 1962 board meeting. A number of groups had joined the NAACP cause, CORE and the Oakland Teachers Association among them; talk of a lawsuit was in the air. The desegregation issue had also inspired the creation of a preponderantly white association of hills parents, vocal in its opposition to redistricting. Desegregation was rapidly becoming politicized.

Outgoing superintendent Selmar Berg sought to blunt the assault. His rejection of the desegregation proposals relied primarily on administrative, not ideological, arguments, and was in this sense designed to defuse the issue. Berg opposed proposals for open enrollment as likely to cause either overcrowding or unwanted specialization within the schools; redrawing attendance zones, he asserted (without offering any documentation), would cost between $1.75 and $4 million and hence was not feasible.[16] To the extent that segregation existed, Berg added, it had not been caused by the schools and was not the schools' responsibility to undo. The chairman of the Oakland board concurred: "No policy [should be] adopted to achieve a structure dreamed by a social planner along the lines of a predetermined racial arrangement."[17] The school board voted to reaffirm the Skyline boundaries.

The board of education did, however, agree to establish a Citizens' Advisory Committee on School Needs charged with studying, among other things, the district's racial problems. That venture proved significant for school governance. Although school district professionals had previously established ties with neighborhood groups, this marked the first time that the Oakland board created a formal mechanism, not under board or administrative control, to review any aspect of school policy. In this sense, the committee was similar in intention to the neighborhood councils established in the late 1950s to review city policy generally; its creation suggested that the board might be able to accommodate structural, if not substantive, change. The advisory committee also served the added and valuable goal of buying needed time for the district to formulate a more considered response to the race question.

Controversy over the advisory committee's mission led to further board concessions. In January 1963, the board charged the committee with "mak[ing] recommendations for reasonable actions, within the purview of the board, concerning the alleviation of minority group concentrations within the schools."[18] The board now publicly recognized that "minority group concentrations" existed in Oakland and viewed them as a source of concern. What "reasonable actions" the board could take to redress the problem of concentration was left for the citizens' committee to determine. Although the generally integrationist bias of committee appointees was itself suggestive of what might emerge,[19] the committee's task would not be a simple one. Even in 1962, Oakland's student population was nearly 40 percent black, and because of residential segregation patterns black students were concentrated in particular schools. Of the city's sixty-six elementary schools, seventeen were three-quarters or more black and thirty were three-quarters or more white; only nineteen were in rough racial balance. Ten of the sixteen junior high schools were similarly imbalanced, as were all but one of the high schools.

The shift in the Board of Education's position on desegregation was also made manifest in more concrete ways. In September

1962, the new superintendent of schools, Stewart Phillips, proposed a limited open enrollment plan, similar to that recommended by board member Nolan and rejected by Phillips' predecessor only six months earlier. Under this plan, parents could request that their children be assigned to any school in which space was available. Yet this action was not viewed as a "victory" by the civil rights groups because of the way the board reached its decision. Even as the board accepted limited open enrollment, it rejected a more ambitious busing and redistricting plan that would have reshaped the Skyline boundaries; the approved plan was thus seen as a compromise, not a triumph. More significantly, although the board's action was expected to promote desegregation, this was not its explicit intention. On the contrary, the limited open enrollment plan had been propounded as an administrative solution to a less glamorous problem, the inefficient use of available classroom space. The plan itself was color-blind, consistent with the view of Superintendent Phillips that the school district had no legal obligation to take any action with respect to persisting racial imbalance. Preference went not to students seeking a desegregated education but to students attending overcrowded schools; the plan was supposed to increase parental choice, not necessarily to lessen racial isolation. At this point in the Oakland desegregation controversy, the fact that the district had actually made greater racial mixing possible mattered less than its unwillingness to assert this as its objective.

In 1963, a speedy and relatively peaceful resolution of the dispute over desegregation was nonetheless conceivable. The Oakland board had acted with considerable dispatch to close the gap between it and those on its left both by its substantive action, adopting open enrollment, and by establishing the citizens' advisory committee. The school district appeared to be moving toward substantial desegregation at a time when the question was only beginning to be aired throughout the North and West. A report commissioned by the U.S. Commission on Civil Rights concluded that Oakland "is on the threshold of dealing in a meaningful way with educational problems of Negro pupils."[20] That hoped-for resolution did not take full account of the volatile character of the issue and hence proved overly optimistic.

It would be more than a year before the citizens' advisory committee released its report. During that time, civil rights groups channeled most of their energies to nonschool issues, among them

Oakland's failure to provide adequate housing for those displaced by urban redevelopment and alleged job discrimination on the part of city agencies, the Alameda Naval Air Station, and local merchants. Not that desegregation was wholly ignored: after a semester-long truce, the NAACP returned to the offensive, demanding the elimination of high school boundaries, "administrative assignment" to relieve de facto segregation, and a variety of other measures, among them courses in minority culture and a much expanded compensatory education program. Were these demands not met, a "direct action" program would commence: "The Oakland NAACP will sit-in, register-in, and attend-in the schools during September 1963 and withhold attendance at the de facto segregated schools. The NAACP will demonstrate at each meeting of the Board of Education and picket the administration offices."[21]

The NAACP efforts were apparently intended to force the board to take immediate additional action concerning desegregation. In that, they were ill timed, for the citizens' advisory committee report on these matters was still some months away from completion, and unimpressive. Direct action amounted to nothing more than a handful of NAACP pickets at September board meetings, and the school boycotts never occurred. At the same time the NAACP picketed, a numerically larger black group under the auspices of the Afro-American Association conducted a "study harder" demonstration at predominantly black McClymonds High School. Although the two efforts were not intended to conflict with each other, they served as a reminder that the NAACP was not the only voice speaking on behalf of Oakland's blacks.

The board did concern itself with racial policy in the fall of 1963. It urged the state, in selecting textbooks, to give preference to materials that accurately portrayed the contribution of minority groups and reviewed its own teacher assignment and transfer practice with an eye to encouraging faculty desegregation. That was insufficient for the NAACP, which vowed to bring a lawsuit.[22] The threat of litigation, which had had limited impact when previously uttered, was now ignored; after 1963, even the threat would be voiced less frequently. Whereas civil rights groups in other cities went to court in the face of the perceived failure of the political process, the school board (and later the school administration) rather than the courtroom remained the focus of attention in Oakland.

Political jockeying over racial issues continued until the publication of the citizens' advisory committee report. The NAACP explored new tactics intended to embarrass the school board into action, while the district went somewhat further in responding to NAACP demands. To commemorate the tenth anniversary of the *Brown* decision, the NAACP, like CORE in Sausalito, proposed a boycott of classes on May 18, 1964. The civil rights group anticipated that 8,000 students would stay away from school. That prospect led the board to revisit the hoary question of attendance at Skyline High School. Within weeks of the NAACP boycott call, and over the vocal protests of parents living in the Skyline attendance zone, the board approved a plan to admit 200 students from other parts of Oakland to Skyline. But this action did not satisfy the NAACP; only the promise of a study of desegregation in Oakland, conducted by the state and paralleling the citizens' advisory committee undertaking, persuaded the NAACP to call off the *Brown*-anniversary boycott. Further political maneuvering would await the citizens' committee and the state reports.

The citizens' advisory committee report, published in May 1964, was a controversial document. It proposed that Skyline High School's attendance zone be contracted to encompass only its immediate neighborhood, with the remaining students reassigned to the other secondary schools, which would thus render them more desegregated. The report also proposed that open enrollment be undertaken to promote desegregation and not just family choice. A minority of the committee went considerably further, urging a return to attendance zones that spanned hill and flatlands neighborhoods.

The recommendation to redraw Skyline's boundaries evoked passionate hostility. Up to this point, the NAACP and its allies in the civil rights movement had had the field almost to themselves; now Skyline parents turned out to oppose the alteration of the secondary school's attendance zone. Reshaping Skyline's boundaries, they declared, would produce not desegregation but massive white flight to the surrounding suburban communities. In October 1964, the board rejected the committee's recommendation. Too much antagonism had been stirred up, for too little apparent benefit, to justify any other course.[23]

This decision was not regarded by the school board as laying the desegregation issue to rest. The board had on its hands a just-issued report of the California Commission on Equal Opportunity in Education, which concluded that Oakland should close its one nearly all-black high school, permit students from three junior highs to attend Skyline if they so chose, and formulate a master plan for desegregation.[24] There also remained the prospect of continuing confrontations with the NAACP, understandably unhappy about losing this round in the policy battle.

The district did in fact undertake further desegregation, but beginning in the mid-1960s, the interest of black community leaders increasingly shifted to other educational goals.[25] In 1962, Oakland had received two million dollars in Ford Foundation Grey Area funds to help counter perceived social disorganization in the largely black West Oakland community. During the next several years, 42 percent of that money went to a variety of school programs, including compensatory education for low-achieving youngsters.[26] The equation of community betterment with educational betterment continued under the Office of Economic Opportunity (OEO) antipoverty program. In the first two years of that program, before the passage of the ESEA preempted the field, 64 percent of Oakland's federal antipoverty grant was spent on education, again mostly for compensatory instruction. These new undertakings had considerable significance. They provided smaller classes and introduced new modes of teaching for Oakland's black youngsters, and furnished jobs to a considerable number of community residents. It was of more than symbolic importance that the first black employed in Oakland's central school administration was the director of compensatory education; the program was from the first a black power base.

A new generation of politically astute radical black activists, trained in the guerrilla theater of the antipoverty programs, came to see themselves as the rightful representatives of Oakland's blacks. They struggled with black professionals, whom they criticized as the "establishment," for control over the Oakland Economic Development Corporation, the community-action program. They also exerted substantial influence over the Model Cities agency, bargaining with city political and administrative officials on behalf of a neighborhood, West Oakland, that they sought to turn into a semiautonomous political entity. The interest of this group lay first in promoting indigenous political participation, second in providing the services that predominantly black neighborhoods needed. Although these leaders did not quarrel publicly with advocates of desegregation, they had little enthusiasm for that goal. When one of their number appeared before the board of education, it was to demand such benefits as free lunches or an improved open enrollment program, of which individual parents could take advantage, not to speak for desegregation.

Interest in desegregation did not suddenly disappear. When coalitions of community groups formed in Oakland throughout the

1960s to make demands of the board of education, desegregation was often among those demands. Through the early 1970s, some continued to lament the ever-growing racial identifiability of Oakland's schools. Both the school board and the administration modestly promoted desegregation, even in the absence of outside urging. Yet a new emphasis could be detected among those who purported to speak for Oakland's blacks. Desegregation ceased to be the preferred racial policy in Oakland as early as 1965. The chance to control the expenditure of substantial public funds and to have some direct say in shaping educational offerings for black youngsters came gradually to displace desegregation as the primary interest.

IV

Desegregation continued to command school board and administration attention throughout the 1960s. But less and less was the issue pressed by outside groups on behalf of a black constituency. Instead, a small group of predominantly white liberals maintained their faith in desegregation as the primary means of achieving racial justice in the schools and thus kept the question alive. Between 1965 and the early 1970s, desegregation was transformed from a matter of paramount importance to the concern of a mere handful of board members and educational professionals. Eventually desegregation mattered to almost no one. It was regarded as a moot point in a school district with proportionately as few white students as Detroit.

This denouement could not have been predicted in late 1964. The Skyline boundary question was again before the board; this time, the proposal was not to reduce the size of the white neighborhood served by the school, as the citizens' advisory committee had urged, but to expand the attendance zone as the California Commission on Equal Opportunity in Education recommended, thereby permitting students from several mostly black junior high schools to enroll at Skyline. The commission proposal was accepted in modified form by the board in January 1965. But, as with the earlier adoption of a district-wide open enrollment plan, the board received little credit from civil rights groups because of the manner in which it acted. Twice during 1964, the plan had been voted down. Board approval was secured only after state education officials publicly rebuked the Oakland board; representatives of the Oakland Federation of Teachers, the NAACP, and the Alameda County Central Labor Council voiced strong support for the action; and CORE picketed the board. The board's action appeared to be merely a response to pressure, which did not please even those who had applied the pressure.

During this period, the board took other measures intended to improve race relations in the schools. It committed itself to preparing a master plan for desegregation of Oakland's schools as recommended by the state commission. Its nondiscriminatory teacher hiring and assignment practices merited praise from the California Fair Employment Practices Commission. The pattern of hiring substantial numbers of minority teachers has continued to the present. Between 1965 and 1980 the proportion of white teachers in the district declined from 77.6 percent to 51.9 percent, and the proportion of black teachers more than doubled, from 17.1 percent to 36.9 percent. The change is even more dramatic in the case of school administrators: in the same period, the proportion of whites dropped from 92.8 to 32.9 percent, while the proportion of blacks rose from 5.8 to 59.6 percent.[27]

The NAACP had still more demands, however. Clinton White, the new president of the organization, assailed the Skyline open enrollment plan as wholly inadequate; only boundary changes, not open enrollment, would end segregation at Skyline. If the board did not adopt a more sweeping desegregation plan, White added, the NAACP would consider retaliating by opposing a proposed increase in the school tax rate, urging the federal government not to aid the school district, and organizing a student boycott. The board also confronted an assault from its right flank. A largely white parents' group accused the board of appeasing the NAACP in adopting open enrollment and the Skyline feeder plan. Those actions were rooted in political expediency, not educational statesmanship, the group asserted.

"Quality Education in Oakland,"[28] the master plan prepared in response to the Commission on Equal Opportunity in Education report, did not quiet these criticisms. It proposed modest junior high school desegregation, involving sixty black students, which was implemented. Its responses to such questions as district-wide de facto segregation, compensatory education, education in human relations, fair employment practices, and school and community relations were vague in formulation and were ignored by the school board.

Although this inaction drew the ire of several community groups, no other approach appeared feasible to the board. By 1966, blacks comprised the single largest group in the district.[29] Holding on to the remaining whites constituted the primary policy challenge. "The concern is the flight of whites. . . . We're trying to maintain faith in the people so we won't have an exodus and at the same time we are keeping at the compensatory education programs to upgrade education in the Negro schools."[30]

Because it was not limited to transfers that promoted desegregation, the open enrollment plan in fact functioned to "maintain faith" among whites. As many whites as blacks took advantage of the transfer option to attend primary and junior high schools in the hills. While black reassignments improved racial mix in the hills schools, white transfers exacerbated segregation in the flatlands. Even at the secondary level, open enrollment led to increased segregation because of the sizable proportion of whites transferring to Skyline. Seymour Rose, the board's most liberal member, unsuccessfully urged that only transfers that had the effect of increasing desegregation be approved. Open enrollment in Oakland has continued until the present, without the limitation that Rose proposed. An estimated fifteen hundred to two thousand students currently participate in the open enrollment plan. Despite board requests for such information, statistics concerning the total number of participants and the racial mix of students exercising the option are not maintained.[31]

In September 1966, Oakland embarked on another small-scale desegregation effort, the so-called Model Integration Plan.[32] This undertaking differed from its predecessors in several significant respects. It was the result of district initiative, not external suasion; by all accounts, the plan was developed entirely by the professional staff. Moreover, it not only guaranteed spaces in predominantly white primary schools for some 360 students enrolled in overcrowded, largely black schools, but also offered free transportation, something otherwise not available in the school system. Because busing was provided, poor black parents living in the designated area who desired a desegregated education for their children could now exercise that choice.

The Model Integration Plan produced the sorts of mixed results that have become commonplace in desegregation ventures.[33] When students were tested two years later, no differences in achievement between bused and nonbused black students were detected; the social acceptance of the bused students in the new environment was, however, quite high, and the atmosphere in the schools was racially harmonious. Yet if this plan was intended as a "model" to be imitated elsewhere in the district, as its name suggests, that eventuality did not come to pass. The $55,000 expended annually for student transportation came from federal, not school district, funds. When that money ran out in 1968, the Model Inte-

gration Plan was permitted to die, the last such initiative under-taken in Oakland. It is a measure of popular sentiment concerning desegregation at that time that abandoning the program evoked no public reaction.[34]

In subsequent years, desegregation was discussed with de-creasing frequency. The school board or administrative staff, not a community group, broached the subject. The administration raised the issue only in the context of proposing cutbacks in the open enrollment plan, citing overcrowding as the reason. It was Seymour Rose, on occasion joined by one of the board's two black members, who prodded his unwilling colleagues to consider new desegregation initiatives. In November 1966, Rose requested that the superintendent explore the possibility of an interdistrict plan, but the idea came to naught. Two years later, a proposed citizens' committee, which would review Oakland's experience with deseg-regation, assess the apparently successful desegregation just un-dertaken in neighboring Berkeley, and offer recommendations to the board, was quashed by the board president, Lorenzo Hoopes. "Let's not be diverted from a general program for good schools by trying to create a divisive issue on integration. Integration has been and is being progressively and substantially achieved in the Oakland schools."[35] The facts, of course, were otherwise: Oakland schools were increasingly segregated. In the view of the board ma-jority, however, desegregation was no longer relevant to Oakland except as a symbol. Its revival as a political issue would generate only heat, not light.

A state attempt to enforce its desegregation guidelines in 1970 focused attention on desegregation one last time.[36] The guidelines called for a racial mix in each school that differed by no more than 15 percent from the racial composition of the school district. If, for instance, a school district enrolled 40 percent black students, a school whose enrollment was between 25 and 55 percent black was, by this criterion, "balanced." Oakland was among the 222 dis-tricts in the state with "imbalanced" public schools: seventy-six of the eighty-nine Oakland schools were imbalanced. Although the state guidelines did not require desegregation, the Department of Education could and did demand that districts make "progress reports." What efforts to relieve this imbalance would Oakland undertake?

The school board acted with dispatch. It proposed creation of a new citizens' committee and adopted a policy statement firmly committing it to the objective of desegregation. When the board heard from representatives of community groups, however, no sup-

port for desegregation was voiced. "The political consequences of the present national busing hysteria," stated Elijah Turner, spokesman for the Black Caucus, a black leadership coalition, "should not be played out in Oakland by busing students to achieve some fixed racial ratio in the city's schools."[37] A state-wide referendum overturning the state's racial balance guidelines ultimately brought this last act of the desegregation drama formally to a close. The real end had come some time earlier. Elijah Turner, speaking to the board, spelled out an agenda concerning race and educational policy very different from that of the 1960s:

The time for integration was in the 1960s. We're in the 1970s now. Frankly, integration is outdated. The black community is now moving in another direction. We don't want the board to get hung up on the process of trying to integrate. What the board should do is provide quality education to the children where the schools are. When they have achieved quality education, then they can start talking about integration. . . . Oakland should have integrated its schools in 1960. I think it may be impossible now. The black community is talking about community control and quality education. The board should spend money it might on busing on providing quality education in the schools.

The Oakland League of Women Voters, historically committed to desegregation, now reminded the board that concern for educational quality properly ought to be linked to any discussion of desegregation.

The irony of this transformation was evident. For years, blacks had criticized the board of education for resisting desegregation; now they warned the board not to revive the possibility. In less than a decade, the moral imperative of desegregation had given way among prominent blacks to other and more pragmatic concerns: politics, educational programs, and jobs. Desegregation in Oakland was an idea whose time had come and gone without its ever becoming much more than a symbol. By 1970, all that it symbolized was controversy. One year later, when Oakland's first black superintendent, Marcus Foster, decentralized the district's administrative structure, he rejected anything that could have been interpreted as a move to desegregate Oakland's schools. "Integration of the Oakland schools was really a moot point, for the school population was almost 75 percent nonwhite. . . . There was no substantial community sentiment—black or white—pressing for school integration."[38]

"Oakland should have integrated its schools in 1960," Elijah Turner stated, and in 1960 there were enough white students to create a genuinely racially mixed school system. Yet Turner's sug-

gestion lacks political realism. In 1960, the politics of race were such that civil rights leaders were not ready to ask for and the Oakland school board was not ready seriously to consider desegregation. At just about the time that desegregation could be discussed in Oakland, it was apparently no longer wanted. Other understandings of sound educational policy had become more salient.

V

Oakland school policymaking changed dramatically during the mid-1960s: that much is certain. School politics evolved from a white-dominated process that excluded minorities to one more open and responsive to minorities. The use of advisory committees to help shape district policy was a structural innovation intended to involve sectors of the city that were otherwise cut off from and hostile toward the school district. It had the effect of seriously engaging blacks for the first time in school affairs. The school board had made substantive changes as well. Although the scale of Oakland's desegregation was small, few northern cities had done more at the time. The timely arrival of new education money from foundations and from the state and federal governments enabled the district to begin rectifying historical inequities in the quality of educational services and facilities. Poor and minority children were now getting a somewhat fairer share of the educational pie.

Whether these efforts and parallel undertakings by other branches of city government could avert a crisis far more serious than anything Oakland had as yet witnessed remained unclear. A secret government report, leaked to the *Wall Street Journal*, identified the racial situation in Oakland as the nation's worst; a riot to rival Watts and Detroit was predicted if unemployment, housing, policy relations, and educational problems were not alleviated.[39] Throughout the balance of the decade, Oakland school politics, like city politics generally, had something of the quality of a time bomb. The question was not whether policy change was occurring but whether in pace and scope that change could forestall a crisis of unknown dimension.

The demand for a radical transformation of substantive school policies and school politics grew in pitch and intensity during this period. Although the Black Caucus constituted a significant source of pressure, the push for participation and policy change was more general. It involved blacks and whites; teachers, students, and parents; hills and flatlands residents; church and neighborhood groups. Between 1966 and 1970, more than one hundred organizations formed and dissolved; a number of coalitions

cut across the political spectrum of these church-related, neighborhood, and community-based entities.

These organizational efforts, unprecedented in a historically apolitical city, suggested both considerable popular interest and substantial disagreement about appropriate educational policy. Several basic groupings were detectable: parent organizations, primarily concerned about what might be described as a "quality" education; such black establishment groups as the NAACP, the Urban League, and black church organizations; and more radical neighborhood-based groups, among them the local community action committees. Present in the background although never directly involved in Oakland school politics was the Black Panther Party.

The nature of these groups' interests varied from a desire for administrative leadership to urging by the Oakland Education Association that a new citizens' committee be formed to review district policy generally, to demands by Black Caucus spokesmen for a reallocation of power away from the board and the central administration into the hands of parents and school-site personnel. As confidence in the board and administration declined, the nature of the demands grew more extreme and the manner in which they were expressed became more shrill.

Unhappiness with school district policy brought a measure of unity to Oakland's dissident groups. "This is the first time since the civil rights movement began in the Oakland schools," the education editor of a local newspaper, the *Montclarion*, remarked, "that a number of groups have joined in a common pursuit with any degree of cohesiveness." In April 1966, twenty-one Oakland organizations constituted themselves as the Ad Hoc Committee for Quality Education, produced a long list of demands, and threatened to resort to the tactics of the early 1960s civil rights movement— including a boycott of the public schools.

Desegregation was one, but only one, of the many concerns. The committee was interested in matters of equity: it wanted, for example, an equalization of curricular opportunities, equipment, and facilities in hills and flatlands schools. It also sought particular changes that in its view would improve the caliber of instruction, including smaller classes, free summer schools, training in intergroup relations, and a coordinated preschool program. The growing Mexican-American population, represented on the committee by the Mexico-American Unity Council, sought the hiring of Spanish-speaking professional personnel, especially school counselors.

The proposals concerning school governance were most disturbing to the board and administration. The committee insisted on parent participation in managing federal education programs. It demanded school-by-school achievement data, which could presumably be used to hold the system accountable for the relatively poorer performance of minority youngsters. Of greatest significance, the committee sought recognition as a legitimate separate constituency, with representation on administration and board committees. Parity of influence, not merely giving advice, was its objective.

Several hundred spectators packed the board meeting to witness the committee's presentation. John George, a veteran civil rights activist and Black Caucus member, spoke of desegregation in phrases reminiscent of Martin Luther King's call to "bring us together."[40] Other speakers pressed a more militant position. One of the new generation of radicals, Curtis Baker, declared: "We are tired of the Uncle Toms and Aunt Jennys who listen and then carry on sweetly and do nuthin [*sic*]. . . . We are going to have a lot in store for this board. We are not going to take your messin' [*sic*] around anymore and I don't care how many taxpayers have to give for it." Acting as a "safety valve" to defuse community pressure would no longer suffice, Robert Scheer, a candidate for Congress, told the board. "If you can't solve the problem, then you should resign and let John George and Curtis Baker take your places."

Although the school board agreed to meet with the committee, the nature of the relationship remained unclear. The board refused to recognize the committee as a group with bargaining status, for that was to surrender too much of its statutory and political prerogative. From the committee's list of demands, the board selected the items that it could support if funds were forthcoming. Further desegregation was not among these, a fact that angered committee leader (and, subsequently, national CORE chairman) Elijah Turner. It was not, however, the persistence of segregation that aroused Turner's ire but the resource inequities attributable to segregation. Because "all the money for quality education is being spent in hill schools," continued segregation meant continued inequality of opportunity for Oakland's blacks.

Subsequent meetings between board of education members and the ad hoc committee in the spring of 1966 produced little by way of formal agreement, aside from a revision of the student disciplinary code. The meetings did, however, legitimate participation in school district decision making by a neighborhood-based, not city-wide organization, a group whose members had not been

selected by district officials. The school district was becoming increasingly permeable, even if the tangible impact of the permeability remained modest.

In the fall of 1966, the ad hoc committee reiterated its policy demands. When the school board did not accede to them, the committee called for a three-day student boycott. "Freedom schools" patterned on institutions set up in the South to instruct blacks in segregated school districts would focus on community concerns during the boycott, suggesting a parallel between the situation in Oakland and the overtly racist South. Boycotts are supposed to be peaceful events in which the power of a group is revealed but not wielded. This one turned out very differently.[41] A violent attack on one high school campus caused $21,000 in damage, and 50 students were arrested. Although 5,000 students more than the number usually absent did not attend school, only about one thousand attended the freedom schools.

The boycott widened the political gap between the community groups represented on the ad hoc committee and the city's political system. The mayor of Oakland, drawn into the fray by the need to stem the violence, condemned the committee as "troublemakers." The school board, determined to bar any repetition of the boycott, voted harsh disciplinary measures. The California Commission on Equal Opportunity in Education, the agency whose intervention had forestalled the threat of boycott in 1964, investigated the circumstances that gave rise to the 1966 riots. In its report, the commission blamed not the ad hoc committee but the board and the administration, which it faulted for not effectively addressing the underlying school problems and the persisting racial tensions.[42] Criticism is, of course, easier to frame than positive policy. In making substantive recommendations, the state commission did not speak in terms of particular reforms but more generally about the virtues of leadership. It did not confront the hard issue of how the school system should cope with the changing character of the city and what the impact of those changes on the educational enterprise would be. With good reason: although numerous cities throughout the country were experiencing similar turmoil, solutions were nowhere to be found.

Measures of the Oakland school system's problems were everywhere at hand. Less money was spent in the schools that black children attended than in the hills schools, even taking into account the influx of federal dollars. Teachers in predominantly black schools were less experienced and more likely to have tempo-

rary status; buildings were shabbier, and a higher proportion of flats students were in portable classrooms; playgrounds were small, supplies few, and classes crowded. Viewed in terms of educational achievement, the picture was even more grim. In general, Oakland students' achievement fell below state levels. Most discouraging was information, released in 1967 in response to one of the ad hoc committee demands, that "children in the Oakland flatland schools slip backwards as they proceed from the first grade on into high school."[43] Although students in the first grade read as well as the state average, by sixth grade minority youngsters were reading at only the fourth-grade level; the hills schools remained above average in performance. This disparity between black and white achievement persisted through secondary school and beyond. One study reported that 40 percent of Skyline pupils went on to college and that only 2 percent were unemployed two years after graduation. In contrast, in an almost entirely black high school, only 5.4 percent of the graduates continued on to college, and 15.5 percent were unemployed.

What, if anything, could be done? The 1966 boycott had revealed that Oakland might explode into violence at any time and that in important respects the city was within no one's control. Oakland's school system had to determine for itself what new policies concerning both substantive programs and participation of community groups fit the circumstances. The chief measure of the district's success in this task was the gradual admission of Oakland's black community groups into a partnership of sorts with the official political system. The appointment of the district's first black superintendent was the key event; from it followed experiments in broadened participation, the decentralization of certain school governance functions, and a shifting of resources away from white and wealthy to poor and black schools. Despite the fact that only two blacks serve on the seven-member school board, Oakland's schools presently do belong largely to its black community. Viewed from the vantage of the mid-1960s, that change represents nothing less than a peaceful political revolution.

Superintendent Stewart Phillips, the insider appointed to maintain prevailing policies at the beginning of the decade, by the mid-1960s was widely perceived as being unable to lead the Oakland school district effectively. Of greatest significance was Phillips' lack of rapport with minority community groups, an obviously serious problem in a predominantly nonwhite school

district. Phillips' resignation, effectively engineered by a coalition organized by board member Seymour Rose, allowed the district the opportunity of selecting a leader more fit for the times.

The selection of a new superintendent became the central issue around which community groups could organize. All could agree that responsiveness was the key attribute and that participation in the selection process was the key concept. At least initially, the board of education was unmoved by community-group coalition building. Appointment of a committee of outside experts to recommend candidates was as far as the board was willing to go in assuring the thoroughness of the search. In May 1969, just two months before Phillips was to depart, the superintendency was offered to James Mason, superintendent in Las Vegas and not one of the candidates proposed by the expert panel. However, Mason had apparently been involved in a conflict-of-interest scandal, his foot-dragging role in the desegregation of Las Vegas' schools upset some Oakland black leaders, and the absence of community participation in the selection process was equally disturbing. The director of the Oakland Economic Development Corporation urged a boycott of the schools in order "to hit the school board over the head with a hammer." Minority leaders demanded Mason's immediate resignation and the selection of a new superintendent "by the community."[44]

Several hundred people packed the next board meeting to reiterate these demands. Spokesmen focused primarily on the board's failure to follow the selection procedures that it had adopted, an action perceived as demonstrating disregard for constituents' wishes. "If the conflict for community involvement in our schools has to be escalated from this board room into our homes, our schools, our churches, and our businesses, then let it be known, this is our Armageddon."[45] The board of education refused to review Mason's hiring and adjourned. Protesters, vowing that the board members would remain until it reconsidered its decision, blocked the doorways to the meeting room. A few minutes later, the Oakland police arrived and used Mace to disperse the crowd. The confrontation was quite enough for Mason, who submitted his resignation shortly thereafter.

The Mason fiasco not only revealed a school board stiffening in its resolve in the face of minority-group pressure but also encouraged sympathy for the "Oakland Five," who were arrested after the board fracas.[46] Revelations about the district's compensatory education program, made public shortly thereafter, were re-

garded by the growing number of dissidents as revealing the consequences of Oakland's perceived indifference to minority student
needs. A state audit of $5.5 million Title I, ESEA funds expended
by Oakland in 1966–67 indicated that, contrary to the purpose of
that legislation, the money had not been spent on educationally
disadvantaged students but had been dispersed generally throughout the district's schools. Moreover, despite staff shortages in the
schools, fully one-third of the funds had been used for administration. The auditors did not suspect malevolence but observed that
"there was no one at the policy-making level who was responsible
and accountable for the implementation of the program." Not even
the black compensatory education director had been able to effectively to defend blacks' interests.

The fact that a great many communities treated Title I monies
similarly, as a no-strings handout from Washington, was both unknown at the time and irrelevant. The Title I audit provoked deep
anger in black leaders. In the meantime, the board persevered in
its efforts to hire a superintendent. Although it appointed a team of
consultants to sound out black spokesmen, those leaders would
have no part of an arrangement in which their influence would be
expressed only through intermediaries. The board was groping for
ways of involving the emergent black leadership in decision making without ceding its statutory responsibility.[47] For its part, when
the Black Caucus spoke of participation, it had in mind something
akin to a veto. As Elijah Turner, representing the Black Caucus,
stated: "If the community isn't involved [in the superintendency
search] the superintendent can't be successful. . . . The only power
we have is to raise hell. And I will raise hell."[48]

The board's second choice for the superintendency was announced in November 1969: Ercell Watson, black superintendent
of the Trenton, New Jersey, school system. Again the Black Caucus,
joined by other groups, including the Oakland Federation of Teachers, protested the action. Their objection was not to Watson but to
the board's continuing failure formally to enlist them in the selection. Vowing to "interview Watson and tell him 'like it is' in Oakland,"[49] Elijah Turner flew to Trenton with other Black Caucus
members. Shortly thereafter, Watson turned down the Oakland
position, asserting that he preferred to stay in Trenton.

Watson's decision left the Oakland Board of Education and
the various minority community groups represented by the Black
Caucus effectively at a standstill. The board had managed to keep
community groups out of the superintendent-selection process de-

spite intense efforts to intervene. For its part, the Black Caucus had indeed been able to "raise hell"; it had twice induced the board's candidate to decline the post.

Of potentially greater moment, the level of black political antagonism to the school board and administration had reached such heights that Black Caucus members could speak seriously about boycotting the school district, not merely for a few days but until the system radically transformed itself. Addressing the board of education shortly after the Title I revelations, Donald McCullum, longtime NAACP leader, asserted: "The agonizing tragedy is that black people and poor people had hoped passionately that these new programs would provide a breakthrough for their children. . . . The next step should be a decision by this community whether their children will attend school in Oakland under the present administration this fall." McCullum proposed the creation of an alternative educational regime—a "people's system. You have demonstrated your indifference so we have no alternative than to establish a parallel school board."[50]

After the effort to appoint Watson, the Black Caucus did preside over the creation of such a body. This new entity was perhaps the most impressive of the education-focused political coalitions to be founded in Oakland. It commanded the allegiance of both the NAACP and the Black Panthers, as well as many other civil rights and black power groups, the two teachers' unions, the League of Women Voters, several church groups, welfare-rights organizations, and the Jewish Community Relations Council.[51] These disparate entities shared a profound dissatisfaction with the existing system. The entity was perceived as a parallel board with a committee structure identical to the board's own. "The board has abdicated," Paul Cobb of the Black Caucus declared, "so we are going to do their job. If people call us militant, let them. We are militant about quality education."[52]

This newest umbrella group, Community United for Relevant Education (CURE), sought unsuccessfully to draw the board of education into its affairs, inviting board members to sit on its committees and proposing discussion of superintendent selection procedures. The board of education regarded CURE's invitation as a threat to its prerogatives. Although the board was willing to discuss "educational policy" questions with CURE members, the board, not CURE, would select the district's next superintendent and make policy for the school district. How long the board could maintain this posture of autonomy was uncertain. It took a most astute appointment to the superintendency—Marcus Foster, black

assistant superintendent in Philadelphia—to exercise the leadership that eventually produced a satisfactory and remarkably stable political resolution. Foster's leadership, coupled with the adaptability of the school board to changed circumstances, made possible the transformation of the Oakland school system into one attentive to the needs of its largely minority clientele.

VI

With the arrival of Marcus Foster as superintendent of schools in 1970, the issue of race and schooling took a very different turn.[53] Foster was able substantially to satisfy the city's black leadership, at war with the school system for the better part of a decade, that the Oakland schools were now treating seriously the educationally and politically rooted concerns of the black majority. Devolution of influence over significant policy decisions and a reallocation of resources from the hills to the flatlands schools marked the transformation of the school system from one unsure of its mission in the face of markedly changed community circumstances into one that redistributed monetary and political resources from rich to poor, white to black.

It is a sign of Foster's success that he was able to begin this transformation without arousing substantial resentment on the part of the remnants of the white community; whites did not protest that they were worse off because blacks were better off. In this sense, Foster preserved the educational system intact, thus managing conflict and insuring needed institutional stability. Neither his regime nor that of his successor, Ruth Love, resolved the educational dilemmas that confront Oakland. These are not, however, dilemmas concerning race and schooling of the sort that constantly engaged the district between 1960 and the early 1970s. Instead, they are policy problems that any urban school district, regardless of the racial composition of its students, is likely to confront today. The racial factor, although rendering these problems more serious and possibly more consequential, nonetheless does not define them.

Quite like the two earlier superintendency nominations, Marcus Foster's appointment in 1970 initially divided Oakland's black leadership. On one side were those concerned about what this selection process revealed about minority powerlessness; on the other side stood those more interested in Foster's capacity to lead a divided school district and anxious to heal the wounds opened by the Black Caucus' battles with the school board. By the time Foster arrived to assume the superintendency, he had already met privately with Black Caucus members, apparently allaying their concerns. During his tenure, Foster managed through near-constant meetings and negotiations adroitly to command the support, or at least not arouse the hostility, of almost all the volatile segments of the community.

Desegregation was not central to Foster's mission. Instead he hoped to manage a process of decision making that involved parents and community groups in shaping school district policy and practice.[54] The superintendent proposed to resolve long-standing conflicts between the school system and its antagonists over the role of outsiders as participants in policymaking. Because Foster's notion of participation came with specifics attached, his position was more credible. Early in his term, for instance, Foster established committees of parents, teachers, and students to recommend new school principals; Foster would make the final choice from among the committees' suggestions. Treating the selection of a new principal as a decision appropriately influenced by community members was consistent with Foster's more general interest in ensuring parental and student support for the school system.

The creation of a new citizens' committee, underwritten by foundation funds to assure its independence from district suasion, was another example of the participation to which Foster was committed. That group of 300—subdivided into task forces to deal with school buildings, finance, curriculum, decentralization, multicultural education, and community resources (but not, as with the predecessor citizens' committee of 1963, desegregation)—churned out dozens of proposals, some of which helped shape district policy. Foster promised only to hear out, not to accept, the recommendations. This arrangement aroused some distrust in those who feared that it would degenerate into mere "reshuffling of staff and numerous meetings of parents," but these fears did not produce public conflict. From Foster's point of view, it was "good for the administration to hedge [on particular proposals]. It keeps the task forces from thinking we've got to go with their recommendations."[55]

Administrative decentralization of the school district into three regions was also part of Foster's design for reform. Decentralization was a more efficient arrangement, a management consulting firm retained by the district reported, for it undid the prevailing concentration of administrative power and made it easier for parents to resolve their grievances. Although decentralization provided a marvelous opportunity to rethink desegregation, the Foster administration refused even to consider the idea for fear of stirring up old quarrels. Each of the three regions was a microcosm of the district; within each, attendance boundaries were essentially untouched. A decade earlier, the creation of Skyline High School as a "bastion of bigotry" had marked the commencement of hostilities between blacks, along with their liberal white allies, and the school district. When Skyline's boundaries remained intact following the 1971 reorganization, the matter passed without notice. By then, black leaders had nothing to say about desegregation. They were waiting instead to see what a new black superintendent would do for them.

One thing Foster could and did accomplish was to hire more minority staff. The proportion of black principals and assistant principals almost doubled, to 49 percent, whereas the proportion of black teachers jumped from one-quarter to one-third. Although these actions continued the efforts of past administrations rather than representing a policy departure, the pace of minority hiring was accelerated.

Resources also flowed into minority schools in substantially higher proportions than in earlier years. A comparison of the allocation of teachers before and after Foster's arrival reveals a startling change.[56] In 1969–70, Oakland distributed state and local money on an approximately equal basis to all schools, whatever their racial or social-class composition; when federal funds were added into the calculation, the poorest and predominantly black schools were most generously treated. In schools with fewer than 10 percent minority students, $370.73 salary dollars were expended for each pupil, as compared with $404.66 in schools with more than 90 percent minority students; the expenditure gap between schools enrolling the richest and the poorest students was even greater, with over one hundred dollars more being spent on the poorest schools.

Foster disequalized distribution of state and local money to favor the poor and preponderantly black schools even more clearly. As a result, in 1970–71 schools with more than 90 percent minority students spent almost two hundred dollars more per pupil on teachers' salaries than predominantly white schools; in schools enrolling the poorest students, $260 more was spent on teachers' salaries for each pupil than in schools enrolling the district's wealthiest students. The weak academic performance of students enrolled in flatlands schools was being addressed by one of the few techniques available to school administrators, budgetary reallocation.

Judged in terms of the impact of specific reforms, the Foster administration was a failure. The Master Plan exercise consumed funds without producing an agenda that Oakland could embrace. Decentralization appeared to some to be just another bureaucratic layer, not a means of making school management more accessible to the clientele, and was substantially modified by Foster's successor. The redistributed resources had little apparent impact on measured achievement. An attempt to introduce budgeting rationality through implementing a Planning, Programming, and Budgeting System (PPBS) did not succeed.[57]

Yet in an important sense, these specifics are not the appropriate yardstick against which to measure this administration's performance. Foster managed what had previously seemed impossible of achievement: he served as a bridge between blacks and whites, and between school board and community groups, in Oakland. In the 1971 elections, two conservative board members ran on Marcus Foster's coattails and were reelected easily. The distrust and hostility that had characterized relations between the school system and those it served noticeably declined during his administration. Black Caucus spokesmen moved on to other issues; the importance of the Black Panthers diminished; the reduced appeal of radical rhetoric and confrontationist strategies in the 1970s was everywhere remarked. Foster himself was able to revive the interest of much of Oakland's black population in the education of its children by reshaping the school system to respond to that population's wants. For the first time, Oakland's less well-organized ethnic minorities, especially the Latinos, received a sympathetic hearing—and an expanded commitment to bilingual education.[58] Political voice, new educational programs, an infusion of resources: these things, not desegregation, are what Oakland's minorities gained from the school system in the 1970s. Foster brought stability to the schools. By his success, he also helped make it possible for black officials to assume positions of leadership, not only in the school system but also throughout city government.

Marcus Foster was assassinated November 6, 1973, by members of a radical fringe group, the Symbionese Liberation Army. It is relevant in assessing Foster's impact to note that the district was effectively paralyzed by this event and was unable to fix a new direction for nearly two years. In December 1975, the school board appointed as superintendent Ruth Love, a black woman who once taught in Oakland and more recently had headed the Right to Read Program in the Department of Health, Education and Welfare. Love, who stayed in the post until 1981, brought a new set of concerns to the position. Although she continued to stress the needs of the minority student population, educational achievement and not power-sharing or administrative decentralization mattered most to her. To that end, Love created an Instructional Strategy Council to develop curriculum guides emphasizing competence in literacy and arithmetic and tried to make teacher accountability turn on student performance. In this undertaking, the school district has a long way to go. Its achievement scores remain very low, even when compared with those reported by California's other large cities. Financial difficulties due to the tax ceiling imposed by Proposition 13 have made this task harder, obliging Oakland to cut back its teaching staff by almost 10 percent.

The substitution of student achievement for participation and decentralization reflects a more general change in the educational policy agendas of big cities since the early 1970s. This change is not in any obvious way animated by race. It is rather a matter of two superintendents, both black, having different views of how to manage an urban school system. While the board of education still has only three black members, it acquired a liberal majority for the first time in 1977, and in time a majority of the board may well be black.[59] That development will be largely irrelevant to the course of educational policy in Oakland, which has been firmly set by Foster and Love, not by the board. The Oakland school system is now perceived as responsive to the black community. How that school system, profoundly altered in the past decade, will make good its hopes for institutional responsiveness or improved student achievement is the unresolved issue. It is a vital issue, but not a question of racial justice.

VII

The Oakland school district did not embrace the moral aspiration of desegregation, however fervently it was pressed during the early 1960s. Nor did the racial issue so escalate as to require resolution in the courts, the one forum that regularly renders ideology into policy. Desegregation in Oakland is now hard to conceive. Only a small proportion of whites, less than 15 percent, is available to produce a racially mixed school system, but this fact does not suffice as an explanation. Other cities with similarly sizable black student enrollments, among them St. Louis and Detroit, were nonetheless haled into court by proponents of desegregation in the 1970s. One needs look elsewhere to understand Oakland's history.

What distinguishes Oakland is the willingness of both the school system and civil rights advocates to turn questions of racial justice into subjects for bargaining. Although the bargaining was conflict ridden and frequently on the verge of collapse, statesman-

ship by both sides kept the process going. The school board gradually accommodated itself to the transformation of school politics
and the consequent reallocation of school resources in Oakland.
For their part, the civil rights groups generally maintained a consistent pressure for reform even in the face of apparent obduracy;
they neither gave up nor escalated the issue to a level at which negotiation would be impossible. As a result, race and schooling politics in Oakland—including current disinterest in desegregation—
reflect the popular will as well as any politically derived solution
may be said to do.

How did the Oakland school board respond to an undeniably
changing political climate? In the middle and late 1960s, before
the appointment of Marcus Foster to the superintendency, the
board's many and diverse critics saw it as an inflexible behemoth.
Because of the undeniable need for reform and the volatile character of the racial issue, this inflexibility was treated as a potentially
fatal weakness.

A 1968 report on Oakland, prepared by the National Education Association and the California Teachers Association at the request of the local union, advances this thesis. The title of the report
conveys the thrust of its argument: "A Community in Transition
with a School District Too Slowly Adapting." The study concludes:
"The Board has revealed its reluctance to acknowledge the seriousness of Oakland's educational problems by maintaining that Oakland has no more troubles than other cities. This tendency to minimize weakness undermines the sense of urgency leaders must
convey to a community expected to provide the means for improvement. . . . The responsibility for establishing priorities has
not been assumed by the administration and the Board. . . . Despite all the words that have been printed and all that has been
said in speeches at meetings, so very little seems to have happened."[60] A similar criticism was propounded in 1968 by liberal
board member Seymour Rose. The focus of his ire was the way in
which Oakland had procrastinated with respect to desegregation:
"If Oakland is achieving integration it's very slow. We still have
children going to schools which are 98 percent white. We may even
be breaking the law. You're not willing to move fast enough. I say to
you, my fellow colleagues, you're making a mistake." Desegregation only illustrated a more general shortcoming, as Rose saw the
matter; the root concern was a failure of leadership. "This board
has not been a good leader. If the board were providing leadership,
the community would follow us. We would have passed our tax increases. I think they haven't passed because we haven't involved

the community. I'm not satisfied as a board member and I represent the part of the community which feels we are not moving fast
enough."[61]

Rose's critique was two pronged. On the one hand, the board
vacillated rather than providing leadership; on the other hand, the
board was not responsive to constituent concerns. One or the other
prong of this argument was accepted by groups ranging from militant black organizations to the Skyline PTA. As Rose observed, in
the context of a board discussion concerning creation of a citizens'
group to review mounting student disturbances, "The trouble is
we've had the opportunity many times in the past to give citizens
participation in things and we haven't done so. They feel we are
not responsive to them. There is a large segment of our community
who do not have confidence in us as a board."[62]

Although this critique of the Oakland school board acquires a
certain authority through repetition, another view of the historical
record is at least equally plausible. The call for leadership generally presupposes the existence of a coherent policy direction that
the district could have pursued. Under the circumstances, however, that seems a most unrealistic presupposition. The wisest
course for a district like Oakland, in the midst of momentous
change, may well be to respond on an essentially ad hoc basis to
situations as they arise rather than shaping the future in conformity to some grand scheme.

A failure of leadership on the part of the board was also asserted by three consultants hired by the school district in its efforts
to woo community support during the superintendency search. In
a remarkable brochure prepared for prospective candidates, the
consultants noted: "For too long, the Board has received a series of
surprises, and has perforce reacted to them defensively. . . . It
should sit in judgment on policy, procedures, and results—and not
as defender of the status quo."[63] Lack of leadership in this instance
is equated with defensive and conservative behavior. It implies doing very little. Yet Oakland's several desegregation initiatives, the
vigorous recruitment of nonwhite teachers and administrators,
and the compensatory education programs established well in
advance of federal funding do not reveal a moribund district.
Whether or not the board was as imaginative as the circumstances
required, it did move well beyond the practices of an earlier and
simpler time.

Nor is it clear that the Oakland Board of Education was unresponsive to the community's wishes. Seymour Rose's dissatisfaction partly reflects the fact that, as he put it, "I represent the part of

the commmunity which feels we are not moving fast enough."
Board president Lorenzo Hoopes offered an instructive rejoinder:
"This board has not moved as fast as some would like, but has
moved faster than others would like. This is not a bad position. The
board has maintained the equanimity of the community."[64]

The board read the election results. Throughout the critical
period, it maintained its stable conservative majority. But it did
not ignore the voting minority that Rose represented. From being
a hermetic institution in the 1950s and early 1960s, the board
evolved into increasing experimentation with forms of participation, drawing a line only where it would formally have had to cede
its legal authority. The establishment of a citizens' advisory committee in 1963, negotiations subsequently conducted with the ad
hoc committee, community involvement in the selection of "human relations assistants" for the high schools, and indirect consultation with Black Caucus leaders in the superintendency search all
illustrate such experimentation. What the Oakland board did *not*
do is equally important. The board of education never promised more than it could deliver; antagonisms were consequently
contained.

Not that the board's behavior in these matters is above criticism. In specific instances, as in designing the superintendency-
selection process, the board should have been more attentive to
constituency concerns. Its tendency to back grudgingly into reform
did not strengthen its reputation. Its chief administrator during
the 1960s, Superintendent Stewart Phillips, was too strongly committed to professional autonomy, too quick to dismiss the value of
participation. On balance, however the board performed adroitly.
Many of the changes demanded in the name of openness—a "community veto" over the new superintendent, for instance—would
have resulted in abdication, not responsiveness; these the board
was wise to reject. When Marcus Foster subsequently pursued similar experiments in limited community participation that preserved the authority of the administration, he acquired a reputation for political astuteness; board members, if not as astute as
Foster, were also far from being as intransigent as is routinely
asserted.

A different set of community spokesmen might well have regarded the board's actions as unacceptably timid and slow and
have sought vindication for their position outside normal political
channels. Judicial condemnation of segregation in Oakland represented the most likely form of such vindication, and indeed the
threat to file suit was frequently voiced during the early 1960s. The

fact that suit was not brought is surprising. The resources to undertake litigation were available. There were competent lawyers among Oakland's civil rights leaders, and the national NAACP might well have offered tangible support. Moreover, the legal case to be made out was quite as good in Oakland as in any northern city. If de facto, or fortuitous, segregation was unconstitutional, as some lower federal courts and the California Supreme Court asserted throughout the 1960s, there clearly was de facto segregation to undo; racial isolation was more prevalent in Oakland's schools than in those of many large cities. Even if the constitution proscribed only deliberate, de jure, segregation, the creation of a predominantly white high school, Skyline, which predictably increased segregation, might well have sufficed to demonstrate the requisite intent.[65]

Oakland's civil rights leaders took a remarkably pragmatic view of litigation. They strategically deployed the prospect of a lawsuit in order to win some concession from the board. It was the threat of a lawsuit that brought about the liberalized attendance requirement for Skyline; another such threat initially opened board policies to external purview by the 1964 citizens' advisory committee. Those trade-offs sufficed to keep the issue out of court through the mid-1960s.

As the nature of black concern shifted from desegregation to specific participatory and educational-program benefits for the black community, the possibility of litigation to secure these objectives disappeared. Such redistributive questions do not readily admit of judicial resolution; they are what politics is supposed to address. Although the frustration of black community groups with the pace and scope of political change was undeniable, these groups persevered in the political arena. They also submerged their considerable differences and thus acted as an effective coalition. Their continuing efforts made possible an eventual political resolution and shaped the substance of that resolution.

Oakland succeeded in resolving momentous questions of racial policy through the political process, and that is a considerable achievement. Whether the substance of that resolution constitutes good policy is a different and harder issue. The difficulties in addressing it are formidable. The reallocation of money and power within the school system secured for Oakland's black community a measure of distributive justice. How does this compare with other possible outcomes? Had the school system been desegregated in the mid-1960s, when there were still a substantial number of white students, would that action merely have accelerated white departure? What other effects might it have had on Oakland schools? The merger of Oakland with the surrounding white suburban communities, another conceivable alternative, would have altered the district's racial composition in a way likely to produce relative racial stability—since whites could not readily have moved to other suburban sanctuaries—and a more equal racial mix than desegregation within Oakland. Yet such a district would have been far larger than Oakland, in terms both of student population and of geographic area, and hence more susceptible to the weaknesses associated with institutional gigantism. How ought those factors be weighed, one against the other?

These doubts about what is "right" for Oakland illustrate broader dilemmas concerning both the substance of race and schooling policy and the way that policy gets fashioned. Part 3 takes up these questions.

PART THREE
The Possibility of Policy

The World was all before them,
where to choose.

> John Milton, *Paradise Lost*

CHAPTER
11

Stays Against Confusion: Understanding the Historical Experience

I

American public schools have been substantially altered, even transformed, in the past quarter-century. Efforts to harness racially rooted concerns to the idea of equal educational opportunity represent a chief cause of that transformation. Changes in school policy and practice directly traceable to race matter in their own right, and race also catalyzed other reforms that have reshaped the schools' broader mission.

The specifics of change vary with the particularities of place, as the case studies confirm: things turned out differently in each of the five Bay Area communities. The attributes of each community—notably the character and strength of civil rights groups and their conservative opposition, the organizational dynamics of the school system, and the civic culture—shaped its experience: in this sense there were many different transformations. But the experiences of the Bay Area communities reveal the significance of commonality as well as the importance of idiosyncrasy, the framework of constraint as well as the ambit for initiative. What is unique deserves attention, even as it needs to be placed in perspective. Although San Francisco, Richmond, Berkeley, Sausalito, and Oakland rarely if ever acted in concert, they did confront comparable pressures. National perceptions similarly evoked common local responses. It is no coincidence, for example, that the mid-1960s marked both the heyday of liberalism in each of these cities and the historical moment when national sentiment was comparably if less profusely liberal.[1] In this respect, one may speak of a single transformation as well as of many different ones.

This chapter explores the substantive transformation of the idea of racial justice, from the initial demand that segregation be taken seriously as a problem to the push for district-wide desegregation coupled with reform of the educational program. With the failure fully to achieve that end, several paths were subsequently followed, among them black separatism, white reaffirmation of the status quo ante, and the redistribution of authority and resources from whites to blacks. Recent initiatives have been designed to link racial and educational concerns, in a time of diminished institutional expectations. If a revolution in the practices of the schools was ultimately the goal of the civil rights forces, that end has been only partly achieved in the five communities. Although national norms emphasizing equality are in place, the substantive successes of the movement have been more modest and place-specific.

The greatest change has occurred in the process of decision making. The race issue catalyzed a crisis of school governance in each district, in which the superintendency lost its unquestioned dominance and school boards and community groups struggled to assert themselves. Although the sense of crisis has passed, governance remains fluid, more accessible to outside influence. Of greatest moment, minority voices, which historically were shut out of the forums of decision, are now given a respectful hearing, as a result of court decisions as well as political initiatives. Minority participation has partly served as a surrogate for substantive reform; in that respect blacks have been coopted by the institution. What emerges most clearly is a richer sense of the diverse outcomes of participatory politics, proceeding in the context of an evolving, nationally defined understanding of racial equality.

II

The protean character of the aspiration to achieve racial justice in education is revealed in the diverse meanings associated with the ideal. Turn back the calendar a decade or so. San Francisco was about to desegregate its schools. In Berkeley and Sausalito, which had taken this step some years earlier, cultural liberation had come to assume greater importance. Oakland, having abandoned desegregation as infeasible and no longer of political interest, sought different ways of responding to black wishes, while Richmond had seemingly abandoned civil rights concerns, behaving as if the 1960s had never existed. These differences do not merely distinguish particularities but represent opposite sides of a great social and political divide. Universalism and racially rooted communitarianism stand as far removed from one another as the ideal societal types of Gemeinschaft and Gesellschaft. Policymaking with respect to race, in the Bay Area as elsewhere, permitted the dreaming of different and conflicting dreams.

These extremes of policy have seemingly vanished. On the one side, the idea of desegregation nowhere arouses bitter white resistance; it is rather a matter of calibrating costs, weighing racial mixing against other social goods. On the other side, black separatism seems a spent force. Although desegregation is not greeted by the black community with the fervor that rendered it the symbol of a movement, neither is it denigrated; in these quarters, too, it entails weighing and balancing on quite different social scales.

Although the evolution of racial equality has not run its course, patterns can be detected in the various responses. Each of the five school districts defined the concept iteratively and with ever-increasing expansiveness. No single and decisive reform fixed the course of policy; instead, policy proceeded step by step, in a search for resolution suited to the circumstances. Over time, the substance of policy combined what was unique to each community with norms and practices prevalent elsewhere. The experience of the five places also confirms that issues of race cannot be disentangled from the larger policy agenda. What started as a quest for racial justice became a far broader and more diffuse crusade for equity, and has subsequently become entangled with a very different drive to limit the reach of government.

When racial concerns were first aired by Bay Area civil rights groups in the late 1950s, the several school districts held a shared and quite conventional understanding of the mission of public education. Humane Progressivism had largely vanished. Gone, for the most part, was the child-centered school that Dewey had urged, gone too the very idea that schools might reshape the social order.[2] The task of the schools, it was felt, was to provide a differentiated education that matched the varied abilities of a heterogeneous population. The most able were given rigorous preparation for college, and the rest were offered vocational training or a terminal "general education" program. Differentiation reached into the primary schools, which often were rigidly tracked. The fact that it was professionals' children who received the advanced education while poor children were assigned to the non-college preparatory classes was taken for granted, if noticed at all, and of course one could always point to the exception, the poor child who graduated as class valedictorian.

Race was factually and normatively irrelevant to this understanding of schooling. Discrimination did not exist, school administrators repeatedly asserted. Although that assertion ignored some inconvenient facts, among them the basis for choosing certain school sites and the practice of assigning black teachers to predominantly black classes, it nonetheless informed policy. Colorblindness was the aspiration, if not the reality. Taking race into account, it was thought, could only work mischief; better that schools adhere to a neutral criterion, such as educational performance. No racial statistics were kept, for it was said that to do so would constitute discrimination.

When the marked educational failure of black youngsters aroused concern, the school systems sought to contain that concern by introducing a pedagogical remedy, compensatory education. This approach, it was believed, would help students to overcome a disability stemming from their deprived backgrounds. To do more by confronting race directly seemed unprincipled and inefficacious. That blacks fared badly in this society was indisputable, but the problem in its full enormity lay well outside the schools' responsibility. It made little difference whether blacks were few in number, as in Berkeley, or numerous, as in Oakland; whether the district was generally regarded as committed to excellence, as was true of San Francisco, or known for its penny-pinching ways, as was Richmond: race was nowhere regarded as a legitimate educational policy concern.

It was this cast of mind that civil rights groups initially sought to alter. Between 1958 and 1963, these groups appeared before the school boards of each of the five communities. Sometimes the precipitating event was a policy decision, ostensibly reached on nonracial grounds, with racial consequences: setting the attendance boundaries of an elementary school in San Francisco or an Oakland high school. Elsewhere, as in Sausalito, concerns that had been voiced nationally by CORE and the NAACP were brought home. What was wanted in each case was much the same: recognition that racial separation existed and that it constituted a problem, and a commitment to do something about that problem.

Reaction to this concern varied from sympathetic support in Richmond (where the demand was stage-managed by the school board) and Sausalito to principled resistance in San Francisco and attempts at diversion in Oakland and Berkeley. Yet even where the demand elicited a positive response from the school board, the resulting policy change was routinely defined in nonracial terms:

open enrollment plans were adopted or school boundary lines altered not to further racial mixing but to relieve overcrowded buildings or promote parental choice of schooling. These rationales were seen as educationally legitimate, but a race-conscious rationale was not. Only in that light can one appreciate the extraordinary struggle in San Francisco to obtain data concerning the schools' racial composition or the obfuscations of the Oakland superintendent called upon to redraw one high school's boundaries.

The reluctance of school boards and administrators to address the racial issue was premised in part on uncertainty about the nature and scope of the question. Race remained very much a symbolic issue in the early 1960s. Official recognition of the fact of racial separation confirmed the concerns of the civil rights movement but did not carry with it any educational agenda. It is one thing to assault a "bastion of bigotry," quite another to contemplate what racial justice might mean in Oakland or Richmond.

Introducing race into the educational policy calculus upset the prevailing order. The Bay Area communities, although initially more attentive to this concern than cities elsewhere, still sought to contain the degree of change. By the mid-1960s, each had recognized the problematic aspects of race and had committed itself to some positive policy. But only Sausalito, by far the smallest, had undertaken to desegregate its schools completely. The reforms adopted elsewhere—voluntary open enrollment, school pairings in which blacks were bused to white schools, and limited school attendance-boundary shifts—were far more modest. They affected relatively few students, relied primarily on volunteers, and placed the burden of change disproportionately on blacks.

The significance of these responses should not be underestimated; at this time, few other cities in the North and West had gone beyond the talking stages.[3] Yet to the civil rights activists, these efforts were just first steps. From the initial, limited undertakings larger ventures emerged, and planning commenced for system-wide change. If at the time one could imagine a substantive resolution of the issue of race and schooling, it would have coupled racial mixing with pedagogical and institutional reform. Such a resolution appeared achievable in each of the five communities at some point during the decade. There existed in each a willingness to take major action with respect to race. Sausalito and Berkeley were among the first school districts in the nation voluntarily to desegregate, and the others seemed well on their way. Not just racial mixing but programmatic change was occurring in systems that had become far more modern in a scant decade. A commitment to universalism was fused with a revived belief in the salutary powers of public schooling.[4] The hoped-for result was an educational system that would make everyone better off.

That resolution did not come to pass. Two communities chose not to desegregate. In Oakland, demography outpaced policy; by the time substantial racial mixing was politically achievable, there were too few white students. Richmond successfully resisted district-wide desegregation, ousting the proponents of the idea and opting instead to limit racial mixing to a voluntary program. The desegregation that ultimately came to San Francisco was an imposed and mechanical undertaking, not the educationally more ambitious and enthusiastically embraced voluntary effort of the 1960s. The era of integrationist possibility was apparently over almost as soon as it could be detected. Division and dissension within and among the communities became the order of the day.

Had this account been written in the early 1970s, it would have been possible sharply to distinguish Berkeley, Sausalito, and San Francisco on the one hand, from Oakland and Richmond on the other. The schools in the first three cities were desegregated, it would have been said, while those in the other two communities remained largely segregated. Yet that description conveys only the barest sense of what was happening. It treats policy outcomes as fixed when policies were little more than stabs in the dark, stays against the confusion caused by wrenching institutional and social upheaval.

Desegregation did not mark a stable point in this dynamic process. Where public schools were desegregated, particularly in Berkeley and Sausalito, blacks came eventually to seek something more—or something other—than integration. Their claims had sometimes coexisted with the drive for desegregation but had been muted in the process; in other instances, they arose from dissatisfaction with specific integration efforts and more broadly with the promise of integration itself. The common curriculum, some said, needed to be changed in order to incorporate a black perspective and to nurture black pride. Others urged "strategic disengagement" from the desegregated schools or emphasis on basic education for black youngsters, whose academic performance did not improve with desegregation.

Each of these proposals makes some pedagogical sense, and

the fact that they were advanced in the name of racial justice made them especially hard to resist. Who could object to the notion that blacks—and whites—should acquire an appreciation for black history and culture as part of genuine integration or that traditional schooling should be supplemented by less structured classes for those who flourished in that looser environment? What caused difficulties were not the ideas themselves but their execution, an altogether grayer domain in which principled issues were harder to locate.[5] Opposing efforts to go beyond "mere integration" came to seem inflexible, old-fashioned; since the proponents of the further reforms were usually black, their opponents could easily and devastatingly be labeled racist.

All educational policy issues were defined for a time as racial, racial issues became confrontations, and confrontations were treated as racist episodes. As a result, the idea of integration—even, in some cases, the very process of education—was put seriously at risk. An undertaking that demanded patience and prudence was scarred by violence and vilification. Only after some years were the schools in Sausalito and Berkeley able to begin making something out of the possibilities presented by desegregation.

This stage in the process of securing racial justice is not inevitable, as San Francisco's experience confirms, but it is understandable. On the one side, blacks were called upon overnight to assume responsibilities for which they had been neither trained nor prepared, to exercise leadership in an uncharted and inherently volatile domain. Blacks in these communities were also caught up in a tide of assertiveness that at the national level had prompted interest in black power. Separatism represented a vision of the future, and in Berkeley and Sausalito, which wished to experience the future before anyone else, the vision was not easily resisted. Prudence is hard to demand in such circumstances. On the other side, white liberals lacked a clearly articulated alternative vision. Integration resembles the Heavenly City toward which Pilgrim sets out in John Bunyan's tale: it acquires definition from the obstacles lying in the way of its achievement. In Berkeley and Sausalito, integration has assumed deeper significance through contrast with black power, separatism, and experimentalism. The present commitment to the idea of racial justice in Berkeley and Sausalito seems less rhetorical, more tempered, and more sincere than its earlier incarnation.

The barriers to achieving integration were not confined to the plane of racial ideology. Administrative opposition or even inattention could work similarly devastating effects. It was one thing to order that a school system be desegregated, quite another to realize the underlying integrationist aspiration in the face of bureaucratic indifference—a lesson learned by civil rights partisans and the federal court in San Francisco. And where, as in Berkeley and Sausalito, the administration's attention lay elsewhere, making integration work was equally hard going. Even in the desegregated districts, integration was less a system-wide reality than something that might transpire inside particular schools or classrooms.

There is yet another twist in this history of iterative policy, and in some respects it prompts the greatest surprise. After the formal undoing of system-wide desegregation in Richmond and the more covert efforts to undermine integration in Berkeley, Sausalito, and San Francisco, one might have thought the idea as good as dead, not just in these Bay Area communities but in the country as a whole. If genuine integration could not prevail here, in an area where it was demographically feasible and politically plausible, what more promising site could commend itself? Yet reports of the demise of universalism have proved premature. Berkeley and Sausalito have returned to tasks left undone at the end of the 1960s. They are exploring the possibilities of integration, drawing on the sometimes distinct educational concerns of whites and blacks within a framework of racial heterogeneity. There are small promising signs—the return of white families to the schools of Sausalito and relative racial stability in Berkeley, improved achievement-test performance in both districts—but it is far too early to report success or even to know just what such a report would include.

The Richmond open enrollment plan, adopted grudgingly by a conservative school board, has permitted a sizable proportion of that city's black population to attend desegregated schools outside their own neighborhoods; there, too, efforts at integration have begun on the bedrock of racial mixing. The continued participation of one-sixth of Richmond's black students in the open enrollment program even after transportation was no longer provided indicates the depth of minority support for integration.

Only in Oakland is integration essentially undiscussed. That city has defined racial justice differently, in terms of a reallocation of authority and resources to the black community. It is hard to imagine what else a city whose schools are so predominantly black might do, hard to generate much enthusiasm for the idea of distributing the few remaining whites equally among the schools. Universalism can be at best a slogan, at worse a delusion, in such a setting; only a political order linking Oakland's fate with that of its neighbors would invite a different conclusion.

III

The interrelationship between uniformity and idiosyncrasy is evident in the range of policies effectuated by the five school districts. In one respect, these policies run the gamut of options taken elsewhere in the nation, and are in that sense exemplars. But policy has also been informed by condition and circumstance, as seemingly similar programs assumed different meanings from place to place.

One can readily fit the choices made by the several communities onto a broader policy map. That map includes a range of approaches to racial mixing from preserving neighborhood schools to securing racial balance, incorporating such intermediate steps as open enrollment and gerrymandering school boundaries; it also includes other race-related efforts, among them decentralization, compensatory programs, and alternative schools.

Three cities—San Francisco, Berkeley, and Sausalito—desegregated their entire systems. San Francisco was the first major Northern city to do so under court order, and in many ways it typifies judicial efforts of the period. The plan adopted stressed racial balance and had little educational content. Berkeley and Sausalito belong to the more select company of school districts that voluntarily desegregated all their schools. Both also have adopted rather conventional pedagogical strategies in recent years; if Progressivism has been revived, it is in these schools. Attention has returned to instruction in literacy and arithmetic, enhancing the quality of the relationship between teacher and student, and maintaining a sense of community within the school. These are old concerns, but no less valuable for that reason.

Richmond exemplifies a limited voluntary response to racial isolation. Open enrollment was a popular idea in the mid-1960s and remains a widely preferred policy. In a nation committed to desegregation but generally unwilling to bus students in order to achieve it, open enrollment is a policy for which widespread support can be mustered; it has replaced a hands-off approach as defining the minimum obligation of the schools.[6] Even in Oakland, more than four-fifths black, an open enrollment program of limited scope survives.

Oakland's primary effort, refocusing administrative energies and resources on the educational problems of the black community, embodies another model. The Oakland alternative has its counterparts in such cities as Atlanta, where a largely black school district stresses hiring black teachers and administrators rather than further token desegregation, and Detroit, similarly predominantly black, where substantial educational program reform, not city-wide racial balance, has been established.[7] When desegregation cannot be accomplished, "do something else" becomes an especially attractive possibility.

The experiences of the Bay Area school districts reflect the history of cities and towns in the North and West, but they are also particular to place. Although in some ways the districts merely adapted formula to circumstance, more substantial variations can also be detected.

Even in San Francisco, where the court-approved desegregation plan was shaped as if by a cookie cutter, the relationship of Third World groups to desegregation—a vital concern in a district where blacks and whites together constitute a minority of the student population—and the development of racially mixed public alternatives to the assigned school reflect community idiosyncrasy. So too in Berkeley education is played out against a political background more liberal, a cultural background at once more sophisticated and exotic, than in most other communities; the egalitarianism that informs Berkeley civic life shapes the schools as well. Sausalito's tiny size turns policy issues into questions of personality. Relationships and not directives count most in a school district with fewer students than the average urban primary school. Oakland's reforms have succeeded in part because of the city's well-organized community groups, which have participated in decision making and provided support for the administration's initiatives. Open enrollment in Richmond functions in a school system whose conservatism about its instructional mission obliges the students taking advantage of the program, not the schools themselves, to bend.

These particularities are in each instance small but not trivial matters. Such substantive variations are the necessary adaptations of formula that any institution will make. Attentiveness to such variations, as well as to those, such as the marked disparity in per pupil expenditures, reported in the Appendix, is also likely to influence the course of a policy reform. The sources of variability need to be appreciated as potential resources to be drawn upon, not obstacles to be overcome in the understandable but misguided aspiration to achieve a uniform solution.

IV

The pursuit of racial equality reached beyond black-white relationships, gathering in its net a host of equity-related concerns. During the past quarter-century, the Bay Area schools became legally and politically obliged to respond to the claims not only of blacks but also of a host of others historically ignored in the calculus of educational decision, and those claims severely strained the institutions' capacities.

As an ideal, racial equality is sometimes thought to stand by itself. Yet because racial concerns are intimately joined to so many other questions, this disentanglement cannot be achieved. Change the racial composition of the work force, for instance, and this affects the unemployment rate, the size of the school population, and the index of housing segregation; conversely, a policy designed to curb inflation will have special impact on blacks. This is not news, but for some reason it is often forgotten in discussions of race and schooling. Those who argued that integration required considering such matters as school financing, the administrative structure, and instructional quality were derided for obscuring a matter of simple justice. The Bay Area histories suggest otherwise.

Civil rights activists allied themselves from the start with others more generally concerned about the backward state of the schools. Desegregation became part of a reform campaign seeking more of what schools already offered—libraries, laboratories, and the like—as well as more visionary futures, such as educational parks or publicly supported alternatives.[8] These proposals were designed variously to make desegregation more palatable or more workable. The prospect of desegregation also permitted administrators to smuggle onto the policy agenda items from their wish lists, for the linkage with race gave them a credibility they would otherwise have lacked.

Although few of the bigger proposed innovations were adopted, they in turn became the impetus for other reforms urged by different groups and also related to race. Third World organizations, especially in San Francisco and to a lesser extent in Berkeley and Oakland, self-consciously emulated the blacks' strategy.[9] They sought the kind of attention and support that blacks had previously won. More quietly but with comparable effectiveness, white middle-class parents promoted programs for able students. Some were racially mixed, such as the alternative schools set up in Sausalito, Berkeley, and San Francisco, but classes for gifted children became disproportionately white enclaves in minority-dominated districts. Other groups launched parallel drives for recognition, among them parents of the retarded in San Francisco and the educationally disadvantaged in Richmond.

Neither grafting onto race a variety of other substantive concerns nor relating the plight of blacks to other have-not groups is peculiar to these communities. Educational policymaking between 1960 and 1980 was in large part a story of growing attention to equity-based concerns, at the state and federal levels even more than at the local level.[10] The handicapped, women, and the limited-English-speaking all acquired a special claim on the attention of the schools, based on legislative or constitutional entitlement.[11] Although a host of factors, such as increased reliance on courts and centralized authority to fashion educational policy, has informed and hastened these developments, the quest for racial justice in the schools was their inspiration. Issues initially presented in the racial context gave life to each of the succeeding aspirations.

The schools' mission has expanded considerably since *Brown*, and racial concerns instigated this change. Instruction that was differentiated on the basis of ability and that stressed the traditional subjects of study, the pattern of a quarter-century ago, no longer suffices. Schools are now supposed to offer an array of courses suited to the interests of a more varied clientele. They are legally required to be nonracist and nonsexist places, hospitable to varied cultures, supportive of students with widely differing aptitudes. Equity in all its richness and complexity informs every aspect of the schools' functioning. The abstract appeal of such an approach is undoubted. But in light of the case studies there remains a nagging substantive question: Can these beleaguered institutions be equal and excellent too?[12]

V

The issue of racial equality has not only worked substantial substantive changes in school policy but has also altered the ways schools are managed and governed. We tend too easily to speak of crisis, but crisis there has been with respect to the capacity of lay boards and professionals to run public schools in a manner that commands general assent. Many things have contributed to this crisis, among them a growing cynicism toward politics generally, a perceived decline in educational standards, diminished deference to expertise, and a concomitantly diminished willingness to cede

substantial discretion to professional decision.[13] These factors figure generally in the political and bureaucratic landscape. In the
school setting as in other areas of social policy, race has added a
powerful additional source of discontent.

The five Bay Area cities, like many other American towns,
were quiescent, almost apolitical in their approach to education a
quarter-century ago. These communities largely shaped their own
educational policies free from state and federal regulation. They
did so with little conflict over the substance of policy, which had
been removed from politics some time earlier and lodged with the
school professionals.

That picture shifted rapidly during the next decade. Educational policymaking turned into a politicized process. Seemingly
unified communities fragmented as dissension became the norm.
Policy initiatives were molded in the cross fire of political pressures. The presence of state and federal agencies was increasingly
felt. Local authorities were accountable not only to their constituencies but also to officials enforcing civil rights and substantive
program standards and to courts that constitutionalized much of
educational policy.[14] The insertion of race into the policy agenda
prompted many of these changes in the process of policymaking,
just as racial concerns affected the substance of policy. The nature
of this transformation can be understood by looking first at the relationships among the chief parties at interest—school administrators, school boards, community groups, and those deriving
their authority from outside the community, including the state
and federal administrative agencies and the courts—and then at
the interaction of politics and law in the crafting of policy.

Although school boards are usually supposed to set policy
that administrators carry out, in practice the line is often blurred.[15]
Administrators understandably desire to convert policy questions,
political in character and so appropriately resolved by school
boards, into questions involving expert judgment on which they
can exercise final say. Realizing this desire depends in good part on
the acquiescence of school boards. When professionals have their
way, the board assumes a different function. From agents of policymaking, boards become instruments of policy transmission,
conveying the decisions of professionals to the community;[16] in the
process, school governance becomes "symbolically democratic."[17]
School boards may, however, entertain their own views of what the
schools should be doing. They may even insinuate themselves into
mundane management, thus breaching the barrier between set-

ting and implementing policy. Relationships between board members and administrators potentially involve an ongoing battle over the exercise of power and control. Each party musters its own resources in the fray: professional skills and the power to evade or avoid dictates on the one side, popular support and the capacity to choose administrative leadership on the other.[18]

School administrators in each of the five Bay Area school districts had succeeded in securing control over significant decision making when race appeared on the policy agenda. Not every district had its Walter Helms, superintendent of Richmond's schools for a half-century, or its Harold Spears, whose reputation in national educational circles served him well in San Francisco, but in each community the superintendency was a stable and powerful post. School board meetings were brief and relatively infrequent; discussion centered on detail, not policy; and on matters of substance the administration's recommendations were routinely adopted by board vote. Administrators did not, to be sure, exercise unconstrained authority. Their discretion was limited by a sense of what was broadly acceptable to the community over whose schools they presided. They looked to the civic elites for guidance, seeking consensus on the parameters of policy.[19]

The end of the era of professional hegemony may be traced directly to the question of race. The racial issue was unlike questions of curriculum or school construction, since by its very nature it transcended educators' professional expertise. It also exposed fissures in communities previously viewed as homogeneous or at least rightly proud of their tolerance for differentness. Administrators sought either to assimilate the issue to more familiar educational concerns or to dismiss it as irrelevant, but school boards took a different approach. Because they saw the matter as vitally important to a new constituency, board members were more responsive. The race question was unique, and so was the way it was handled.

Changes in the composition of the school boards also made them more receptive. Board members had historically been drawn from the conservative business and professional establishment, and their political views reflected these backgrounds. In some cities, board members were appointed; even if they were obliged to run for office, the campaign was a formality, for nominees were handpicked by the board itself or by a coalition of community leaders. New issues, notably race, encouraged a different sort of candidate. Those who challenged the 1950s regimes were cosmopolitans, not locals, veterans of the Stevenson campaign and later of the War on Poverty, new professionals, and nonwhites. The political liberalism of the challengers reflected a shift in Bay Area politics generally, and their activism was symptomatic of the era. The liberals, who formed a majority on the boards of every community except Oakland at some point during the 1960s, were not content to treat their jobs as ceremonial. They campaigned on the basis of dissatisfaction with the pace of racial reform and the apparent inability of the school systems to modernize themselves, committing themselves to do things differently. The insurgents were activists, and race was high on their agenda.

The appearance of race as an issue confronting school administrators, coupled with the changing character of school board members during this period, upset the old pattern of relationship between school boards and administrators. The struggle to redefine that relationship marked the decade of the 1960s. Boards increasingly seized the initiative, framing substantive directives, recruiting outsiders to the superintendency, and otherwise attempting to reassert control over policy. Administrators drew upon their own sources of power. Unlike board members, they were used to running things. In Richmond and to a lesser extent elsewhere, administrators mobilized resistance to board efforts from within the ranks. But school administrators did not merely resist and retard reform. They too were a changing breed. A new generation of administrators altered the traditional priorities and practices of the school systems, allying them with new aspirations. Some of these changes were substantive, including novel instructional efforts. Others were organizational: hierarchies were flattened, human relations strategies introduced, advice from management and policy analysts sought.

The balance of power between school board and school administration has subsequently undergone another wave of adjustment. Domination by the administration in Richmond, Sausalito, and Oakland is superficially reminiscent of the 1950s; in San Francisco and Berkeley disputes over authority persist, although less vehemently than in an earlier day. Yet things are actually very different. The line between administration and governance has everywhere been blurred. The superintendency has become a largely political and managerial job. Administrators have bent themselves to the task of survival in the face of new pressures from without and within, becoming knowledgeable about law, accounting, and negotiation. Educational decision making remains politicized, but the form of politics is new. In place of an essentially ideological politics, more pragmatic concerns are expressed in a manner that reflects the give and take of pluralist bargaining.[20]

The relationship between school and community is informed by a central paradox. Because public schools are usually governed not by a general-purpose body but by an elected board responsible only for the schools, they are potentially the most accessible of all institutions. Nonetheless, schools are routinely regarded as impervious to outside influence.

School governance during the 1950s corresponded to this common perception. Policymaking was the exclusive prerogative of the school board and administration. Parent involvement was confined to PTAs, which ran bake sales and chaperoned dances; as outsiders, parents were not regarded as meriting a say in policy. The very appearance of civil rights organizations before school boards was a novelty.

When school boards began aggressively to assert their policymaking prerogatives, they also opened the process to outside intervention. The typical vehicle was the citizens' advisory committee, a device rarely used in the past but heavily relied on during this era. No community was without at least one such committee, and in San Francisco, Berkeley, and Oakland, advisory groups were appointed on several occasions.

Citizens' committees appealed to the school boards for various reasons.[21] They protected the board on both political flanks. On the one hand, they offered a way to buy time, easing the pressure from civil rights groups for change and deflecting that pressure from the school board and administration to the new entity. On the other hand, they screened the board from unhappy conservatives, who mounted recall campaigns against board members in three of the five Bay Area towns. Citizens' committees also functioned as stalking-horses for new initiatives. They were selected with the expectation that their recommendations would coincide with the views of the school district; their supposed independence gave them added credibility. Sometimes the advisory committee fulfilled its ostensible mandate and offered instructive guidance, providing information needed by harrassed school officials.

Whatever the motivation for its creation, this new instrument of participation assumed a life of its own, especially as a means of aiding blacks and other minorities in their drive for inclusion. Board receptivity to community participation encouraged groups to form and build coalitions. Community leaders recognized that specific substantive policy recommendations might ultimately matter less than the institutionalization of advisory committees and other new forms of participation. That concern over process and power, not educational substance, underlies disagreements over the composition of citizens' committees and the boards' receptivity to their recommendations.

Schools were not, of course, the only institution of government where battles over the form and nature of participation were played out. The federally sponsored community-action programs of the 1960s were as much struggles over say as disputes over program.[22] In the Bay Area, this governance issue first emerged in the schools. Desegregation was in effect a primary school for political activists, introducing minority leaders to the facts of political life in the established system and involving more people in running schools.

Participation begets participation. The involvement of pro-civil rights groups in decision making induced those hostile to the demands of these groups to mobilize. School policymaking, once an elite affair, came to embrace a wider mix of partisans pressing contending viewpoints. The input of the several sources of pressure varied from place to place. Reactive forces prevailed in Richmond; minority groups effectively stymied the efforts of the Oakland school district to select a superintendent; pro-civil rights coalitions in Sausalito and Berkeley convincingly triumphed; and in San Francisco the court took the decision out of the partisans' hands. The political process in each instance drew upon voices that had in the past gone unheard.

Organized interest groups have been less visible during the 1970s. Although community concerns have not been allayed, as the furor generated by San Francisco's modification of its desegregation plan and the bitterness in Richmond suggest, they are less frequently and less vociferously expressed. Some activists stopped caring or were worn down. Many of those who concerned themselves with education have either moved on to other issues or have withdrawn from the political wars altogether. Yet their impact continues to be felt. The 1960s struggles for inclusion redirected the energy and attention of the schools, and (with the possible exception of Richmond) there has been no serious subsequent attempt to restore the narrower and more elitist institutional focus of an earlier time. Reformist aims have been institutionalized, even as the possibility of major reform has been lessened by diminished resources. One measure of this institutionalization is the participation within the school system of one-time community spokesmen, especially in Oakland and Berkeley. It is uncertain whether these activists have been coopted,[23] the energies of the various pressure groups drained, or whether they can ultimately work consequential changes in the bureaucracy.

VI

Educational decision making reaches beyond local interests—school boards, administrators, and community groups—to include all the participants in the federal system. State and national as well as local agencies, courts, legislatures, and administrative agencies: all have a hand in decision making. This federal system formally allocates authority in complex and confusing ways; informal allocations of power defy classification.[24] To speak of American federalism as a "marble cake," as political scientists commonly do,[25] recognizes this complexity and the inaptness of a hierarchical metaphor without making federalism more coherent.

The impact of intervention by state and federal agencies needs to be appreciated from two perspectives. The direct influence of the upper reaches of government was surprisingly small, but as value shapers the authority of federal agencies was more substantial.

The involvement of the nonjudicial branches of state and federal government was particularly modest in the five school districts. Federal administrative efforts had been instrumental in securing the desegregation of Southern school districts, and elsewhere in the North the Justice Department and the Office of Civil Rights prodded school districts into responding to racial demands.[26] Not so in the Bay Area. Among the five school districts, only in Berkeley did the Office of Civil Rights take action, forcing the closure of Black House. A Justice Department investigation of alleged deliberate segregation in Richmond came to naught.

With few exceptions, states have sought to skirt the race and schooling question, fearing the predictable whirlwinds. In California, the state board of education might have preferred a more activist stance but lacked the legal authority to intervene. The Department of Education was at best a marginal presence in the politics of race, able to exhort but not enforce. Only in Sausalito, where its help was actively solicited by a school district committed to desegregation, could the department have acted decisively—and even there, further study was all that it urged. Elsewhere, the department's involvement was more modest. Departmental recommendations helped tip the political balance in Oakland, at a time when the issue was very much in flux. The state agency found no allies in San Francisco, and its advice was ignored, but the state's suggested standard for racial balance was incorporated into the district's remedy framing and the court decree.

The state and federal courts were another story. In San Francisco, policy was fashioned by a federal district court decision, the first such opinion to order system-wide desegregation in a major Northern city, and the fate of Richmond's open enrollment plan rested for some years with the state courts. The role of these courts was significant but hardly decisive. The issue was politically framed in both instances, and political considerations proved vital in implementing the remedy ordered by the court in San Francisco. In this respect, the San Francisco experience mirrors that of numerous other communities, confirming the blurring of constitutionalism and politics.[27]

The hope in these circumstances is that the courts can shape a politically acceptable and pedagogically sensible resolution within the limits of the constitutional command of equality. The separation of the judiciary from the local political system, the tradition of respect for authoritative pronouncements of law, and the non-bureaucratic character of the court all potentially aid it in this task.[28] Judicial involvement in race and schooling controversies has been most effective when political bargaining has broken down. The court, having determined the parties' legal rights and obligations, can encourage renewed bargaining. If that negotiation fails, the judge is well situated to devise a remedy responsive both to the constitution and the parties' preferences.[29]

Or so experience elsewhere suggests. In San Francisco and Richmond, the courts' efforts were less exemplary. In its haste to resolve the case, the San Francisco court may have misapplied prevailing law. By adopting a narrow definition of the dispute, the court ignored closely related issues—notably the treatment of limited-English-speaking youngsters under the desegregation decree—and so fragmented the process of decision making. The remedy, although prepared by the school district, embodied a technician's response to an educator's and politician's and judge's problem; the short period that the judge permitted for remedy framing almost guaranteed this result. The Richmond case confounded decision making by conveying inconsistent and weakly explained messages to the partisans.

These failings are understandable. Because San Francisco's was the first major Northern desegregation suit, it was likely that miscalculations would be made, particularly that the court would be overly reluctant to abandon the illusion of authority for the reality of effectiveness. The Richmond case was so badly mangled by the advocates that no court could have rescued it. These assessments themselves do not settle the proper role of courts in race and schooling, an issue taken up in the next chapter. They do reveal just how vulnerable to misuse the courts are, and how widely estimates of judicial success vary from place to place. In this respect, too, the system of governance turns out to be highly variable.

If the direct influence of federal and state government was slight and more often than not misdirected, the indirect influence appears more beneficial. Even where no lawsuit was filed and no administrative action taken, political discourse was shaped by the language of equality, language derived from the United States and California constitutions and the 1964 Civil Rights Act. It was not mere power that carried the day, but power tamed by values directly traceable to the constitutional concern for fairness. As a result, "local elites that could have turned their leadership to the ends of separatism have instead been induced to give limited commitment to national values."[30] Doing something, it was frequently urged, was not merely right but also a right secured by law. Threatened recourse to higher levels of government, pointed reminders of other cases and administrative efforts elsewhere, also galvanized fruitful political activity. It may well be that Washington and Sacramento had their greatest impact not in dictating policy outcomes but in helping to formulate policy values.[31]

VII

A pattern runs through these recountings. Race becomes an item on the policy agenda of a school system and in short order develops its own momentum. The pitch of argument escalates as its substance evolves. Official responses beget disquiet, not satisfaction, and this disquiet in turn keeps the matter alive. That reaction has little to do with the content of the government's response. As Murray Edelman writes: "In the field of race relations the talk . . . is in terms of liberty and equality on one side and in terms of the prevention of social disorder . . . on the other side. Neither of these ostensible goals . . . specifies a condition that is objectively definable in the sense that there can be a consensus that it has been achieved. . . . Their semantic ambiguity . . . is precisely what makes them potent symbols."[32] A system in equilibrium is consequently thrown into disorder. Where previously there had been apparent consensus, there is now disaffection and division. Where formerly the substantive agenda of the schools had been relatively clear and limited, priorities are scrambled. In that process, blacks cease being the invisible men of public schooling.

The attendant tension was immense in each city; given the character and intensity fostered by the issue, it could not have been otherwise. What was being demanded was no less than that blacks be admitted into full partnership in the educational regime and that policy decisions be made with the concerns of black children kept unblinkingly in mind.

The several school systems reacted in different ways to this challenge. Richmond ultimately responded with excessive constraint. In that city, the kind and quality of the education that blacks receive, including the possibility of a desegregated education, remains very much the prerogative of whites. The substance of blacks' educational experience there deserves a mixed evaluation. Those who govern the Richmond system deny this sizable minority a voice and fail to take seriously blacks' own aspirations. At an earlier stage in the process, the white working-class majority was similarly shut out. They had no voice in determining the nature or scope of desegregation, and the plan adopted by the liberal board drastically affected schools in their neighborhoods.

In Berkeley and Sausalito, in contrast, the decision-making apparatus seemed for a time to lack a governor. Minority and radical demands provoked little resistance or even challenge, but were acquiesced in by a white liberal majority incapable of asserting its own legitimate interests. A healthy and necessary constraint born of a sense of what public schools ought to be doing was missing. The processes of decision making were consequently corrupted as racial preference and reverse racism prevailed, and apparent hurt was done to the children who were made hostages to ideological excess.

Both communities have now achieved a more satisfactory equilibrium. Was such unfairness a necessary corrective for past injustice? The Oakland history indicates that a school system can overcome its past history without first submitting to this kind of Jacobinism. Negotiations among the parties at interest never ceased in Oakland. What did change was the relative strength of the parties, and consequently the substantive solutions that were reached. Oakland, regarded at the time as under the greatest strain, may have made the most successful political adaptation to rapidly evolving circumstances. San Francisco's history is similar in some respects. There, each side retained effective counters throughout, ultimately including recourse to the courts and the capacity to shape implementation of the court decree. Debate among the adversaries went on before, during, and after the litigation.

Demography and politics explain these differences. Changing demography suggests one reason why the Oakland history turned out as it did. It is hard to imagine how, in a city rapidly becoming predominantly black, minority desires to make Oakland "ours" could forever be denied; what remained was to fix the terms on which power was transferred. This is at least a narrower issue than that confronting the other cities, where no policy option was foreclosed by racial composition.

Political culture has more pervasive significance. Richmond is not a community at all but the offspring of a shotgun wedding joining discrete entities with distinct agendas. Political identities remained bound to Kensington and El Sobrante and Pinole, not to the school district, and alliances were formed within the smaller entities. Because there was little sense of the whole, solutions in which one coalition of the like-minded imposed its will on the rest came naturally. In contrast, Oakland and San Francisco have rich community traditions—a commitment to efficient management in the one, civility and tolerance in the other—which served them well under duress. Berkeley and Sausalito converted reform itself into a tradition—what was new was presumed good—and this permitted them to change, even as in changing they forsook their own recently adopted reforms.

The balance struck by the political culture between ideological and pragmatic considerations, and between the claims of narrowly defined self-interest and universalist aspiration, figures importantly in these resolutions. Liberalism unalloyed with more self-centered concerns was acutely vulnerable to accusations of racism and consequently to unbecoming manipulation. Such naive liberalism idealized the abstraction of desegregation rather than focusing on the immense challenges that desegregation posed in the concrete. It also idealized the process of transformation, stressing the place of rationality and humane relationships in that process, rather than accepting and making effective use of the more mundane tools of politics.

It is one thing to make an institution more responsive to its constituency, something altogether less commendable for the managers of a system to refuse to exercise authority or leadership. The line between self-centeredness and universalism is exceedingly fine. On one side lies sentimentality, on the other lack of caring. To abandon idealism works a kind of political tyranny, as in Richmond. Adherence to the sort of idealism that prompted a Sausalito parent to declare that her children could "live with black militancy" is to blind oneself to sorry truths, hardly less real for being inconvenient.

If we can't obtain the things we want, we come eventually to accept what we can get. That "strategic retreat from objectives"[33] is much in evidence in the tendency to substitute a concern about how the issue of race and schooling was confronted for attention to the results of that confrontation. Appraising the robustness of a political system seems an achievable task. Whether that system fostered good outcomes for its students seems in contrast a matter about which certainty comes harder; the evidence concerning pupil achievement in the five Bay Area districts set out in the Appendix sheds some light on this. "All our work had been very little, no great change had been made. . . . I'd been so fascinated by the motion that I'd forgotten to measure what it was bringing forth." So declares the narrator of Ralph Ellison's *Invisible Man*; might not the same be said about the emphasis on the how, rather than the what, of racial justice?

Deficiencies in process may signal bad outcomes. It is hard, for instance, to imagine how the racial issue could satisfactorily be resolved in a community such as Richmond, where narrow self-interest is the overriding motivation, for race and schooling policy necessarily has too much of the quality of a public good. The converse, that vital pluralism will yield a good result, does not necessarily follow. It is in the nature of public goods that individual bargaining, however vigorous, may not yield the right solution for the community.[34] Is that true here?

Consensual resolution is appealing not only because it accords with contemporary democratic aspirations but also because our presently muddled perception of racial justice causes us to stress process rather than substance. "The typical issue in liberal politics is over the legitimacy or the representativeness of the government, not over its goodness."[35] In this instance, though, the dichotomy between process and substance is false, since political give-and-take has clear substantive consequences. In Oakland, where the process may have worked best, the outcome involved not integration but the redistribution of money and power; there was almost no interest in enlisting surrounding communities in an integrationist solution. This result reorients our sense of what racial justice dictates.

Confronting substantive concerns head-on poses the deepest

of the issues that the five communities' histories evoke. Does the integrationist aspiration still deserve respect? Is redistributing money and authority from white haves to black have-nots an objective that can succeed the univeralist vision, not only as pragmatically more achievable but also as morally preferable? Does the fact that a viable political system supported this result shape or shake our convictions? To consider these questions fully demands placing the histories of the Bay Area school districts in broader perspective, once again relating idiosyncrasy to uniformity. How ought the process of decision making be designed to encourage genuinely political resolutions? And what substantive limits, what uniform standards, should constrain those resolutions?

CHAPTER

12

Self-Interest and Public Good: Reshaping Race and Schooling Policy

I

At the outset, the quest for racial equality centered on a substantive entitlement. Equality was the premise of *Brown v. Board of Education*,[1] the rallying cry in efforts to turn the *Brown* decision into a present and functioning reality. The quest was also, if less explicitly, procedural in nature. The call for equality included a demand that attention be paid, respect accorded. It entailed participation in the institutions that shape policy for the republic, involvement in the political and judicial processes of decision.

Both the substantive and the procedural aspects of the quest have been complex, the results mixed. Could it have been otherwise, when the change both in values and practices was of such magnitude? There are some unambiguous successes to report. As a social norm, the idea of equality has come to command broad popular acceptance. Surveys conducted over the past two decades report that Americans increasingly declare color blindness to be the appropriate policy in education, as in a host of issues including the provision of housing and employment opportunities.[2] The shift has been marked—some 20 to 40 percent of the white population, depending upon the issue, has abandoned its old prejudices and come to accept the rights of blacks as persons. That transformation has made racial equality the professed belief of most Americans, with support for government-sanctioned segregation confined to 5 percent of the populace.

These changes in belief and attitude, although spurred by *Brown*, have been brought about largely through the informal mediating processes of the culture, not through direct governmental imposition. The development represents an essentially private policy, the aggregation of individual preferences, not public policy.[3] Efforts to reform schooling in ways consistent with the ideal of racial equality are informed by a quite different set of institutional dynamics, and here too there have been noteworthy successes. As compared with a quarter-century ago, blacks and whites are more likely to attend racially mixed schools; resources are more equitably shared by black and white students; blacks are far more likely to stay in school beyond the minimum leaving age (indeed, the college attendance rates of blacks and whites are essentially the same),[4] and the gap between the educational achievement of blacks and whites, although still sizable, has narrowed considerably.[5] Yet the implementation of policy reforms has been a problematic enterprise. Efforts to remake the old ways have, unsurprisingly, encountered considerable and persistent resistance. More interestingly, as the case studies reveal, the meaning of racial justice—the end being pursued—has itself proved evanescent. The core commitment to end governmentally imposed racial separation endures, but beyond that disagreement prevails. The meaning of equality in education has evolved over time, and proponents of equality advance inconsistent understandings of the aspiration.

This fragmentation with respect to the idea of equality has occurred within a system of decision making—embracing the political and judicial branches, at all levels of government—that has, in the main, become more open to participation by blacks. Although in *An American Dilemma* Gunnar Myrdal could fairly characterize Northern blacks as unnoticed and invisible men,[6] blacks now exert a role in shaping policy more closely proportional to their numbers. This is a considerable accomplishment. It begins to approximate the state of affairs Michael Walzer has in mind when he writes:

> If no one is invisible, the state is not immoral. The recognition of its members as concrete individuals with needs and desires may seem a minimal requirement of any political system and hardly capable of producing significant moral attachments. In fact, however . . . the liberal state that finally recognizes all men and women and grants them their humanity will inherit from those centuries [of past struggle] an extraordinary moral power.[7]

That transformation may be at least as consequential as the substantive policy changes that have occurred.

Substantive variability, coupled with an increasing emphasis on the manifold processes of decision making, assures that there is no single American policy toward issues of race and schooling, but instead multiple and variable policies. This diversity is apparent in the present array of substantive resolutions. In one community, compensatory education programs are clustered in predominantly black schools; a neighboring town has racially balanced its schools; and its neighbor rests content with an open enrollment plan in which 15 percent of the black children (and none of the whites) participate. The forms of decision making are similarly various. Decisions are at once centrally and locally motivated, informed by political realities and constitutional norms.

This disorderly universe has been thoroughly savaged. As a society, we are scored for being either too much or too little committed to bringing together black and white schoolchildren, overly judicialized or excessively politicized in the way we formulate policy. Criticism has at times swelled in pitch and intensity, calling into question not merely the effectiveness of present practice but the legitimacy of the system of government producing that practice.

Although the critics are themselves various, they can be loosely grouped into conservative and liberal camps. Conservatives, who regard self-governing local governments as the norm, decry federal intervention as a heavy-handed and ill-advised attempt to level healthy differences.[8] They have for this reason spearheaded the altogether successful effort to turn Congress into a naysayer, content to defang the Office of Civil Rights and latterly the Justice Department.

The judiciary arouses the deepest conservative ire. Although there is no argument with the core proposition of the *Brown* decision that state-imposed segregation is unconstitutional, *Brown* is read narrowly with respect both to the definition of the wrong and to the specification of the remedy.[9] Although it is appropriate, say conservative critics, to require that school districts undo whatever segregation can fairly be attributed to official mischief—for such mischief perverts the purposes of majoritarian democracy—it makes no sense to sweep into the judicial net segregation that seems to have transpired naturally. This has supposedly happened, through disingenuous judicial efforts to expand the idea of intentional segregation to embrace almost all racial separation. Such judicial imperialism converts what should be treated as a political issue, a decision concerning how schools ought to be run, into a legal matter. The kind of give-and-take that characterizes local politics consequently cannot occur, and the scope of maneuver for democratic decision making is wrongly confined.

Court-ordered busing is the conservatives' bête noire, for it is perceived as both inconsistent with the ideal of a color-blind constitution and violating popular preference. Judicial decisions affecting the administration and educational program of school districts also offend, for these undermine the capacity of local authority to turn local desires into policy; indeed, such decisions are sometimes regarded as imperiling the very legitimacy of the courts. In short, the conservative aspiration is for decentralized and politically responsible decision making with respect to race and schooling.

Liberal critics, on the other hand, regard present policy as insufficiently constitutionalized, and deeply distrust the decentralization and politicization that now exist.[10] Treating race as a regional and political concern, they point out, produced Jim Crow laws in the South and their informal (and sometimes official) equivalent in the North. Only an authoritative decision of the Supreme Court occasioned even the semblance of fairness, and that decision marked the beginning of a protracted struggle for equity in which a national commitment would continually be needed.

By its nature, liberals say, racial justice is a public value rooted in an underlying moral concern, an idea with meaning for the society at large and not just for particular communities or regions; for that reason it requires national definition.[11] Determinations of racial policy cannot as a practical matter be confined to a given setting. The actions of one community will be widely felt, since "[b]lack children in San Francisco do not escape the stigma when the state calls blacks in Los Angeles inferior."[12] Differences in treatment will necessarily seem iniquitous to blacks who regard themselves as having lost out.

The observation that such differences result from the workings of a healthy pluralism in naturally defined political communities does not allay these liberal concerns, for both smallness and pluralism are deeply suspect. When conservatives look at communities they see Arcadia, whereas liberals envision Sinclair Lewis's *Main Street*, with all its attendant babbitry. To the liberal, smallness betokens small-mindedness, an emphasis on self-interest over general interest, exclusion of minority views, intolerance of dissent.[13] Pluralist decision making is derided as characterizing a world in which nothing of value exists: "There is no substance. Neither is there procedure. There is only process."[14] Pluralism at its best brings about modest reform, inadequate in face of the scope of the need for change, and more typically buttresses the status quo. Far from accommodating the range of interests affected by a particular issue, pluralism is said to favor the haves over the have-nots, the organized over the historically disenfranchised. In attending only to adjustment at the margin, pluralism denies the reality of deeper fissures; in stressing the pragmatic, pluralism leaves no room for healthy ideological conflict. As Wilson Carey McWilliams writes: "Groups which must endeavor to change not merely the distribution of values but the values themselves, not their position in the [pluralist] system but the moral assumptions of the system, find themselves at a disadvantage. The bias of the system works against them."[15]

Race is what McWilliams has specifically in mind: "What else is the lesson of race relations in American life?"[16] For that reason, politicizing and localizing race policy spells disaster to liberals. It diminishes the prospect of racial balance. It respects school district boundaries that, by separating black cities from white suburbs, reduce the possibility of meaningful policy change. As a historical fact, Theodore Lowi asserts in speaking of the 1960s community-action effort, politicization "converted the revolutionary moral force of the civil rights movement to a geographically segmented, economically defined, and negotiable set of goals, around which locally oriented, well-organized groups could form for purposes of negotiation."[17] This outcome is unfortunate from the liberal perspective, since it defuses the quest for equality.

Central government is the liberals' preferred setting for policy, the courts their instrument of choice. Because the issue of racial equality is defined in normative terms, it is thought best handled by the judiciary, the chief norm-setting institution of the society. Reason and principle are the commodities in which judges are held to traffic, and out of reasoned interchange just values can best be derived. The court's professed impartiality and the relative permanence of constitutionally based judicial decision as opposed to political action underscore the liberal argument for "juridical democracy," in which such matters as racial equality are removed entirely from the political arena.[18]

The conservative and liberal challenges to the prevailing pattern of decision both draw on widely shared societal norms. Political accountability and constitutional justice, participation and equity, racial mixing and personal preference: in the context of race and schooling, these aspirations pull in opposing directions. Different processes of decision will resolve them differently. And who can confidently say that any of them is inherently misguided? Concern for educational quality—or student safety, for that matter—is not properly dismissed as racist; nor, on the other side, is interest in integrated schools rightly viewed as turning students into "pigmented pawns."[19] Politics as well as constitutionalism marks the checks and balances built into the American system of governance.

The evident weakness of the liberal and conservative viewpoints is that each forces a choice between interest politics and constitutionalism. What is needed instead is an amalgam of political and constitutional processes of decision making and the acceptance of bounded substantive diversity that the amalgam portends. The variability of the present fully reflects our inability to specify a single vision of the Good Society, either politically or constitutionally powered. "A judicial model would serve well," Grant McConnell observes, "if standards existed on which men agreed and which could be readily applied," but these circumstances are not at hand.[20] A political resolution would similarly be acceptable if the full gamut of possible political action commanded broad assent, but that is not the situation.

Constitutionalism and politics, centralism and localism strain against one another as ideals of decision, and so maintain a certain balance among competing social goods. A wholly politicized world might rob minorities of rights that affect their dignity, whose source lies deeper than the momentary will of the electorate, even as a wholly judicialized world could overwhelm the reality of circumstance with the force of principle. Law "tempers the erratic impulses of our pluralist democracy";[21] politics reintroduces specificity into the law. The tension between these keeps policy at once pragmatic and principled. So too with the parallel tension between central and local authority. Central government has been the source of redistributive, equity-based efforts, while local governments have emphasized efficient action. Both elements are properly present in policy calculus.[22]

Policy concerning race and schooling has been extraordinarily dynamic in the years since *Brown*, and the deliberate maintenance of tension among the processes of decision making has fueled that dynamism. The judiciary has historically exercised varying degrees of influence; it has not been the single-mindedly imperialist institution that conservative critics decry. The courts' role has shifted from one of social control in the context of Southern desegregation during the 1960s to managing a reinvigorated polity within a constitutionally fixed framework in the 1970s. The relationship between central and local government has similarly varied over time. These tugs and pulls have kept the course of policy loosely in touch with social learning. In that sense, bounded variability, although less coherent than either the conservative or liberal models, may more reliably guarantee a policy that approximates the wishes of a constitutionally informed and shifting consensus.

The present process of decision does not work badly, and its variability contributes importantly to its success. Not that we couldn't do better. In substantive terms, what is wanted is a policy combining uniform minimum guarantees of equal treatment—including the chance to obtain a genuinely integrated education—with idiosyncratically developed school programs building on the preferences of particular communities. In procedural terms, enhancing the opportunities for black participation in shaping those idiosyncratic decisions and in monitoring uniform minima is the desired end. Although those policy objectives will not command universal assent, they are fairly derived from the detailed recounting of the Bay Area communities' experience and more generally from the evolution of national race and schooling policy; in that, they make historical sense. This evidence speaks to the use and limits of rules and discretion, and to the appropriate locus of decision for the several issues that, taken together, constitute race and schooling policy.

Such a policy perspective, which favors an energetic federalism capable of shaping a national commitment to integration within the very different possibilities presented by local circumstance, enlists the several branches of government at each of its levels. It demands changes in the ways the courts and the political system do business. Constitutional doctrine, as developed by the Supreme Court in the context of Northern segregation, is excessively devoted to faultfinding, insufficiently attentive to the underlying issues of equitable treatment. Lower courts' efforts may jeopardize the distinction between political and judicial action. The negativism of national-level politics since the mid-1970s has hindered efforts to develop sane policy. At the local level, policy seems increasingly driven by self-interest, less attentive to the claims of the larger community. Each of these assertions is developed in succeeding sections of this chapter, with the aim of indicating a plausible policy direction for the 1980s.

II

Because the judiciary determines the constitutional bounds within which political activity surrounding race and schooling occurs, an appraisal of the present logically starts with the courts. As chapter 3 argues, all judging is itself political as well as legalist in character. Nonetheless, one can usefully distinguish between the judiciary as shaper of doctrine, the conventional understanding of the

Supreme Court's mission, and the judiciary as superintendent of constitutionally constrained negotiations, as often occurs in the lower courts. Aspects of each enterprise pose dilemmas.

For nearly two decades following the *Brown* decision, the Supreme Court decided only Southern school desegregation cases.[23] The cause of racial separation in those cases seemed, plainly enough, the officially maintained dual school system, whose effects lingered after its formal abolition. The justices did not belabor this point, but instead stipulated what remedies were constitutionally necessary to undo the continuing effect of segregation.

By 1971, however, when *Swann v. Charlotte-Mecklenburg Board of Education*[24] was decided, the nexus between pre-1954 segregation and the present racial composition of the schools, so long presumed, had become attenuated. The Charlotte-Mecklenburg school district had some years earlier abandoned the evasions of *Brown*, which predictably produced dual schools. Other considerations contributed to racial identifiability in the schools, notably an increase in residential segregation coupled with the maintenance of neighborhood schools. In this respect, Charlotte-Mecklenburg did not seem so very different from Northern districts that, although untainted by a history of mandated dual schools, nonetheless operated substantially segregated school systems in which school attendance was largely determined by place of residence. *Swann* emphasizes the persisting consequences of the pre-1954 regime, but that portion of the opinion is factually unconvincing. Its very unpersuasiveness prompted speculation that the Supreme Court might abandon entirely the premise that only deliberate segregation was unconstitutional, treating desegregation as an affirmative constitutional right regardless of the cause of racial separation.[25]

In *Keyes v. School District Number 1, Denver*[26] the Court refused to adopt such an approach. In a community with no history of Jim Crow laws, the majority maintained, deliberate intent to segregate had to be shown before a court would grant relief; the mere fact of racial isolation was constitutionally irrelevant. Proof of intentional segregation affecting a substantial portion of a district presumptively demonstrated that deliberate segregation had a district-wide effect, and for that reason district-wide desegregation, including busing if necessary, was appropriate. The Court has been largely preoccupied since *Keyes* with elaborating the meaning of intent and refining the connection between wrong and remedy. Both are confusing enterprises.[27]

Because Northern school districts had not been formally authorized in modern times to separate students on racial grounds, intentional segregation had to be inferred from the actions of the school board, its decisions concerning attendance boundaries, construction of new schools, teacher assignment, and the like. But how was this inference to be drawn? Was it sufficient to prove that school policy had the predictable effect of segregating students, or did intent carry a stronger meaning, implying some additional element of culpable conduct? Opinions after *Keyes* first contracted and later expanded the possibility of proving intentional segregation. The Court's determinations were similarly accordionlike with respect to the fit between wrong and remedy, increasing and diminishing plaintiffs' legal burdens.

The Supreme Court's vagueness and vacillation, the latter plainly visible in the Court's two very different decisions in the Dayton school case,[28] has caused considerable trouble. Lower courts, unsure of what standard to apply, have reached varying decisions without being able clearly to communicate an explanation for the differences: Why should Pontiac and Kalamazoo, but not Grand Rapids, have to bus students? Policymakers have been baffled and infuriated by these turnabouts. *Brown v. Board of Education* was premised on values understandable and persuasive to the intelligent layman. *Keyes* and its progeny, by contrast, float in a sea of murky technicality, barely comprehensible to anyone, not obviously anchored to principles of fairness.

The constitutional standard propounded in *Keyes* is the chief culprit. Requiring proof of intentional segregation before calling for any remedy is a defensible reading of the Fourteenth Amendment—the language of equal protection is sufficiently capacious to tolerate a range of understandings—but not the most sensible reading. The injury that children suffer from racial separation has nothing to do with its cause. Does a black fourth grader know that her school is 95 percent black only because officials gerrymandered the attendance zone? Does it matter? The emphasis on intent also ignores the obvious point that segregation always results from official action—assigning children to particular schools. Intent is peculiarly susceptible to a host of different interpretations, in a policy universe where uniformity with respect to the bedrock of constitutional obligation seems an essential element of fair policy. Most important, because intentional segregation as the judges have defined the concept is neither a consistent nor a readily understandable basis for judicial intervention, the very legitimacy of the Court's effort is jeopardized. Why should people obey a decision whose rationale they cannot grasp and whose authoritativeness they doubt?

A preferable constitutional approach, well within the Supreme Court's discretion in interpreting the Equal Protection Clause, would recognize the irrelevance of fault-finding with respect to most aspects of segregation. Justice Powell's opinion in the Denver case follows this course in proposing:

> a right, derived from the Equal Protection Clause, to expect that once the state has assumed responsibility for education, local school boards will operate integrated school systems.... A system would be integrated in accord with constitutional standards if the responsible authorities had taken appropriate steps to (i) integrate faculties and administration; (ii) scrupulously assure equality of facilities, instruction, and curricular opportunities throughout the district; (iii) utilize their authority to draw attendance zones to promote integration; and (iv) locate new schools, close old ones, and determine the size and grade categories with this same objective in mind.[29]

This approach, uniform minimum integration, attempts to distinguish between the principle-based and policy-based components of the idea of racial justice, assigning only the former exclusively to the courts. It locates a core substantive right, not appropriately subject to testing against the competing concerns of the larger community, and distinguishes that right from more obviously policy-based claims. The latter type of claim advances an essentially utilitarian argument—the benefit to the community as a whole justifies the proposed policy—and hence contemplates comparison with rival claims. This comparison is most fittingly carried out politically, whereas claims of principle, derived from the Constitution, are more evidently the business of courts. Racial equality spans both sorts of contentions. Ronald Dworkin, from whom the principle-policy distinction is borrowed, notes: "A program that depends chiefly on principle, like an antidiscrimination program, may reflect a sense that rights are not absolute and do not hold when the consequences for policy are very serious."[30] Beyond the uniform minimum obligation, racial concerns are, as Justice Powell notes, properly weighed against "other, equally important educational interests which a community may assert."[31] Although policy and principle cannot neatly be distinguished, Justice Powell's approach offers a helpful way of focusing judicial efforts on concerns of principle.

Uniform minimum integration is also attentive to the need for articulate consistency. Although the scope of the constitutional obligation remains disputable in the marginal instance—there will inevitably be disagreements over the "scrupulousness" of equalization efforts or the feasibility of drawing boundaries in ways that promote further racial mixing—the range of differences from place to place is substantially narrowed. The standard takes into account objections leveled at the fault-centered approach of *Keyes*. It is clear, comprehensible, and intuitively plausible. Since every school district would have a constitutional responsibility to bring black and white students together, the distinction between North and South, now almost wholly lacking any factual basis, would be abandoned. The scope of that responsibility would be bounded in a manner consistent with both the constitutional command of equal treatment and popular perceptions of fairness. This approach accords with growing popular acceptance of the rightness of desegregation. In 1975, 76 percent of Northern and 62 percent of Southern parents said they would willingly send their children to half-black schools; just ten years earlier, 68 percent of Northern parents and only 32 percent of Southern parents would not have objected.[32] In this sense, the standard offers a sensible, acceptable, and understandable constitutionally premised minimum.

Uniform minimum integration, although specifying the most important judicial task, needs to be augmented in several respects. Because entitlement to an education free from racial stigma is an individual constitutional right—it is, after all, the rights of "persons" that the Fourteenth Amendment secures—any child, black or white, should be able to attend a school other than the one to which he or she is assigned if that choice reduces racial isolation.[33]

The rights of minority children also encompass freedom from intentionally imposed segregation that causes existing racial isolation. In this respect, the concern for intent that animates the Supreme Court's opinions has continuing vitality. Intent is used here in the strong sense, referring to demonstrable official *design*, not just to inferences made from the *effect* of a particular practice. Before intent becomes legally relevant, the causal connection between a policy of deliberate segregation and segregation itself would also have to be proven; in other words, the wrong has to be consequential. A school district that deliberately and effectively separates blacks and whites robs them of their constitutional rights. Only a remedy that restores those rights, undoing what the district has done, fairly fits the circumstances.

Similarly, where segregation can be shown to result from the willful acts of state government or from several districts' scheming, remedies may ignore the boundaries of a particular district. Neither district-wide relief of the sort ordered in Denver nor metropolitan-wide relief should be routinely contemplated. These

remedies trench on longstanding, legitimate state and local political prerogatives; they also strain the distinction between policy
and principle. That is the reason for insisting on a strict showing of
intent. Whether intent can be defined sufficiently narrowly to minimize abuse of the standard or with sufficient specificity to reduce
inconsistency is uncertain, and recent judicial attempts are not encouraging. Nonetheless, the effort needs to be made. Where deliberate official action has materially contributed to walling off black
ghettos from white neighborhoods or black central cities from
white suburbs, judicial abstention works too great an injustice.[34]

Uniform minimum integration, the right to choose a less segregated school, a broader race-conscious remedy where there is
proof of deliberate and effective efforts to separate black and white
students within school districts or metropolitan areas: these are
the elements of a judicial role that at once respects the civil rights
of individuals and the policy interests of communities. How might
the application of this approach affect the Bay Area communities?
San Francisco would not have been required to bus students in
order to improve the racial mix of the schools—at least not without a fuller showing of intentional segregation than was adduced
at the trial. Since the *Johnson* order is no longer in effect, the existing busing program is a voluntary effort, which the proposed standard permits—indeed encourages. The voluntary racial-balance
efforts in Berkeley and Sausalito would similarly be unaffected.
Richmond's open enrollment plan would constitute part of what
was minimally required; whether sufficient efforts had been made
to encourage integration through attendance zone revisions, equalization efforts, and teacher assignments would have to be judicially determined. Oakland would clearly need to do more if challenged in the courts. At the least, its modest open enrollment
program would have to be expanded and restricted to transfers
that improved the racial mix of the students. The boundaries of
Skyline High School, for so long the focus of blacks' unhappiness,
would not withstand scrutiny; far from promoting desegregation,
they have separated blacks from whites.

The challenge confronting the lower courts is different, for
they are less the inventors of doctrine than the overseers of institutional reform in the schools. The courts have done reasonably well
in setting in motion a new mode of decision, one with noteworthy
effects on social policy. Nathan Glazer, speaking generally of in-
stitutional-reform litigation, notes that courts:

are beginning to shape the entire structure of social policy. They are determining which of the factions disputing policies and their implementation
are to be strengthened, and which weakened. . . . They are significantly determining how resources within any given branch of social policy are to
be distributed, and how they are to be distributed among the several
branches of social policy.[35]

But what licenses judges to act in this fashion? Certainly not the
traditional conception of adjudication, which sharply distinguishes
judging from politics.[36] Lower courts themselves have sought to
maintain this conception. Even as they act in a political setting,
they emphasize unbroken links to past legalist behavior. Even as the
courts goad a political process, they issue orders; even as they seek
to balance interests, they refer to rights.[37]

   Yet in the context of contemporary desegregation problems, a
trial court that attempted to function in exclusively legalist terms,
confining its concerns to matters directly derivable from authoritative rule, could not respond effectively to the issue at hand, and
hence could in no sense vindicate the rights at stake in the controversy. A rigidly legalist judiciary courts uselessness. It risks turning the "least dangerous branch" into an institution that traffics exclusively in symbols, not in consequential reality.[38] Such a posture
of forbearance could well bring about its own crisis of institutional
legitimacy.

   We tend to forget just how adaptive the federal judiciary
has historically been in finding a place for itself in the political
maelstrom. In this quest for relevance, rights have often been
rooted in the realities and beliefs of the day.[39] And the consequences
of court decisions matter, as the justices themselves well understand. During the oral argument in the *Brown* case, Justice Frankfurter inquired: "Does anyone know . . . where we can go to find
light on what the practical consequences of these decisions have
been?"[40] Consequences are an abiding concern to a judiciary as
deeply enmeshed in political discourse as the federal courts. Attending to consequences requires that courts be able to adapt in
the face of altered circumstances. In the context of desegregation,
the newly perceived relationship between institutional restructuring and the undoing of discrimination, and the concomitant necessity for framing remedies extending beyond racial mixing, warrant
the judicial adaptiveness evident in many district court decisions.
This point is recognized by Justice Powell's *Keyes* opinion, which
expresses concern for "equality of instruction and curricular
opportunities."[41]

Yet as a justification for institutional reform litigation, the need for adaptiveness proves too much. It is not the case that the court can assume *any* posture or confront *any* question, as long as the outcome promises to be efficacious. Were it otherwise, there would be neither place nor need for majoritarian government, no distinction whatsoever between principle and politics. Hence the core question: How can the judiciary reconcile the need to act effectively with the importance of retaining the qualities that distinguish it from the coordinate branches of government?[42]

While no bright line demarcates the activities of courts, judicial decision making is distinctive in two respects. The decisions themselves emerge from interchange between the judge and those directly affected by the issue; they derive from actual controversies, not from the desire to undo imagined mischiefs. And those decisions are premised not on the judges' beliefs but on the positive law.

The desegregation cases may be understood as an attempt to preserve these distinctively judicial attributes even as the form and nature of the litigation evolves. Consider first the process of decision. The very sweep of the cases makes the actual participation of all those affected a practical impossibility, which is why "classes" are represented not by all their members but by named individuals. But even within the courtroom, the idea that representative participation is preserved amounts to scarcely more than a conceit.[43] The entire class, usually the minority students of the school district, is never formally notified of the litigation. The named plaintiffs are essentially figureheads. Discordant voices within the larger class—those who might be interested in securing black separatism, for example, or in exempting Hispanic students from the decree—are discouraged, for they introduce complications not readily resolved in the adversarial setting.

In adapting the process of adjudication, shaping a more political resolution of the controversy through negotiation, the trial court is attempting more fully to recognize the range of affected interests, thus relating process to substance. Within the context of negotiations over remedy, it is possible to involve affected outsiders, and in so doing to create a counterpart to the dialogue usually carried out in the courtroom. This negotiation does not mirror the politicking that transpires prior to the lawsuit. It offers those who were likely to have been frozen out of the earlier give-and-take—the racial minorities who suffered the consequences of nonrepresentation—a chance to participate. Judicial solicitude for the constitutional wants of "discrete and insular minorities," a familiar enough explanation for court intervention, is given renewed significance in these cases.[44] Where the participation succeeds, where the court-initiated negotiations in fact revitalize a pluralist system of decision making, it is "representation reinforcing" action. Such negotiation unclogs for minorities the channels of government, giving them some say over their own lives.[45]

Process matters greatly in the constitutional scheme of things. As John Ely has written, the Constitution "is overwhelmingly concerned . . . with ensuring broad participation in the processes and distributions of government." But the Constitution does not speak only to the nature of representation. It encompasses broad substantive rights as well, among them the right to equal treatment. "By its explicit concern with equality among the persons within a state's jurisdiction it constitutes the document's clearest . . . recognition that technical access to the process may not be sufficient to guarantee good-faith representation of all those putatively represented."[46] That command to fairness serves as the substantive basis for the desegregation cases. The constitutional language is, of course, not tightly bounded; that seems appropriate, when a value as durable and as public as equality is at issue. The breadth of the constitutional provision permits judges to notice ever more subtle forms of inequity. It also licenses attending to the strategic elements of remedy, taking into account such factors as the complaisance of the school district, the feasibility and acceptability of the alternatives, and the need to speak not just to the manifestations but also to the source of the threat to equality.[47] Equal protection is not, however, an unbounded concept; nor can it be equated with the good society. In this case, the standard of uniform minimum integration provides some check on the scope of trial court efforts.

Finally, the process of participation and the substance of decision do not occupy separate spheres. Where the substantive basis for decision—here, equality—is very much in flux, and where consensus is itself a good, the effort to assure opportunities for participation further enhances the legitimacy of the outcome.[48] Within constitutional bounds, equality means what those affected concur that it means. In process and substance, justice is importantly idiosyncratic. Its meaning evolves with changes in circumstance and with altered understandings of the core value of equality.

In race and schooling litigation, trial courts are continuously learning not only what works, but also how they may intervene effectively while still performing a distinctive function within the constitutional system of governance. There is no ready way to hold them accountable for their missteps: indeed, it is the absence of obvious mechanisms of accountability that prompts the concern about the legitimacy of courts' actions. Impeachment is a rare event, constitutional amendments to overturn particular judicial decisions even rarer, and attempts to constrict the jurisdiction of the federal courts—in order to deny district courts original jurisdiction in desegregation cases, for example—have been unsuccessful.

Yet the courts, if not formally accountable, are nonetheless subject to restraints, both imposed externally by the larger system of governance and self-imposed. When a court acts within the uniquely judicial domain, its opinions enjoy considerable deference, if not obeisance. When, however, a court departs from its familiar script and speaks essentially as an actor in the political arena, its pronouncements necessarily compete for attention with other voices in that arena. Judicial decisions of this sort constitute a form of pressure and influence, and although they are not unimportant they are less likely to be determinative. The consequent diminution of authority may at least lessen the consequences of misused authority, if not curb its appearance.

Judicial self-restraint is of at least equal moment.[49] Within the federal system, higher courts check the excesses of lower courts. In the very act of deciding race and schooling cases, judges sense the limits of their capacity to refashion the existing order. This perceptiveness is apparent in the actions both of the Supreme Court[50] and of the district courts hearing this most controversial species of case.[51] That federal courts refer to the limits of their office matters less than that they believe in those limits. Such self-restraint cannot wholly resolve the problem, for self-imposed limitations, however salutary, are themselves too varied and situation-specific to allay the larger, more systemic fears. Yet the idiosyncratic character of the cases argues against any more general and formulaic approach. The courts—and the society—may simply learn how to live with the strains on institutional legitimacy inherent in the contemporary race and schooling cases, cases that are at once political and constitutional events.

III

During the mid-1960s, when moral vision was infused by a capacious sense of the politically possible, the legislative and executive branches of the federal government joined with the courts to undo Southern school segregation. In contrast, in the 1970s Congress warred with the executive branch and especially with the courts over the scope of the federal presence. Well over one hundred bills and constitutional amendments were introduced in Congress during the decade, each intended to constrict the authority of the judiciary, the Office of Civil Rights, and the Justice Department.[52]

The present congressional posture disappoints because it embodies a default in leadership, an ability to specify only what *isn't* wanted without any sense of a usefully positive federal presence. Returning to the activism of an earlier time would be neither appropriate nor imaginable, for the civil rights issues that need to be resolved are different, as is our sense of what Washington can usefully do. Not that the past is irrelevant. It teaches us that questions of race and schooling can only be confronted with some hope of ultimate success if the national will to do so is shared by all of the several branches of government, which together can articulate the uniform elements of policy. The combined efforts of Congress, the executive, and the judiciary made the rapid desegregation of Southern schools possible during the Johnson presidency. Circumstances are now different—can anyone seriously imagine that even a unified federal government would have the last say in such matters without the full involvement of state and local governments?—but the necessity for national collaboration remains a vital element of responsible thinking about policy.

During the past decade we have learned a great deal about the relevance of race in this society and about the capacity of government to shape social behavior. That knowledge sobers. It is discomfiting to realize that the American dilemma does not vanish in the face of visions of progress and that social problems acquire new complexities even as they seem finally amenable to solution. The Supreme Court's declaration in the second *Brown* decision, that desegregation had to occur with "all deliberate speed"[53] rather than at once, may have been as misguided as is now generally supposed. But in reaching their decision the justices recognized that achieving racial justice in schools constitutes a revolution in the practices, if not the principles, of the republic. For that reason, race and schooling reform cannot be brought about instantly or painlessly. Nor can attending seriously to questions of race, even if that effort is fused with educational purpose, achieve miracles. Despite the lingering popular faith in the curative powers of education, schooling cannot overcome all of the divisions between blacks and whites, or the effects of those divisions on children. This realization counsels restraint on the part of the political as well as judicial branches of the national government, a recognition of what cannot be done well by Washington. It does not justify abdication.

There remains a significant federal role, if the political

branches choose to assert it. Congressional and executive support for uniform minimum standards of the sort propounded by Justice Powell in *Keyes* would strengthen their claim to political as well as constitutional legitimacy. Washington can also raise and redistribute substantial sums of money to encourage local experimentation with diverse approaches. The Emergency School Assistance Act (ESAA), the one modest source of federal funds presently available to aid school districts in the throes of desegregation, has been at least a minor success in this regard. Though the program has been hobbled with congressionally imposed restraints born of Congress's dislike for busing, some six hundred districts have spent their ESAA allotments on badly needed improvements in the school curriculum and on earnest efforts to reduce racial tensions. The thoughtfulness of many district efforts—as well as their apparent success in producing modest gains in achievement—suggests that local governments may do best if left free from detailed federal requirements.[54]

The federal government can, in addition, offer technical assistance directly to school districts. It might consider borrowing from Britain the idea of an education inspectorate that collaborates closely with professionals in the field, sharing ideas that have worked elsewhere and helping to implement new programs. Such undertakings have not fared well in the history of American education. The Department of Education does not fancy itself a helpmate. It has sought to impose its priorities on local officials, using its authority to promote compliance with federal directives. A variety of process-oriented devices, specifying the ways in which decisions are to be reached and the information that must be made available, have been deployed to encourage lower levels of government to embrace Washington's perspective. The threat of cutting off federal funds has been relied on for the same purpose.

Where rights are at issue, compliance is indeed what is wanted: if the minimum integration standards are national rules, they ought to be followed nationally. But beyond the minima, an orientation to compliance as distinguished from assistance makes little sense. Compliance has nothing to do with improving the quality of educational practice; such efforts are a form of craft, which cannot be reduced to a matter of following rules. Moreover, compliance efforts don't work well. At best, as with Title I, ESEA, Washington can induce the appearance of compliance.[55] Mandating substantive change is beyond its grasp.[56] The effort to do so is counterproductive, for it provokes resentment and distrust between levels of government, and so makes a useful national role harder to fashion. The ends of race and schooling policy would be better served were the Department of Education largely to abandon the carrot-and-stick mentality. Instead of threatening local officials as would-be miscreants who need policing, Washington might better regard them as fellow professionals sharing common concerns.

Distribute money, provide technical support, establish uniform minimum standards for a fair race and schooling policy: that much might be accomplished at the national level. Beyond that, Washington can only encourage state and local educators, working within their own political frameworks, to identify how best to resolve questions of race and schooling, selecting among the numerous alternatives adopted elsewhere or adopting an approach more precisely attuned to local needs. These alternatives are sufficiently different to warrant leaving specific choices to state and local institutions, whose grasp of nuance is necessarily better than Washington's. Courts should continue to enforce constitutional minima and can usefully nurture political bargaining among the interested parties. Only where that process stalls should the judiciary assume a more activist posture, particularly to secure a fully participatory regime. For the rest, trusting to the variability of local wants seems the wisest course.

IV

The critical question remains: Will honoring constitutionally bounded local wants promote good policy? The recent historical record is generally cheering. The past quarter-century has been filled with delay and disappointment, but viewed in retrospect these seem to reflect the enormity of the transformation sought in the name of racial equality, not a breakdown of governmental capacity. Political actions taken in numerous school districts, including the five Bay Area towns, confirm a remarkable capacity for change at the community level. A variegated political order, goaded by the norms of constitutionalism and less abstractly by court decisions, reformed its rules and reshaped its policies to confront the concerns of the civil rights movement. In so doing, passions were domesticated and rendered fit for political resolution.

Will attention to racially rooted inequities in an arena of decision increasingly open to black participation persist in the 1980s? Social policy predictions are about as reliable as reading tea leaves, especially for an issue as volatile as race and schooling, and our long and sorry history of race relations may make us especially sensitive to the smallest sign that progress toward the full inclusion of blacks in the social order is eroding. Nonetheless, the portents disturb. There is detectably diminished enthusiasm for reforms designed to bring about greater racial equality or a fuller measure of equal educational opportunity. Moreover, the norms of civic loyalty that made the idea of racial equality in education properly a concern not just of minorities but of everyone now have less force, and that may diminish the authority of the polity.

The very success of the drive for racial equality may have dampened prospects for further government-initiated reforms. The destructive passions of a decade ago have dissipated, and this is all to the good. This surface harmony, coupled with tangible signs of prosperity in the growing black middle class, has persuaded many whites that "total equality of opportunity has been achieved."[57] In 1976, 63 percent of white Americans believed that the position of blacks in the society had changed greatly during the past few years; twelve years earlier, only 39 percent held that view.[58] Yet that perception may lead whites to resist further civil rights initiatives as mere special pleading. When queried about the propriety of the federal government's making "every possible effort to improve the social and economic position of blacks," just 15 percent were strongly supportive in 1978, a decline from 20 percent in 1970.[59] Why pursue further government action, white Americans seem increasingly inclined to ask, if there no longer remains a significant problem? Skepticism about the utility of federal intervention also may contribute to an unwillingness to rely on government action. Fewer than one-third of the white population believes that the "1960s programs" actually helped minorities; 60 percent thought these initiatives had either no impact or made things worse.[60]

A similar pattern can be detected in white attitudes toward race and schooling. The temptation is to dismiss the task of achieving racial equality in the schools by regarding it either as already achieved or as unachievable. Although only one in twenty Americans now professedly favors segregation, government policy designed "to insure integration" is another story. Support for such a policy reached its highest point in 1972, when 41 percent of the white population endorsed it; by 1978, the ranks of the aggressively prointegrationists had thinned to 34 percent. The majority wanted "something in between" integration and segregation—presumably governmental noninvolvement.[61]

Blacks perceive a different world, with different social possibilities. For the black community, the great change came with the symbolic affirmation of their rights as citizens, in 1964: that year, three-fifths of the black population reported substantial change in the position of blacks. But even as continuing progress was made, black skepticism increased. By 1976, only 32 percent believed that considerable change in their status had occurred during recent times. Although blacks remain far more enthusiastic than whites about government efforts to integrate the schools—55 percent favor this policy—disillusionment with government efforts in general seems to have carried over into this realm. Support among blacks for integration declined from 77 percent in 1964 to 55 percent in 1978.[62] Blacks now more frequently associate equality in education with successful black schools and apparently have less interest in an integrated system of public education.

Black skepticism and white resistance need to be balanced against the institutionalization of attentiveness to race in many districts, the growth of minority participation in school governance, and the diminution of overt racial hostilities. These signs may presage further reform, at least in some locales. Whether this happens will largely depend on the parlous state of educational policy, for like other social policy questions, racial issues are hostage to political and economic circumstance.

During the liberal social reformist period of the 1960s and early 1970s, it was possible to summon the resources of talent and money needed to modernize education. As in the common school and Progressive eras, education was widely regarded as a panacea for the nation's ills. Support for schooling increased dramatically at every level of government.[63] Expenditures on public schools grew from 3.8 percent to 4.6 percent of the gross national product between 1960 and 1975. During the same period, per pupil expenditures doubled (taking inflation into account).[64] The ideas of racial equality and educational reform were closely intertwined. The demand for racial justice formed part of the call for modernization, and the availability of new resources made attentiveness to race-specific issues politically more palatable.

The present state of public education presents a more sobering picture. The decline in enrollment has forced many school systems to contract; communities are selling off their schools, not building new ones. Between 1971 and 1976, only half as many school bond issues—designed to finance new programs, usually construction—were put before the voters as during the period 1961–66, and during the same interval voter-approval rates fell from approximately 70 percent to about 50 percent. Budgets already strained by taxpayer reluctance to approve tax increases have been further constricted by voter-approved ceilings, in a number of states, on local tax rates and state expenditures.[65] Taking inflation into account, per pupil expenditures declined slightly between 1975 and 1978, an event without modern precedent.[66] Public schools were not the chief target of taxpayers' unhappiness; four-fifths of California voters, surveyed after the passage of Proposition 13, which limits local districts' taxing capacity, favored maintaining or even increasing educational expenditures, and the evidence from other states is similar.[67] Yet the schools have been among the major losers in the wake of the taxpayers' revolt. Sizable teacher layoffs in each of the five Bay Area communities— most dramatically in San Francisco and Berkeley, where teaching staffs were cut by almost one-quarter between 1975 and 1979— and ending district financial support for busing in Richmond bring home the consequences of the new fiscal conservatism and its impact on minorities.

Budget trimming potentially encourages institutions to rethink their mission—not a bad idea in the case of the schools—but there is little evidence of this happening. Cutbacks in staff and resources have produced uncertainty, bred division among teachers, and increased pressure on school administrators and board members. Reform demands at least a modest vision, hard to summon when survival seems the preeminent concern; rethinking requires energy in an institution whose ablest younger members are being laid off and whose remaining staff understandably emphasize the bread-and-butter questions of salary and security. There are exceptions to these discouraging tendencies, but the pressure to retrench and the fortress mentality that this invites within schools is everywhere felt, if not routinely dominant.[68] It is harder to attend to racial equality when the maintenance of the institution can no longer be taken for granted.

It required a resurgence of political interest in education to modernize the public schools. The emergence of the race and schooling question played a key part, for "the heightening of black consciousness which began with the Supreme Court desegregation decision" has been "the most unalloyed example of 'democratic surge'" in our nation's history,[69] but it was not just civil rights groups whose involvement was critical. The willingness of long-quiescent individual citizens and interest groups to contribute what Albert Hirschman terms "voice"—to speak out in order to influence policy—animated this institutional transformation.[70] When such participation occurs, it strengthens the political order by legitimating the process of decision making. Present signs point to a slackening of shared commitment and a focus on narrower self-interest. In the school context, this entails "exiting"—moving to a more homogeneous community or removing one's children from the public schools. One consequence is diminished interest in racial equality.

Since the earliest days of the republic, education has been regarded as a public good whose consequences affect us all. As a nation, it is conventionally supposed, we pay the price for producing benighted drudges and reap the rewards of training excellence.[71] This conception of schooling as a shared responsibility powered the common school movement; it also underlies the willingness of the populace to tax itself for the provision of education and to participate in setting its direction. As members of the affected community, citizens assume some responsibility—premised on what Hirschman terms loyalty—for the quality of education, and this leads them to rely on voice, not just the more usual option of exit, to register discontent. That commitment forms part of a more general civic identity, a sense of oneself as part of the polity "over and above the divisive effects of private roles and life."[72]

This commitment to sustain American public institutions through acts of loyalty is not new, nor is it peculiarly the province of education. In *Democracy in America*, Alexis de Tocqueville writes: "The Americans have combated by free institutions the tendency of equality to keep men asunder, and they have subdued it."[73] Participation in the affairs of the republic, most vitally at the local level, makes this outcome possible. "The legislators of America," Tocqueville notes, "thought that it would be well to infuse political life into each portion of the territory in order to multiply to an infinite extent opportunities of acting in concert for all members of the community and to make them constantly feel their mutual dependence."[74] Americans did not preach about "the close tie that unites private to general interest"[75]—they practiced it, through immersion in politics. "The free institutions which the inhabitants of the United States possess, and the political rights of which they make so much use, remind every citizen, and in a thousand ways, that he lives in society."[76]

Tocqueville's portrayal of American politics romanticizes the American experience by treating "unitary democracy"[77] not as the creature of special circumstance but rather as the American norm. If enlightened self-interest underlies a good deal of American policy, so too does self-interest understood in more conventional and narrow terms. Yet citizen involvement in the effort to secure racial equality in the schools was very much a public-regarding act. Narrow self-interest did not disappear—for parents remained deeply concerned about their children's futures—but it ceased to enjoy unquestioned pride of place. Many of those who spoke out believed that, as Richard Hofstadter has written with reference to liberal politics more generally, "political life ought to be run, to a greater degree than it was, in accordance with general principles apart from and superior to personal needs . . . government should be in good part an effort to moralize the lives of individuals. . . ."[78] This is a problematic view of politics. It asks citizens to surrender some of their personal prerogatives and factions to subordinate their parochial aspirations in the search for the larger good. Such a conception is susceptible to abuse by being converted into a tool of oppression by the enlightened. Yet this commitment to principled action did spur the schools to respond, however imperfectly, to the needs of all their members. Widespread reliance on voice has, in that respect, powerful egalitarian consequences.

Exit has subsequently become more evident than voice, as parochialism has reasserted itself. Not that the exit option ever disappeared: some parents sent their children to private schools throughout this period, and a steady stream of white and middle-class families has left the cities for the suburbs since the 1950s. Yet the pace of exit has quickened. Affluent parents seek out suburban school systems where they anticipate that their children may be expected to learn more;[79] within urban systems, affluent youngsters are isolated in the few remaining islands of excellence.[80] Private schools, which attract twice the proportion of well-to-do students as public schools,[81] now enroll some 11 percent of the school-age population, a modest increase over the past five years. The most promising educational nostrums of the 1960s presumed that change would occur within urban public schools. In contrast, educational vouchers and tuition tax credits, which have recently attracted considerable political support, contemplate substantial government aid to private schools and well-off families.[82]

Race is pivotal here. Studies of whites who have left desegregating districts reveal that they moved because they opposed busing, resisted submitting their children to the policy, and had the money to go elsewhere; self-interest tinged with racism motivated their actions.[83] Only where school systems enjoy an effective monopoly over education, by serving an entire metropolitan area, has this phenomenon not occurred, and even in those instances private alternatives have expanded. Christian academies have more than doubled their enrollment during the past decade, and although the resurgence of fundamentalist Christianity partly explains this growth, these schools also afford havens for whites fleeing desegregation.

The racial schism separating city and suburban schools means that the community that makes policy decisions grows ever narrower, more clearly a congregation of the like-minded, more evidently divided by race and class, indifferent to the plight of outsiders. In 1968, four of the largest ten school districts in the nation, sixteen of the largest thirty, had a majority-white enrollment. Just eight years later, only eight of the biggest thirty and one of the largest ten had white majorities.[84] The line dividing city from suburb is treated as impenetrable by suburbanites, who deny any responsibility for the fate of central cities. "A lot of people moved out here because they didn't want to live in the Houston district," a suburban school board member observed, explaining why the community he represented wanted no part of any metropolitan-wide desegregation initiative. "Now why don't they just leave us alone."[85] Yet if the suburbs *are* left alone, if they are not induced to open their schools to blacks living in the neighboring city, increased racial separation is inevitable. Oakland will represent not just one conception of racial fairness but the only available option, an inevitability and not an option. That eventuality impoverishes the idea of racial equality.

A quarter-century ago, American public schools were run on a two-track system, with whites predominating in the upper track and blacks peopling the lower track. That equilibrium, shattered by the protracted campaign for racial equality, has in some respects been restored. The two tracks are again in place, with blacks and whites now separated between as well as within school systems. Yet in contrast to the earlier era, blacks exercise political and administrative dominion over the lower track. Although the importance of that change should not be minimized, one may wonder if this represents the best we might hope for.

An urban school system that has become predominantly non-middle-class and nonwhite no longer resembles the common schools of historic memory and symbolic moment. Such a transformation jeopardizes our sense of the public school as an institution critical to the nation's well-being, which we maintain out of enlightened self-interest. These schools may instead come to be regarded as a welfare service, provided as a matter of largesse to the less favored members of the society. That perception of public schools as charity schools was strongly resisted by American educators a century and a half ago. With good reason: if this view becomes widely held, it can only hasten the decline of the institution.[86]

It is easier to suggest in broad terms what is wanted than to imagine how this might presently be pursued: a commitment to an understanding of equity, in education as elsewhere, that "gives all persons a sense of fairness and inclusion in the society and which promotes a situation where . . . people become more equal so that they can be treated equally,"[87] and a polity willing to assume significant responsibility for defining the task of the schools. The courts can explicate core constitutional values and police the political process, but they cannot impose detailed solutions—at least not without a radical revision of our understanding of democratic institutions. The professionals need to rethink their mission, to learn from what has worked elsewhere how to nurture a "climate of institutional expectation"[88] and not to treat failure as inevitable. The influence of the professionals is most salutary if it coexists in healthy tension with legalist and political impulses.[89] A return to the politically quiescent days of the 1950s, when professionals dominated the apparatus of policy, is neither imaginable in light of subsequent history nor especially desirable, for professional hegemony encourages a narrowing of vision very much at odds with what is presently needed. The grandest hope is that restructuring the governance of schools, through the kinds of judicial and political reforms suggested here, becomes not an end in itself, a celebration of constitutionally bounded pluralism, but instead a means of redesigning the schools in order to better the lives of children. In this conception, process and substance interact to secure a richer understanding of racial fairness.[90] That seems at once a very tall and a very important order.

"The spirit of a commercial people," John Stuart Mill once wrote, "will be . . . essentially mean and slavish, whenever public spirit is not cultivated by extensive participation of the people in the business of government in detail";[91] so too with the furtherance of racial justice. In this respect present prospects are not cheering. Yet this is a decidedly short-run perception. The past quarter-century has been marked by nearly continuous attention to racial justice in the schools, and a period of respite and consolidation may be needed.[92] In any event, the issue will not vanish. The quest for racial equality is a long-standing one, the end elusive, the dilemmas deep and likely to endure.

Appendix

Racial Composition of General Population, Students, Faculty, and Staff; Pupil Achievement; and Per Pupil Expenditures in San Francisco, Oakland, Berkeley, Richmond, and Sausalito

TABLE 1: Racial Composition of Students, 1977–78 and 1979–80

	San Francisco				Oakland				Berkeley				Richmond				Sausalito			
	1977–78		1979–80		1977–78		1979–80		1977–78		1979–80		1977–78		1979–80		1977–78		1979–80	
	Number	%	Number	%	Number	%	Number	%	Number	%	Number	%	Number	%	Number	%	Number	%	Number	%
American Indian	364	.6	366	.6	418	.8	390	.8	16	.1	127	1.2	113	.3	121	.4	0	0	0	0
Asian	15,367	24.0	15,764	27.4	3,157	5.9	3,329	6.8	779	6.8	434	5.2	1,514	4.6	1,547	5.2	5	1.0	8	1.8
Filipino	6,581	10.3	5,208	9.1	709	1.3	568	1.2	96	.8	46	2.0	344	1.0	604	2.0	0	0	0	0
Black	18,469	28.8	15,586	27.4	36,834	68.6	33,425	69.9	5,011	43.5	4,504	38.7	11,805	35.8	11,531	38.7	217	44.5	193	33.7
White	14,166	22.1	11,373	19.8	8,254	15.4	6,857	13.9	5,184	45.0	4,714	45.0	16,481	50.0	13,405	45.0	263	53.9	239	54.1
Hispanic	9,180	14.3	9,198	16.0	4,331	8.1	4,633	9.4	428	3.7	449	8.6	2,730	8.3	2,550	8.6	3	.6	2	.5
Total	64,127		57,495		53,703		49,202		11,514		10,274		32,987		29,758		488		442	

NOTE: Percentages will not always total 100.0 because of rounding off.
SOURCE: Office of Intergroup Relations, California State Department of Education, "Racial and Ethnic Survey of Students and School Level Staff," 1977–78 and 1979–80.

TABLE 2: Achievement Test Performance: Percentile and Comparison Band Percentile, 1975–76 and 1979–80

	San Francisco				Oakland				Berkeley				Richmond				Sausalito			
	1975–76		1979–80		1975–76		1979–80		1975–76		1979–80		1975–76		1979–80		1975–76		1979–80	
	Percentile	Comparison Band[a]	Percentile	Comparison Band	Percentile	Comparison Band	Percentile	Comparison Band	Percentile	Comparison Band	Percentile	Comparison Band	Percentile	Comparison Band	Percentile	Comparison Band	Percentile	Comparison Band	Percentile	Comparison Band
Reading, Grade 3	30	17–24	40	12–29	16	24–39	11	13–29	58	60–75	63	47–70	39	35–49	36	27–49	40	28–50	49	25–26
Reading, Grade 6	17	13–21	22	15–24	13	15–23	15	16–25	54	41–60	69	33–52	43	31–46	25	29–49	32	10–28	39	17–45
Reading, Grade 12	22	16–27	15	23–38	5	12–23	11	13–23	79	53–76	59	75–91	35	32–50	39	35–53	...†	...	...	...
Math, Grade 12	56	15–28	56	24–40	14	12–25	18	13–25	77	55–80	76	83–92	47	33–56	43	37–57	...	...	...	...

[a]Comparison band is the state-calculated range of expected achievement scores for school districts with students of similar social and economic status.
†Sausalito operates only primary schools.
SOURCE: California Assessment Program, California State Department of Education, "Profile of District Performance," 1975–76 and 1979–80.

TABLE 3: Racial Composition of Teachers, 1977–78 and 1979–80

| | San Francisco | | | | Oakland | | | | Berkeley | | | | Richmond | | | | Sausalito | | | |
| | 1977–78 | | 1979–80 | | 1977–78 | | 1979–80 | | 1977–78 | | 1979–80 | | 1977–78 | | 1979–80 | | 1977–78 | | 1979–80 | |
	Number	%	Number	%	Number	%	Number	%	Number	%	Number	%	Number	%	Number	%	Number	%	Number	%
American Indian	27	.9	19	.7	4	.2	5	.2	1	.2	2	.5	8	.6	6	.5	0	0	0	0
Asian	308	10.7	302	11.1	124	5.9	142	7.1	34	6.7	26	6.4	66	5.0	65	5.3	0	0	0	0
Filipino	72	2.5	70	2.6	28	1.3	33	1.6	5	1.0	5	1.2	17	1.3	15	1.2	0	0	0	0
Black	287	10.0	228	8.3	754	35.7	781	36.9	119	23.4	94	23.3	154	11.6	158	12.8	6	17.6	5	16.7
White	2,026	70.7	1,965	71.9	1,117	52.9	1,062	50.2	326	64.0	256	63.4	1,025	77.5	935	76.0	28	82.4	25	83.3
Hispanic	146	5.1	149	5.5	84	4.0	94	4.2	24	4.7	21	5.2	53	4.0	52	4.2	0	0	0	0
Total	2,866		2,733		2,111		2,117		509		604		1,323		1,231		34		30	

NOTE: Percentages will not always total 100.0 because of rounding off.
SOURCE: Office of Intergroup Relations, California State Department of Education, "Racial and Ethnic Survey of Students and School Level Staff," 1977–78 and 1979–80.

TABLE 4: Racial Composition of Administrators, 1977–78 and 1979–80

| | San Francisco | | | | Oakland | | | | Berkeley | | | | Richmond | | | | Sausalito | | | |
| | 1977–78 | | 1979–80 | | 1977–78 | | 1979–80 | | 1977–78 | | 1979–80 | | 1977–78 | | 1979–80 | | 1977–78 | | 1979–80 | |
	Number	%	Number	%	Number	%	Number	%	Number	%	Number	%	Number	%	Number	%	Number	%	Number	%
A. Principals																				
American Indian	0	0	0	0	0	0	0	0	0	0	0	0	0	0	0	0	0	0	0	0
Asian	7	6.6	11	11.2	5	3.6	4	4.8	3	13.6	3	14.3	3	5.2	2	3.6	0	0	0	0
Filipino	1	.9	3	3.1	1	.7	0	0	0	0	0	0	0	0	0	0	0	0	0	0
Black	22	18.8	17	17.3	84	60.0	43	51.8	7	31.8	10	47.6	7	12.1	8	14.5	1	50.0	1	100.0
White	76	65.0	57	58.2	46	32.9	35	42.2	12	54.5	8	38.1	48	82.8	45	81.8	1	50.0	0	0
Hispanic	11	9.4	10	10.2	4	2.9	1	1.2	0	0	0	0	0	0	0	0	0	0	0	0
Total	117		98		140		83		22		21		58		55		2		1	
B. Assistant Principals																				
American Indian	2	2.5	1	1.6	0	0	0	0	0	0	0	0	0	0	0	0	0	0	0	0
Asian	3	3.7	4	6.3	0	0	1	1.8	2	14.3	0	0	0	0	0	0	0	0	0	0
Filipino	0	0	0	0	0	0	1	1.8	0	0	0	0	0	0	1	4.3	0	0	0	0
Black	10	12.5	10	15.9	0	0	38	69.1	10	71.4	4	66.7	5	20.0	6	26.1	0	0	0	0
White	61	76.2	42	66.7	0	0	12	21.8	2	14.3	2	33.3	20	80.0	16	69.6	0	0	0	0
Hispanic	4	5.0	6	9.5	2	100.0	3	5.5	0	0	0	0	0	0	0	0	0	0	0	0
Total	81		63		2		55		14		6		25		23		0		0	

NOTE: Percentages will not always total 100.0 because of rounding off.
SOURCE: Office of Intergroup Relations, California State Department of Education, "Racial and Ethnic Survey of Students and School Level Staff," 1977–78 and 1979–80.

TABLE 5: Expenditures per Pupil (Based on Average Daily Attendance), 1975–76 and 1979–80

	San Francisco		Oakland		Berkeley		Richmond		Sausalito	
	1975–76	1979–80	1975–76	1979–80	1975–76	1979–80	1975–76	1979–80	1975–76	1979–80
	$2,006	$2,620	$1,579	$2,220	$2,242	$2,723	$1,497	$2,092	$2,612	$3,457

SOURCE: Local Assistance Bureau, California State Department of Education, "Selected Statistics," 1975–76; 1979–80 from unpublished data provided by the California State Department of Education, Local Assistance Bureau.

TABLE 6: Racial and Ethnic Composition of the General Population, 1980

	Total Individuals	White		Black		American Indian, Eskimo, and Aleut		Asian and Pacific Islands		Other		Spanish Heritage*	
		Number	%	Number	%	Number	%	Number	%	Number	%	Number	%
Oakland	339,288	129,690	38.2	159,234	46.9	2,199	.7	26,341	7.8	21,824	6.4	32,491	9.6
San Francisco	678,794	395,082	58.2	86,414	12.7	3,548	.5	147,426	21.7	46,504	6.8	83,373	12.3
Richmond**	74,676	29,664	39.7	35,799	47.9	452	.6	3,642	4.9	5,119	6.9	7,713	10.3
Berkeley	103,328	68,198	66.0	20,770	20.1	445	.4	9,897	9.6	4,018	3.9	5,219	5.1
Sausalito***	7,090	6,739	95.0	60	.8	28	.4	152	2.1	111	1.6	168	2.4

*Includes Mexican, Puerto Rican, Cuban, and other Spanish, and is counted here as an ethnic, not a racial group. These persons are therefore also counted in one of the five racial categories.

**Does not include surrounding communities incorporated into Richmond Unified School District.

***Does not include Marin City.

SOURCE: 1980 census printout, State Census Data Center, Department of Commerce, Bureau of the Census.

Notes

Chapter 1 / *(Pages 3–12)*

1. 347 U.S. 483 (1954).
2. See, e.g., Nathan Glazer, *Affirmative Discrimination: Ethnic Inequality and Public Policy* (New York: Basic Books, 1975); Lino Graglia, *Disaster by Decree: The Supreme Court Decisions on Race and Schools* (Ithaca: Cornell University Press, 1976); Harvey R. Rodgers, Jr., and Charles S. Bullock III, *Coercion to Compliance* (Lexington, Mass.: D. C. Heath, 1976); U.S. Commission on Civil Rights, *Fulfilling the Letter and Spirit of the Law* (Washington, D.C.: Government Printing Office, 1976); Symposium, *Is School Desegregation Still a Good Idea?*, 84 *School Review* 309 (1976); Ray Rist, "On the Future of School Desegregation: A New American Dilemma," in *School Desegregation: Past, Present, and Future*, ed. Walter G. Stephan and Joe R. Feagin, 117 (New York: Plenum, 1980).
3. See Jack Peltason, *Fifty-Eight Lonely Men* (Urbana: University of Illinois Press, 1961).
4. Compare Robert Kagan, *Regulatory Justice* (New York: Russell Sage, 1978).
5. See Gary Orfield, *The Reconstruction of Southern Education* (New York: John Wiley, 1969); Beryl Radin, *Implementation, Change, and the Federal Bureaucracy: School Desegregation Policy in HEW, 1964–1968* (New York: Teachers College Press, 1977).
6. See, e.g., Ronald Dworkin, *Taking Rights Seriously* (Cambridge: Harvard University Press, 1977).
7. Ibid., at xi.
8. M. G. Jean de Crèvecoeur, *Letters from an American Farmer* (New York: Fox, Duffield & Co., 1904 ed.); Alexis de Tocqueville *Democracy in America* (New York: Vintage, 1954 ed.); James Bryce, *American Commonwealth* (New York: Macmillan, 1976 ed.); D. W. Brogan, *The American Character* (New York: Knopf, 1944).

9. Gunnar Myrdal, with Richard Sterner and Arnold Rose, *An American Dilemma: The Negro Problem and Modern Democracy* (New York: Pantheon, 1972 ed.).

10. *Green v. County School Board*, 391 U.S. 430, 442 (1968).

11. Eugene Rostow, "The Democratic Character of Judicial Review," 66 *Harvard Law Review* 193, 208 (1952).

12. *Cooper v. Aaron*, 358 U.S. 1 (1958).

13. Howell Raines, *My Soul Is Rested: Movement Days in the Deep South Remembered* (New York: G. P. Putnam's Sons, 1977).

14. See Frank T. Read, "Judicial Evolution of the Law of School Integration since *Brown v. Board of Education*," 39 *Law and Contemporary Problems* 7 (1975); Michael Namorato, ed., *Have We Overcome? Race Relations since Brown* (Jackson: University of Mississippi Press, 1979).

15. See David Kirp, "School Desegregation and the Limits of Legalism," 47 *Public Interest* 101 (1977).

16. De Tocqueville, *supra* note 8, at vol. 2, p. 510.

17. Compare J. R. Pole, *The Pursuit of Equality in American History* (Berkeley and Los Angeles: University of California Press, 1979).

18. See Orfield, *supra* note 5; Radin, *supra* note 5.

19. See Charles Lindblom, *Politics and Markets* (New York: Basic Books, 1977).

20. *U.S. v. Carolene Products Co.*, 304 U.S. 144, 152, n. 4 (1938).

21. See John Hart Ely, *Democracy and Distrust* (Cambridge: Harvard University Press, 1980).

22. Daniel Bell, *The Cultural Contradictions of Capitalism* 185 (New York: Basic Books, 1976).

23. See Philippe Nonet and Philip Selznick, *Law and Society in Transition: Toward Responsive Law* (New York: Harper Colophon, 1978), for a general discussion of these themes.

24. See the discussion of "public values" in Owen Fiss, "Foreword: The Forms of Justice," 93 *Harvard Law Review* 1 (1979).

25. On federalism see, e.g., Morton Grodzins, *The American System: A New View of Government in the United States* (Chicago: Rand McNally, 1966).

26. See Richard Kluger, *Simple Justice* (New York: Knopf, 1976).

27. See National Academy of Education, *Pride and Prejudice* (Washington, D.C.: Government Printing Office, 1978), for a sample of the contending views.

Chapter 2 / *(Pages 13–30)*

1. Gunnar Myrdal, with Richard Sterner and Arnold Rose, *An American Dilemma: The Negro Problem and Modern Democracy* (New York: Pantheon, 1972 ed.).

2. Ibid., at lxix.

3. Ibid., at lxxii.

4. Ibid., at 23 (quoting Kelly Miller, *Out of the House of Bondage* 134 (New York: Neale, 1914).

5. Ibid., at lxxv (italics deleted).

6. M. G. Jean de Crèvecoeur, *Letters from an American Farmer* (New York: Fox, Duffield & Co., 1904 ed.).

7. Yehoshua Arieli, *Individualism and Nationalism in American Ideology* 19–20 (Harmondsworth, England: Penguin, 1966 ed.).
8. Quoted in ibid., at 86–87.
9. Thomas Jefferson, Third Annual Message, October 17, 1803, in 3 *Writings* 353, Andrew A. Lipscomb (Washington: Thomas Jefferson Memorial Association, 1905).
10. Number 10, *The Federalist Papers* 77 (New York: New American Library, 1961 ed.). See Garry Wills, *Explaining America: The Federalist* (New York: Doubleday, 1981).
11. Jefferson, letter to George Flower, September 12, 1817, 15 *Writings* 140, *supra* note 9.
12. Myrdal, *supra* note 1, at lxx.
13. Louis Hartz, *The Liberal Tradition in America: An Interpretation of American Political Thought since the Revolution* (New York: Harcourt, Brace & World, 1955). See also Lionel Trilling, *The Liberal Imagination* (New York: The Viking Press, 1950).
14. Nathan Glazer, *Affirmative Discrimination: Ethnic Inequality and Public Policy* 5 (New York: Basic Books, 1975).
15. 42 U.S.C. 2000 et seq.
16. See, e.g., Robert Wiebe, *The Segmented Society: An Introduction to the Meaning of Equality* (New York: Oxford University Press, 1975); William Appleman Williams, *The Contours of American History* (New York: Frank Watts, 1973); Rowland Berthoff, *An Unsettled People: Social Order and Disorder in American History* (New York: Harper & Row, 1971).
17. Winthrop Jordan, *The White Man's Burden: Historical Origins of Racism in the United States* 33 (New York: Oxford University Press, 1974). See also Edmund Morgan, *American Slavery, American Freedom: The Ordeal of Colonial Virginia* (New York: Norton, 1975).
18. Ibid., at 117.
19. George M. Frederickson, *The Black Image in the White Mind: The Debate on Afro-American Character and Destiny, 1817–1914* 323 (New York: Harper & Row, 1971).
20. J. R. Pole, *The Pursuit of Equality in American History* 150 (Berkeley and Los Angeles: University of California Press, 1978).
21. Alexis de Tocqueville, *Democracy in America* 373 (New York: Vintage, 1954 ed.).
22. See Pole, *supra* note 20, at 149–68.
23. Robert Somers, *The Southern States since the War, 1870–71*, quoted in Christine Bolt, *Victorian Attitudes to Race* 113 (London: Routledge and Kegan Paul, 1971).
24. See Frederickson, *supra* note 19, at 320–25.
25. See Harvey Wish, ed., *Ante-Bellum* (New York: G. P. Putnam's Sons, 1960).
26. Myrdal, *supra* note 1, at 1002.
27. Ibid., loc. cit.
28. Frederickson, *supra* note 19, at 325.
29. See Clement E. Vose, *Caucasians Only: The Supreme Court, the NAACP, and the Restrictive Covenant Cases* (Berkeley and Los Angeles: University of California Press, 1959), and Leon Mayhew, *Law and Equal Opportunity* (Cambridge: Harvard University Press, 1968).

30. William Graham Sumner, *Folkways* (Boston: Ginn & Co., 1906 ed.).
31. James Sundquist, *Politics and Policy: The Eisenhower, Kennedy, and Johnson Years* 243 (Washington, D.C.: Brookings Institution, 1968).
32. Thomas Brooks, *Walls Come Tumbling Down: A History of the Civil Rights Movement 1940–1970* (Englewood Cliffs, N.J.: Prentice-Hall, 1974).
33. A more cynical view is advanced by Charles Silberman: "The tragedy of race relations in the United States is that there is no American dilemma. White Americans are not torn and tortured by the conflict between their devotion to the American creed and their actual behavior. They are upset by the current state of race relations, to be sure. But what troubles them is not that justice is being denied but that their peace is being shattered and their business interrupted" (*Crisis in Black and White* 9–10 [New York: Random House, 1964]).
34. August Meier, *Negro Thought in America, 1880–1915* 51 (Ann Arbor: University of Michigan Press, 1963).
35. Myrdal, *supra* note 1, at 929 (italics deleted).
36. Ibid., at 928 (italics deleted).
37. See Meier, *supra* note 34, at 278. The durability of black values, even under slavery, is recounted in Eugene D. Genovese, *Roll, Jordan, Roll: The World the Slaves Made* (New York: Pantheon, 1974). See also Lawrence W. Levine, *Black Culture and Black Consciousness: Afro-American Folk Thought from Slavery to Freedom* (New York: Oxford University Press, 1977).
38. "Remarks of President on Nationwide Radio and Television," press release, June 11, 1963.
39. Quoted in Richard Kluger, *Simple Justice* 757 (New York: Knopf, 1976).
40. Quoted in Brooks, *supra* note 32, at 215.
41. Thomas Pettigrew, *Racially Separate or Together?* 318 (New York: McGraw Hill, 1971).
42. Mark Yudof, "Equal Educational Opportunity and the Courts," 51 *Texas Law Review* (1973). See also Owen Fiss, "Racial Imbalance in the Schools: The Constitutional Concepts," 78 *Harvard Law Review* 564 (1965).
43. See, e.g., Thomas Pettigrew, "Race and Equal Educational Opportunity," in *Equal Educational Opportunity*, ed. Harvard Educational Review, 69 (Cambridge: Harvard University Press, 1969); and David K. Cohen, Thomas F. Pettigrew, and Robert T. Riley, "Race and the Outcomes of Schooling," in *On Equality of Educational Opportunity* ed. Frederick Mosteller and Daniel P. Moynihan, 343 (New York: Random House, 1972).
44. See David Kirp and Mark Yudof, *Educational Policy and the Law* (Berkeley: McCutchan, 1982).
45. Quoted in Lee Rainwater and William Yancey, *The Moynihan Report and the Politics of Controversy* 126 (Cambridge: MIT Press, 1967).
46. Kenneth Clark, *Dark Ghetto: Dilemmas of Social Power* (New York: Harper & Row, 1965).
47. Thomas Pettigrew, *A Profile of the Negro American* (Princeton, N.J.: D. Van Nostrand, 1964).
48. Daniel Moynihan, "The Negro Family: The Case for National Action," in Rainwater and Yancey, *supra* note 45.

49. Clark, *supra* note 46, at 107.
50. For historical accounts of the War on Poverty, see Daniel Moynihan, *Maximum Feasible Misunderstanding* (New York: Free Press, 1969); James Sundquist, *supra* note 31 at 111–54; Sar Levitan, *The Great Society's Poor Law* (Baltimore: Johns Hopkins University Press, 1969); J. David Greenstone and Paul Peterson, *Race and Authority in Urban Politics: Community Participation and the War on Poverty* (Chicago: University of Chicago Press, 1976).
51. Moynihan, *supra* note 48.
52. Glazer, *supra* note 14, at 38.
53. See, e.g., Ronald Dworkin, *Taking Rights Seriously* 223–40 (Cambridge: Harvard University Press, 1977), and Bruce Ackerman, *Social Justice in the Liberal State* (New Haven: Yale University Press, 1980), for two attempts to craft such a justification in "liberal" terms.
54. See Owen Fiss, "Groups and the Equal Protection Clause," 5 *Philosophy and Public Affairs* 107 (1976).
55. The fullest statement of the black power argument by those who developed it appears in Stokeley Carmichael and Charles Hamilton, *Black Power: The Politics of Liberation in America* (New York: Random House, 1967). See also Wilson Carey McWilliams, *The Idea of Fraternity in America* 570–617 (Berkeley and Los Angeles: University of California Press, 1973); Benjamin Muse, *The American Negro Revolution: From Nonviolence to Black Power, 1963–1967* (Bloomington: Indiana University Press, 1968); Robert Scott and Wayne Brockriede, *The Rhetoric of Black Power* (New York: Harper & Row, 1969).
56. Carmichael and Hamilton, *supra* note 55, at 54.
57. McWilliams, *supra* note 55, at 570–617.
58. Greenstone and Peterson, *supra* note 50.
59. Rainwater and Yancey, *supra* note 45, at 11.
60. See, e.g., Michael Novak, *The Rise of the Unmeltable Ethnics* (New York: Macmillan, 1972); Richard Gambino, *Blood of My Blood: The Dilemma of the Italian American* (New York: Doubleday, 1974). But see D. Garth Taylor, Paul Sheatsley, and Andrew Greeley, "Attitudes Toward Racial Integration," 238 *Scientific American* 42 (1978).
61. See, e.g., Glazer, *supra* note 14.
62. See, e.g., "The Black Plight: Race or Class? A Debate Between Kenneth B. Clark and Carl Gershman," *New York Times Magazine*, October 5, 1980, p. 22.
63. See Irving Welfeld, "The Courts and Desegregated Housing: The Meaning (If Any) of the Gatreaux Case," 45 *Public Interest* 123 (1976).
64. *Supra* note 62, at 24.
65. See *Fullilove v. Klutznick*, 448 U.S. 448 (1980).
66. *New York Times*, p. 69, col. 5, 6–7 (March 1, 1970).
67. *Supra* note 62, at 24.
68. William Julius Wilson, *The Declining Significance of Race: Blacks and Changing American Institutions* 142 (Chicago: University of Chicago Press, 1978).
69. Dorothy K. Newman, Nancy J. Amidei, Barbara L. Carter, Dawn Day, William J. Kruvant, and Jack Russell, *Protest, Politics, and Prosperity: Black Americans and White Institutions, 1940–1975* (New York: Pantheon, 1978).
70. Ibid., at 29.

71. Glazer, *supra* note 14, at 62–63.
72. Wilson, *supra* note 68, at 142.
73. Glazer, *supra* note 14, at 40.
74. 438 U.S. 265 (1978); *Fullilove v. Klutznick*, 448 U.S. 448 (1980).
75. For a discussion of the competing positions, see Allan Sindler, *Bakke, DeFunis, and Minority Admissions* (Philadelphia: Longmans, 1979); Marshall Cohen, Thomas Nagel, and Thomas Scanlon, eds., *Equality and Preferential Treatment* (Princeton: Princeton University Press, 1977).
76. Wilson, *supra* note 68, at 88, 116. See also Thomas Blair, *Retreat to the Ghetto* (New York: Hill and Wang, 1977).
77. Peter Roggemann, "When Blacks Win Municipal Elections," 11 *Social Policy* 46 (March-April 1981).
78. Edwin Dorn, *Rules and Racial Equality* 53 (New Haven: Yale University Press, 1979).
79. See Martin A. Levin and Barbara Ferman, "Why Some Programs Were Effectively Implemented: The Implementation of Nine Youth Employment Programs" (paper presented at Northeast Political Science Association meeting, November 1980).
80. Orlando Patterson, *Ethnic Chauvinism: The Reactionary Impulse* 168 (New York: Stein and Day, 1977). Cf. Oliver C. Cox, *Race Relations: Elements and Social Dynamics* (Detroit: Wayne State University Press, 1976).
81. Noel Epstein, *Language, Ethnicity, and the Schools* (Washington, D.C.: Institute for Educational Leadership, 1977). See Nathan Glazer and Daniel P. Moynihan, eds., *Ethnicity* (Cambridge: Harvard University Press, 1975).
82. See David Kirp, *Doing Good by Doing Little: Race and Schooling in Britain* (Berkeley and Los Angeles: University of California Press, 1979).

Chapter 3 / *(Pages 31–49)*

1. Henry Steele Commager, *The American Mind* 10 (New Haven: Yale University Press, 1950). See also Robert Wiebe, "The Social Functions of Public Education," 21 *American Quarterly* 147 (1969).
2. See Carl Kaestle, "'Between the Scylla of Brutal Ignorance and the Charybdis of a Literary Education': Elite Attitudes Toward Mass Schooling in Early Industrial England and America," in *Schooling and Society: Studies in the History of Education*, ed. Lawrence Stone (Baltimore: Johns Hopkins University Press, 1976).
3. Gunnar Myrdal, with Richard Sterner and Arnold Rose, *An American Dilemma: The Negro Problem and Modern Democracy* 882 (New York: Pantheon, 1972 ed.).
4. For a discussion of symbolic politics, see Murray Edelman, *Politics as Symbolic Action* (Chicago, Markham, 1971).
5. See James S. Coleman, "The Concept of Equality of Educational Opportunity," in *Equal Educational Opportunity*, ed. Harvard Educational Review, 9 (Cambridge: Harvard University Press, 1969).
6. See Samuel Bowles and Herbert Gintis, *Schooling in Capitalist America: Educational Reform and the Contradiction of American Life* (New

York: Basic Books, 1976); Colin Greer, *The Great School Legend: A Revisionist Interpretation of American Public Education* (New York: Viking, 1973); Michael Katz, *Class, Bureaucracy, and the Schools: The Illusion of Educational Change in America* (New York: Knopf, 1971).

7. See, e.g., Raymond Boudon, *Education, Opportunity, and Social Inequality: Changing Prospects in Western Society* (New York: John Wiley, 1974).

8. 347 U.S. 483, 493 (1954).

9. See, e.g., James S. Coleman et al., *Equal Educational Opportunity Survey* (Washington, D.C.: Government Printing Office, 1966).

10. Horace Mann, *Twelfth Annual Report of the Board of Education, Together with the Twelfth Annual Report of the Secretary of the Board* (1849), quoted in Lawrence Cremin, *The Transformation of the School: Progressivism in American Education, 1876–1957* 9 (New York: Knopf, 1961).

   For discussions of these differing ends of education, see David Tyack, *The One Best System: A History of American Urban Education* (Cambridge: Harvard University Press, 1974); Patricia Graham, *Community and Class in Urban Education* (New York: Wiley, 1974); Raymond Callahan, *Education and the Cult of Efficiency* (Chicago: University of Chicago Press, 1962); Frances Fitzgerald, *America Revised: History Textbooks in the Twentieth Century* (Boston: Atlantic-Little, Brown, 1979).

11. Benjamin Rush, "Thoughts upon the Mode of Education Proper in a Republic," quoted in David Tyack, ed., *Turning Points in American Educational History* 102, 103 (Waltham, Mass.: Blaisdell, 1967).

12. Thomas Jefferson, "Bill for the More General Diffusion of Knowledge," quoted in Tyack, *supra* note 11, at 109.

13. Henry Barnard, in *Henry Barnard on Education* 96, ed. John S. Brubacher (New York: McGraw Hill, 1931), quoted in Arthur Bestor, *Educational Wastelands: The Retreat from Learning in our Public Schools* 26 (Urbana: University of Illinois Press, 1953).

14. Ibid. For assessments of the common school movement, see Lawrence Cremin, *The American Common School: An Historic Conception* (New York: Bureau of Publications, Teachers College, Columbia University, 1951); Michael Katz, *The Irony of Early School Reform: Educational Innovation in Mid-Nineteenth Century Massachusetts* (Cambridge: Harvard University Press, 1968).

15. See Diane Ravitch, *The Great School Wars: New York City, 1805–1973* (New York: Basic Books, 1974).

16. George E. Baker, ed., *The Works of William H. Seward* (1853), quoted in Rush Welter, *Popular Education and Democratic Thought in America* 85 (New York: Columbia University Press, 1962).

17. On education in the Progressive Era, see Cremin, *supra* note 14; Clarence Karrier, Paul Violas, and Joel Spring, *Roots of Crisis: American Education in the Twentieth Century* (Chicago: Rand McNally, 1973).

   On the Progressive Era generally, see Richard Hofstadter, *The Age of Reform* (New York: Knopf, 1955); David Noble, *The Paradox of Progressive Thought* (Minneapolis: University of Minnesota Press, 1958); Robert Wiebe, *The Search for Order, 1877–1920* (New York: Hill and Wang, 1967); David Noble, *The Progressive Mind, 1890–1917* (Chicago: Rand McNally, 1970); Morton White, *Social Thought in America: The Revolt Against Formalism* (Boston: Beacon, 1957).

18. See Tyack, *supra* note 10, at 66–77.
19. David Nasaw, *Schooled to Order: A Social History of Public Schooling in the United States* 100 (New York: Oxford University Press, 1979).
20. Welter, *supra* note 16, at 208.
21. Cremin, *supra* note 10, at 126.
22. Ibid.
23. John Dewey, *Democracy and Education* 377 (New York: Macmillan, 1916).
24. See, e.g., Joel Spring, *Education and the Rise of the Corporate State* (Boston: Beacon, 1972); and Leon Kamin, *The Science and Politics of IQ* (New York: John Wiley, 1974).
25. Quoted in Nasaw, *supra* note 19, at 131.
26. Coleman, *supra* note 5, at 9, 15.
27. National Educational Association, Commission on the Reorganization of Secondary Education, *Cardinal Principles of Secondary Education* (1918), quoted in Richard Hofstadter, *Anti-Intellectualism in American Life* 335 (New York: Vintage, 1963).
28. Ibid.
29. Tyack, *supra* note 10, at 232.
30. William Maxwell, *A Quarter Century of Public School Development* (1912), quoted in ibid., at 233.
31. Quoted in ibid., at 238–39. See also Robert Carlson, *The Quest for Conformity: Americanization Through Education* (New York: John Wiley, 1975).
32. Hofstadter, *supra* note 27, at 343–45.
33. Ibid., at 343.
34. Bestor, *supra* note 13, at 26.
35. Ibid., at 36.
36. H. G. Rickover, *Education and Freedom* 115 (New York: E. P. Dutton, 1959).
37. James Conant, *The American High School Today* 15 (New York: McGraw Hill, 1959).
38. James Conant, *Education and Liberty: The Role of the Schools in a Modern Democracy* 56 (Cambridge: Harvard University Press, 1953).
39. Quoted in Michael Olneck and Marvin Lazerson, "Education," in *Harvard Encyclopedia of Ethnic Groups*, ed. Stephan Thurnstrom, Ann Orlov, and Oscar Handlin (Cambridge: Harvard University Press, 1980).
40. This discussion draws upon Meyer Weinberg, *A Chance to Learn: A History of Race and Education in the United States* (New York: Oxford University Press, 1977); Horace Mann Bond, *The Education of the Negro in the American Social Order* (New York: Prentice-Hall, 1934); Tyack, *supra* note 10, at 109–25; Sarah Lawrence Lightfoot, *Worlds Apart: Relationships Between Families and Schools* 125–55 (New York: Basic Books, 1978); Henry A. Bullock, *A History of Negro Education in the South* (New York: Praeger, 1970); Diane Ravitch, "Desegregation: Varieties of Meaning," in *Shades of Brown*, ed. Derrick Bell, 31 (New York: Teachers College Press, 1980); Thomas Webber, *Deep like the Rivers: Education in the Slave Quarter Community, 1831–1865* (New York: Norton, 1978).

41. Lightfoot, *supra* note 40, at 153.
42. See John Kaplan, "Segregation Litigation and the Schools—Part II: The General Northern Problem," 58 *Northwestern University Law Review* 162 (1963).
43. For a discussion of this case, see Richard Kluger, *Simple Justice: The History of Brown vs. Board of Education and Black America's Struggle for Equality* (New York: Knopf, 1976).
44. Quoted in Leon F. Litwack, *North of Slavery: The Negro in the Free States, 1790–1860* 113 (Chicago: University of Chicago Press, 1961).
45. Ibid., at 116.
46. Ibid., at 137.
47. Quoted in Tyack, *supra* note 10, at 114.
48. *Roberts v. City of Boston*, 50 Massachusetts 198 (1849).
49. Quoted in Litwack, *supra* note 44, at 142–43.
50. Timothy Smith, "Native Blacks and Foreign Whites: Varying Responses to Educational Opportunity in America, 1880–1950," 6 *Perspectives in American History* 309 (1972).
51. President's Commission on Higher Education, 1 *Higher Education for American Democracy* 27 (New York: Harper & Brothers, 1948).
52. Quoted in Henry Perkinson, *The Imperfect Panacea: American Faith in Education, 1865–1965* i (New York: Random House, 1968).
53. See the discussion in chapter 2, at notes 40–47.
54. See Charles Valentine, *Culture and Poverty: Critiques and Counterproposals* (Chicago: University of Chicago Press, 1968), and Eleanor Leacock, ed., *Culture of Poverty: A Critique* (New York: Simon & Schuster, 1971).
55. See Thomas Sowell, "Patterns of Black Excellence," 43 *Public Interest* 26 (1976).
56. See Robert Rosenthal, *Pygmalion in the Classroom: Teacher Expectation and Pupils' Intellectual Development* (New York: Holt, Rinehart and Winston, 1968). See also Ray Rist, *Invisible Children: School Integration in American Society* (Cambridge: Harvard University Press, 1978).
57. James Conant, *Slums and Suburbs* 10 (New York: McGraw Hill, 1961).
58. See Stephen K. Bailey and Edith K. Mosher, *ESEA: The Office of Education Administers a Law* (Syracuse: Syracuse University Press, 1968).
59. 42 U.S.C. 2000 et seq.
60. For a discussion of the different constituencies that mobilize the federal, as opposed to the state or local, level, see Gary Orfield, *The Reconstruction of Southern Education: The Schools and the 1964 Civil Rights Act* (New York: John Wiley, 1969); Martha Derthick, *New Towns in Town: Why a Federal Program Failed* (Washington, D.C.: Urban Institute, 1972); Jeffrey Pressman and Aaron Wildavsky, *Implementation: How Great Expectations in Washington Are Dashed in Oakland* (Berkeley and Los Angeles: University of California Press, 1973).
61. See Joel Spring, *The Sorting Machine: National Educational Policy since 1945* 211–23 (New York: David McKay, 1976).
62. Coleman, *supra* note 9.
63. These evaluations are thoughtfully analyzed in Richard Light and Paul Smith, "Social Allocation Models of Intelligence: A Methodological Inquiry," 39 *Harvard Educational Review* 3 (1969), and Alice Riv-

lin, "Forensic Social Science," 42 *Harvard Educational Review* 6 (1973).

64. Coleman, *supra* note 5, at 9, 20.

65. Christopher Jencks et al., *Inequality: A Reassessment of the Effect of Family and Schooling in America* (New York: Basic Books, 1972). See also Frederick Mosteller and Daniel P. Moynihan, eds., *On Equality of Educational Opportunity* (New York: Vintage, 1972).

66. Senator Robert Kennedy, quoted in Milbury McLaughlin, *Evaluation and Reform: The Elementary and Secondary Education Act of 1965, Title I* 2 (Cambridge, Mass.: Ballinger, 1975).

67. Christopher Lasch, *The Culture of Narcissism: American Life in an Age of Diminishing Expectations* 143 (New York: W. W. Norton, 1978).

68. United States Commission on Civil Rights, *Racial Isolation in the Public Schools* (Washington, D.C.: Government Printing Office, 1967).

69. Only later did it emerge that social class rather than race was the decisive factor. This confusion of race and class reflected a broader unwillingness to disentangle the two or to define policy in social-class terms. See Nancy St. John, *School Desegregation: Outcomes for Children* (New York: Wiley, 1975).

70. See chapter 6 for a discussion of the San Francisco case.

71. Gary Orfield, *Must We Bus? Segregated Schools and National Policy* 113–18 (Washington, D.C.: Brookings Institution, 1978).

72. See ibid.; Charles Willie and Susan Greenblatt, *Community Political and Educational Change: Ten School Districts under Court Order* (New York: Longman, 1980); Howard Kalodner and James Fishman, eds., *Limits of Justice: The Courts' Role in School Desegregation* (Cambridge, Mass.: Ballinger, 1978).

73. See Al Smith, Anthony Downs, and M. Leanne Lachman, *Achieving Effective Desegregation* (Lexington, Mass.: D. C. Heath, 1973); Norman Miller, "Making School Desegregation Work," in *School Desegregation: Past, Present, and Future*, ed. Walter G. Stephan and Joe R. Feagin, 305 (New York: Plenum, 1980).

74. On community control in schools, see Leonard Fein, *The Ecology of the Public Schools: An Inquiry into Community Control* (New York: Pegasus, 1971); Alan A. Altschuler, *Community Control: The Black Demand for Participation in Large American Cities* (New York: Pegasus, 1970); Henry Levin, ed., *Community Control of Schools* (Washington, D.C.: Brookings Institution, 1970); Mario Fantini, Marilyn Gittell, and Richard Magat, *Community Control and the Urban School* (New York: Praeger, 1970); David Kirp, "Community Control, Public Policy, and the Limits of Law," 68 *Michigan Law Review* 1355 (1970); David Cohen, "The Price of Community Control," 48 *Commentary* 23 (July 1969).

75. In the case of community control, a movement played out with particular force in New York City, this default was quite specific: one Harlem school, supposed to be integrated, instead opened all-black. If the school was going to be segregated, parents argued, at least they should have a decisive say in running it. See Maurice Berube and Marilyn Gittell, *Confrontation at Ocean Hill-Brownsville: The New York School Strikes of 1968* (New York: Praeger, 1969).

76. Nasaw, *supra* note 19, at 243. See also Carl Kaestle, "Social Reform

and the Urban School," 12 *History of Education Quarterly* 211 (1972): "What we need and do not yet have is a new synthesis that will account for the school as the focal point of idealism as well as self-interest, an institution at once the object of public scrutiny and public ignorance, an institution that evolves more by mundane accretion than dramatic reform and yet continually arouses herculean efforts and exaggerated expectation" (p. 217).

See also Diane Ravitch, *The Revisionists Revised: A Critique of the Radical Attack on Schools* (New York: Basic Books, 1978).

Chapter 4 / *(Pages 50–71)*

1. See Anna Holden, *The Bus Stops Here: A Study of Desegregation in Three Cities* (New York: Agathon, 1974); Harrell Rodgers and Charles Bullock, *Coercion to Compliance* (Lexington, Mass.: D. C. Heath, 1976); Howard Kalodner and James Fishman, eds., *Limits of Justice: The Courts' Role in School Desegregation* (Cambridge, Mass.: Ballinger, 1978); Charles Willie and Susan Greenblatt, *Community Political and Educational Change: Ten School Districts under Court Order* (New York: Longman, 1980); Lino Graglia, *Disaster by Decree: The Supreme Court Decisions on Race and the Schools* (Ithaca: Cornell University Press, 1976); United States Commission on Civil Rights, *Fulfilling the Letter and Spirit of the Law* (Washington, D.C.: Government Printing Office, 1976); United States Commission on Civil Rights, *Desegregation of the Nation's Public Schools: A Status Report* (Washington, D.C.: Government Printing Office, 1979).

2. For a discussion of this history, see Gary Orfield, *Must We Bus? Segregated Schools and National Policy* (Washington, D.C.: Brookings Institution, 1978); J. Harvie Wilkinson III, *From Brown to Bakke: The Supreme Court and School Integration* (New York: Oxford University Press, 1979); Adam Yarmolinsky, Lance Liebman, and Corinne Schelling, eds., *Race and Schooling in the City* (Cambridge: Harvard University Press, 1981); Walter G. Stephan and Joe R. Feagin, eds., *School Desegregation: Past, Present, and Future* (New York: Plenum Press, 1980).

3. 347 U.S. 483 (1954).

4. See Morroe Berger, *Equality by Statute* (Garden City, N.Y.: Doubleday, 1968).

5. Millicent Cox, *A Description of School Desegregation since 1965* 30 (Santa Monica, Calif.: Rand Working Note 10436-HEW, 1979).

6. See David Kirp and Gary Babcock, "Judge and Company: Court-Appointed Masters, School Desegregation, and Institutional Reform," 32 *Alabama Law Review* 313 (1981).

7. This proposition appears to hold true for "institutional reform" litigation generally. See, e.g., Abram Chayes, "The Role of the Judge in Public Law Litigation," 89 *Harvard Law Review* 1281 (1976); Colin Diver, "The Judge as Political Power Broker," 65 *Virginia Law Review* 43 (1979); Note, "Implementation Problems in Institutional Reform Litigation," 91 *Harvard Law Review* 428 (1977).

8. Cf. Robert Dahl, "Decision Making in a Democracy: The Supreme Court as a National Policy-Maker," 6 *Journal of Public Law* 279 (1957)

and Jonathan Casper, "The Supreme Court and National Policy-Making," 70 *American Political Science Review* 50 (1976).

9. Wilkinson, *supra* note 2, at 62.
10. 349 U.S. 294 (1955). Cf. Gerald Gunther, "Some Reflections on the Judicial Role: Distinctions, and Prospects," 1979 *Washington University Law Quarterly* 817.
11. 349 U.S., at 301.
12 Ibid., at 300–301.
13. Ibid., at 299.
14. *Cooper v. Aaron*, 385 U.S. 1 (1958).
15. Ibid., at 20 (Frankfurter, J., concurring).
16. 42 U.S.C. §2000.
17. *U.S. v. Jefferson County Board of Education*, 1372 F. 2d 836 (5th Cir. 1966); *aff'd*, 380 F. 2d 385 (5th Cir. 1967) (*en banc*). See also Note, "The Courts, HEW, and Southern School Desegregation," 77 *Yale Law Journal* 321 (1967).
18. 391 U.S. 430 (1968).
19. 369 U.S. 19 (1969).
20. 402 U.S. 1 (1971).
21. 391 U.S. 430 (1968).
22. 396 U.S. 19, 20 (1969).
23. 402 U.S., at 14–16.
24. Ibid., at 27.
25. Ibid., at 30–31.
26. Ibid., at 26.
27. Ibid., at 15.
28. See, e.g., *Reynolds v. Sims*, 377 U.S. 533 (1964); *Miranda v. Arizona*, 384 U.S. 436 (1966); *Roe v. Wade*, 410 U.S. 113 (1973).
29. See Gary Orfield, *The Reconstruction of Southern Education* (New York: John Wiley, 1969); Beryl Radin, *Implementation, Change, and the Federal Bureaucracy: School Desegregation Policy in HEW, 1964–1968* (New York: Teachers College Press, 1977).
30. 413 U.S. 189 (1973).
31. See, e.g., *Dayton Board of Education v. Brinkman*, 433 U.S. 406 (1977). But cf. *Dayton Board of Education v. Brinkman*, 439 U.S. 1357 (1979).

  For a discussion of the linkage between residence patterns and school segregation, see Franklin Wilson and Karl E. Tauber, "Residential and School Segregation: Some Tests of Their Association," in F. Bean and W. Parker Frisbee, eds., *The Demography of Racial and Ethnic Groups* 51 (New York: Academic Press, 1978); Karl E. Tauber and Franklin Wilson, "The Demographic Impact of School Desegregation Policy," in *Population Policy Analysis: Issues in American Politics*, ed. Michael C. Kraft and Mark Schneider (Lexington, Mass.: D. C. Heath, 1978).

  See Steven B. Kanner, "From Denver to Dayton: The Development of a Theory of Equal Protection Remedies," 72 *Northwestern University Law Review* 382 (1977).
32. 433 U.S. 267 (1977).
33. The district courts' fact-finding was also extended extraordinary deference in *Columbus Board of Education v. Penick*, 439 U.S. 1348 (1979).

34. *Columbus Board of Education v. Penick*, 439 U.S. 1348 (1979); *Dayton Board of Education v. Brinkman*, 439 U.S. 1357 (1979).
35. See, e.g., *U.S. v. Montgomery County Board of Education*, 395 U.S. 255, 231–32 (1969): "The dispute deals with faculty and staff desegregation, a goal that we have recognized to be an important aspect of the basic task of achieving a public school system wholly free from racial discrimination." See also *Milliken v. Bradley*, 418 U.S. 717, 764 (1974) (White, J., dissenting): "The task is not to devise a system of pains and penalties to punish constitutional violations brought to light. Rather it is to desegregate an *educational* system in which the races have been kept apart, without at the same time, losing sight of the central *educational* function of the schools."
36. Wilkinson, *supra* note 2, at 310.
37. Ibid., at 308.
38. *Terminiello v. Chicago*, 337 U.S. 1, 37 (1949) (Jackson, J., dissenting).
    For a more critical view of the role of political considerations in these decisions, see Alan Freeman, "Legitimating Racial Discrimination Through Antidiscrimination Law: A Critical Review of Supreme Court Doctrine," 62 *Minnesota Law Review* 1049 (1978); Derrick Bell, "*Brown v. Board of Education* and the Interest-Convergence Dilemma," 93 *Harvard Law Review* 518 (1980).
39. See Cox, *supra* note 5.
40. See the discussion of this issue, in the San Francisco and Oakland settings, in chapters 6 and 10. For a discussion of the relationship between law and bargaining in another context, see Robert Mnookin and Lewis Kornhauser, "Bargaining in the Shadow of the Law: The Case of Divorce," 88 *Yale Law Journal* 950 (1979).
41. *Keyes v. School District No. 1, Denver*, 413 U.S. 189, 217 (1973) (Powell, J., concurring in part and dissenting in part).
42. See, e.g., David Hulburd, *This Happened in Pasadena* (New York: Macmillan, 1951).
43. See Robert L. Crain, *The Politics of School Desegregation* (Garden City, N.Y.: Doubleday, 1969).
44. Cox, *supra* note 5, at 31.
45. See Paul Peterson, *School Politics, Chicago Style* (Chicago: University of Chicago Press, 1976).
46. See Mark Yudof, "Implementation Theories and Desegregation Realities," 32 *Alabama Law Review* 441 (1981).
    See also Richard Elmore, "Organizational Models of Social Program Implementation," 26 *Public Policy* 185 (1978); Paul Berman, "The Study of Macro- and Micro-Implementation," 26 *Public Policy* 157 (1978); and Richard Elmore, "Backward Mapping: Implementation Research and Policy Decisions," 94 *Political Science Quarterly* 601 (1979).
47. 276 F. Supp. 834, 846–47 (E.D. La. 1967).
48. *NAACP v. Lansing Board of Education*, 429 F. Supp. 583, 631 (W.D. Mich. 1976).
49. *Amos v. Board of School Directors of the City of Milwaukee*, 408 F. Supp. 765 (E.D. Wis. 1976).

322 Notes to Pages 50–71

50. *Pasadena Board of Education v. Spangler*, 427 U.S. 424 (1976).
51. See Mitchell Feigenberg, "Pasadena," in David Kirp, Nancy Borow, Mitchell Feigenberg, Tim Gage, Elliott Marseille, and Dorothy Robyn, "Judicial Management of School Desegregation Cases" 41 (unpublished report prepared for the National Institute of Education, 1979).
52. Ralph Smith, "Two Centuries and Twenty-Four Months: A Chronicle of the Struggle to Desegregate the Boston Public Schools," in *Limits of Justice: The Courts' Role in School Desegregation*, ed. Howard Kalodner and James Fishman, 25, 84–85 (Cambridge, Mass.: Ballinger, 1978).
53. See Owen Fiss, "The Supreme Court, 1978 Term, Foreword: The Forms of Justice," 93 *Harvard Law Review* 1 (1979).
54. See, e.g., Robert Goldstein, "A *Swann* Song for Remedies: Equitable Belief in the Burger Court," 13 *Harvard Civil Rights–Civil Liberties Law Review* 1 (1978).
55. See, e.g., Nancy Borow, "Minneapolis," in Kirp et al., *supra* note 51; see the discussion of this issue in chapter 6.
56. See Nancy Borow, "Atlanta," in Kirp et al., *supra* note 51.
57. See Tim Gage, "Dallas," in ibid.
58. See Elliott Marseille, "Denver," in ibid. at 47.
59. *Kelly v. Guinn*, 456 F. 2d 100, 110 (9th Cir. 1972).
60. For a discussion of these organizational issues, see, e.g., Karl E. Weick, "Educational Organizations as Loosely Coupled Systems," 21 *Administrative Science Quarterly* 1 (1976); James G. March, "American Public School Administration: A Short Analysis," 86 *School Review* 217 (1978); and Seymour Sarason, *The Culture of School and the Problem of Change* (Boston: Allyn and Bacon, 1971).
61. *Northcross v. Board of Education, Memphis City Schools*, 341 F. Supp. 583 (597) (W.D. Tenn. 1972).
62. Compare E. P. Thompson, *Whigs and Hunters: The Origin of the Black Act* 265 (New York: Pantheon, 1975) referring to the rule of law: "The rhetoric and rules of a society . . . may disguise the true realities of power, but, at the same time, they may curb that power and check its intrusions. . . . [Thus, law] imposes inhibitions upon power or pure politics."
63. See Fiss, *supra* note 53.
64. 269 F. Supp. 401, 517 (D. D.C. 1967).
65. Kenneth Karst and Harold Horowitz, "*Reitman v. Mulkey*: A Telophase of Substantive Equal Protection," 1967 *Supreme Court Review* 39, 79. See also Lawrence Tribe, "Seven Pluralist Fallacies in Defense of the Adversary Process: A Reply to Justice Rehnquist," 33 *University of Miami Law Review* 43, 57–58 (1978).
66. Glendon A. Schubert, *The Judicial Mind: The Attitudes and Ideologies of Supreme Court Justices, 1943–1963* (Evanston, Ill.: Northwestern University Press, 1965), notes that judges differ in their perception of the constraints imposed by prior decisions. See Lon Fuller, "Positivism and Fidelity to Law," 71 *Harvard Law Review* 630 (1959). Cf. Martin Shapiro, "Toward a Theory of *Stare Decisis*," 1 *Journal of Legal Studies* 125 (1972).
67. See Peter D. Roos, "Bilingual Education: The Hispanic Response

to Unequal Opportunity," 42 *Law and Contemporary Problems* 111 (1978); and Gary Orfield, *Must We Bus? Segregated Schools and National Policy* (Washington, D.C.: Brookings Institution, 1978).

68. *Clark v. Board of Education*, 328 F. Supp. 1205, 1217 (E.D. Ark. 1971).
69. See Marseille, *supra* note 58, at 22.
70. See Dorothy Robyn, "Wilmington,"in Kirp et al., *supra* note 51.
71. Ibid., at 99.
72. Ibid., at 51.
73. Ibid., at 52.
74. Ibid., at 53–55.
75. See, e.g., Frank T. Read, "Judicial Evolution of the Law of School Integration since *Brown v. Board of Education*," 39 *Law and Contemporary Problems* 7 (1975).
76. Mark Yudof, "School Desegregation: Legal Realism, Reasoned Elaboration, and Social Science Research in the Supreme Court," 42 *Law and Contemporary Problems* 57 (1978).
77. Fiss, *supra* note 53, at 47.
78. See, e.g., Kirp and Babcock, *supra* note 6.
79. U.S. v. Hendry County School District, 50 F. 2d 550, 554 (5th Cir. 1974).
80. See Elwood Hain, "Sealing Off the City: School Desegregation in Detroit," in Kalodner and Fishman, *supra* note 52, at 223.
81. *Bradley v. Milliken*, 402 F. Supp. 1096, 1101 (E.D. Mich. 1975).
82. Hain, *supra* note 80, at 292.
83. Susan Greenblatt and Walter McCann, "Courts, Desegregation and Education: A Look at Boston" (unpublished paper, Harvard Graduate School of Education, 1979).
84. See also Kalodner and Fishman, *supra* note 52, at 23.
85. See Theodore Lowi, *The Politics of Disorder* (New York: Basic Books, 1971).
86. See, e.g., Donald Horowitz, *The Courts and Social Policy* (Washington, D.C.: Brookings Institution, 1977); Archibald Cox, *The Role of the Supreme Court in American Government* (New York: Oxford University Press, 1976); Nathan Glazer, "Should Judges Administer Social Services?," 50 *Public Interest* 64 (1978); and Paul Mishkin, "Federal Courts as State Reformers," 35 *Washington and Lee Law Review* 949 (1978).
87. Fiss, *supra* note 53.
88. See Grant McConnell, *Private Power and American Democracy* (New York: Random House, 1966 ed.); and Paul Peterson, *School Politics Chicago Style* (Chicago: University of Chicago Press, 1976).
89. See Bell, *supra* note 38.

Chapter 5 / *(Pages 75–81)*

1. For descriptions of the Bay Area, see James Vance, Jr., *Geography and Urban Evolution in the San Francisco Bay Area* (Berkeley: Institute of Governmental Studies, 1964); Mel Scott, *The San Francisco Bay Area: Metropolis in Perspective* (Berkeley and Los Angeles: University of California Press, 1959); Wlliam Chapin, Alvin D. Hyman, and Jonathan Carroll, *The Suburbs of San Francisco* (San Francisco: Chronicle

Books, 1969); and Stanley Scott and John Bollens, *Governing a Metropolitan Region: The San Francisco Bay Area* (Berkeley: Institute of Governmental Studies, 1968).

2. Statement of Vote, General Election, November 7, 1972 (compiled by Edmund G. Brown, Jr., Secretary of State); Statement of Vote, State of California, General Election, November 5, 1968 (compiled by Frank M. Jordan, Secretary of State).

3. U.S. Bureau of the Census, *Statistical Abstract of the United States, 1978* 143 (Washington, D.C.: Government Printing Office, 1978).

4. U.S. Bureau of the Census, *Census of Population and Housing: 1970 PHC(1)-189 San Francisco–Oakland, California SMSA* 217–19 (Washington, D.C.: Government Printing Office, 1972).

5. Ibid.

6. Ibid., at 145–47.

7. *U.S. Census, 1950*, vol. 2, pp. 162–65, 179; *U.S. Census, 1940*, vol. 2, pp. 540–43; San Francisco Bay Area Council, *The Bay Area 1970 Census Series*, vol. 1, tables 1 and 7.

8. Wilson Record, "Willie Stokes at the Golden Gate," *The Crisis* 56 (June 1949), reprinted in Roger Daniels and Spencer Olin, Jr., *Racism in California* 277–78 (New York: Macmillan, 1972).

9. U.S. Bureau of the Census, *supra* note 4, at 289–91, 73–75.

10. Ibid., at 289–318.

11. Karl Tauber and Alma Tauber, *Negroes in Cities* 32–34 (Chicago: Aldine, 1965).

12. Association of Bay Area Governments, *Regional Housing Study, Supplemental Reports RA-4* 208–9 (Berkeley: ABAG, October 1969) (hereafter *Housing*). Kenneth Clark makes the same comparison in *Dark Ghetto: Dilemmas of Social Power* 25 (New York: Harper & Row, 1965).

13. Tauber and Tauber, *supra* note 11, at 223–31.

14. Wilson Record, *Minority Groups and Intergroup Relations in the San Francisco Bay Area* 4 (Berkeley: Institute of Governmental Studies, 1963); the 1965 data is cited in *Housing, supra* note 12, at 218.

15. The 1959 study is cited in *Housing, supra* note 12, at 10.

16. Cited in ibid., at 219. The results of the survey were published by the Citizens Committee to Study Discrimination in Housing in Berkeley, *Housing Discrimination in Berkeley, Report to the County Welfare Commission* (mimeo, July 1972).

17. *Housing, supra* note 12, at 220.

18. See the discussion of these issues in chapters 6 and 8.

19. *Housing, supra* note 12, at 220.

20. See, e.g., Arthur Hippler, *Hunter's Point: A Black Ghetto* (New York: Basic Books, 1974); and Robert Kapsis, "Continuities in Delinquency and Riot Patterns in Black Residential Areas," 23 *Social Problems* 567 (1976).

21. Tom Wolfe, *Radical Chic and Mau Mauing the Flak Catchers* 97 (New York: Farrar, Straus and Giroux, 1970).

22. Quoted in Record, *supra* note 14, at 47.

23. For a discussion of school segregation in California, see Charles M. Wollenberg, *All Deliberate Speed: Segregation and Exclusion in California Schools, 1855–1977* (Berkeley and Los Angeles: University of California Press, 1977).

24. For a discussion of the legacy of Progressivism in California politics

generally, see Eugene Lee, *The Politics of Nonpartisanship* (Berkeley and Los Angeles: University of California Press, 1960); Willis Hawley, *Nonpartisan Elections and the Case for Party Politics* (New York: John Wiley, 1973).

25. See Rufus Browning, Dale Marshall, and David Tabb, "Blacks and Hispanics in California City Politics: Changes in Representation," 20 *Bulletin of the Institute of Governmental Studies* 1 (June 1979); and Rufus Browning, Dale Marshall, and David Tabb, "Minority Mobilization and Urban Political Change, 1960–1979," (paper prepared for the 1979 Annual Meeting of the American Political Science Association).

26. Vance, *supra* note 1, at 78.

27. See Appendix for a summary of data for the five districts concerning: composition of the student body; composition of teaching and administrative staffs; performance on state-wide achievement tests; and per pupil expenditures.

Chapter 6 / *(Pages 82–116)*

1. 339 Fed. Supp. 1315 (N.D. Cal. 1971), *vacated and remanded*, 500 F 2d 349 (9th Cir., 1974).

2. Each of the case studies relies heavily on primary source material: school district reports, board of education minutes, court transcripts, and the like. In order to keep footnotes to a manageable number, these materials and interviews are cited only where essential to document an event or argument. More readily accessible materials are fully cited.

   Doris Fine assisted in gathering and analyzing the data for an earlier version of this chapter.

3. See Howard Becker, ed., *Culture and Civility in San Francisco* (Chicago: Aldine, 1971); and Frederick Wirt, *Power in the City: Decision-Making in San Francisco* (Berkeley and Los Angeles: University of California Press, 1974).

4. The census data are drawn from the 1950 and 1970 U.S. censuses and from 1979 estimates of the San Francisco Health Department. The category "white" does not include Spanish-surnamed persons, whose number is derived from data for "white foreign stock," "foreign-born," or "native of foreign or mixed parentage" (for 1950) and from the 1970 census report.

5. "Status Report of the Office of Integration, San Francisco Unified School District" 6 (1975); "ESAA Program Review," San Francisco Unified School District (1979).

6. San Francisco's 1905 decision to create separate schools for Chinese and Japanese students, ultimately reversed only through the personal intervention of President Theodore Roosevelt, reveals the historical roots of this prejudice. See David Brudnoy, "Race and the San Francisco School Board Incident: Contemporary Evaluations," 50 *California Historical Quarterly* 295–312 (1971).

7. See Lee Dolson, "Administration of the San Francisco Public Schools" (Ph.D. dissertation, School of Education, University of California, Berkeley, 1964).

8. Larry Cuban, *School Chiefs under Fire: A Study of Three Big City Super-*

intendents under Outside Pressure (Chicago: University of Chicago Press, 1976). Spears made this observation in 1957, contrasting the policies of Little Rock, Arkansas—then in the midst of racial turmoil—with those of San Francisco. In 1961, in the wake of a federal court decision striking down the boundary gerrymandering of a Northern school district (*Taylor v. Board of Education*, 294 F.2d 36 [2d Cir. 1961], *cert. denied*, 368 U.S. 940 [1961]), Spears stated: "We have not manipulated boundaries to segregate racial groups nor to integrate them. . . . We . . . are trying to treat everyone fairly" (*San Francisco Examiner*, March 17, 1961, p. 6, col. 1).

9. *Hearings of the United States Commission on Civil Rights*, San Francisco, September 19, 1960, at 816–17.

10. This civil rights history is recounted in Robert L. Crain et al., *The Politics of School Desegregation: Comparative Case Studies of Community Structure and Policy Making* 81–94 (Chicago: Aldine, 1968).

11. San Francisco Board of Education, transcript, Dec. 5, 1961, at 23–24; interview with Ruth Kadish, founder of the Coordinating Council for Integrated Education.

12. Harold Spears, "The Proper Recognition of a Pupil's Educational Background, Superintendent's Report to the Board of Education" (mimeo, June 19, 1962).

13. San Francisco Board of Education, transcript, Sept. 18, 1962, is the primary source for this section. See also Congress of Racial Equality, "Relationship Between Racial Balance and Sound Education in the San Francisco Unified School District" (unpublished paper, San Francisco, September 1, 1962; on file at the Alexander Meikeljohn Library, Berkeley).

14. See Council for Civic Unity, Race and the Schools, September 5, 1962, at 21 (submitted but not orally presented to the board).

15. *Brock v. Board of Education*, No. 71034, (N.D. Cal. October 2, 1962).

16. San Francisco Board of Education, "Final Report of the Ad Hoc Committee" (unpublished paper, April 2, 1963).

17. *San Francisco Chronicle*, April 3, 1963, p. 1, col. 7.

18. San Francisco Board of Education–San Francisco Human Rights Committee Joint Conferences, transcript, vol. 1, August 23 and 26, 1965, pp. 51–54, 95–97.

19. Crain, *supra* note 10, at 92.

20. Ibid., at 93.

21. Harold Spears and William L. Cobb, "Selected Data for Study in the Challenge to Effect Better Racial Balance in the San Francisco Public Schools" (unpublished paper, San Francisco Unified School District, November 1965).

22. Craine, *supra* note 10, at 13–28, 75–84.

23. Two other related studies were undertaken at this time: the State Fair Employment Practices Commission and the San Francisco Human Rights Commission reviewed district employment practices, and the United States Commission on Civil Rights included San Francisco in the national assessment of *Racial Isolation in the Public Schools* (Washington, D.C.: Government Printing Office, 1967).

24. Stanford Research Institute, *Improving Racial Balance in the San Francisco Schools* (Menlo Park, Calif.: SRI, 1967).

25. The discussion of OMI is based on interviews with Laurel Glass,

school commissioner, 1967–72; Donald Kuhn; and Charlotte Berk, secretary of OMI. For data on the ethnic composition of the OMI community, see San Francisco Fair Housing Planning Committee for the Racial, Ethnic and Economic Integration of Residential Neighborhoods in San Francisco, "One City or Two?" 6 (mimeo, October 1973).

26. *1965–1975: OMI Schools Ten Years Later*, 6 *OMI News* 4–5 (March 1975).

27. See Arthur Hippler, "The Game of Black and White at Hunter's Point," in Becker, *supra* note 3, at 53.

28. See statement of Rev. Charles Lee, director of Southeast Educational Development (SEED) in *Hearings of the Senate Select Subcommittee on Equal Educational Opportunity*, part 9B, pp. 4277–78 (Washington, D.C.: Government Printing Office, 1971); interview with Robert Fisher, formerly education director of SEED.

29. Robert Jenkins, "EE/Q Report #1: Program Alternatives" (mimeo, San Francisco Unified School District, December 19, 1967).

30. San Francisco Board of Education, Policy Statement, transcript, June 10, 1968.

31. Citizens' Advisory Committee, "EE/Q Progress Report" (mimeo, San Francisco Unified School District, May 19, 1970).

32 Robert Jenkins, "EE/Q Schools for Living: An Adventure in Education" (mimeo, San Francisco Unified School District, December 15, 1969).

33. *San Francisco Chronicle*, February 12, 1970, p. 1.

34. The recounting of Mayor Alioto's role derives largely from interviews with John DeLuca, executive deputy to Mayor Alioto; Leroy Cannon, counsel to the board of education; Terry Francois, NAACP board member and former member, board of supervisors; and Howard Nemerowski, former member, board of education. Unsurprisingly, those interviewed offered markedly different assessments of Alioto's actions.

35. Wirt, *supra* note 3, at 266.

36. *San Francisco Chronicle*, February 4, 1970, p. 1, col. 1.

37. Ibid.

38. *Nelson v. San Francisco Unified School District*, No. 618–643, San Francisco Super. Ct., June 15, 1970.

39. Interview with Robert Jenkins, former San Francisco superintendent of schools.

40. This and subsequent quotations are drawn from the record, both of papers filed and transcripts of oral argument, which is available at the Office of the Clerk of the Court for the Northern District of California, San Francisco. Only references to published opinions of the court are specifically footnoted.

41. *Davis v. School District*, 309 F. Supp. 734 (E.D. Mich. 1970).

42. James S. Coleman et al., *Equal Educational Opportunity Survey* (Washington, D.C.: Government Printing Office, 1966). Although the Coleman Report was used by plaintiffs to demonstrate the educational benefits of racial desegregation, the report's broader conclusion, that the socioeconomic background of the individual student is the strongest predictor of school achievement, was not noted by plaintiffs, nor was the relevance of the report questioned by the defendant school district.

43. This and subsequent appraisals of the board of education are drawn from the record of board meetings and from interviews with former board of education members, including Lucille Abrahamson, Zuretti Goosby, Laurel Glass, Claire Lilienthal, Howard Nemerowski, and David Sanchez. Perceptions of the board's role varied among those interviewed.
44. This assessment derives both from the record of the case and from an interview with George Krueger.
45. Judge Weigel himself raised the community-control issue. Weigel posed a number of questions he hoped the hearings would answer. "I [also] want you gentlemen to consider and provide me answers [to]. . . . this question. . . . Assuming minority groups desire separate schools, and assuming they can show that such schools would not be inferior, should that desire, if it is manifested to this Court, be considered by the Court?" Weigel elaborated on his question. "There's something new that's coming along. . . . There [is] beginning to emerge a demand on the part of large segments of minority groups, particularly among the blacks, that they run their own schools and [that] they have black schools" (transcript, *Johnson v. San Francisco Unified School District*, July 30, 1970).
46. Ibid., July 30, 1970; August 6, 1970.
47. Ibid., August 25, 1970.
48. 402 U.S. 1 (1971).
49. Order Setting Aside Submission, *Johnson v. San Francisco Unified School District*, September 22, 1970.
50. This list is drawn from Steven Weiner, "Educational Decisions in an Organized Anarchy" 437–70 (Ph.D. dissertation, School of Education, Stanford University, 1972).
51. The discussion of school administration in San Francisco derives from interviews with ex-superintendents Thomas Shaheen and Robert Jenkins, as well as with board members, lower-echelon administrators (among them Irving Breyer, for forty years legal counsel to the school district, and Donald Johnson, director of the Office of Integration, 1971–73), and such participants as James Ballard, president of the San Francisco American Federation of Teachers.
52. *Anderson v. San Francisco Unified School District*, 357 F. Supp. 248 (N.D. Cal. 1972). See also Earl Raab, "Quotas by Any Other Name," *Commentary* 41 (Jan. 1972).
53. See Weiner, *supra* note 50.
54. Interview, Theodore Neff, Bureau of Intergroup Relations, California Department of Education.
55. See Equal Educational Opportunities Project, *Data Processing Requirements for School Desegregation: A Case Study of the San Francisco Unified School District* (Washington, D.C.: Council of Great City Schools, 1973).
56. Weiner, *supra* note 50, at 77.
57. 402 U.S. 1 (1971).
58. Ibid., at 15.
59. Ibid., at 25.
60. *Johnson v. San Francisco Unified School District*, 339 F. Supp. 1315, 1326–27 n. 3 (N.D. Cal. 1971).
61. Ibid., at 1329–39.

62. Ibid., at 1332.
63. "Intervenor's First Objections to Plan Filed on June 10, 1971," *Johnson v. San Francisco Unified School District*, June 14, 1971.
64. 339 F. Supp. 1315, 1327 (N.D. Cal. 1971).
65. The analysis of the citizens' advisory committee work draws on the documents the committee produced and on interviews with the one professional staff member, Donald Johnson, in Sausalito and with committee members, including Chairman Donald Kuhn and Nicki Salan. See also Weiner, *supra* note 50.
66. Title V, Calif. Adm. Code, § 14020–21. Sections 5002–3 of the Education Code, which declared the state policy of eliminating racial balance in California schools and thus served as a statutory warrant for the board of education's regulations, were repealed by initiative in 1972. That repeal was upheld by the California Supreme Court in *Santa Barbara School District v. Mullin*, 13 Cal. 3d 315. 530 P. 2d 605 (1975).
67. Analysis of the NAACP's planning effort derives from the plan itself and from interviews with former NAACP Education Committee members Lois Barnes and Ann Bloomfield.
68. The observations concerning Chinatown and the Big Six Companies are drawn from a variety of sources, among them: Victor G. Nee and Brett de Bary Nee, *Longtime Californ'* (New York: Pantheon, 1973); and Stanford M. Lyman, "Red Guard on Grant Avenue," in Becker, *supra* note 3, at 20.
69. *San Francisco Examiner*, June 4, 1971, p. 1, col. 4.
70. Complaint of Plaintiffs in Intervention, *Johnson v. San Francisco Unified School District*, June 18, 1971, at 1.
71. Transcript, *Johnson v. San Francisco Unified School District*, June 3, 1971.
72. 339 F. Supp., at 1322.
73. Transcript, *Johnson v. San Francisco Unified School District*, June 24, 1971.
74. Ibid., at 1321.
75. Ibid., loc. cit.
76. 404 U.S. 1214, 1216–17 (1971).
77. Order, August 19, 1972.
78. No. C-72-808-RFT (N.D. Cal. May 5, 1972).
79. 500 F. 2d 249 (9th Cir., 1974).
80. 413 U.S. 189 (1973).
81. 500 F. 2d, at 252.
82. The data for 1965–76 are drawn from the "status reports" of the Integration Department, San Francisco Unified School District. Data for 1976–79 are drawn from San Francisco Unified School District, "ESAA Program Review" (April 23, 1979).
83. Tom Wolfe offered a somewhat romantic rendering of the Chinese Freedom School movement, "Bok Gooi, Hok Gooi and T'ang Jen: Or, Why There Is No National Association for the Advancement of Chinese Americans," *New York*, September 21, 1971, p. 36. See also *Hearings of the Select Subcommittee on Equal Educational Opportunity of the United States Senate* (Washington, D.C.: Government Printing Office, 1971), part 9B, pp. 4223–28.
84. Memorandum from Margery J. Levy, director, Integration Depart-

ment and ESAA, to Lane De Lara, associate superintendent, operations and research, "Evaluation of Elementary School Desegregation: Report #2, Resegregating Tendencies in Special Programs," San Francisco Unified School District, October 2, 1975.

Racial disproportionality in the programs for educable mentally retarded (EMR) students was successfully challenged in federal court. *Larry P. v. Riles*, 343 F. Supp. 1306 (N.D. Cal. 1972), 502 F. 2d Dist. 963 (9th Cir. 1974), 495 F. Supp. 926 (N.D. Cal. 1979). As a result of that lawsuit, student enrollment in EMR classes has dropped sharply, but the problem of racial disproportionality has not been solved.

85. 339 F. Supp. at 1325.
86. *O'Neill v. San Francisco Unified School District*, No. C-72-808 RFT (N.D. Cal. May 5, 1972).
87. *San Francisco Chronicle*, February 24, 1972, p. 15.
88. *Report of the 1971 Grand Jury of the City and County of San Francisco* (San Francisco, n.d.).
89. Although four incumbents were elected to the board, two had been appointed after the trial court decision in Johnson was handed down, both of whom spoke out against busing. The other two elected incumbents supported the board's decision to appeal *Johnson*.
90. San Francisco Public Schools Commission, "Statement of William Matson Roth, Chairman," *San Francisco Chronicle*, May 15, 1975, p. 23.
91. The discussion of the Educational Redesign is drawn from newspaper accounts in the *San Francisco Chronicle*, the *San Francisco Examiner*, and the *San Francisco Progress*, and from reports of the district, including "Educational Redesign: A Proposal," January 1978.
92. *San Francisco Chronicle*, April 29, 1978, p. 1.
93. Interviews with former school board member Zuretti Goosby and board president Peter Mezey.
94. *San Francisco Examiner*, July 5, 1977, p. 34.
95. *San Francisco Progress*, July 13, 1977, p. 10.
96. *San Francisco Examiner*, February 1, 1978, p. 1.
97. No. C-70-1331 SAW, "Memorandum and Order of Dismissal," *Johnson v. San Francisco Unified School District*, June 22, 1978.
98. Interview with former school board member Zuretti Goosby.
99. Jane Mercer, "Evaluating Integrated Elementary Education" (unpublished paper prepared for San Francisco Unified School District, September 1973).
100. *San Francisco Chronicle*, June 13, 1979, p. 3.
101. 414 U.S. 563, 566 (1974).
102. "Report of the Citizens' Task Force for Bilingual Education," San Francisco Unified School District, January 21, 1975.
103. Interview, school board president Peter Mezey.

Chapter 7 / *(Pages 117–147)*

1. An earlier version of this chapter was coauthored by Doris Fine and Steven Angelides. Lillian Rubin's *Busing and Backlash: White Against White in a California School District* (Berkeley and Los Angeles: Uni-

versity of California Press, 1972) provides both useful source materials and an alternative interpretation of the Richmond history up to 1970.

2. Richmond Unified School District, minutes, June 4, 1969 (hereafter minutes).

3. *Richmond Independent*, July 2, 1969.

4. Richmond Unified School District, "Racial Distribution of Enrollment," 1967–1976.

5. "In Action" (superintendent's newsletter), March 1970, speaks of "reasonable" racial balance as a criterion for school attendance boundaries. On inexplicitness as a criterion for policymaking with respect to race, see David Kirp, *Doing Good by Doing Little: Race and Schooling in Britain* (Berkeley and Los Angeles: University of California Press, 1979).

6. Minutes, August 30, 1978.

7. The description of Richmond draws generally on Joseph Whitnah, "A History of Richmond, California" (Richmond, Calif.: Richmond Chamber of Commerce, 1944); Lee Friedel, "The Story of Richmond" (mimeo, Richmond Union High School District, 1954); John Enos, "Local Government in Greater Richmond" (mimeo, Richmond Union High School District, 1964); Robert Wenkert et al., *An Historical Digest of Negro-White Relations in Richmond, California* (Berkeley: University of California Survey Research Center, 1967); Richmond City Planning and Community Development Staff Report, *Neighborhood Profiles*, 1973.

8. Contra Costa County Planning Department, "1975 Countywide Special Census of Contra Costa County—Racial/Ethnic Distribution" (mimeo, February 1977).

9. Richmond League of Women Voters, "A Study of Housing" (mimeo, 1972); Richmond Model Cities Agency, "Richmond Facts" (mimeo, 1974).

10. The early Richmond school history draws primarily on Hubert O. Brown, "The Impact of War Worker Migration on the Public School System of Richmond, Ca., 1940–45" (Ph.D. dissertation, School of Education, Stanford University, 1973).

11. *Berkeley Gazette*, January 31, 1971.

12. Ibid.

13. Irate local residents expressed resentment that the "burden of building schools for these trailer families brought here to work in defense industries is falling entirely on the permanent residents and property owners of the district" (*Richmond Independent*, June 4, 1972).

14. NAACP letter to the board of education, March 31, 1958, cited in Wenkert, *supra* note 7, at 44.

15. Interview with Betty Stiles, member of the Richmond Union High School District Board prior to unification, and the Richmond Unified School District Board, 1965–69.

16. James Conant, *The American High School Today* 15 (New York: McGraw Hill, 1959). See also chapter 3.

17. Interview with George Blumenson, public information officer, Richmond Unified School District.

18. Ibid.

19. State of California Education Code, Section 17654, as amended by Stats. 1963, Ch. 2163, and Stats. 1963, Ch. 14.
20. Quoted by Rubin, *supra* note 1, at 26.
21. See, for example, the comments of Richmond High School board member Earl Cheit, Richmond Union High School District, minutes, May 12, 1964.
22. See Richmond Union High School, minutes, July 29, 1964.
23. The vote is recorded in Richmond Union High School District, minutes, November 10, 1964.
24. Rubin, *supra* note 1, at 152.
25. Richmond Unified School District, "Racial Distribution of Enrollment, 1965" (mimeo, October 1969).
26. See Douglas Maher, "The Pattern of a Generation: History of Post-War Community Organization in North Richmond" (Ph.D. dissertation, School of Education, University of California, Berkeley, 1966).
27. Minutes, September 1, 1965.
28. Minutes, September 1, 1965. See chapters 6 and 10 for a discussion of the San Francisco and Oakland histories.
29. Minutes, September 22, 1965.
30. Rubin, *supra* note 1, at 91.
31. See minutes, November 22 and December 17, 1965.
32. See Richmond Unified School District, "Report of the Citizens' Advisory Committee on De Facto Segregation" 11 (mimeo, March 4, 1967).
33. Minutes, May 26, 1966.
34. Minutes, March 23 and May 11, 1966.
35. See minutes, February 23, January 12, and March 9, 1966.
36. Minutes, May 11, 1966.
37. Minutes, May 25, 1966.
38. Interview, George Blumenson, *supra* note 17.
39. Minutes, September 14, 1966. Also interview, Leo Gaspardone, director until 1977 of the Richmond Integration Program.
40. Rubin, *supra* note 1, at 114.
41. Ibid., at 106.
42. Ibid., at 98–99. "We sought to lead the community . . . to encourage busing to relieve overcrowding [in order] . . . to get people used to the idea of integration. . . . We wanted to keep trying."
43. Minutes, June 21 and July 19, 1967.
44. Minutes, November 24, 1967 (board member Maurice Barusch, Superintendent Denzil Widel, and board member Margaret Berry).
45. Minutes, November 29, 1967 (Milton Vail, chairman, Citizens Committee for Neighborhood Schools).
46. See, e.g., minutes, September 20, November 15, December 20, 1967, and January 31, March 20, May 1, May 14, and June 5, 1968.
47. Minutes, November 29, 1967.
48. Minutes, January 3, 1968.
49. Minutes, January 17, 1968.
50. *Richmond Independent*, April 15, 1968.
51. Marcus R. Peppard, "School Desegregation: A Case Study of Polarization Within a Community (Richmond Unified School District), July, 1968 to July, 1969" 26 (unpublished manuscript, 1969).

52. Information concerning legal services strategy is drawn from interviews with staff attorney Marcus Peppard and director Eugene Swann, and from Peppard, *supra* note 51.

53. *LaTina Johnson v. Richmond Unified School District*, No. 112094, Superior Court, Contra Costa County, filed October 16, 1968.

54. *Jackson v. Pasadena City School District*, 29 Cal. 2d 876, 31 Cal. Reptr. 606, 382 P.2d 878 (1963).

55. See Maher, *supra* note 26, for a discussion of black community attitudes on the issue.

56. Rubin, *supra* note 1, at 129; also interviews, Maurice Barusch, member, Richmond Union High School District Board prior to unification and chairman, Richmond Unified School District Board, 1965–69, and Betty Stiles, *supra* note 15.

57. Peppard, *supra* note 51, at 48.

58. Barusch interview, *supra* note 56.

59. *Richmond Independent*, November 21, 1968.

60. Minutes, November 20, 1968.

61. Minutes, December 18, 1968.

62. Order, *LaTina Johnson v. Richmond Unified School District*, No. 112094, Superior Court, Contra Costa County, November 25, 1968.

63. Memorandum of Decision, *LaTina Johnson v. Richmond Unified School District*, No. 112094, Contra Costa County, January 27, 1968.

64. The opinion can be interpreted in several different ways, none of which wholly satisfies:

   a. Liability for existing segregation is deemed admitted by the district, which is ordered to remedy that segregation. Because the district has already acted, no additional order is required. The decision does not so read. It does not deem liability to be admitted, even though that should have been the consequence of the district's answer in the case, nor does it require any remedy.

   b. The entire action is moot, because the district's voluntary adoption of the desegregation plan leaves no role for the court; any constitutional violations that may once have existed are no longer present. That is the legal effect of the decision, if read liberally. But in fact the district had not yet implemented its plan; even if it had, the familiar rule is that voluntary cessation of illegal activity is not grounds for holding an action moot. Plaintiffs were entitled to a ruling that the district's conduct violated the Constitution, even if that conduct had already ceased.

   c. Only the order to show cause, not the entire action, is moot. Although the court enters no finding against the district, the complaint remains valid and can be revived if the district misbehaves in the future. This interpretation is illogical. To distinguish between the order to show cause and the action as a whole is spurious, since in the case the former is the essence of the latter.

   d. The decision is designed to end the case, without binding the district in future circumstances to the actions of this board. The adversary system is not designed to promote judicial paternalism of this sort. The parties, not the court, bear primary responsibility for protecting their own interests.

65. Rubin, *supra* note 1, at 133–40.

66. Peppard, *supra* note 51, at 45–46.
67. Minutes, November 6, 1968.
68. Rubin, *supra* note 1, at 148.
69. Minutes, July 1, 1969.
70. *Richmond Independent*, July 2, 1969. A decade later, Gay would publicly declare that he had only supported the plan as "the lesser of two evils" (minutes, August 3, 1978).
71. *Richmond Independent*, July 11, 1969.
72. *The Voice*, a publication of the Committee for Educational Excellence, August 1, 1968.
73. Data for this section are drawn from two publications of the Richmond Unified School District: "School Enrollment Trends" (mimeo, 1965) and "Racial Distribution of Enrollment, 1967–71" (mimeo, 1971).
74. "In Action" (superintendent's newsletter), November 1969.
75. Rubin, *supra* note 1, at 160.
76. "In Action" (superintendent's newsletter), March 1970.
77. Richmond Unified School District, "Racial Distribution of Enrollment, 1967–71" (1971).
78. Minutes, June 4, 1969.
79. Memorandum of Decision, *LaTina Johnson v. Richmond Unified School District*, No. 112094, Superior Court, Contra Costa County, July 28, 1969.
80. *Melvin v. Richmond Unified School District*, No. C-69561-WTS, United States District Court, Northern District California, filed December 11, 1969.
81. Memorandum of Decision, *Melvin v. Richmond Unified School District*, No. C-69561-WTS, United States District Court, Northern District California, March 26, 1970.
82. Motion to Permit Filing of First Amended Answer, *LaTina Johnson v. Richmond Unified School District*, No. 112094, Superior Court, Contra Costa County, January 29, 1971.
83. Minute Order, *LaTina Johnson v. Richmond Unified School District*, No. 112094, Superior Court, Contra Costa County, March 10, 1971.
84. First Amended Answer, *LaTina Johnson v. Richmond Unified School District*, No. 112094, Superior Court, Contra Costa County, March 15, 1971.
85. Reporter's Transcript, *LaTina Johnson v. Richmond Unified School District*, No. 112094, Superior Court, Contra Costa County, November 5, 1971 (hereafter Reporter's Transcript).
86. Ibid., at 1246–47.
87. Interview with Judge Raymond Sherwin.
88. Reporter's Transcript, at 1650, 2405–6, 3102.
88. Ibid., at 1650, 2405–6, 3102.
89. Clerk's Transcript, *LaTina Johnson v. Richmond Unified School District*, No. 112094, Superior Court, Contra Costa County, filed Oct. 16, 1968.
90. Ibid., at 36–42.
91. Opinion, *LaTina Johnson v. Richmond Unified School Distict*, No. 1/Civil 32853, First District Division 1, California District Court of Appeal, June 7, 1972.
92. Opinion, *LaTina Johnson v. Richmond Unified School District*, No. 1/

Civil 32853, First District Division 1, California District Court of Appeal, August 28, 1972.

93. *Richmond Independent*, February 11, 1974.

94. *2 Bare Facts*, no. 8 (1973).

95. *2 Bare Facts*, no. 9 (1973).

96. *Oakland Tribune*, March 9, 1977.

97. District officials also argue that "closing a school does not save money unless a district is absolutely certain it will never be used again and unless it can get top dollar for its sale" (minutes, November 9, 1977).

98. Interview, Superintendent Richard Lovette, Richmond Unified School District.

99. The data are drawn from Richmond Unified School District, "Racial Distribution of Enrollment," an annual mimeographed publication (1968–78), "R.I.P. and Open Enrollment Count" (1969–78); the 1978–79 information comes from an internal district memorandum, prepared July 25, 1979.

100. Interview, Billie Alexander, community activist and unsuccessful school board candidate.

101. Richmond *Independent-Gazette*, August 31, 1978.

102. Interview, James Shattuck, member, board of education, 1969–present.

103. Lovette interview, *supra* note 98.

104. Interview, Virgil Gay, member, board of education, 1967–present.

105. *Richmond Independent*, April 4, 1979.

106. Alexander interview, *supra* note 100.

107. Shattuck interview, *supra* note 102.

108. This discussion draws on interviews with three black candidates for the Richmond school board: Ron Boldin, Billie Alexander, and George Harris.

109. *Richmond Independent*, August 15, 1978.

110. California State Department of Education, Bureau of School Apportionments and Reports, *Annual School District Employee Ratio Report* (1980).

At the request of a group of black parents, the Department of Justice undertook in 1978 to investigate charges that the district was in violation of the 1964 Civil Rights Act (*Richmond Independent*, September 9, 1978).

111. Rubin, *supra* note 1, at 174.

112. Minutes, November 9, 1977.

113. Rubin, *supra* note 1, at 5.

114. Cf. David Sears, Carl Hensler, and Leslie Speer, "Whites' Opposition to 'Busing': Self-Interest or Symbolic Politics?" 73 *American Political Science Review* 369 (1979). See also chapters 11 and 12.

Chapter 8 / *(Pages 148–193)*

1. Patrick Hayashi and Doris Fine provided substantial assistance in gathering and analyzing data for this chapter.

Berkeley's handling of the race and schooling issue, particularly through the desegregation of its schools in 1968, has been much discussed. See especially Harriet Nathan and Stanley Scott, eds., *Experi-*

ment and Change in Berkeley (Berkeley: Institute of Governmental Studies, 1979); Neil Sullivan with Evelyn Stewart, *Now Is the Time: Integration in the Berkeley Schools* (Bloomington: Indiana University Press, 1969); Carol Sibley, *Never a Dull Moment: The History of a School District Attempting to Meet the Challenge of Change: Berkeley, California 1955–1972* (Berkeley: Documentation and Evaluation of Experimental Projects in Schools, 1972); Daniel Freudenthal, "Evolution of School Desegregation in Berkeley, California," in *Man as the Measure: The Crossroads*, ed. Daniel Adelson, 108 (New York: Behavioral Publications, 1972); U.S. Senate, *Hearings Before the Select Committee on Equal Educational Opportunity of the United States Senate*, 92d Cong., 1971 (Washington, D.C.: Government Printing Office, 1971) (hereafter EEO Hearings); Jay Ball, "A Study of Organizational Adaptation to Environmental Pressures: The Demand for Equal Educational Opportunity (Ph.D. dissertation, School of Education, University of California, Berkeley, 1966); Thomas Parker, "The Berkeley Epilogue," in *School Desegregation in the North*, ed. Frederick Wirt and Thomas B. Edwards, 74 (San Francisco: Chandler, 1967).

The period since 1968 has, in contrast, been less fully addressed. The publications of the League of Women Voters, including "About Berkeley Schools," organize data in helpful ways. Because much of the district's energy during the period 1971–76 was focused on the ESP, evaluations of that project speak more generally of school district and community matters. See Berkeley Experimental Schools Project, "Final Report 1971–1976" (Berkeley: Berkeley Unified School District, 1976) (hereafter BESP Report); Institute for Scientific Analysis, "Educational R & D and the Case of Berkeley's Experimental Schools," (San Francisco: Scientific Analysis Corp., 1976) (hereafter ISA Report). See also U.S. Commission on Civil Rights, *School Segregation in Berkeley, California* (Washington: Government Printing Office, 1977).

The author was employed by the school district as a consultant in conjunction with the dispute between Berkeley and Office of Civil Rights, Department of Health, Education and Welfare, over the legality of two racially exclusive experimental schools, Black House and Casa de la Raza, and served as an external project reviewer for National Institute of Education, assessing the Berkeley Experimental Schools Project.

2. The account of the first day of elementary school desegregation is drawn primarily from Sibley, *supra* note 1, Sullivan, *supra* note 1, and the *Berkeley Gazette*, Sept. 11, 1968; other events noted in the introduction are more fully explored in the body of the text.
3. Sullivan, *supra* note 1, at 193.
4. BESP Report, at 50.
5. Interview, Marc Monheimer, former member, Berkeley school board.
6. The question was first posed by education historian George Counts a half-century ago, speaking generally about American education. The school district suggested that the ESP would provide an affirmative answer to the question (Berkeley Unified School District, Office of Project Planning and Development, "The Rationale for Sub-Systems in an Integrated School District" [mimeo, February 1, 1971]).

7. Roger Rapport, "Death of the Berkeley Dream," 3 *New West* 26 (February 13, 1978).
8. Foreword to Sullivan, *supra* note 1, at ix.
9. Berkeley Unified School District, "Experimental Schools Educational Plan," as revised (mimeo, June 8, 1971).
10. Sibley, *supra* note 1, at 13.
11. Quoted in ISA Report, at 32.
12. U.S. Bureau of the Census, *Statistical Abstract of the U.S., 1978* 24 (Washington, D.C.: Government Printing Office, 1979).
13. See Joseph Lyford, *The Berkeley Archipelago* (Chicago: Regnery-Gateway, 1981); and Nathan and Scott, *supra* note 1.
14. Mary Metz, *Classrooms and Corridors: The Crisis of Authority in Desegregated Secondary Schools* (Berkeley and Los Angeles: University of California Press, 1978).
15. Ibid., at 45.
16. See Lyford, *supra* note 13, and Sibley, *supra* note 1, at 12–14.
17. Tom Hayden, "The Trial," 9 *Ramparts* 55 (July 1970).
18. For early background on Berkeley schools, see S. D. Waterman, "History of the Berkeley Schools," in *The Professional Press*, ed. S. D. Waterman, 18 (Berkeley: Berkeley School District, 1918). The history of the Nelson era is drawn from interviews with former Berkeley school administrator Daniel Freudenthal and Carol Sibley, former member, Berkeley Unified School District Board of Education, and from Sibley, *supra* note 1, at 1–11. Mary Metz, *supra* note 14, provides background from the vantage point of junior high schools.
19. Sibley, *supra* note 1, at 10–13.
20. Two outside reports—one prepared by University of California professor Theodore Reller in 1956, the second a citizens' advisory committee "Study of the Reller Report" completed in 1957—had spoken of the need for new school construction or correction of major deficiencies in existing buildings.
21. Ball, *supra* note 1, at 52.
22. Sullivan, *supra* note 1, at 37.
23. Sibley, *supra* note 1, at 15.
24. Berkeley Unified School District, "Protection of Enrollment" (mimeo, June 20, 1956). Unlike other Bay Area communities, Berkeley was not reluctant to make racial estimates prior to the passage of the 1965 Civil Rights Act.
25. Sibley, *supra* note 1, at 2.
26. See Ball, *supra* note 1, at 43–48.
27. Citizens' Advisory Committee, Berkeley Unified School District, "Interracial Problems and Their Effect on the Education in the Public Schools of Berkeley" (mimeo, October 19, 1959).
28. Ball, *supra* note 1, at 49–67.
29. Berkeley Unified School District, "Interracial Gains and Goals" (mimeo, August 1961); "Growth and Change in an Interracial Community" (mimeo, June 1962).
30. Almost one hundred groups participated in the workshops; for a list, see the appendix to "Growth and Change in an Interracial Community," *supra* note 29.
31. Freudenthal, *supra* note 1, at 34.

32. Ball, *supra* note 1, at 103–4.
33. Berkeley Unified School District, "De Facto Segregation Study Committee Report" 3 (mimeo, November 19, 1963) (hereafter "Study Committee Report").
34. Sibley, *supra* note 1, at 40.
35. "Study Committee Report," at 28.
36. See Sullivan, *supra* note 1, at 44; Freudenthal, *supra* note 1, at 39.
37. Berkeley Unified School District, "Desegregation of the Berkeley Public Schools: Its Feasibility and Implementation" 3 (mimeo, May 1964) (hereafter Desegregation Report).
38. Ibid., at 2.
39. Ball, *supra* note 1, at 45, n. 11.
40. Sibley, *supra* note 1, at 52–60; and Freudenthal, *supra* note 1, at 41–42, recount the struggle.
41. Sibley, *supra* note 1, at 52.
42. Freudenthal, *supra* note 1, at 44.
43. Sullivan, *supra* note 1, at 79.
44. Ibid., at 72.
45. Sibley, *supra* note 1, at 36.
46. Letter from Neil Sullivan to U.S. Civil Rights Commission, Nov. 17, 1966, quoted in U.S. Civil Rights Commission, *Racial Isolation in the Public Schools* 131 (Washington, D.C.: Government Printing Office, 1967).
47. Ibid.
48. Sullivan, *supra* note 1, at 93.
49. Ibid., at 108.
50. Sibley, *supra* note 1, at 88.
51. Sullivan, *supra* note 1, at 119.
52. Robert Frelow, "The Berkeley Plan for Desegregation" (mimeo, May 16, 1969).
53. Sullivan, *supra* note 1, at 151.
54. *Oakland Tribune*, April 5, 1967.
55. Parker, *supra* note 1, at 76.
56. Sullivan, *supra* note 1, at 155.
57. Sibley, *supra* note 1, at 105–9, describes this period.
58. Frelow, *supra* note 52, at 86.
59. Sullivan, *supra* note 1, at 167.
60. *Berkeley Gazette*, January 19, 1968, p. 18.
61. Sibley, *supra* note 1, at 109–20; Frelow, *supra* note 52, at 53–55; and Sullivan, *supra* note 1, at 170–78, recount this era.
62. Berkeley Unified School District, board minutes, February 9, 1971 (hereafter minutes).
63. Sullivan, *supra* note 1, at 165.
64. Ibid., at 164.
65. Marc Monheimer (shortly thereafter to be elected to the school board), quoted in Sullivan, *supra* note 1, at 168.
66. Berkeley Unified School District, "Report of Group Test Results 1967–68" (mimeo, 1968).
67. Sibley, *supra* note 1, at 133.
68. Sullivan, *supra* note 1, at 182.
69. Ibid., at 182–84.

70. Sibley, *supra* note 1, at 135.
71. These programs are described in Sibley, *supra* note 1, at 128–53; and ISA Report, *supra* note 1, at 34.
72. Letter from Neil Sullivan to School Master Plan Committee, June 8, 1965.
73. Interview, former Berkeley Unified School District superintendent Neil Sullivan.
74. Ibid.
75. Monheimer interview, *supra* note 5.
76. Sibley, *supra* note 1, at 139.
77. Ibid., loc. cit.
78. The phrase was coined by Hazaiah Williams, as justification for the creation of Black House as an all-black publicly supported school. See board of education minutes, Feb. 9, 1971.
79. *San Francisco Chronicle*, March 3, 1976, p. 4.
80. BESP Report, at 52–54.
81. Interviews with Berkeley Unified School District administrators, including Jay Manley, John Newton, and Thomas Parker.
82. BESP Report, at 52–53.
83. Minutes, June 17, 1969.
84. Sibley, *supra* note 1, at 147.
85. Interviews, Samuel Markowitz, former member, Berkeley Unified School District Board of Education, and Monheimer, *supra* note 5.
86. Minutes, February 9, 1971.
87. BESP Report, at 54.
88. Sibley, *supra* note 1, at 153, 168.
89. Peter Jansen, "Evaluation of ESP [NIE] External Project Review Team, December 25, 1973"(xerox).
90. Interview transcript on file with the University of California Oral History Project Office, University of California, Berkeley (hereafter Foster transcript).
91. See BESP Report and ISA Report for discussions of this period.
92. Interview, Mary Jane Johnson, former member, Berkeley Unified School District Board of Education.
93. Interview, former Berkeley Unified School District superintendent, Richard Foster.
94. ISA Report, at 37.
95. Ibid., at 36–37.
96. Ibid., at xi.
97. Ibid., at 12.
98. EEO Hearings, at 4110.
99. Jansen, *supra* note 89.
100. See minutes, June 15, 1971, and July 7, 1971, from which the quotations in the next three paragraphs are drawn.
101. Minutes, August 4, 1971.
102. Comment, "Alternative Schools for Minority Students: The Constitution, The Civil Rights Act and The Berkeley Experiment," 61 *California Law Review* 879 (1973).
103. Newton interview, *supra* note 81.
104. ISA Report, at 74.
105. See BESP Report, at 56–57. Board member Marc Monheimer noted

and condemned "the hiring on a racial basis for the specific program."

106. Berkeley Unified School District, "Certificated Personnel by Racial Subgroups for Years 1968 Through 1977" (mimeo, n.d.); Berkeley Unified School District, "Certificated Personnel Count in BUSD from HEW Report-10/72" (mimeo, n.d.).
107. *Report of the National Advisory Committee on Civil Disorders* 203 (New York: E. P. Dutton, 1968).
108. ISA Report, at 35.
109. *Berkeley Gazette*, July 8, 1971, p. 1.
110. See Sullivan, *supra* note 1, at 185. Also Manley interview, *supra* note 81.
111. Parker and Manley interviews, *supra* note 81, as well as a review of sample curricular material.
112. Interview, John Matlin, teacher, Berkeley Unified School District.
113. *Berkeley Gazette*, January 21, 1971, p. 1.
114. Interview, Louise Stoll, former member, Berkeley Unified School District Board of Education.
115. *Berkeley Gazette*, July 6, 1972, p. 1.
116. Ibid., February 4, 1971, p. 1.
117. Ibid., May 21, 1971, p. 1.
118. BESP Report, at 47.
119. Louise Stoll, "Confessions of a Board Member" 4 (unpublished manuscript, 1977).
120. Minutes, April 18, 1972.
121. Interview transcript on file with the University of California Oral History Project Office, University of California, Berkeley.
122. *San Francisco Chronicle*, March 3, 1976, p. 4.
123. Stoll, *supra* note 119, at 4.
124. Letter from Margaret Ann Watson to school board directors, March 31, 1971, p. 2.
125. *San Francisco Sunday Examiner and Chronicle*, April 18, 1976, A-14.
126. Stoll, *supra* note 119, at 5.
127. Ibid., at 7.
128. Foster interview, *supra* note 93.
129. Berkeley Unified School District, "Progress Report of the Citizens Fiscal Analysis and Review Committee" 17 (mimeo, July 22, 1975).
130. Stoll, *supra* note 119, and interviews with James Guthrie, former member, Berkeley Unified School District Board of Education; Louise Stoll; Marc Monheimer; and former Berkeley Unified School District superintendent Laval Wilson.
131. Foster interview, *supra* note 93, and Wilson interview, *supra* note 130.
132. Ibid.
133. *Berkeley Gazette*, January 21, 1971, pp. 1–2.
134. *San Francisco Chronicle*, March 3, 1976, p. 4.
135. *North East Bay Independent and Gazette*, October 17, 1979, p. 1.
136. Guthrie interview, *supra* note 130.
137. Berkeley Unified School District, "Comparison of Selected Group Achievement Test Results, 1967–1973" (mimeo, 1973).
138. *San Francisco Sunday Examiner*, March 21, 1976, A-15.
139. *Berkeley Gazette*, July 12, 1976, p. 1; Guthrie and Wilson interviews, *supra* note 130.

140. *Daily Californian,* Jan. 13, 1981, p. 10.
141. Guthrie interview, *supra* note 130.
142. *San Francisco Examiner,* March 21, 1976, A-15.
143. Lionel Trilling, *The Liberal Imagination* xii (New York: Doubleday, 1953 ed.).

Chapter 9 / *(Pages 194–216)*

1. Donna Leff coauthored an earlier version of this chapter.
2. Marin County Grand Jury, "Final Report" (mimeo, February 1970) (hereafter Grand Jury Report).
3. The district's racial census in the relevant years is confusing, because no formal records were kept. Percentages were culled from various sources—the school district, the county, and the 1969 Marin County grand jury. For years for which no racial data were available, district reports giving enrollment by location were used, since Marin City residents are virtually all black. This approach distorts the figures somewhat, since the military population includes a small number of Spanish-surnamed children who in subsequent tabulations are identified as nonwhite. In a larger district, these discrepancies would be trivial and the percentages fairly accurate, but since the population of the Sausalito district is so small, errors in counting even a few children are significant, and for that reason trends, not specific percentages, are emphasized. Of greatest note, the proportion of white students, which fell from 58 percent to 44 percent between 1966 and 1971, rose to 54 percent by 1980.
4. In every case in which a conflict between Sausalito School District and county figures exist, county reports were relied on, since those reports are the official record for determining state aid. Enrollment was reported in Marin County Superintendent of Schools, "Statistical Bulletin #1, 10-year comparison, July 1967 to July 1977" (mimeo, 1977).
5. All population figures are from U.S. Bureau of the Census, *Census of Population and Housing* (Washington, D.C.: Government Printing Office, 1972).
6. Interview, Mel Wax, former mayor, City of Sausalito.
7. California Commission on Equal Opportunity in Education, "Ethnic Problems in the Sausalito School District" 8 (mimeo, July 1964) (hereafter Riles Report).
8. Data for Marin City are drawn from interviews with Royce McLemore, former director, Marin City Learning Center, and Susie Edwards, director, Marin City Project Area Committee, and from Marin County Human Rights Commission, "Analysis of Black Population" (mimeo, 1973).
9. Marin County Human Rights Commission, *supra* note 8.
10. The financial data are drawn from Sausalito School District budgets for the years cited.
11. Citizens' Advisory Committee, "Educational Needs of the Sausalito School District" (mimeo, June 1965) (hereafter "Educational Needs").
12. Marin City Project Area Committee, "Grant Proposal" (mimeo, March 1977).
13. 347 U.S. 483 (1954).

14. CORE Education Committee, "Letter to Parents of Children in Sausalito Schools" (mimeo, May 14, 1964).
15. Riles Report, at 9.
16. Interview, David Freedheim, former president, Sausalito School District Board of Trustees.
17. "Educational Needs," at 8.
18. This was also the racial mix propounded by the Commission on Equal Opportunity in Education in its 1964 report. It was premised on the assumption that, were the proportion of blacks kept relatively low, assimilation could be more readily achieved.
19. Interview, Jackie Kudler, Sausalito parent and co-founder, North Bay Alternative School.
20. "Educational Needs," Appendix G, "Sausalito District Teachers Association Report for the Citizens Advisory Commission."
21. William H. Grier and Price Cobbs, *Black Rage* (New York: Basic Books, 1968).
22. Because Toliver lacked the state-required credentials to become a vice principal, the board named him "Assistant to the Principal and Staff at MLK School"; as such, he performed all the functions and duties of a vice principal. In September 1968, the board retroactively corrected June and July minutes to reflect the appointment, then destroyed the original minutes. Toliver's annual salary was increased from $9,224 to $12,500, which required board approval, but none was reflected in the minutes (Grand Jury Report, at 32).
23. *Independent Journal*, August 28, 1969.
24. Interview, Barbara S. Harris, member, Sausalito School District Board of Trustees.
25. Valerie Joy, quoted in the *Independent Journal*, May 27, 1969.
26. Sidney Walton, *The Black Curriculum: Developing a Curriculum in Afro-American Studies* (East Palo Alto: Black Liberation Publishers, 1969).
27. Jackie Kudler, quoted in the *Independent Journal*, February 19, 1970.
28. Grand Jury Report, at 48.
29. If the grand jury had found willful or corrupt misconduct, it could under state law have recommended to the presiding judge of the Marin County Superior Court that the report be referred to the district attorney for prosecution.
30. Quoted in the *Ebb Tide*, February 25, 1970.
31. Quoted in the *Independent Journal*, February 28, 1970.
32. *Independent Journal*, May 5, 1970.
33. Martha Freebairn-Smith, quoted in the *Independent Journal*, May 6, 1970. Despite Ms. Freebairn-Smith's resignation, her name remained on the recall ballot, and she was defeated.
34. Interview, Philip Schneider, former superintendent, Sausalito School District.
35. Midge Lester, quoted in the *San Francisco Chronicle*, June 1, 1970.
36. Barbara Nelson, an organizer of CEIE, quoted in the *San Francisco Chronicle*, June 1, 1970.
37. The recall campaign was not directed against Johnson, the board's black member, or against Gerald Clear. Clear, who had been elected the year before, was considered by all sides to be divorced from the controversy, although he generally voted with the majority. The fifth

board member, John Muldoon, was the most conservative and had CEIE backing. Both Clear and Muldoon, however, apparently had had enough of controversy and chaos, and resigned the night after the election. Freebairn-Smith and Freedheim, both of whom supported Walton and Schneider until almost the very end, took the brunt of the voters' fury. In a statement made after the grand jury report was issued, CEIE's governing body said that the two members "have either initiated or supported all extreme measures. We feel these two members have brought about social and political experimentation that we and the Grand Jury object to. Therefore we feel these two members must be recalled and replaced with more responsible and objective trustees" (unpublished statement, mimeo, n.d.).

38. Sidney Walton was offered a half-year's severance pay. Toliver was fired, then reinstated, and left the district in 1972. The contract of William Bradley (Chaka) was not renewed for the 1970–71 school year.

39. Kudler interview, *supra* note 19.

40. See Appendix for details of test score data.

41. The publicity attendant on the school's return attracted parents of both races. To maintain racial balance, administrators at first gave preference to blacks when vacancies occurred through normal attrition (interview, Donald W. Johnson, superintendent, Sausalito School District).

42. Schneider interview, *supra* note 34.

43. Tom Wolfe, "Radical Chic and Mau-Mauing the Flak Catchers," in *The New Generation*, ed. Tom Wolfe, 377 (New York: Harper & Row, 1973).

Chapter 10 / *(Pages 217–250)*

1. Louis Myers, Kenneth Bloch, Robert Gamble, and Kevin Koshar collaborated in the preparation of an earlier version of this chapter.

2. Larry Joyner, member of the East Oakland–Fruitvale Planning Committee, quoted in an interview with Elliot Medrich, assistant to Superintendent Marcus Foster.

3. On the politics of symbols, see Murray Edelman, *Politics as Symbolic Action* (Chicago: Markham, 1971); Joseph Gusfield, *Symbolic Crusade: Status Politics and the American Temperance Movement* (Urbana: University of Illinois Press, 1963).

4. On pluralist politics, see Robert Dahl, *A Preface to Democratic Theory* (Chicago: University of Chicago Press, 1956); Robert Dahl, *Polyarchy* (New Haven, Yale University Press, 1971); Robert Dahl, *Who Governs?* (New Haven: Yale University Press, 1961); Charles Lindblom, *The Intelligence of Democracy* (New York: Free Press, 1965).

5. See Arnold Meltsner, *The Politics of City Revenue* 12–13 (Berkeley and Los Angeles: University of California Press, 1971); and Harriet Ziskind, "The School Board and Community Control of the Schools" 114–28 (Ph.D. dissertation, School of Education, University of California, Berkeley, 1972), for descriptions of Oakland.

6. The population has decreased even further, to 339,288 in 1980, according to preliminary census data. The 1950 Asian population includes only Chinese and Japanese. The 1970 figure includes Filipinos, Koreans, Hawaiians, and others. Population estimates more recent

than 1970 are drawn from preliminary data; earlier estimates are taken from published census data.

7. See Judith May, "Struggle for Authority: A Comparison of Four Social Change Programs in Oakland" (Ph.D. dissertation, University of California, Berkeley, 1973). The treatment of Oakland neighborhood politics draws heavily on May.

8. Meltsner, *supra* note 5, at 50.

9. See Edward Hayes, *Power Structure and Urban Policy: Who Rules in Oakland?* (New York: McGraw Hill, 1972).

10. Quoted in May, *supra* note 7, at 87. The view of Oakland as an "administrative city" is supported by the fact that the programs established by the city manager and administrative officials were undertaken without the approval of the city council; only when the Ford Foundation expressed a willingness to finance these ventures did the political system come to play a role.

11. See Daniel P. Moynihan, *Maximum Feasible Misunderstanding: Community Action in the War on Poverty* (New York: Free Press, 1969).

12. See Ziskind, *supra* note 5, and Jesse McCorry, "The Political Economy of Leadership: Innovation in the Oakland Public Schools" (Ph.D. dissertation, University of California, Berkeley, 1974).

13. See Ira M. Heyman, "Oakland," *Civil Rights U.S.A.: Public Schools: Cities in the North and West: 1963*, pp. 4–5 (Washington, D.C.: United States Civil Rights Commission, 1963); Robert Crain et al., *The Politics of School Desegregation* 29 (Garden City, N.Y.: Doubleday, 1969). Crain refers to Oakland as "Lawndale."

14. Discussion of the Skyline High School issue is drawn primarily from Heyman, *supra* note 13; Crain, *supra* note 13; and *Oakland Tribune* accounts.

15. Crain, *supra* note 13, at 32.

16. Selmar H. Berg, "Superintendent's Report on School Boundaries" (Oakland Unified School District, mimeo, May 1962).

17. Quoted in Heyman, *supra* note 13, at 38.

18. Quoted in ibid., at 43.

19. The chairman of the advisory committee, Charles Howard, had previously chaired the successful bond issue campaign that led to the building of Skyline; he was generally regarded as a conservative on racial matters and may have been expected to keep committee proposals within the bounds of the politically acceptable.

20. Heyman, *supra* note 13, at 50.

21. The NAACP materials are drawn from the personal files of Donald McCullum, then president of the organization.

22. The impact of visits from national NAACP leadership was not confined to Oakland; similar expansion of civil rights efforts accompanied Carter's appearances in San Francisco and in Portland, Oregon.

23. See Crain, *supra* note 13, at 36.

24. The Commission on Equal Opportunities in Education, California State Department of Education, "Recommendations to the Oakland Board of Education on Certain Ethnic Problems in the Oakland Unified School District" (mimeo, Sacramento, September 1964).

25. These programs are treated in May, *supra* note 7.

26. In 1963, funds for compensatory education were also made available by the state for the first time; some $125,000 in state and matching

local moneys was expended that year on a variety of programs, including secondary school remedial instruction and a project designed to bolster achievement and motivation at the primary level.

27. Oakland Public Schools, Office of Administrative Research, "Report on District Racial Composition of Certificated and Classified Staff" (mimeo, October 1969); Oakland Public Schools, Research Department, Division of Planning, Personnel and Research, "Report on District Racial-Ethnic Composition: Certificated and Classified Staff" (mimeo, October 1978). These reports were prepared for the Oakland Unified School District.

28. Oakland Public Schools, "Quality Education in Oakland: Guidelines for Improving Educational Opportunity" (mimeo, Office of Research and Evaluation, Oakland Public Schools, February 1966).

29. Oakland Public Schools, Office of the Superintendent, "Racial Composition of Student Bodies, November 1962–March 1966" (mimeo, Office of Research and Evaluation, Oakland Public Schools, 1966).

30. *Montclarion*, April 13, 1966.

31. The school district maintains records only for new admissions to the open enrollment program, not for total participants in the program; the estimate derives from interviews with school district officials and site administrators.

32. Information on the Model Integration Plan is drawn from the Oakland chronology and from the files of the League of Women Voters.

33. When the plan was adopted, hope was expressed that "the opportunity for education progress could be significantly enhanced through the integration process.

34. In summer 1968, the Model Integration Plan did become an issue. The parents of twenty-six sixth-grade pupils (eleven black, fifteen white) who had participated in the program wanted to attend Montera Junior High School and Skyline High School, the schools to which those who lived in the attendance area of the "host" elementary school were assigned; on the recommendation of the California Bureau of Intergroup Relations—which considered only implications for racial balance—the parents' request was denied, and students in the Model Integration Program were split up according to residence (*Montclarion*, September 11, 1968).

35. *Montclarion*, October 9, 1968.

36. Cal. Admin. Code, Title V, 2010–61.

37. *Montclarion*, March 11, 1970. This is also the source of the passage quoted below.

38. McCorry, *supra* note 12, at 213.

39. Quoted in the *Montclarion*, January 12, 1966. See also Jeffrey Pressman and Aaron Wildavsky, *Implementation* (Berkeley and Los Angeles: University of California Press, 1973); Amory Bradford, *Oakland's Not for Burning* (New York: McKay, 1968).

40. The quotations come from Oakland Board of Education, minutes, April 26, 1966; and the *Montclarion*, May 4, 1966.

41. The account of the boycott and subsequent rioting is drawn from newspaper reports and from interviews with Electra Price, twice-defeated candidate for the Oakland Board of Education, now director of public relations for the Oakland Unified School District, and with Ralph Capolungo, member, Ad Hoc Committee for Quality Education,

and member, East Oakland's Inter-Faith Citizens' Committee for Social Action.

42. California Commission on Equal Opportunities in Education, "Report and Records of Commission on Equal Opportunities in Education Concerning Disturbances in East Oakland on October 19, 1966," quoted in the *Montclarion*, July 26, 1967, p. 1.

43. *Montclarion*, December 27, 1967.

44. *Montclarion*, May 21, 1969.

45. *Montclarion*, May 28, 1969.

46. The "Oakland 5" included the director of the Oakland Economic Development Corporation, the president of the Oakland Federation of Teachers, the chairman of Blacks for Justice, and the cochairmen of the Black Caucus. They were tried in spring 1970 and acquitted on seven counts; the jury was hung on ten counts, which were later reduced to misdemeanors. The story is recounted in Marcus Foster, *Making Schools Work* (Philadelphia: Westminster Press, 1971).

47. This concern extended beyond the superintendency. When in 1969 the school district decided to hire "human relations assistants" to ease racial tensions at the high schools, the board agreed with parents groups' requests that the assistants be nonprofessionals and live in the neighborhood being served. Over administration objection, candidates were not selected by professional staff alone but were reviewed by mixed community-professional boards, which made recommendations to the school board. This appointment process involved neighborhood constituencies in actual decision making more directly than had any previous undertaking.

48. Quoted in the *Montclarion*, August 20, 1969.

49. See McCorry, *supra* note 12.

50. Both remarks are quoted in the *Montclarion*, August 13, 1969.

51. The roster of member organizations included the American Taxpayers Union, Baptist Ministers Union, Bay Area Urban League, Baymon Community Council, Black Panther Party, Blacks for Justice, California Teachers Association, Citizens for Responsive Government, CORE, East Oakland–Fruitvale Planning Committee, East Oakland Welfare Rights Organization, Filipino Coalition, Interdenominational Ministers' Alliance, Jewish Community Relations Council, League of Women Voters, Legal Aid Society, Lockwood Improvement League, Men of Tomorrow, NAACP, Oakland Business and Professional Women, Oakland Education Association, Oakland Federation of Teachers, Oakland New Careers Association, St. Matthew's Missionary Baptist Church, and Student Committee on Oakland Schools.

52. *Montclarion*, November 19, 1969.

53. McCorry, *supra* note 12, is the primary source for this section.

54. Foster, *supra* note 46, at 158.

55. See McCorry, *supra* note 12, at 97.

56. See Frank Levy, Arnold Meltsner, and Aaron Wildavsky, *Urban Outcomes* 81–87 (Berkeley and Los Angeles: University of California Press, 1974).

57. Compare McCorry, *supra* note 12.

58. See Oakland Public Schools, "District Response to Spanish Speaking Unity Council's Educational Objectives" (mimeo, January 1972).

These "objectives" primarily concerned increases in Spanish-speaking personnel and bilingual instruction; desegregation was not mentioned.

59. In August 1970, the Oakland Legal Aid Society filed suit attacking the at-large system of electing the Oakland Board of Education as "discriminatory against ghetto residents of the city who are poor and in racial minority" and proposing district voting. The complaint noted that candidates who received more than three-quarters of the "ghetto" vote, as had Electra Price in 1965, nonetheless lost elections. Among the asserted consequences of this lack of ghetto representation were resource inequities and the preservation of Skyline High School as a largely white school (*Godinez v. Murphy et al.*, No. 70-1636, U.S. Dist. Ct. [N.D. Cal. August 3, 1970]). The suit, dismissed by the district court, had not been developed in consultation with leaders of the "racial minority" communities, whose attention had shifted at least temporarily from electoral to administrative politics.

60. National Education Association, Commission on Professional Rights and Responsibilities, *Oakland, California: A Community in Transition with a School District Too Slowly Adapting, Report of Investigation* 30 (Washington, D.C.: National Education Association and California Teachers Association, Personnel Standard Commission, 1968).

61. The two remarks by Rose were made at a board of education meeting (*Montclarion*, October 9, 1968).

62. *Montclarion*, November 20, 1968.

63. Untitled brochure, on file with the Oakland League of Women Voters.

64. *Montclarion*, October 9, 1968.

65. See the discussion of the evolution of the meaning of de jure segregation in chapter 4.

Chapter 11 / *(Pages 253–276)*

1. On the national context, see chapters 2–4.

2. See Lawrence Cremin, *The Transformation of the School: Progressivism in American Education, 1876–1957* (New York: Random House, 1964), and the discussion of this era in chapter 2. Superintendent Spears in San Francisco is a conspicuous exception to this statement. See the discussion of his superintendency in Larry Cuban, *School Chiefs under Fire* (Chicago: University of Chicago Press, 1976).

3. See, e.g., Robert Crain, Morton Inger, Gerald McWorter, and James Vanecko, *The Politics of School Desegregation* (Chicago: Aldine, 1968), and chapter 4.

4. Mark Yudof, "Equal Educational Opportunity and the Courts," 51 *Texas Law Review* 411 (1973).

5. Black House in Berkeley is a possible exception: one might well have found the idea of black separatism objectionable, especially since it was so baldly put. See chapter 8.

6. See John McAdams, "Can Open Enrollment Work?," 37 *Public Interest* 69 (1974).

7. See Nancy Borow, "Atlanta," in David Kirp, Nancy Borow, Mitchell Feigenberg, Tim Gage, Elliot Marseille, and Dorothy Robyn, "Judicial

Management of School Desegregation" (unpublished report prepared for the National Institute of Education, 1979); and Elwood Hain, "Sealing Off the City: School Desegregation in Detroit," in *Limits of Justice: The Courts' Role in School Desegregation*, ed. Howard Kalodner and James Fishman, 223 (Cambridge, Mass.: Ballinger, 1978).

8. See Hugh Calkins and Jeffrey Gordon, "The Right to Choose an Integrated Education: Voluntary Regional Integrated Schools—A Partial Remedy for De Facto Segregation," 9 *Harvard Civil Rights–Civil Liberties Law Review* 171 (1974); and Gordon Foster, "Desegregating Urban Schools: A Review of Techniques," 43 *Harvard Educational Review* 5 (1973).

9. See Carlos Ovando, "School Implications of the Peaceful Latino Invasion," 59 *Phi Delta Kappan* 230 (1977).

10. See, e.g., Michael Timpane, ed., *The Federal Interest in Financing Schooling* (Cambridge, Mass.: Ballinger, 1978); John F. Hughes and Anne O. Hughes, *Equal Education: A New National Strategy* (Bloomington: Indiana University Press, 1972); and Frederick Wirt and Michael Kirst, *The Political Web of American Schools* (Boston: Little, Brown, 1972). This era may be drawing to a close.

11. See David Kirp, "Law, Politics, and Equal Educational Opportunity: The Limits of Judicial Involvement," 47 *Harvard Educational Review* 104 (1977).

12. See Philippe Nonet and Doris Fine, "Just Schools" (unpublished report prepared for the National Institute of Education, Washington, D.C., 1979).

13. Cf. Michel Crozier, Samuel Huntington, and Joji Watanuki, *The Crisis of Democracy* (New York: New York University Press, 1975), and Alan Wolfe, *The Limits of Legitimacy* (New York: Free Press, 1977). See Sidney Verba and Norman Nie, *Participation in America* (New York: Harper & Row, 1972); and E. Redford, *Democracy in the Administrative State* (New York: Oxford University Press, 1969).

14. See David Kirp and Mark Yudof, *Educational Policy and the Law* (Berkeley: McCutchan, 1982 ed.).

15. See Alan Rosenthal, ed., *Governing Education* (New York: Knopf, 1964).

16. See Norman Kerr, "The School Board as an Agency of Legitimation," in ibid., at 137; and M. Kent Jennings and Harmon Ziegler, with Wayne Peak, *Governing American Schools* (North Scituate, Mass.: Duxbury, 1974).

17. Roscoe Martin, *Government and the Suburban School* 89 (Syracuse: Syracuse University Press, 1962).

18. See, e.g., Donald McCarty and Charles Ramsey, *The School Managers* (Westport, Conn.: Greenwood, 1971); Joseph Cronin, *The Control of Urban Schools: Perspective on the Power of Educational Reformers* (New York: Free Press, 1973); Lawrence Iannacone and Frank Lutz, *Politics, Power, and Policy: The Governing of Local School Districts* (Columbus: Charles Merrill, 1970); Michael Katz, *Class, Bureaucracy, and Schools: The Illusion of Educational Change in America* (New York: Praeger, 1971); and Harvey Tucker and L. Harmon Ziegler, *Professionals Versus the Public: Attitudes, Communication, and Response to School Districts* (New York: Longman, 1980).

19. See Cuban, *supra* note 2. Cf. the accounts of school-community relationships in an earlier era in August Hollingshead, *Elmtown's Youth: The Impact of Social Classes on Adolescents* (New York: John Wiley and Sons, 1949); and in Robert Lynd and Helen Lynd, *Middletown: A Study in American Culture* (New York: Harcourt, Brace, and World, 1956 ed.).
20. On the distinction between ideological and pluralist politics in the school setting, see Paul Peterson, *School Politics, Chicago Style* (Chicago: University of Chicago Press, 1976).
21. Contemporary analysis took a dim view of this politicization. See Morton Inger and Robert Stout, "School Desegregation—the Need to Govern," 3 *Urban Review* 35 (1968). Cf. Michael Lipsky and David Olson, *Commission Politics: The Processing of Racial Crisis in America* (New Brunswick, N.J.: Trans-Action Books, 1976).
22. See, e.g., Daniel P. Moynihan, *Maximum Feasible Misunderstanding: Community Action in the War on Poverty* (New York: Free Press, 1969); J. David Greenstone and Paul Peterson, *Race and Authority in Urban Politics: Community Participation and the War on Poverty* (Chicago: University of Chicago Press, 1976); and S. M. Miller and Martin Rein, "Participation, Poverty and Administration," 29 *Public Administration Review* 15 (1969).
23. Cf. Philip Selznick, *TVA and the Grass Roots: A Study in the Sociology of Formal Organization* (Berkeley and Los Angeles: University of California Press, 1953).
24. See John Meyer, "Organizational Factors Affecting Legalization in Education" (unpublished paper prepared for the Institute for Research on Educational Finance and Governance, Stanford University, 1981).
25. See Daniel Elazar, R. Bruce Carroll, E. Ester Levine, and Douglas St. Angelo, eds., *Cooperation and Conflict: Readings in American Federalism* (Itasca, Ill.: F. E. Peacock, 1969); Daniel Elazar, *American Federalism: A View from the States* (New York: Thomas Y. Crowell, 1966); and Robert A. Goldwin, ed., *A Nation of States: Essays on the American Federal System* (Chicago: Rand-McNally, 1963).
26. See Gary Orfield, *The Reconstruction of Southern Education: The Courts and the 1964 Civil Rights Act* (New York: Wiley-Interscience, 1969), and Gary Orfield, *Must We Bus? Segregated Schools and National Policy* (Washington: Brookings Institution, 1978).
27. See chapter 4.
28. See Colin Diver, "The Judge as Political Powerbroker: Superintending Structural Change in Public Institutions," 65 *Virginia Law Review* 43 (1979); and Abram Chayes, "The Role of the Judge in Public Law Litigation," 89 *Harvard Law Review* 1281 (1976).
29. See generally David Kirp and Gary Babcock, "Judge and Company: Court-Appointed Masters, School Desegregation, and Institutional Reform," 32 *Alabama Law Review* 313 (1981).
30. See Grant McConnell, *Private Power and American Democracy* 357 (New York: Random House, 1970).
31. On courts as value shapers generally, see Ronald Dworkin, *Taking Rights Seriously* (Cambridge: Harvard University Press, 1977).
32. Murray Edelman, *Politics as Symbolic Action* 16 (Chicago: Markham,

1971); see also Murray Edelman, *The Symbolc Uses of Politics* (Urbana: University of Illinois Press, 1964).

33. Aaron B. Wildavsky, *Speaking Truth to Power: The Art and Craft of Policy Analysis* (Boston: Little, Brown, 1979).

34. See, e.g., Walter Nicholson, *Microeconomic Theory* 611–39 (Hinsdale, Ill.: Dryden Press, 1978).

35. Harvey Mansfield, Jr., *The Spirit of Liberalism* 45 (Cambridge: Harvard University Press, 1978).

Chapter 12 / *(Pages 277–302)*

1. 347 U.S. 483 (1954).

2. The survey data are collected in Philip Converse, *American Social Attitudes Data Sourcebook, 1947–1978* (Cambridge: Harvard University Press, 1980), and Tom W. Smith, *A Compendium of Trends of Social Survey Questions* (Chicago: National Opinion Research Center, 1980).

3. U.S. Department of Health, Education and Welfare, Office for Civil Rights, *Distribution of Students by Racial/Ethnic Composition of Schools, 1970–1976* (1978). In 1970, 28.7 percent of black students attended 0–49 percent minority schools, and 46.9 percent attended 90–100 percent minority schools; in 1976, the comparable percentages were 32.7 and 39.5.

   This idea is developed in David L. Kirp, *Doing Good by Doing Little: Race and Schooling in Britain* (Berkeley and Los Angeles: University of California Press, 1979).

4. Michael Kirst, "Loss of Support for Public Secondary Schools: Some Causes and Solutions," 110 *Daedalus* (1981), p. 45.

5. See, e.g., Paul Peterson, "Federal Policy and American Education," (unpublished paper prepared for the Twentieth Century Fund, New York, 1981).

6. Gunnar Myrdal, with Richard Sterner and Arnold Rose, *An American Dilemma: The Negro Problem and Modern Democracy* 600 (New York: Pantheon, 1972 ed.).

7. Michael Walzer, *Radical Principles* (New York: Basic Books, 1980).

8. See, e.g., Nathan Glazer, *Affirmative Discrimination: Ethnic Inequality and Public Policy* (New York: Basic Books, 1975); and Lino Graglia, *Disaster by Decree: The Supreme Court Decisions on Race and Schools* (Ithaca: Cornell University Press, 1976).

9. See, e.g., Graglia, *supra* note 8.

10. See, e.g., Ray Rist, "School Integration: Ideology, Methodology, and National Policy," 84 *School Review* 417 (1976); and Gary Orfield, *Must We Bus? Segregated Schools and National Policy* (Washington, D.C.: Brookings Institution, 1978).

11. On the process of defining public values, see Bruce Ackerman, *Social Justice in the Liberal State* (New Haven: Yale University Press, 1980).

12. Charles Lawrence, "'One More River to Cross'—Recognizing the Real Injury in *Brown*: A Prerequisite to Shaping New Remedies," in *Shades of Brown: New Perspectives on School Desegregation*, ed. Derrick Bell, 48, 53 (New York: Teachers College Press, 1980).

13. See Grant McConnell, *Private Power and American Democracy* (New York: Random House, 1970).

14. Theodore Lowi, *The End of Liberalism* 97 (New York: W. W. Norton, 1969). See also William Gamson, *The Strategy of Social Protest* (Homewood, Ill.: Dorsey Press, 1975).
15. Wilson Carey McWilliams, *The Idea of Fraternity in America* 110–11 (Berkeley and Los Angeles: University of California Press, 1973).
16. Ibid.
17. Theodore Lowi, *The Politics of Disorder* 60 (New York: Basic Books, 1971).
18. The phrase appears in Lowi, *supra* note 14. See Owen Fiss, "The Supreme Court, 1978 Term, Foreword: The Forms of Justice," 93 *Harvard Law Review* 1 (1979).
19. Judge DeMascio, in the Detroit litigation, quoted in Elwood Hain, "Sealing Off the City: School Desegregation in Detroit," in *Limits of Justice: The Courts' Role in School Desegregation*, ed. Howard Kalodner and James Fishman (Cambridge, Mass.: Ballinger, 1978).
20. McConnell, *supra* note 13, at 360.
21. Stuart Scheingold, *The Politics of Rights* 25 (New Haven: Yale University Press, 1974).
22. See Paul Peterson, "Voice, Exit, and Equity" (unpublished paper prepared for the National Institute of Education, 1980).
23. These cases are reviewed in J. Harvie Wilkinson, *From Brown to Bakke: The Supreme Court and School Integration* (New York: Oxford University Press, 1979).
24. 402 U.S. 1 (1971).
25. See, e.g., Owen Fiss, "The Charlotte-Mecklenburg Case—Its Significance for Northern School Desegregation," 38 *University of Chicago Law Review* 697 (1971).
26. 413 U.S. 189 (1973).
27. These cases are discussed in David Kirp and Mark Yudof, *Educational Policy and the Law*, chapter 5 (Berkeley: McCutchan, 1982); see also Steven Barrett Kanner, "From Denver to Dayton: The Development of a Theory of Equal Protection Remedies," 72 *Northwestern University Law Review* 382 (1977).
28. Cf. *Dayton Board of Education v. Brinkman*, 433 U.S. 406 (1977) and *Dayton Board of Education v. Brinkman*, 439 U.S. 1357 (1979).
29. *Keyes v. School District No. 1, Denver*, 413 U.S. 189, 226 (1973) (Powell, J., concurring in part and dissenting in part). In subsequent opinions, Justice Powell reverts to a narrower, intent-focused standard, implicitly abandoning the theory he propounds in his *Keyes* opinion.
30. The principle-policy distinction is developed in Ronald Dworkin, *Taking Rights Seriously* (Cambridge: Harvard University Press, 1977).
31. 413 U.S. 217, 240 (Powell, J., concurring in part and dissenting in part).
32. Orfield, *supra* note 10, at 108.
33. Compare Frank Goodman, "De Facto Segregation: A Constitutional and Empirical Analysis," 60 *California Law Review* 275 (1972).
34. See Charles Lawrence, "Segregation Misunderstood: The *Milliken* Decision Revisited," 12 *University of San Francisco Law Review* 15 (1977).
35. Nathan Glazer, "Should Courts Administer Social Services?" 50 *Public Interest* 64, 67 (1978).
36. See, e.g., Robert F. Nagel, "Separation of Powers and the Scope of

Federal Equitable Remedies," 30 *Stanford Law Review* 661 (1978); Alexander Bickel, *The Morality of Consent* (New Haven: Yale University Press, 1975); and Gerald E. Frug, "The Judicial Powers of the Purse," 126 *Pennsylvania Law Review* 715 (1978).

37. Judges themselves believe legalism to be their source of strength. As an eminent jurist remarked: "Judges will serve the public interest better if they keep quiet about their legislative function. No doubt they will directly contribute to changes in the law, because they cannot do otherwise, even if they would. But the judge who shows his hand, who advertises what he is about, [is] doing more harm to general confidence in the law as a constant, safe in the hands of the judges, than he is doing to the law's credit as a set of rules nicely attuned to the sentiment of the day" (Lord Radcliffe, *The Law and Its Compass* 16 [1960], quoted in Louis Jaffe, *English and American Judges as Lawmakers* 7–8 [New York: Oxford University Press, 1969]).

38. On symbolic politics, see, e.g., Murray Edelman, *Politics as Symbolic Action* (Chicago: Markham, 1971).

39. On courts as essentially political institutions, see C. H. Pritchett, *The Roosevelt Court: A Study in Judicial Politics and Values 1937–1947* (New York: Macmillan, 1948); Glendon Schubert, "Behavioral Jurisprudence," 2 *Law and Society Review* 407 (1968); and Walter Murphy, *Elements of Judicial Strategy* (Chicago: University of Chicago Press, 1964).

40. Quoted in Theodore Becker, ed., *The Impact of the Supreme Court Decisions* 1 (New York: Oxford University Press, 1969).

41. 413 U.S. at 226 (1973).

42. See the discussion of courts' "special mission" in Ackerman, *supra* note 11, at 312.

43. See Derrick Bell, "Serving Two Masters: Integration Ideals and Client Interests in School Desegregation," 85 *Yale Law Journal* 470 (1976); and Steven Yeazell, "From Group Litigation to Class Action, Part II: Interest, Class, and Representation," 27 *UCLA Law Review* 1067 (1980).

44. *U.S. v. Carolene Products Co.*, 364 U.S. 144, 152 n. 4 (1938).

45. See John Ely, *Democracy and Distrust* (Cambridge: Harvard University Press, 1980). Cf. Hans Linde, "One Process of Lawmaking," 55 *Nebraska Law Review* 197 (1976); Lawrence Tribe, "Structural Due Process," 10 *Harvard Civil Rights–Civil Liberties Law Review* 269 (1975).

46. Ely, *supra* note 45, at 87, 98.

47. See "Note: Implementation Problems in Institutional Reform Litigation," 91 *Harvard Law Review* 428 (1977).

48. See Lawrence Tribe, "The Emerging Reconnection of Individual Rights and Institutional Design: Federalism, Bureaucracy and Due Process of Lawmaking," 10 *Creighton Law Review* 433 (1977).

49. See Archibald Cox, "The Effect of the Search for Equality upon Judicial Institutions," 1979 *Washington University Law Quarterly* 795; and Walter Murphy and Joseph Tanenhaus, *The Study of Public Law* 140–44 (New York: Random House, 1972). But see Walter Berns, "The Least Dangerous Branch, But Only If . . . ," in *The Judiciary in a Democratic Society*, ed. Leonard Thaberge (Lexington, Mass.: D. C. Heath, 1979).

50. See, e.g., Robert McCloskey, *The American Supreme Court* (Chicago: University of Chicago Press, 1961); Robert Woodward and Scott Armstrong, *The Brethren* (New York: Simon and Schuster, 1979); and David Danelski, "Conflict and Its Resolution in the Supreme Court," 11 *Journal of Conflict Resolution* 76 (1967).
51. See, e.g., Jack Peltason, *Fifty-Eight Lonely Men* (Urbana: University of Illinois Press, 1961); and Howard Kalodner and James Fishman, eds., *Limits of Justice: The Courts' Role in School Desegregation* (Cambridge, Mass.: Ballinger, 1978).
52. See Orfield, *supra* note 10, at 233–318; and United States Civil Rights Commission, *Desegregation of the Nation's Public Schools: A Status Report* 8–13 (Washington, D.C.: Government Printing Office, 1979).
53. 349 U.S. 294, 301 (1955).
54. 20 U.S.C. §3191 et seq. For evaluations of ESAA, see Ann MacQueen and John E. Coulsen, *Emergency School Act Evaluations: Overview of Findings from Supplemental Analyses* (Santa Monica, Calif.: System Development Corporation, 1978); and Stephen M. Smith, *An Assessment of Emergency School Aid Act Program Operations: The Targeting of ESAA Grants and Grant Funds* (Washington, D.C.: Applied Urbanetrics, Inc., 1978).
55. Michael Kirst and Dick Jung, "The Utility of a Longitudinal Approach in Assessing Implementation: A Thirteen Year View of Title I, ESEA" (Report No. 80B18, Institute for Research on Educational Finance and Governance, Stanford University, 1980).
56. Paul Berman and Milbury McLaughlin, *Rethinking the Federal Role in Education* (Santa Monica, Calif.: Rand, 1978); Paul Hill, "Enforcement and Informal Pressure in the Management of Federal Categorical Programs in Education," (Santa Monica, Calif.: Rand, 1979); Jerome T. Murphy, "The Education Bureaucracies Implement Novel Policy: The Politics of Title I of ESEA, 1965–72," in *Policy and Politics in America*, ed. Allan P. Sindler (New York: Little, Brown, 1973).
57. Vernon Jordan, president of the National Urban League, quoted in *New York Times*, December 2, 1978, p. 68.
58. Philip Converse, *American Social Attitudes Data Sourcebook, 1947–1978* 78 (Cambridge: Harvard University Press, 1978).
59. Ibid., at 75.
60. See Kathleen Maurer Smith and William Spinrao, "The Popular Political Mood," 11 *Social Policy* 37 (March-April 1981).
61. Converse, *supra* note 58.
62. Ibid., at 61.
63. On this period, see Dale Mann, *Making Change Happen* (New York: Teachers College Press, 1978); Edith Mosher and Jennings Waggoner, eds., *The Changing Politics of Education* (Berkeley: McCutchan, 1978); and Paul Peterson, "The Politics of American Education," in *Review of Research in Education*, ed. Fred Kerlinger and John Carroll, 348 (Itasca, Ill.: Peacock, 1974).
64. Eric Hanushek, "Throwing Money at Schools" (Discussion Paper 8004, Public Policy Analysis Program, University of Rochester, December 1980).
65. On the impact on education of Proposition 13 and similar efforts in other states see Peter May and Arnold Meltsner, *Strengthening Local*

Governance in a Post-Proposition 13 World (Berkeley: University of California, Graduate School of Public Policy, 1979). Interviews with school board members in San Francisco, Berkeley, and Oakland confirm this perception.

66. See Peterson, *supra* note 5.

67. Robert Palaich, Jim Kloss, and Mary Fraser Williams, "The Politics of Tax and Expenditure Limitations" (Working Paper 23, Education Finance Center, Education Commission of the States, Denver, Colorado, 1980). In contrast, only a third favored maintaining social services expenditures. In four other states, support for maintaining or increasing education expenditures did not fall below 61 percent of the voters. Only support for police and fire services was a consistently higher priority.

68. Mary Lee McCune, "The Impact of Proposition 13 in the Berkeley Unified School District" (M.P.P. dissertation, University of California, Berkeley, Graduate School of Public Policy, June 3, 1979).

69. Peter Steinfels, *The Neoconservatives: The Men Who Are Changing America's Politics* 263 (New York: Basic Books, 1979).

70. Albert Hirschman, *Exit, Voice and Loyalty: Responses to Decline in Firms, Organizations, and States* (Cambridge: Harvard University Press, 1970).

71. Compare Sidney Webb, *Grants-in-Aid: A Criticism and a Proposal* (1920), quoted in Charles Benson, *The Economics of Public Education* 218 (Boston: Houghton Mifflin, 1961): "We cannot afford to let the inhabitants of Little Pedlington suffer the penalties of their own ignorance or their own parsimony, because the consequences fall, not on them alone, but also upon the neighboring districts, upon everyone who passes through this benighted area, upon all those who have intercourse with them, even upon the community as a whole, whose future citizens they are producing. . . . If they are permitted to bring up their children in ignorance . . . it is not the Little Pedlingtonites alone who will have to bear the inevitable cost of the destitution and criminality thus produced."

72. McWilliams, *supra* note 15, at 71.

73. Alexis de Tocqueville, *Democracy in America*, vol. 2, p. 110 (New York: Harper & Row, 1966 ed.).

74. Ibid.

75. Ibid., at 111.

76. Ibid., at 112.

77. Jane Mansbridge, *Beyond Adversary Democracy* (New York: Basic Books, 1981). Contrast Edward Banfield, *The Moral Basis of a Backward Society* 85 (Glencoe, Ill.: Free Press, 1958), which depicts a world in which everyone acts only to "maximize the material, short-run advantage of the nuclear family" and assumes "that all others will do likewise."

78. Richard Hofstadter, *The Age of Reform* (New York: Knopf, 1955).

79. See, e.g., Harvey S. Rosen and David J. Fullerton, "A Note on Local Tax Rates, Public Benefit Levels, and Property Values," 85 *Journal of Political Economy* 433 (1977); and Gerald S. McDougall, "Local Public Goods and Residential Property Values: Some Insights and Extensions," 20 *National Tax Journal* 436 (1976).

80. See Peterson, *supra* note 22.
81. Daniel Sullivan, *Public Aid to Nonpublic Schools* 69 (Lexington, Mass.: D. C. Heath, 1974).
82. See John Coons and Stephen Sugarman, *Education by Choice: The Case for Family Control* (Berkeley and Los Angeles: University of California Press, 1978).
83. See Michael Giles and Douglas Catlin, "Mass-Level Compliance with Public Policy: The Case of School Desegregation," 42 *Journal of Politics* 722 (1980).
84. Diane Ravitch, "The Evolution of School Desegregation Policy, 1964–1979," in *Race and Schooling in the City*, ed. Adam Yarmolinsky, Lance Liebman, and Corinne Schelling, 9 (Cambridge: Harvard University Press, 1981).
85. Jordan, *supra* note 57.
86. See David Kirp, "Poor School System?" (London) *Times Educational Supplement*, August 15, 1980.
87. Daniel Bell, *The Cultural Contradictions in Capitalism* (New York: Basic Books, 1976).
88. Ronald Edmonds, "Effective Education for Minority Pupils: *Brown* Confounded or Confirmed," in Bell, ed., 108 *supra* note 12. See William Brookaver, Charles Beady, Patricia Flood, John Schweitzer, and Joe Wisenbaker, *School Social System and Student Achievement: Schools Can Make a Difference* (New York: Praeger, 1979); and Edward McDill and Leo Rigsby, *The Academic Impact of Educational Climates: Structure and Process in Secondary Schools* (Baltimore: Johns Hopkins University Press, 1973).
89. See David Kirp, "Professionalization as a Policy Choice: British Special Education in Comparative Perspective," *World Politics* (forthcoming, 1982).
90. On the relationship between governance and policy outcomes, see Judith Gruber, "Authority and Exchange in the Control of Public Bureaucracies" (unpublished paper prepared for the National Institute of Education, 1981); and Frank Levy, Arnold Meltsner, and Aaron Wildavsky, *Urban Outcomes* (Berkeley and Los Angeles: University of California Press, 1974).
91. John Stuart Mill, "M. de Tocqueville on Democracy in America," in Marshall Cohen, ed., *The Philosophy of John Stuart Mill: Ethical, Political, and Religious* 141 (New York: Modern Library, 1971). See Glenn Tinder, *Community: Reflections on a Tragic Ideal* (Baton Rouge: Louisiana State University Press, 1980).
92. Cf. Kirp, *supra* note 3.

Index

370 *Index*

and educational policy changes, 67,
68–70, 97, 105, 271; efficacy of,
271–272; incremental approach to,
61, 62; legalism in, 64–68; on racial
balance in schools, 63–64, 68, 100,
104–105, 107; school board participation and response to, 61–63, 64, 97,
100–101, 103, 105–106, 131; in Supreme Court decisions, 52–56, 97,
99–100, 101; and uniform minimum
integration, 287–288
Republican Party, 154, 220
Residential segregation: in Bay Area
communities, 77, 78; in Marin
County, 197, 199–200; in Oakland,
223
Richmond, California, 77, 117–147, 256,
258, 260, 267, 269; busing in, 118, 127,
128, 132, 134; case study of, 117–147;
compared to Berkeley, 79, 145, 150;
court cases on school desegregation
in, 117–118, 129–131, 136–141, 271,
272; creation of the unified school
district in, 122–123; decision making
on racial justice in, 273, 275; district-
wide desegregation plan in, 121, 128,
130, 131, 136, 137; inner-city schools
in, 146–147; Integration Plan, 118,
134, 136, 138, 142–147; level of school
desegregation achieved in, 142–147;
model desegregation plan for, 128;
open enrollment in, 142–146, 260,
261, 262, 271, 288; political culture of,
274; school board's efforts for racial
justice in, 117–118, 124–129
Richmond Complex, in San Francisco,
91–97 *passim*, 102, 109; concept of,
91; opposition to, 93, 96; success and
failures of, 98–99
Richmond Independent, 130, 134
Rickover, Hyman, 38
Riles, Wilson, 111
Riots, 43, 218; causes of, 181; effects of,
78; predicted in Oakland, 233
Robeson, Paul, 150
Robinson, Melinda, 190
Rose, Seymour, 230, 231, 238; Oakland
school board evaluated by, 246–
248
Rush, Benjamin, 33
Russell, James, 36

Sanazaro, Paul, 155, 156
San Francisco, 75, 78, 256, 257, 258,
259, 262; busing in, 91, 93, 101, 102,
103, 108, 110, 112, 288; case study of,
82–116; compared to Oakland, 79;
court case on school desegregation
in, 64, 82–83, 88, 93–97, 100–101,
104–107, 113, 261, 262, 271 (see also
*Johnson v. San Francisco School Dis-
trict*); demographic changes in, 84;
desegregation of schools urged by
civil rights groups in, 85–88, 92–94;
education of ethnic groups in, 111,
114–115; educational crises in, 97–
98, 110–111; educational equality
linked with educational quality in,
90–91; "educational lighthouse"
school in, 109; federal funds for
neighborhood schools in, 90; housing
discrimination in, 77, 78; level of
school desegregation achieved in,
107–113; SRI report on school desegregation in, 89–90, 95; and uniform
minimum integration, 288; U.S. Supreme Court's decision on education
of Chinese students in, 114; "zone" vs.
"city-wide" approaches to school desegregation in, 102–103, 109
San Francisco Board of Education, 84,
110–111
San Francisco Chronicle, 109, 111
San Francisco Examiner, 112
San Francisco Human Rights Commission, 77
San Francisco Public Schools Commission, 110
San Francisco State College, 109
San Francisco State University, 114
San Pablo, California, 119, 122, 133
Sausalito, 12, 78, 194–216, 245, 257,
258, 259, 262, 270, 274; black power
in schools of, 194, 204–211, 214–216;
case study of, 194–216; compared to
Berkeley, 194, 195; decision making
on racial justice in, 273; development
of school desegregation in, 200–203;
encounter groups for teachers in,
204; grand jury report on education
in, 207–208; role of parents in educational policies of, 203, 208, 209–210,
211; school district budget of, 198,